DEMOLISHING A HISTORIC HOTEL

MAIN STREET, DAVIS, CALIFORNIA C4161

DEMOLISHING A HISTORIC HOTEL

A Sociology of Preservation Failures in Davis, California

John Lofland

Davis Research
Davis, California
2003

This book is dedicated to

The Davis Enterprise and to

Heather Caswell and civic-minded people everywhere

Generations of *Davis Enterprise* editors, reporters and other news-workers have created an indispensable chronicle of Davis history in the pages of that newspaper. Without that chronicle, this book would not be possible.

Heather Caswell catalyzed the energy to save the Terminal Building. She is one of those continually emerging community-spirited people upon whom the civic health of societies depends.

For information on obtaining
additional copies of this book contact:

Davis Research
523 E Street
Davis, California 95616

530-758-5258
davisres@dcn.org

The front cover photograph was taken by the author. It displays an especially dramatic moment in the September 28, 2000 ripping apart of the Davis Arch Mural painted on the north wall of the Terminal Building.

The back cover photograph is an excerpt from a postcard on which the photographer is not credited or the publisher indicated. Taken about 1940, the entire picture is shown on the verso page of the title page leaf. David Herbst owns the postcard that was scanned for this image and the author is very appreciative of his permission to use it here.

BRIEF CONTENTS

DETAILED CONTENTS

1

INTRODUCTION

This book tells the story of a historic hotel in Davis, California, a structure variously called the Terminal Building, the Terminal Hotel and the Hotel Aggie. The major parts of this building's story are: its heyday and neglect decades (Chapters 2 through 6); four failures of preservation regarding it (Chapters 7 through 11); it's demolition and burial (Chapters 12 and 13); and, consequences and causes of its demise (Chapters 14 and 15).

1) TO WHOM IS THIS AN INTERESTING STORY?

Few if any stories are of interest to "everyone." People differ and there is therefore always the question, "To whom might this story be interesting?" Let me suggest some kinds of interests to which this story might appeal.

These interests divide into three categories, with variations on each: (a) the **historic preservation puzzled or involved,** (b) **local and town history enthusiasts,** and (c) **social science methodologists.**

<u>THE HISTORIC PRESERVATION PUZZLED OR INVOLVED.</u> Especially promoted by the National Historic Preservation Act of 1966, there has arisen in the United States what we might call a "preservation establishment." While it is not large enough to be termed a "vast army," there are a great many people making a living from it and wielding power in its name. As an idea and an organizational presence, "historic preservation" reaches almost every section of the United States.

Those most involved in it consider themselves "professionals" who practice a complicated discipline. This fact separates them from lay people in the same way other "professionals" are separated from laity. Important markers of the separation include speaking an arcane argot. There are "historic resources," a "National Register," "SHPOs" (pronounced "ship-os"), and so forth, as in other specialized occupations.

(1) All this creates lay people who ask, **"What in the world is 'historic preservation' anyway?"** If you are a person asking this question, this story is for you. I take you "on the ground" though the playing-out of historic preservation in the case of the Terminal Building, a structure about which there was much controversy. One technique used on this tour is to reproduce (especially in the Chapters of Part II) many of the documents of which historic preservation practice consists and indicating how these documents intersect with various groups for and against their application. If you seek to penetrate the seemingly remote and foreign topic of historic preservation, this is your guide.

(2) Oddly, historic preservation as a field has not been strong on generating detailed case studies of how people actually do it (a notable exception being Longstrech, 1998). The

tendency, instead, is to vignettes of triumphs (as in "five minute success stories") or abstract exhortations about proper practice. Clearly, though, descriptions of the "real thing," warts and all, are needed if people are to learn about mistakes and how to avoid them. This book is written very much in this empirical vein. I hope that anyone who can say **"I am seriously involved in historic preservation"** will learn a great deal about how to do it (and how *not* to do it) from reading this account.

(3) True to the ethnographic ethic of the social scientist, I try to convey the grittier realities of historic preservation. If you are a person who says **"I want to be a preservation professional,"** the story of the Terminal Building is a story you should know. It is often and rightly warned that no one should enter medical school without first working in a hospital and accepting the realities routinely encountered there. In kindred fashion, a prospective preservationist-for-hire should read this story and to come to emotional grips with its less-than-cheerful facts.

(4) The story of the Terminal Building is also a technical one in the sense of asking and answering this question: **"How and why did preservation fail in the case of the Terminal Building?"** Unlike the first and third interests, just described, this kind of interest is that of the preservation insider—a person seriously **committed** to or seriously **opposed** to preservation. For such people, answers to this question can help guide action in future preservation struggles.

As I will elaborate in the second section of this Chapter, posing and answering this question of "why preservation failure" is the organizing principle of this book.

LOCAL AND TOWN HISTORY ENTHUSTIASTS. While the rise and vicissitudes of historic preservation are major elements of this story, they are far from all of it. In order adequately to contextualize the historic preservation aspects, I have had to include a great deal of Davis history per se, particularly in the five chapters of Part I, those that cover the eight decades of the building's life. That is, historic preservation did not (and does not) operate in a social vacuum. The larger social matters surrounding it were and are important.

I hope this larger (albeit selective) history will be of interest in at least two ways.

(1) I have been surprised and heartened to observe a rising interest in the histories of towns, and cities (as eloquently voiced and reviewed by Amato, 2002, for example). Less surprising, much of this interest focuses on the great and often cataclysmic changes that took place in so many of them in the decades following World War II. With very high frequency, these changes involved the decimation of their downtowns (Davies, 1998; Fogelson, 2001).

Of signal import, decimation in the usual way did not happen in Davis. Why it did not provides an intriguing case for further and comparative study of towns. However, Davis people **did** engage in a vast devastation of their own sort that I chronicle in Chapter 5. Put tersely, in addition to leveling much of their old downtown, they leveled a good portion of the rest of the town.

(2) One of my pet peeves about the civic life of Davis is it that too many of its participants are afflicted with public life amnesia. The same kinds of problems and successes happen over and over, but any current crop of people in public life react as though THIS (whatever the this) is an entirely new kind of "crisis" (or triumph) for Davis. Very often, it is not. So, one of the aims of this book is to provide Davis people with at least a little historical perspective.

In a more positive vein, the history of Davis—defects and all—is actually quite interesting. In it, we can follow how a town and then city were constructed bit-by-bit. Each juncture in that construction was a point of contest over what best to do. It is clear that events need not have gone the way they did. Given how problematic the outcome of the whole assemblage clearly was, it is a marvel that it came out as well as it did. I hope that I have conveyed just how problematic and "iffy" are processes of change and development.

SOCIAL SCIENCE METHODOLOGISTS. This book is unusual among social science reports in the degree to which it reproduces photographs, newspaper reports, government documents, and other items for the purpose of telling its story. This innovation takes place because, among other reasons, it has recently become practical to do so.

The "doing" of this literally "documentary sociology" presents new kinds of strengths, but also raises new kinds of problems. Those strengths and problems of presenting data in this and other ways are the concerns of social science methodologists, among whom I count myself. I hope that this book will be of interest to such people. (And, I will address this topic again later in this chapter.)

2) PRESERVATION FAILURE(S)

Although I ask many questions along the way, one question provides the principle around which this book (this story) is organized. As previously indicated, that question is: **"Why did preservation fail in the case of the Terminal Building?"**

THE ARGUMENT THERE WAS SOMETHING TO PRESERVE (CHAPTERS 2-6). To speak of preservation having "failed" is to assume there was something worthy of preservation. But, as we will see in Chapters 6 through 11, this was a contested assertion.

The City of Davis Historical Resources Management (HRMC) voted in 1984 and 1999 that the building should be designated a historic resource. But, the nomination was rejected by the Davis City Council both times (2 to 3 in 1984 and 1 to 4 in 1999).

Because a City Council twice thought otherwise, an analyst such as myself bears a special burden to show that the historical record reasonably meets what are called "The National Register's Criteria of Evaluation." For reference, these criteria are reproduced in Fig. 1.1.

Using all the materials developed by the HRMC and city staff and going beyond them with my own research, the five chapters of the Part I are intended to provide empirical evidence that is much more than sufficient to say that the building met at least one of the four criteria (all that is needed) shown in Fig. 1.1. (The details of this documentation and the assessment done by Davis officials in 1999 appear in Chapter 7.)

THE "HOWS" OF PRESERVATION FAILURE (CHAPTERS 7, 8, 10, 11). While, in the end, a building is preserved or it is not, the on-going process leading to an outcome is more complicated. In the Terminal Building case, there was preservation failure-in-increments or by degree.

Viewing failure as a process, there seemed to me to be four major stages (or forms) in this sequence: (1) designation failure, (2) feasibility study failure, (3) facadectomy failure, and (4) freeze failure. These four stages/forms of preservation failure are the topics of the four main chapters of Part II, specifically, Chapters 7, 8, 10, and 11.

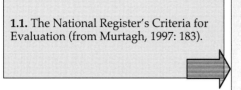

1.1. The National Register's Criteria for Evaluation (from Murtagh, 1997: 183).

The National Register's standards for evaluating the significance of properties were developed to recognize the accomplishments of all peoples who have made a contribution to our country's history and heritage. The criteria are designed to guide state and local governments, federal agencies, and others in evaluating potential entries in the National Register.

The quality of significance in American history, architecture, archeology, engineering and culture is present in districts, sites, buildings, structures, and objects that possess integrity of location, design, setting, materials, workmanship, feeling, and association and:
 (a) that are associated with events that have made a significant contribution to the broad patterns of our history; or
 (b) that are associated with the lives of persons significant in our past; or
 (c) that embody the distinctive characteristics of a type, period, or method of construction, or that represent the work of a master, or that possess high artistic values, or that represent a significant and distinguishable entity whose components may lack individual distinction; or
 (d) that have yielded, or may be likely to yield, information important in prehistory or history.

Designation Failure. In the world of historic preservation, the primordial act of preservation is that of "designation" by a government body. As indicated, this was the first form of failure to which the Terminal Building was subjected. The details of these events are presented in Chapters 6 and 7.

Feasibility Study Failure. Irrespective of success or failure in designation, owners can still decide that they will rehabilitate a building in a way that meets what are called, in preservationist lingo, "the Secretary's standards." The "Secretary" in this phrase is the Federal Government's Secretary of the Interior. This Secretary operates the National Park Service, which includes historical preservation activities. The "Secretary's standards" are, in their simplest form, a set of ten practices with which an owner strives to comply when working with a building. (For reference, I reproduce them in Figure 1.2.)   Or, an owner may decide to rehabilitate a building using looser criteria and broader goals.

Whenever historic preservation is considered, courses of action need to be assessed. This is commonly done with what is called a "feasibility study" or "feasibility analysis." A fairly elaborate undertaking, it is coordinated by a specialist in such studies. It ordinarily consists of the three logical parts of (1) costs, (2) demands, and (3) return on investment (Stevens and Sherwood 1982).

Regarding **costs**, the physical facts of the building are assessed and construction possibilities laid out. "An architect and structural engineer [are commonly] hired to assess the existing condition of the building and then provide schematic drawings of remodel scenarios with input from the property owner, city, and community (ideally). A cost estimate would be provided for each scenario. A financial specialist . . . complete[s] a 'development budget' for each of the scenarios, that includes the 'hard construction costs' . . . and including all the other costs associated with the development" (Wilkinson, 2001).

Regarding **demands**, market potential income is analyzed. "The analyst . . . recommend[s] various funding sources to make the project either financially feasible or infeasible . . . . [For example, [a] project might prove infeasible with a large bank loan, but feasible with a low-interest loan from the Redevelopment Agency or a federal source" (Wilkinson 2001).

Regarding **return on investment**, "a cash-flow analysis [is] developed showing which scenarios pencil out with the various funding sources and which don't . . . . The results of [a study of the Terminal Building] might have shown, for example, that [it . . .] was feasible with second story affordable housing (using a loan from the city and a grant from the state housing office) and the ground floor as commercial. . . ." (Wilkinson, 2001).

In the period when a feasibility study for the Terminal Building was relevant, such studies took several months to conduct and cost in the neighborhood of $20,000.

Despite the urgings of many credible people and organizations, such a study was never performed. This was the second preservation failure. The details are presented in Chapter 8.

Facadectomy Failure. In some situations, compromises that save only a portion of a building are struck. One form of this is to save only the facade and to replace the building behind it. Among strict preservationists, this is referred to derisively as "facadectomy."

Even so, a considerable number of instances of it exist. Although preservation purists decry it, many other people, including myself, find it acceptable, even if not preferable.

In the Terminal Building case facadectomy was part of the discussion, but never achieved truly serious consideration. This third form of failure is chronicled in Chapter 10.

Freeze Failure. The Terminal Building story had the curious feature that the demolition contractor knocked down the rear walls of the building and then stopped in order to have workers salvage the brick dislodged from those walls. The ambiguity of what might be the next steps created at least the hope of a "freeze" on further demolition that might result in some (limited) form of preservation. This freeze also failed and it was the final form of preservation failure. The story is told in Chapter 11.

WHY PRESERVATION FAILED (CHAPTER 15). These four, sequential forms of preservation failure tell us the **hows** of the process. But, we do not yet clearly know **why** it happened. This is a separate question that I try to answer after presenting all the pertinent materials.

Getting all the pertinent materials before us requires 14 chapters. So, Chapter 15 is on the causes of preservation failure.

CONSEQUENCES OF PRESERVATION FAILURE (CHAPTER 14). The processes of preservation failure (Part II) and why it did (Chapter 15) are the central features of the Terminal Building story. But, I would feel remiss if I did not also address a number of ancillary but still important aspects.

One of these is to speak to the question of what happened after the building was gone? What difference did its demolition make? This book went into the publication process a little more than two years after the building was demolished. Therefore, many of the larger and longer term consequences still had not happened (or were at least hard then to see).

Nonetheless, a number of interesting things had occurred in those two years, and I describe them in Chapter 14.

DEMOLITION DRAMA (CHAPTERS 12 and 13). Buildings are not easily demolished and do not immediately disappear. Instead, they have to be smashed and bludgeoned into submission This aspect is, I think, also very much a part of the story of the failure to preserve a historic building. Therefore, I observed the demolition processes and events, which spanned a period of

The Secretary of the Interior's Standards for Rehabilitation

The Secretary of the Interior's Standards for Rehabilitation are ten basic principles created to help preserve the distinctive character of a historic building and its site, while allowing for reasonable change to meet new needs.

The Standards (**36 CFR Part 67**) apply to historic buildings of all periods, styles, types, materials, and sizes. They apply to both the exterior and the interior of historic buildings. The Standards also encompass related landscape features and the building's site and environment as well as attached, adjacent, or related new construction.

Rehabilitation projects must meet the following Standards, as interpreted by the National Park Service, to qualify as "certified rehabilitations" eligible for the 20% rehabilitation tax credit.

The Standards are applied to projects in a reasonable manner, taking into consideration economic and technical feasibility.

1. A property shall be used for its historic purpose or be placed in a new use that requires minimal change to the defining characteristics of the building and its site and environment.

2. The historic character of a property shall be retained and preserved. The removal of historic materials or alteration of features and spaces that characterize a property shall be avoided.

3. Each property shall be recognized as a physical record of its time, place, and use. Changes that create a false sense of historical development, such as adding conjectural features or architectural elements from other buildings, shall not be undertaken.

4. Most properties change over time; those changes that have acquired historic significance in their own right shall be retained and preserved.

5. Distinctive features, finishes, and construction techniques or examples of craftsmanship that characterize a historic property shall be preserved.

6. Deteriorated historic features shall be repaired rather than replaced. Where the severity of deterioration requires replacement of a distinctive feature, the new feature shall match the old in design, color, texture, and other visual qualities and, where possible, materials. Replacement of missing features shall be substantiated by documentary, physical, or pictorial evidence.

7. Chemical or physical treatments, such as sandblasting, that cause damage to historic materials shall not be used. The surface cleaning of structures, if appropriate, shall be undertaken using the gentlest means possible.

8. Significant archeological resources affected by a project shall be protected and preserved. If such resources must be disturbed, mitigation measures shall be undertaken.

9. New additions, exterior alterations, or related new construction shall not destroy historic materials that characterize the property. The new work shall be differentiated from the old and shall be compatible with the massing, size, scale, and architectural features to protect the historic integrity of the property and its environment.

10. New additions and adjacent or related new construction shall be undertaken in such a manner that if removed in the future, the essential form and integrity of the historic property and its environment would be unimpaired.

73 days. These events and processes are analyzed in Chapter 12 and 13. The former depicts the time sequences of the demolition. The latter focuses on special moments in the demolition. and oblivion. Or, to use another metaphor, they have to be hacked to death, butchered, and the bleeding parts of the carcass hauled away.

PRESERVATION CAMPAIGN (CHAPTER 9). As will become evident, the story of preservation failure is also a story of citizens campaigning for preservation. But, in the same way that many other topics are ancillary to the central question of preservation failure (e.g. Chapter 14 on consequences), the story of the citizen's campaign is pertinent but not treated as a story in itself.
Instead, I mostly focus on the campaign's actions as they play on the question of preservation failure or success.

But, as with the other ancillary topics, I would feel remiss if I totally ignored the campaign itself. In this spirit, in Chapter 9 I give special attention to one of the most important moments in the campaign. This was a celebration of the Terminal Building on Sunday, June 11th, 2000.

In fine, I have in this section indicated the question around which this story revolves (why did preservation fail?) and how the various other parts of the story (the book) relate to that central question. In other words, this section summarizes this book.

3) TWO OTHER FRAMES FOR THIS STORY

I acknowledge that the question—"Why did preservation fail?"—is not the only way to phrase or conceive these materials. There are at least two other (and kindred, but different) linguistic renderings.

The first of these might be called **demolition success**. Instead of asking, "Why did preservation fail?" we could ask, "Why and how did demolition overcome the benighted and woolly-minded forces arrayed against it?" This book's title might then be something like: *How Glorious Profit-Maximization Overcame Soft-minded Sentimentalism in the Dreadful People's Republic of Davis, California.*

Rather than bemoan the loss of a historic building, the analyst would celebrate liberation from an archaic past and ugly architecture, the virtues of unfettered private property and the free market, and a victorious strike against demented leftists.

The second alternative framing might be called **parties in conflict**. Instead of taking one side or the other in the struggle--as the above two frames do--one could attempt to stand outside both sides and to be judiciously neutral and uncommitted. This is a rather common frame in early social science studies of conflict (e.g. Kreisberg, 1982; Hierich, 1971).

So conceived, this book's title might be something like *Preservation Conflict in Davis, California.* I did, in fact, experiment with writing this story using this second frame.

As "in principle" ways to proceed, I have no quarrel with either of these two alternative ways to tell this story. The problem with both of them, though, is that neither is my point of view. Instead, I do not believe the first and I am not neutral, which is required by the second. To write this story in other than the way I have would be a lie and inauthentic.

4) STORY-FRAMES AND BRUTE FACTS

Story-frames such as the three I have just described make a difference: in (1) the questions one asks or fails to ask, in (2) some of the facts and that one elects to include or exclude from one's account, and in (3) the interpretation one makes of some facts.

Even so, I want also to stress that the greatest portion of what one reports is not affected by the story-frame one uses. For example:

- The first part of the Terminal Building was constructed in 1925 or it was not.
- The Hotel declined after World War II or it did not.
- The Davis City Council denied historic resource designation to the building in September, 1999 or it did not.

It happens that the bulk of the story of anything is at this brute level of empirical fact. This brute level is more-or-less immune from change by the author's story-frame.

In the present case, I think that while I promote the approach signaled in the phrase "preservation failure," the sheer history I write differs little if at all from one written using either of the other two story-frames.

5) THE BROADER SOCIOLOGICAL PERSPECTIVE

For readers who may not be familiar with it, let me add that, more broadly, this inquiry is informed by the sociological perspective. This study is, I hope, an example of it. By "sociological perspective" I mean the point of view that exhibits the three features of focusing on human behavior or social organization, asking generic questions about these, and applying a skeptical mindset.

First, the focus is human behavior and social organization in their myriad forms. In this inquiry, the human behavior of central interest is an episode or event, that of "preservation failure" (Cf. Lofland and Lofland, 1995: Ch. 4, on "episodes").

Second, the inquirer asks at least one of the eight generic empirical questions sociologists ask about human behavior and organization and makes a serious effort to develop an answer or answers (Lofland and Lofland, 1995: Chapter 7).

One of the eight generic empirical questions asked in this inquiry is, "What are the causes of X?" As reported above, the application here is, "What are causes of preservation failure?" An answer is offered in Chapter 15. Others questions asked and answered include the questions of social process (Chapters 7, 8, 10, 11, 12) and of consequences (Chapter 14).

This second feature sets the sociological perspective off from a large portion of other writings and reports on social behavior and social organization. These other works commonly provide descriptions and abundant moralizing, but little or no effort seriously to ask and answer generic empirical questions.

Third, in his classic primer, *Invitation to Sociology*, Peter Berger rightly declares: "the first wisdom of sociology is this—things are not what they seem." He elaborates that this statement is itself "deceptively simple," for, "social reality turns out to have many layers of meaning. The discovery of each new layer changes the perception of the whole"(1963:23).

If this is true, answering questions about human behavior and organization requires the unwavering application of a critical, questioning or skeptical mindset. The surface or official appearance of things cannot be taken as "the" true or complete account—nor can any dissent from any surface or official account. In the quest to know, the questioning of the questioning is unending. In this study, I have had to question any number of surface realities, to question those questionings, and to question those questionings, in infinite regress (Lofland and Lofland, 1995:153-156).

Even so, every inquiry has to end sometime. But this does not mean questioning and skepticism end. It only means one has, for the moment, run out of time, patience, and resources. The skepticism itself has to go on. I am uncertain about many aspects of the answers to questions I offer here. This has to be and this is how it should be.

So also, readers have an obligation to bring a skeptical mindset to what is presented here—and to what they make of what they think they see here.

6) DIGITAL DOCUMENTARY EVIDENCE

As everyone knows, the silicon chip joined with the computer has begun a "digital revolution" in encoding and transmitting information. Specifically, it has become possible for people of ordinary means (such as myself) to encode, manipulate, and reproduce words and images in ways heretofore either not possible or prohibitively expensive.

This book consists largely of resized and edited reproductions of original documents and pictures that make up the story of the Terminal Building. Only a few years ago, it was not, as a practical manner, possible to compose a story in the documentary manner seen in the pages of this book.

Instead—and as I did many times in empirical studies I performed in the 1960s through the early 1990s—I would have had to provide my own textual/verbal representations of the documents and pictures. But now, "digitizing," (commonly termed "scanning") has transformed what is routinely possible in the pages of a book.

We are still at the beginning of this transformation, which means that ways to use the new possibilities to best advantage are undefined and unknown. Like children with new toys, though, we stumble ahead with glee (e.g. Lepore, 2001).

Therefore, the "digital documentary" way I tell the Terminal Building story is in the nature of an experiment—a groping forward into new ways of presenting evidence.

Nonetheless, even though "digital documentary" is experimental and groping, I cannot but believe that reproductions of originals provide a historical authenticity that is likely stronger than an author's textual representation of those documents. Indeed, I think the veracity and vigor with which one can present "brute facts" (mentioned above) is much strengthened.

I might also mention that I view the use of these new "visual" materials as marvelous but only a technical extension of sociological inquiry as we know it (just explained in section 5, above), rather than as a radical epistemological departure or leap. That is, some versions of what is termed "visual sociology" or "visual studies" tend to view "the visual" as a step across a great divide of some kind (discussed but not necessarily endorsed by, for example, Becker, 1974, 1995, 2002)). I do not. It is a leap and a big one, but one that primarily increases the detail with which we can present evidence and the credibility of that evidence.

7) MY ROLE

Looked at from the point of view of methods of social research, this study is an instance of what sociologists call, variously, "fieldwork," "participant-observation," or "participatory research."

Whatever the rubric, the hallmark of the method is the researcher's direct participation in the social life under study.

It is useful to distinguish among such studies in terms of whether or not the researcher began involvement with research in mind or not. In this case, I developed research objectives only on September 18, 2000, the day the demolition began.

Before that, I was only and simply an involved citizen. Along with many other people, I was attempting to preserve the Terminal Building in some manner. This also explains why there are so few photographs in this book taken by me before that date, but many after that date. I had then begun seriously to document what was going on with a camera and field notes.

Therefore, questions of "informed consent" (now so often raised regarding research) were not pertinent before September 18. After that day, it was my practice to indicate to everyone I encountered that I was "writing a book" about the building.

The topic of this research has one unusual feature I want to call attention to because it bears on issues of ethics, privacy and disclosure that are so often raised regarding sociological fieldwork. That unusual feature is that all the people and events involved in this book took place in the political arena and they were events of public life. In our society at this time, at least, people and events that are political and public are, by definition, proper objects of observation and comment by anyone. Indeed, the contents of this book offer ample evidence that many residents of Davis were not shy about observing and commenting.

Therefore, with materials of this kind, my relation to the social life under study was the same as that of everyone else who cared to pay attention.

Some of the documents I reproduce show that I was a rather involved partisan in the Terminal matter. The depth and intensity of my involvement is a two-edged sword. On the one edge, my involvement provided me with a view closer than that of some other people. I was one type of "insider." This means I could gather data of certain sorts that were not available to the less involved.

On the other edge, my partisanship clearly poses the threat of bias. I have always been aware of this, and I have tried my best to correct for it. But, in the end, I cannot be the final judge. Each reader will have to form her or his own assessment. I can hope, however, that the "digital documentary" evidence I mention above helps the story tell itself, so to speak. It makes the reader less dependent on me than is the case with some other methods of representing what happened.

8) DAVIS HISTORY IN A NUTSHELL: POPULATION AND GEOGRAPHICAL EXPLOSION

The history of Davis I present in the chapters that follow is necessarily specialized and selective. It is therefore important to provide a larger context into which the reader can fit these several pieces. That is, the full meaning of events—in 1960, for example—cannot be appreciated unless one knows the relation of that or any year to the years and decades before and after it.

In my view, the two most important dimensions of this larger context are Davis' 1) population growth and 2) geographical size viewed over time from the beginning in 1868 to the 21st century. This is a span of some fourteen decades. Inspecting only these two variables over these decades provides us, I think, indispensable perspective on the machinations we observe in Davis in any year.

POPULATION EXPLOSION. In column 1 of Fig. 1.3 we see the population of Davis at the start of each of fourteen decades of its history. At the start of the first decade, it was zero (for there was no Davis) and in 2000 (the start of the fifteenth decade), it was 60,308.

Let us first look at the population figures for the first five decades, 1860-1900. We see they run: 0, 500, 600, 700, and 700. This was the era of Davis as a small and even stagnating agricultural **VILLAGE**. Indeed, in 1900 there were only about 175 residential and commercial structures.

But, in 1906, Davis was selected as the site of the University of California experimental farm. A small installation was built and began slowly to grow. This influence is seen in the population figures for the next four decades of 1910-40: 850 to 1,040 to 1,243, to 1,672. This was a new era for Davis. In it, many if not most, of the structures people later regarded as classically and quintessentially Davis were fashioned. Most pertinent here, this was the period in which the Terminal Building was constructed. With this growth and construction, Davis was changing from a village to a **TOWN**.

But all these population figures were truly small and even pathetic compared to what happened over the next five decades—the 1950s through the 1990s. Looking again at column 1 of Figure 1.3, we see leapfrog jumps in the population numbers. From 3,554 in 1950, the population increased to 60,308 in 2000. Davis had changed once again, this time from a town to a **CITY**.

For perspective, consider the average per year increase in population from the village to the town to the city periods. In the village decades, the population grew about seven people a year, on average. In the town decades, this increase was about 70 a year. But then, in the new city decades, Davis was adding some 1,200 new residents every year.

So, when reading about the struggles of the Terminal Building in the "neglect decades" chronicled in Chapters 5 and 6, for example, bear in mind that one is reading about a new-city-in-the-making constructed by a new mix of players. A hoard of highly educated and sophisticated newcomers was combining with the old-boy G Street merchants to build a futuristic Davis. (In the above sketch, I have used without specific citation snatches of text from the introduction to Lofland and Haig, 2000:7-8.)

GEOGRAPHICAL EXPLOSION. The slowness of Davis' growth before World War II meant that the number of developed blocks changed little from the original grid of 1868. The boundaries that became official with incorporation in 1917 were virtually the same as the original 1868 grid and these did not change until after World War II! In the map of Davis' geographical growth shown in Fig. 1. 4, this "original city" area is shown in solid black in the lower middle.

As the *Davis Enterprise* graphic makes clear, the city was enlarged in wave after wave of annexations over the 1950s-90s.

These population and annexation facts provide, then, the context in which to view both (1) demolition zeal and (2) rising concern for local history and preservation.

1.3. Davis Population and UC Davis Enrollment over 14 decades. (Reproduced from Lofland, 1999: 35. Technical notes [signaled by * and **] omitted.)

Decade ↓	1 Davis population at start of decade*	2 Decade increase in population	3 Average yearly increase in population (rounded)	4 Farm/ UC Davis enrollment at start of decade**	5 Decade increase in Farm/ UC Davis enrollment	6 Average yearly increase in enrollment (rounded)
1860s	0	500	50			
70s	500	100	10			
80s	600	100	10			
90s	700	0	0			
1900s	700	150	15	0	125	12
10s	850	190	20	125	175	17
20s	1,040	203	20	300	200	20
30s	1,243	429	50	500	700	70
40s	1,672	1,882	200	1,200	500	50
50s	3,554	5,356	500	1,700	1,100	100
60s	8,910	14,578	1,500	2,800	9,800	980
70s	23,488	13,152	1,300	12,600	4,500	450
80s	36,640	9,569	1,000	17,000	5,000	500
90s	46,200	11,591	1,200	22,000	3,000	300

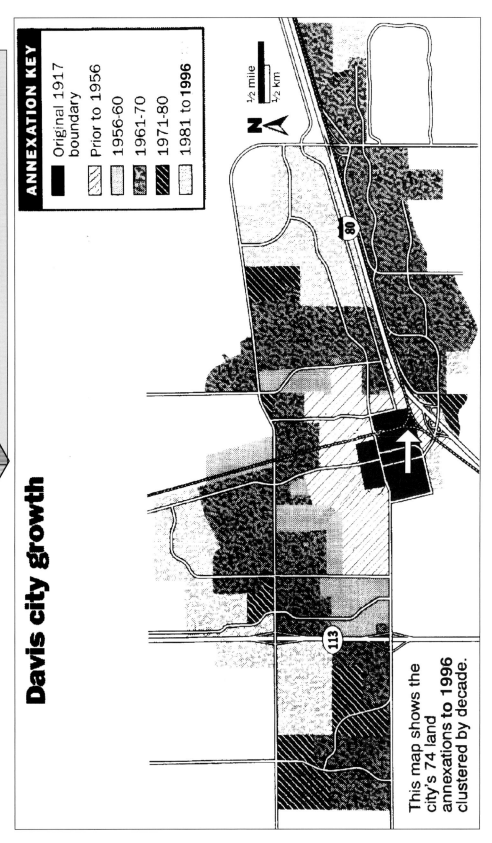

1.4. The 1917 city incorporation area of Davis is shown in black in the lower middle of this map.

The Terminal Building at Second and G streets was next to the railroad track in the lower right of the black area. The white arrow points to the location.

(Map reproduced with my deletions and revisions from a graphic by Nathaniel Levine appearing in the *Davis Enterprise* of October 4, 1996.)

Davis city growth

ANNEXATION KEY

- ■ Original 1917 boundary
- Prior to 1956
- 1956-60
- 1961-70
- 1971-80
- 1981 to 1996

½ mile
½ km

N

This map shows the city's 74 land annexations to 1996 clustered by decade.

❖❖   ❖❖   ❖❖

In this chapter, I have suggested how the story of the Terminal Building can be significant; explained the central concept of "preservation failure" that will explored; indicated how this book is organized; and, placed this undertaking in sociological and methodological perspective.

With, in addition, a sketch of Davis' population and geographical explosion, we are ready to get on with the story itself.

I

A HISTORIC HOTEL
EIGHT DECADES, 1920s–1990s

To label the Terminal Building demolition a "preservation failure" is to claim that, for historical, cultural, or other reasons a case can be made for its "significance" and, therefore, its "designation" and, perhaps, preservation.

The chapters in Part I try to make that case. In addition, each chapter is designed to provide some of the larger, Davis context.

• **Chapter 2** describes the site on which the Terminal Building sat **before** it was there.

• The building itself was erected in two phases in 1924 and 1926–27 and opened with great Davis fanfare (**Chapter 3**).

• Through the 1930s and '40s, the Terminal Cafe, retail stores in the building, and the hotel were central institutions of Davis life (**Chapter 4**).

• Along with downtowns elsewhere, after World War II the Davis downtown went into what was perceived as decline and this decline included the Terminal Building. As was done in downtowns across the nation, the "cure" for decline was "redevelopment" and "urban renewal." This also happened in Davis in the 1950s–70s, although a few G Street buildings were spared (**Chapter 5**).

• Demolition slowed towards the 1980s and programs of local history and historic preservation picked up. Strong policies to keep the Davis downtown economically vibrant worked, except for the Terminal Building, which continued to decline through the turn of the millennium (**Chapter 6**).

2

BEFORE THE BUILDING

L aid out in 1868, Davisville/Davis existed some five and one-half decades before the 1924 construction of the first part of the Terminal Building at the northeast corner of Second and G streets. Because the location was proximate to the railroad depot, we can correctly guess that there were prior uses of the site. For the sake of historical depth and context, I want in this chapter to describe uses about which we know at least a little.

There are only a few early photographs of the northeast corner of Second and G. We are therefore especially fortunate that the Sanborn Map Company, which made maps of American towns and cities for fire insurance companies, included Davis in its mapping from the fairly early year of 1888.

This company periodically updated its maps. For Davis, we have such "snapshots" of the town for at least nine different years between 1888 to 1955. Of these, in this chapter I excerpt the relevant portions of six years that show the site before the construction of the Terminal Building. (The six excerpts are from the digital scans on Chadwyck-Healey's compact disk titled *Davis, California Sanborn* Maps [Chadwyck-Healley, Inc., 1999].)

In Fig. 2.1 we see the portion of the 1888 map that shows the northeast corner of Second and G. The approximate footprint of the future Terminal Building is shown with a thick-line rectangle on this map (and on subsequent maps). Here, we see that the three occupants of the site were a barber shop, saloon, and outdoor toilet.

On the 1891 map (Fig. 2.2), the barber shop building has been removed, although the outhouse remains. (In all likelihood, it burned down, as fires were frequent in this era.)

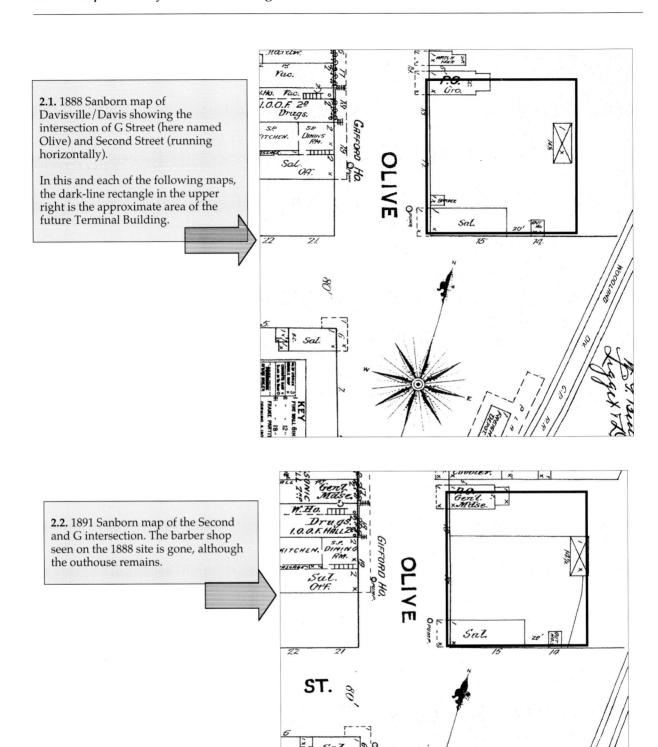

2.1. 1888 Sanborn map of Davisville/Davis showing the intersection of G Street (here named Olive) and Second Street (running horizontally).

In this and each of the following maps, the dark-line rectangle in the upper right is the approximate area of the future Terminal Building.

2.2. 1891 Sanborn map of the Second and G intersection. The barber shop seen on the 1888 site is gone, although the outhouse remains.

2. 3. Circa 1895 view looking north from the southern end of G Street, which is just beyond the tracks running across the middle of the picture. The black arrow points to the fire alarm bell tower at Second and G, an installation also shown on the 1907 Sanborn map reproduced in Fig. 2.6. The building on the left is the Lillard Hotel that was built in 1884 and burned down in 1898.(Larkey Collection.)

2.4. 1900 Sanborn map of the G (here called Olive) and Second intersection.

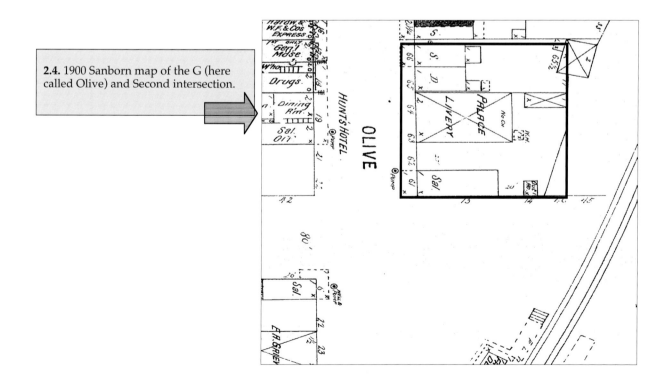

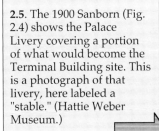

2.5. The 1900 Sanborn (Fig. 2.4) shows the Palace Livery covering a portion of what would become the Terminal Building site. This is a photograph of that livery, here labeled a "stable." (Hattie Weber Museum.)

2.6. 1907 Sanborn map of the Second and G intersection.

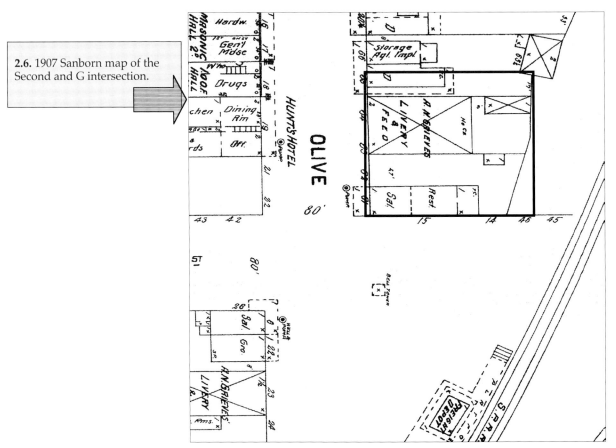

2. 7. This circa 1907 photo was apparently taken to show the delivery of the first almond huller to Davis, shown in the lower foreground. But it also shows G Street looking north from Second. The fire bell tower in the middle distance also appears in Figs. 2.3, 2.6, and 2.8. (Larkey Collection.)

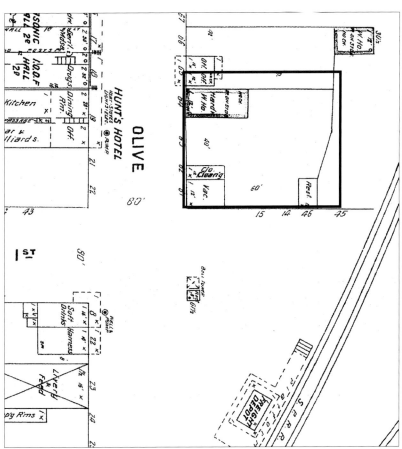

2.8. 1911 Sanborn map of the Second and G intersection. The three previous maps show a "saloon" on the Terminal Building site, together with a second saloon on the southeast corner of this intersection.

Here, the Terminal site saloon is vacant and the southwest corner building has become "soft drinks." These closings—and the closing of several other saloons north of here on G Street—were the result of a successful effort by Davis Prohibitionists to get the state legislature to ban the sale of alcohol in Davis as a way to protect "fragile" University Farm students from Demon Rum.

2.9. Circa 1915 view looking north up "Main Street" (the everyday but unofficial name of Olive/G Street). The building on the extreme right occupies the Terminal Building Site. The recently (1914) constructed Anderson Bank Building is on the left (with its original corner door). (David Herbst.)

2.10. Circa 1918-19 view looking west through the Davis Arch on Second and toward the University Farm. This photograph is reproduced from the 1919 edition of the University Farm yearbook, *El Rodeo*. The building seen on the far right in Fig. 2.9 is just out of view to the right in this photograph.

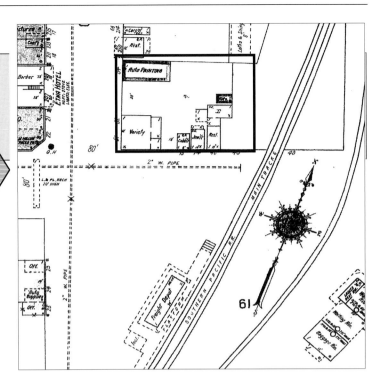

2.11. 1921 Sanborn map of the Second and G intersection. There has been a flurry of construction on the Terminal site since the 1911 map (Fig. 2.8). According to the labels on the buildings, the new activities include a cobbler, jeweler, restaurant, and a dwelling.

2.12. Circa 1919 photo of the structure that will be moved in 1924 to make way for the new Terminal Building. Before Tingus and Belenis opened the Terminal Cafe in this building, its uses included those of a pool hall and variety store. (Larkey Collection.)

2.13. 1921 view of the corner door of the Terminal Cafe at Second and G. This photograph and caption are reproduced from the *Davis Enterprise* of December 18, 1958.

The year 1921 is based on the claim in the caption that this photograph was taken 37 years before this publication in 1958.

37 YEARS AGO IN DAVIS—From left, Jim Belenis, Pete Belenis and John Tingus, partners for 24 years in the old Terminal Cafe, are shown standing under their new electric sign. The cafe was located on the corner of Second street across from the SP Depot, where the Aggie Hotel is now located.

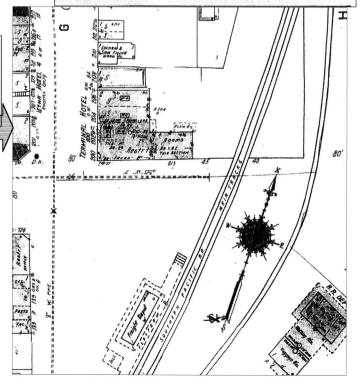

2.14. 1945 Sanborn map of the Second and G intersection. As will be elaborated in the next chapter, the Terminal Building was erected in two phases in 1924 and 1926.

This, then, was the location at which the Terminal Building was constructed. We turn now to the coming of the building itself.

3

HEYDAY DECADES, 1920s

Using items appearing in the *Davis Enterprise*, I want in this chapter to chronicle the two phases of the Terminal building's construction and to suggest something of the richness and variety of social life that began to center on the Terminal Cafe just after its new opening on November 12, 1924.

This chapter focuses on the four years of 1924–27—roughly the mid and late 1920s. In the next chapter, I survey the subsequent two decades.

1) CONSTRUCTION AND OPENING IN 1924

Although the building's construction did not begin until August, 1924, the briefly displaced Terminal Cafe was re-opened well in time to have a strong finish in 1924.

3.1. Published August 1, 1924, the story appearing on the next page is the first *Davis Enterprise* report on a new building at the northeast corner of G and Second streets. In the right-hand column, we are told that the building will be one story, but constructed so that a second story and a wing can be added later. This was, in fact, undertaken in 1926 (and described later in this chapter).

GEORGE TINGUS, JAS. D. BELENIS LET CONTRACT

For $20,000 Building at the Corner of Second and G. Streets, Davis

OF BRICK CONSTRUCTION

With 75 Feet Front on G. and 57 Feet on Second Sts. Three Occupancies

Messrs. George Tingus and Jas. D. Belenis, proprietors of the Terminal Cafe, have let a contract for the construction of a brick building that will be located at the corner of G and Second Sreets and will cost $20,000.

A building project that means considerable to The City of Davis, has reached the stage of contract let and work under way.

Chas. S. Mabry of Sacramento was awarded the contract for the construction, Tingus and Belenis to remove the building that now occupies the corner to be built upon. The old structure has been disposed of to J. D. Grieve and will be immediately removed to a point facing G street and to the south of the Liggett Garage.

We are informed the contractor will rush construction at once and is allowed 35 working days within which to complete the structure.

Those gentlemen state that their plans call for a structure one story in height, but sufficiently strong to support not less than three additional stories that in all probability will be added later. The building will be so arranged that it may later be utilized for hotel purposes if desired.

The walls will be of brick, faced with pressed brick somewhat similar to the outside finish of the Bank of Davis building, with a main entrance at the south west corner.

The cafe business will be transferred into the corner room of the new building, to be an up-to-the-minute eating house with all the modern equipment, including a refrigerating plant and the latest in kitchen apparatus, everything modern and sanitary to the last word.

In addition to the section of the new building that will be occupied as an eating department, there will be also, two store rooms to the north and also facing upon G street, that have not as yet been leased, but the owners announce it is their policy to have the rooms so occupied that present business houses will not be injured from the point of competition.

They also requested us to say that notwithstanding the fact that an outside firm was awarded the contract for construction, sub-contract will be open to local bidders, and it is hoped all will be done by local people.

Transformed Into An Auto Display Room

Once more the old corner at north east corner of Second and G is vacant. The same thing has occurred a number of times during the history of Davis. The vacator on previous occasions has been the fire demon, but this time the building occupying said corner was raised from its foundations and moved intact to the J. D. Grieve property to the south of the Liggett Garage, having been purchased by Grieve who has leased same to Frank Liggett to be used, he says as a display room for his cars-for-sale, for which use the structure is well adapted, being faced with an all-glass front.

The building was formerly occupied as a pool hall and later by C. M. Ray as a grocerstore.

It was the first building to be saved from destruction from fire by the new water system.

FRIDAY, AUGUST 8, 1924

3.2. The building at Second and G streets was moved just to the north of 139 G Street, which is now a hotel parking lot.

3.3. The existing Cafe apparently continued to operate in its old building in its new location.

HOPE TO BE IN NEW BUILDING ABOUT OCTOBER FIRST

Construction of the Tingus-Belini building at the corner of Second and G streets, is coming right along and the owners hope to be able to occupy about the first of October. They will be ready to move from present quarters immediately when the new building is finished.

FRIDAY, AUGUST 22,

3.4. Progress on the new building is reported in the second paragraph.

3.5. In this first ad for the Cafe, Davis is so small that one does not have to include the address.

BUILDING ACTIVITY

The additional wing for Davis Grammar School is coming along rapidly; the basement in and the walls up. The roof no doubt will soon be on which will protect the work from the winter storms.

Good progress is being made on the new structure at the north east corner of second and G streets, being erected by the proprietors of the Terminal Cafe. The building will be ready for occupancy sometime early in November.

The construction of the Julius Oeste dwelling, located near the highway junction, a mile west of Davis, is coming along with the basement in and frame coming up.

FRIDAY, OCT. 8, 1924

Formal Opening New Terminal Cafe, Nov. 12

The NEW TERMINAL CAFE will throw open its doors to the public on Next Wednesday evening, November 12. On this occasion special dinners will be served, both turkey and chicken, or guests will be served regularly from the menu. In other words, any service desired will be given in addition to special dinners.

The new Terminal Cafe, as new in every respect, other than the proprietorship, the owners being, Messrs. Tingus and Holinis who have conducted so satisfactorily the Terminal Cafe at the old stand on the corner since war times.

The management announce that not only the building, but all the furnishings and equipment will be sparkling new and perfectly adapted to first class service in every respect. They tell us that Davis will now have a cafe up-to-the-minute all the way. That the same service will be rendered as heretofore found only in the large cities. In addition to regular service they will be prepared to serve special dinners for parties, with a seating capacity up to 130 plates per sitting. With popular prices.

On next Wednesday evening, the opening night, the doors will be thrown open at 6 o'clock and if desired reservations of tables may be made for that hour.

The enterprise and business sagacity displayed by the Terminal Cafe people is most commendible, and will prove a big asset to Davis and they are deserving of unqualified success and it is to be hoped they will get the encouragement due them thru a liberal patronage. That our citizens will come out strong on the opening night, thereby showing them that we are with them in their new departure and that we appreciate their efforts.

3.6. William Henry Scott, who owned and edited the *Davis Enterprise,* was unabashedly partisan on many matters he reported. In this November 7th article he is unequivocally enthusiastic about this new establishment.

3.7. Cleanliness in restaurants was a serious issue in the 1920s. This November 14th ad seeks to assure people on this matter by offering them "a visit of inspection."

A VISIT to our new commodious, airy, well-lighted quarters will bring to you a realization of the comforts and service that go with a meal served here.

YOU are welcome at all times to pay us a visit of inspection. . . . . .

THE TERMINAL CAFE

Fresh Oysters Daily   Steaks, Chops, Poultry

GRAND OPENING TERMINAL CAFE WEDNESDAY EVE

Pronounced Success With An Overflow Demand For Reserved Tables

The opening night of Terminal Cafe in the new place in the new building at the corner of Second and G Wednesday night, proved a most auspicious occasion. The attendance with demands for tables in reserve for the dinner, was far beyond the expectations of the management, with the result that the facilities were taxed to the limit during the evening.

It was quite apparent that the towns people were out to give expression to their appreciation of the enterprise displayed by Messrs Tingus and Belenis, in the giving to the city so fine a cafe, modernly equipped in every way. Davis Business Men's Association presented them with a beautiful floral piece. Each table was decorated with carnations. The special menu included a choice of chicken, turkey and Virginia ham.

The management was handicapped somewhat in giving the service they would liked to have given, owing to the unexpected number of guests and the fact that everything was absolutely new, and some hitches occurred during the afternoon in mechanical connections.

The management requests the Enterprise to assure the towns people that they appreciate to the limit the excellent spirit of co-operation and good will so apparent, and to say that their aim will be to give the best service possible. That they are for and with the town. Also that their entire place, kitchen included, is open for inspection. They are anxious to convince the people that cleanliness is one of their slogans and nothing so convincing as seeing.

3.8 The Terminal Cafe seated 130, but Davisites apparently turned out in numbers much greater than this. In 1924, the town population was about 1,100. This report of crowding suggests that perhaps some twenty percent of the Davis population turned out to eat at the grand opening.

3.9. The B and B Meat Company opening announced in this December 5th article was the first of a series of meat shops that occupied the northern-most retail space up to and after World War II.

Announcement Of A New Business

The B. & B. Meat Company announce the opening of their new Meat Market at Davis will take place next Monday morning, Dec. 8. That they have obtained a lease on the north store room of the Terminal Cafe building for a term of years and plan to conduct a market that will meet with the approval of the people of Davis and vicinity. Their purpose will be to offer only high quliaty meats at right prices. They invite the public to pay their market a visit and see for themselves, and especially seek a reasonable share of patronage and promise to show appreciation in good service.

2) THE NEW DAVIS SOCIAL CENTER IN 1925

Reports in the 1925 *Davis Enterprise* suggest that the new Terminal Cafe almost instantly became "the" place to "meet and greet" among Davis elites and the civic-minded. The following is a sample of these reports for 1925. Because my focus is the Terminal Building rather than the particular groups, I have edited out much of what is reported about what groups did at their meetings. I hope readers will find this frustrating enough to propel them to research these groups.

3.10. This meeting on January 23rd was one of a great many held in this period in order to wrestle with the question of adopting a "city plan." Such a plan implied, among other things, "zoning," a scheme for telling people where they could build what kind of structures.

3.11. The "Men's Class" consisted of adult male members of the Community Church. It was a "Sunday School" group that seemed mostly to discuss civic affairs at their meetings.

The matter of City Planning for Davis was given great impetus at a gathering of local citizens, 60 in number and representative of the various Civic and Fraternal organizations of Davis at a meeting Held Monday evening at the Terminal Cafe, and which was staged as the result of action taken previously by the Davis Business Men's Association.

MONTHLY DINNER ON JANUARY 25

The monthly dinner of the Men's class at the new Terminal Cafe comes on next Wednesday evening. There will be reports of standing committees that will interest every member of the community. Also some brief special talks by Harry Shepherd and Tracy Storer about some of the things to be done about our homes and about the town at this time of the year to help make Davis a more beautiful home town. We want Davis to be known as the best home town in California. The Committee of the men's class are working toward this.

All men are welcome to the dinners. They are "Dutch" at 50 cents a plate. Ask Cal Covell, or Maghetti or Dewey Song to see that a place is reserved for you at the table. The hour is 6:30.

3.12. The evening of March 6th, 1925, the Davis Business Men's Association changed its name to the Chamber of Commerce.

As a direct aftermath of the decision Monday evening of Davis Business Men's Association to adopt a new name that of Chamber of Commerce, and undoubtedly a very wise move, the merchants, or as might be properly termed those whom are considered strictly business men, in the way of actually selling something to the public, proceeded to hold a get-together luncheon on Wednesday.

The attendance as above indicated was held to mean those only engaged in business in the business section of the town, with the exception of the service stations, Professional men not not included.

The get-together was held at the Terminal Cafe and during the luncheon purpose of the occasion was discussed and the purpose briefly outlined as that of discussion frankly among themselves business matters of interest to both merchant. It is the announced idea to go to the bottom of things to the end that patrons will be given the best possible service for the least possible prices, and the merchant at the same time placed in a position he protected to some degree at least from bad accounts and any other avoidable business drains.

3.13. The Merchants Club, apparently a group different from the Chamber of Commerce, also met at the Terminal Cafe.

Merchants Congregate At Luncheon

What is termed the Merchants Club, assembled at luncheon for the second time Wednesday noon at the Terminal Cafe. As arranged at the previous meet, a week earlier, Mayor A. C. Anderson presided. C. M. Ray will be Master of ceremonies next Wednesday. A few matters of local business interest were discussed, such as the matter of license fees for outside venders, peddlers, etc. Messrs. C. A. Maghetti and Otto Bruhn were appointed a committee for investigation and to report at the next meeting.

3.14. In the 1920s, it appears to have been common for local adults to sing before groups in quartets and solo (March 26th).

MEN'S CLASS IN REGULAR SESSION MONDAY EVENING

The Men's Class of Davis Community Church held their monthly meet Saturday evening, opening up with a dinner at the Terminal Cafe as the first number on the program.

A male quartett, Covell, MacAfee Finke and Long, rendered a vocal solo and answered an encore with another.

C. A. Covell preside, calling the session to order.

3.15. The speaker on sheep at this meeting, Professor H. F. Miller, lived in the house at the southwest corner of B and Eighth streets.

3.16. This is another of the many meetings at the Terminal Cafe on the topic of city planning (April 24th).

MEN CLASS HOLD EAT WED'Y EVE

The regular monthly dinner meeting of the men's class at the Terminal Cafe on Wednesday was a most enjoyable affair. The place of the sheep in the economic development of the community was the general topic of discussion. H. F. Miller spoke of the wonderful recent development of the early lamb industry in California and the place of Yolo County in this industry.

FRIDAY, APRIL 17, 1925

CITY PLANNING COMMITTEE IN FIRST MEETING

Local merchants assembled in a get-together at Terminal Cafe Wednesday noon luncheon. Sixteen gathered about the tables. F. P. Wray, presided for the session.

The committee previously appointed in the matter of formation of a credit information bureau, reported progress but was not ready for complete report on findings but stated that it was hoped to have things shaped up for launching on the first of May.

3.17. Oysters and Abalone were widely popular foods in the 1920s (November 13th advertisement).

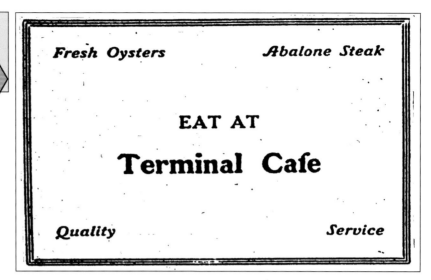

3.18. *Davis Enterprise* Advertisement, November 20, 1925.

Merchants Give Aggies Trophy

Davis merchants assembled at the Terminal Cafe for their weekly luncheon Wednesday. Gus Gerson, representing the California Aggies at Davis, in the matter of working up a boxing team for the coming season, was present.

[November 27, 1925]

3.19. This story goes on to report that the merchants were so enthusiastic about a boxing team they voted to offer a trophy cup to be contested for annually.

3.20. The Davis Rotary Club was organized out of this meeting at the Terminal Cafe on December 4, 1925.

Shall Davis Develop A Rotary Club

The weekly luncheon of the Merchants club, gathered at the Terminal Cafe Wednesday at 12:15.

E. S. McBride presided and had arranged for a pleasant bit of entertainment in that he had present Messrs. Ed. Roby of Auburn and Carl Lamus of Sacramento. These gentleme, it developed are very enthusiastic Rotarians, and were invited to do a little talking upon the subject

Mr Roby was first introduced, and declared he admired the spirit of coperation that seemed apparent with Davis merchants, and introduced Mr. Lamus, as the big talk on that subject

Mr. Lamus opened his talk with the question, "What would a Rotary Club do for Davis, and the community.' The speaker declared Rotary clubs are now functioning in 33 of the nations of the earth and that there are nearly three thousand clubs going in the U. S. Club membership incluudes but one of each particular vocation in a community. One of the particular objects of rotarianism is the breaking down of formal barriers between men. One of the provisions that members must address each other by their given names.

3) THE TERMINAL HOTEL ADDED IN 1926-27

Apparently bolstered by the success of their Terminal Cafe, Messrs. Belenis and Tingus embarked, in November, 1926, on the previously envisioned expansion of the building into a hotel.

3.21. Before that heady addition work, though, restaurant life went on. This greeting of the season is one of about a dozen occupying an entire page of the *Enterprise* dated January 1, 1926.

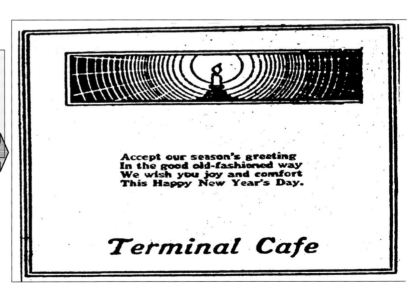

Accept our season's greeting
In the good old-fashioned way
We wish you joy and comfort
This Happy New Year's Day.

Terminal Cafe

Terminal Cafe Is Robbed

Monday evening the Terminal Cafe was visited by one who carried away some of the lucre accumulated during the evening. The place is operated by Messrs. Tingus and Belenis. Mr. Tingis had retired to his bed for the night and Mr. Belenis, leaving the change in the till, had attended the screening of the "Vanishing American." planning to reenter the cafe and to pick up the change. At about 10:45 he returned from the show and entered the cafe. As he entered the front door he noticed a bit of noise within and observed a door connecting the kitchen with the dining room swinging, indicating that someone had just passed thru. This followed by the slamming of the rear screen door.

The investigation that followed disclosed the fact that the intruder had been helping himself to the contents of the cash register, but seemingly had been interrupted in the procedure as he overlooked rolls of dimes and nickels amounting to $7.50. A total of about $35.00 was missing from the register.

Rifling the cash register was the only thing disturbed so far as it could be ascertained. The intruder had apparently entered thru the door by the aid of a pass or skeleton key of some kind, as the door did not show any evidence of being forced. A screen over a rear window had been cut but the latch was not lifted. The proprietors are somewhat puzzled over the circumstances, but without any clue as to the identity of the burglar.

3.22. *Davis Enterprise,* January 15, 1926. Although apparently not common, crimes such as this were not rare in Davis, either.

3.23. *Davis Enterprise,* January 29, 1926. Public sanitation was a key issue in California in the 1920s. The State had begun programs of inspection and found Davis eating places—the Terminal Cafe excepted—wanting.

Community Men's Class Hold Session

TERMINAL CAFE HIGHEST RATING IN CALIFORNIA

The Mens Class Davis Community Church assembled in regular monthly session at the Terminal Cafe on Wednesday evening. The meeting was quite well attended and considerable enthusiasm displayed relative to local matters of public concern.

C. A. Covell presided in the absence of Prof. G. H. True, and he did not permit of a dull moment.

Dr. Bates chairman of the local committee on sanitary conditions, reported a visit of an inspector of California State Board of Health Bureau of Foods and drugs. That a number of local places were inspected, such as serve the public with food and drink. That the conditions found, were what might be termed fair to good. That said inspector declared that he found the conditions at the Terminal Cafe so far as sanitation and cleanlines is concerned, the best he had inspected in California Dr. Bates concluded his report with a resume of the annual inspection and clean-up campaign in which the Boy Scouts have been accustomed to assist. will be carried thru again this spring, and he asked that the Class back him up in the campaign.

Terminal Cafe to Erect Modern 35-room Hotel

Davis has been particularly favored the past few years with the installation and operation of a first class cafe, the buildling, a substantial and attractive brick struuoture, conducted most successfully by Messrs. Tingus and Belenis. These gentlemen have conducted an eating emporium that has been and is still a credit to Davis, both as one of the cleanest places to eat, as found by the State Inspector, to' be seen anywhere.

But this is not all. Tingus and Belenis have been planning to enlarge the scope of their operations. They have from their/xperience as caterers, become convinced that there is a good opening here for a modern hotel. This they have planned for and final arrangements have been made with the builder.

The addition to the Terminal Cafe means that the space to the rear of the present building will be cleared of the buildlings and a structure brought up alongside the present oneand then the entire construstion carried two stories.

The plans of these modern caterers are to work out plans for a very nice hotel with a total of 35 rooms added. There will be included a few suites and apartments so arranged that they will be convertible to the requirements of the tenants., so that two or more rooms may be thrown together as desired.

They tell us that they propose to have a first class, modern hotel in every respect. The buildling will be wired for telephones, hot and cold water will be in each room, electric bells, steam heat and some of the rooms with private baths. A little later we plan to tell the public more of the interesting details as the plans are more mature.

Messrs Tingus and oBlenls are giving evidence of their faith in the future of Davis, and as an example of business enterprise rather exceptional, to say the least, and which will undoubtedly be appreciated and this appreciation shown by co-operation.

3.24. *Davis Enterprise*, November 12, 1926.

3.25. *Davis Enterprise*, December 10, 1926.

Work Started On Terminal New Addition

Work has been started on the the proposed improvement planned by Tingus and Belenls, owners of the Terminal Cafe. The plans are for clearing away from the rear all of the frame buildings now standing there to make room for the new addition. A force of carpenters are engaged preparing the front of the room fartherst to the north, and a part of the cafe building for W. Alter, as a shoe and repair shop, in order to make a place for him to move into. His old place will be torn down to make room for the new addition. Mr. Alter plans to move into the new building not later than Monday next.

The old buildings at the side of the cafe that must be cleared are alld laposed of but one, and that is expected to be sold soon.

It is hoped to have everything ready for active operations on the new building not later than next Monday, and to rush the consthuction rapidty. The addition will be a great improvement to this already popular block.

With the old buildings to the rear cleared away, that sector of the new structure will be brought up to the level of the present one, and then the entire building carried up a second story. Davis Lumber company is supplying the materials in their line for the new building.

DAVIS ENTERPRISE

THE PURPLE CIRCLE HAS MORE BLOODED STOCK THAN ANY SIMILAR SIZE AREA IN THE WORLD

HAVE YOU SOME THING TO SELL? ADVERTISE IN THE ENTERPRISE

THIRTIETH YEAR   DAVIS ENTERPRISE, DAVIS, YOLO COUNTY, CALIFORNIA, APRIL 1, 1927   PUBLISHED WEEKLY   No. 18

Down Town Section Gets Addition In New Hotel

Tomorrow evening, Davis will witness the adition of another permanent asset in the way of comfort an convenience, aapted particularly for the pleasure and comfort of those who chance to be within our gates. We have in mind the opening for business of the Hotel Terminal, at the north east corner of G and Second Streets.

It will be remembered hat, originally upon this corner was situate what has been known as the Terminal Cafe, with Messrs. Tingus & Belenis, proprietors. This cafe has been conducted the past three years, and so successfull, that the owners were encouraged to carry out their original plan, that of going up another story, and converting the second floor into an up-to-the-minute hotel.

Construction has been under way for some months, and while the lobby on the first floor is scarcely set in its coat of paint, the rooms will be ready for occupancy and will be thrown open to the public tomorrow evening and Davis, for the first time in a long period of years, will have a down town hostelry, and what is particularly pleasing, the fact that the finish, and the furnishings are such that it is very creditable to our little city, in fact would be classy in a metropolitan city, and to the credit and good judgment of the management as well. The proprietors are men of extended experience in catering to the public in this line and undoubtedly will make the place home-like and the patrons comfortable.

Just a word as to the furnishings will not be amiss here. It is not overdrawing the facts to say that the Hotel Terminal is furnished in a first class manner in modern stlsr. The rooms have all the modern conveniences, and the furniture, in steel in a walnut finish, the only article in the room of a wood a com fy rocker; the mattresses, springs, and beddstead, "Simmons Best." The window drapes and curtains were fashioned by Miss Theo Palmer and are very nice indeed. There are eight suites of rooms, arranged for the convenience of families particularly, also, a few single rooms.

The lobby is situate on the first floor, with the netrance off G street the main stairway to the second floor leading therefrom. All rooms are outside rooms, and well ventilated. The management is having installed appropriate and attractive electric signs.

In short, Davis is prepared, as she has not been in years to offer hotel accommodations to visitors, to those who stop over when visiting the University Farm etc.

3.26. *Davis Enterprise* front page, April 1, 1927. The banner headline, above, has been reduced to fit on this page. The accompanying front page story has been enlarged to make it easier to read.

3.27. The above opening day advertisement also appeared on the April 1, 1927 front page. Unlike the opening of the Terminal Cafe, which received, as seen, a rather detailed write-up, there was no follow-up *Enterprise* report on the Hotel opening. But, then, and unlike eating, checking into a hotel just a few blocks from one's home is not something many Davis people were likely to do.

3.28. This is the earliest known photograph of the Terminal Building. It is reproduced from a 1928 University Farm promotional booklet and was probably taken in 1927 or 1928. (The booklet is in the California Promotion Collection of the UCD University Library Special Collections.)

4) CONCLUSION

I have in this chapter reported the beginnings of the Terminal Cafe and Hotel and the building that housed them. By means of excerpts from news stories I have suggested that the Terminal Cafe was a key venue in the social life of Davis in the 1920s. In the next chapter, we look at the next two decades.

HEYDAY DECADES, 1930s–40s

The pages of the *Davis Enterprise* continued to feature meetings of leading groups at the Terminal Cafe up to (and beyond) World War II. Because of the repetition, I will not provide many further examples of these happenings.

Instead, I want to focus on photographs. Curiously, there are almost no known pictures of the Terminal Building dating from the 1920s—or even of G Street more generally. This began to change in the 1930s and beyond, and I want to feature those photographs in this chapter.

1) SECOND AND G STREETS AS ICONIC DAVIS

The importance of these images resides, in the first instance, in the very fact that their takers made them and included the Terminal Building. The fact that there are so many pictures of the area at and near the intersection of Second and G streets—but not of many other Davis locales—suggests to me that the picture-takers believed that they were picturing "Davis" in these photos.

But they were not just picturing Davis. The fact of the pictures means that they thought Davis was important enough to warrant photographing **and/or** that people to whom they might sell the pictures were of that belief.

Specifically, the period before World War II was still an era—albeit then waning—of the "real photograph" postcard. Camera and print technology made it possible for postcard-entrepreneurs to make and sell photographs of town scenes at affordable prices. Several of the photographs in this chapter were taken for the purpose of making such real photograph postcards. Entrepreneur decisions to make cards of Davis tells us they believed there was a market. The fact that these cards center on Second and G tells us their assessment of what **"was"** Davis to them. The featured buildings, **which regularly included the Terminal Building**, were, to them, the defining or iconic features of the town.

4.1. *Davis Enterprise*, August 21, 1931. The structure is called "The Terminal Hotel Building" in this ad. Some telephones now have three rather than only the two digits we saw in the 1920s. But, a street address is still not needed.

Rotary Club Addressed by Prof. Wilson

Davis Rotary Club met as usual at Terminal Cafe for luncheon Monday. Sam Brinley, president of the club, occupied the chair. Chester Roadhouse led the singing, and gave Jack Vest, one of the new members, an opportunity to display his ability as a vocalist in the rendering of "Sweet Adeline."

President Brinley announced that he had received a message of appreciation from Prof. J. F. Wilson, of the telegraphic message sent him while at Laramie, Wyoming, in attendance upon the funeral of his brother who was accidently drowned while attempting to save a friend who was about to drown in a lake.

Prof W. M. Regan of the University Farm staff, was the principal speaker and he chose for his subject, "Care of Livestock." Mr. Regan said that he had been connected with several colleges, but that he found the cooperative spirit between the college and the adjoining town here at Davis, the best that he had witnessed anywhere.

4.2. August 7, 1931. Into the 1930s, the custom of opening and closing meetings with solo singing performances by local people continued.

4.3. September 4, 1931. People not only sang solo at local meetings, they performed songs written by local people. "Dr. Roadhouse" and "Dr. Hayes" were prominent faculty at the University Farm.

ROTARY WOULD FOSTER INTER-CITY ATTENDING

Assembly Meeting at Lake Tahoe Outlines Work of Year

Davis Rotary Club, Sam Brinley as president, in the chair, enjoyed an interesting luncheon season at Terminal Cafe Monday. Quite a contingent of Woodland Rotarians were present.

Dr. Roadhouse, song leader, offered two new songs, stating they had been prepared by Dr. Hayes, and both went over good.

APPRAISAL OF PROPERTY

Located at ___2nd & G___ Street, Assessed to ___Tingus & Belinis___

Occupied by ___Terminal Hotel___ Year built ___1925___

DESCRIPTIVE INFORMATION

Stories ___2___ Major rooms ___36___ Minor rooms ___27___

Ceiling height—1st floor ___14'___ 2nd floor ___8'6"___

Roof pitch ___Flat___ Cornice projection ___Fire wall___

Size joists—1st floor ___2n8___ 2nd ___2x2___ Double floors ___Yes___

Hardwood floors ___40x40___ In how many rooms _____

Plastered walls ___Yes___ If not, what kind _____

Outside finish ___Brick___ Roof ___Hot___ Size basement ___20x75___
___Cement___

Foundation _____ Size _____

Garage _____ Size _____

Rate per plan No. _____ Other buildings ___16x49x10___

Main part—size	@		30,000	00
Projecting rooms	@			
Bay windows	@			
Dormers	@			
Porches	@			
	@			
	@			
	@			
Foundation _____ prm.				
Difference for arch style				
Basement walls _____ L. F.	@			
" floor _____ S. F.	@			
" excavation	@			
Fireplace ___No___				
Plumbing ___Regulation___				
Heating ___Oil Heating Plant___				
Wiring and elect. ___Regulation___				
Cabinet work ___Little in kitchen___				
Garage				
Other outbuildings ___16x49 Old restaurant, in rear___			700	00
Total present day replacement value			30,700	00
Less depreciation ___7 Years___			2,150	00
Assessed value			28,550	00

Dated ___March 30___ , 19__3__

4.4. 1933 "Appraisal of Property" sheet for the "Terminal Hotel." This one of a set of 464 such sheets, one for each developed structure in Davis in 1933. The complete set is housed in the UC Davis University Library Department of Special Collections. The "year built" of 1925 shown here is apparently a negotiated date since we know that the first part of the building was built in 1924 and the second in 1926-27.

4.5. From the first issue of the University Farm yearbook to today, many Davis businesses bought advertisements that appeared in a special section at the back. This is the Terminal Hotel and Cafe ad in the *El Rodeo* of 1934..

Hot and Cold Water Steam Heat
All Outside Rooms

TERMINAL HOTEL & CAFE
Home of the California University Farm

"The Leading Hotel and Cafe"

Phone 83 Davis, Calif.

4.6. On March 26, 1936, A. E. Gilmore photographed Davis from a Goodyear blimp. The above is an excerpt from that photo, showing the Terminal Hotel on the left. The entire picture is printed on page 10 of Lofland and Haig, 2000. (The print from which I scanned the picture is owned by Pete Richards of the Davis Gold and Silver Exchange.)

4.7. Davis looking east in a photo taken ~1939. College Park is in the lower left and the University Farm Quad is in the lower right. I include this view here to draw attention to just how small Davis was even on the eve of World War II. (Scanned from photograph number 3789 in the UC Davis University Library Special Collections.)

2) DAVIS' ONLY ALL-NIGHT ESTABLISHMENT

In 1939 and for a while later, it appears that Davis had a **single** establishment that stayed open all-night and that was the Terminal Hotel. In this sense, the Terminal Building housed the watcher of the night, the single entity awake to sound the alarm in the case of emergency.

This came to be because in November of 1939 the telephone system changed from a live operator to an automatic system. Prior to that, there was an all-night live telephone operator in Davis who served as the watcher of the night and to whom people reported fire and other emergencies. The operator then relayed the calls to the right authority.

Having no operator, the first Fire Department response was to hook the Department's phone directly to the alarm. This was quickly abandoned because pranksters rang up only to make the alarm sound. One mother even instructed her children that it was time to come home when they heard the fire alarm, for she would call up in order to set it off.

The solution then devised was to have an extension on the Fire Department phone (number 456), near the cash register at the Terminal Hotel and Cafe. Someone was always there when it rang. The employee who answered that phone took the call and then called the unlisted number that set off the fire alarm.

This system was not perfect, though. There were only 999 numbers on the system in Davis and teenagers made it a game to call numbers until they hit it. This made it necessary to change the unlisted number "about every four months" (Miller, n.d., 132).

All this gaming became unnecessary when Davis grew large enough to justify paying people to be at the fire station twenty-four hours a day. (I draw the above from pages 131 and 132 of Charles Miller's delightful compilation of materials on his father's service as the Davis Fire Chief from mid-1934 to late 1940 (Miller, no date).

For Over 17 Years

The Leading Hotel and Cafe in Davis

TERMINAL HOTEL & CAFE

4.8. This 1939 *El Rodeo* yearbook ad fudges on the time period because the first part of the building had stood for 15 years and the hotel for 12 years. The reference is likely to the Belenis and Tingus Cafe, which preceded the building.

MAIN STREET, DAVIS, CALIFORNIA   C4101

4.9. Taken ~1940, this photo depicts "Main Street" Davis close to its fullest "town" development. (This image is scanned from a postcard owned by David Herbst..)

4.10. Downtown Davis in 1941. The business district mostly stops at F Street on the west and Third on the north. (Larkey Collection.)

4.11. Excerpt from Fig. 4.10 providing a closer view of the Terminal Building.

4.12. Excerpt from a photo in the Delay Family Collection in the Hattie Weber Museum Archives. Taken about 1944, it shows two of the business buildings next to the Terminal Building that would be demolished in the "cowboy" 1950s–70s. Notice the welding shop, a farm-oriented type of business that disappeared from the "downtown."

4.13. Taken in 1944, this photo is from the UCD University Library Special Collections Eastman Collection, B-2123. Eastman titled the full picture "Main Street, Davis, California" and published it as a postcard.

4.14. Photographed by Eastman Studios in 1945 (B-3153), the building's brick south wall has been covered with stucco. (UCD Special Collections.)

4.15. In aerial photographs taken in September, 1946, Eastman Studios likely captured Davis at its fullest small town development. Below is an excerpt from one of those pictures that sold widely as a picture postcard. (Eastman B-4705, UCD Special Collections.)

3) AN OLD WORLD ENDS

The photographs in this chapter depict aspects of the last stage of small town America. Even though the country was rapidly urbanizing, across the nation towns such as Davis still retained a certain economic and social integrity.

But following World War II, this all changed very rapidly. In the next two chapters we will see how these changes played out in Davis in general and, specifically, with regard to the Terminal Building.

5

NEGLECT DECADES, 1950s–70s

The history of Davis (and of virtually the entire world) divides into "before" and "after" World War II. As a part of Davis, the history of the Terminal Building also divides into decades before that war (three of them) and decades after it (five of them).

The five decades after that war must themselves be separated into the some three decades in which a new Davis downtown was constructed by demolishing a good part of the existing town (1950s-70s) and the two decades of relatively little new construction or demolition (1980s-90s).

This chapter addresses the three decades of the 1950s-70s. The next chapter deals with the 1980s-90s.

Unlike the larger downtown, through all five decades of the 1950s-90s, the Terminal Building was in decline.

In order to understand this long-term decline, we need first to understand what else was happening in the downtown. This context helps to explain the building's neglect, which was part of a more general G Street "problem."

1) BUILDING A NEW DOWNTOWN

The events of World War II destroyed the "old world," both literally and symbolically. The late 1940s were the beginning of a "new world," in the United States, a world of fresh starts, new enterprises, and rapid economic development.

For California in general and Davis in particular, this meant rapid population growth and decisions about how to accommodate such growth. In a great many if not most towns and cities, accommodation took the form of encouraging (or at least allowing) peripheral shopping malls that had the effect of drawing business away from and ultimately decimating traditional, pre-World War II downtowns. As everyone knows from her or his own observation, the three-part complex of (1) the dead downtown, (2) the highway retail strip, and (3) the large shopping mall at the edge of or outside town is a virtually defining feature of the American landscape (Davies, 1998; Rome, 2001).

For complex reasons still not well understood, the economic and political elites of Davis reacted differently to explosive population growth than did those of many other communities. The G Street business crowd early-on viewed growth as a threat to the downtown. While they favored rapid **residential** growth at the edges of the town, they saw that large-scale retail at the periphery would undercut them. Indeed, this threat was so obvious to them and spoken about so often in the pages of the *Davis Enterprise* that one wonders why other downtown elites did not more often react like those in Davis.

One reason for this difference in reaction may reside in the nature of the Davis downtown as compared to the downtowns of other towns and cities. And, the nature of Davis' downtown has to be understood in the context of the nature of Davis itself.

This "nature" was that Davis in its entirety, including its downtown was, still in the late 1940s, **very small**. Its population of some 3,000 (Fig. 1.3) fit into an area well less than one square mile. The entire town barely spanned six blocks north to south and twelve blocks east to west. **The "downtown" of this late 1940s Davis was little more than one (or perhaps portions of a few) of the some seventy blocks making up the whole town!**

The reader can see this tiny Davis in its entirely in Figure 4.7. The downtown itself as it existed in 1941 is shown in Figure 4.10. The abrupt transition from commercial to residential shown in the upper portion of Figure 4.10 is particularly striking.

In a strict and traditional sense, when we speak of "saving" Davis' downtown we should be speaking of the area around G and Second streets (the area shown in Figure 4.10), for, only that area was the "classic" downtown.

But, the "downtown" that people commonly now think as having been "saved" in Davis refers in only a minor way to the historic G Street area. Instead, the geographic referent of the term has become, to a great extent, what was previously much of the entire town. This shift in meaning and referent had already taken place by the early 1960s. By then, the "downtown" was becoming a large part of the twenty-four blocks bounded by First and Fifth and B and G. **Many of what were previously residential blocks were now thought of as commercial blocks and, therefore, the "downtown."**

The upshot was that Davis not so much "saved" its downtown (defined as the immediate Second and G area) as it started over and built an entirely new downtown on ground to the north and west of the tiny old downtown.

From the founding of the town in 1868 up to the late 1940s, the "center" of the downtown was undisputedly the intersection of G and Second streets. With the 1950s-70s expansion, the center was consciously shifted two blocks west and one block north (which is shown in Fig. 5.1). In addition, Second Street had formerly been the main corridor from the train station to the UC campus. Corridor thinking now shifted north and centered on Third Street and the idea of a "Third Street Parade" or perhaps shopping mall (Fig. 5.1).

One can well ask, "How did all this happen?" The short answer is that the public and private political and economic elites formed a funding partnership that hired a San Francisco planning firm to create a plan for a new downtown. Significantly, the firm was provided a fairly detailed set of guidelines that were developed by a 50-member Core Area Citizen's Advisory Committee (*Davis Enterprise*, February 2, 1961).

In Fig. 5.1, a Mr. Blayney from that firm is shown giving a public lecture on the just-delivered written plan. The caption to the photograph in Fig. 5.1 sums up the plan nicely: almost complete, large-scale reconstruction of residential areas adjacent to the old downtown and a Davis population of 75,000 by 1985.

The term "core area" that became standard in the Davis lexicon, meaning roughly the new, twenty-four block "downtown," was introduced by this planning firm. Indeed, their plan was titled *Davis Core Area Plan* (Livingston and Blayney City and Regional Planners, 1961). When the plan was under development in the early 1960s, *Davis Enterprise* editors often put quotes around "core area," suggesting that the newspaper thought the term an odd expression. (Notice that the caption in Fig. 5.1 places the term in quotes.) By the late 1960s, though, this was no longer done.

On reflection, Livingston and Blayneys' renaming much of the original town of Davis the Core Area was a clever piece of strategic labeling. By means of this new name they sidestepped issues of what one "really" meant by such old terms as "downtown" and "business district." Instead, one was talking about something new: the CORE AREA!

Perhaps, also, this re-naming functioned in a way similar to the renaming that sometimes accompanies a person who undergoes a radical change of identity and self-conception, typically a radical religious transformation of identity. Among many examples, Malcolm Little became Malcolm X, the intent being to repudiate his now-rejected previous identity. In a similar fashion, Davis elites broke with and rejected their "old fashioned" and out-of-date past by going from the stodgy "downtown" to the hip Core Area.

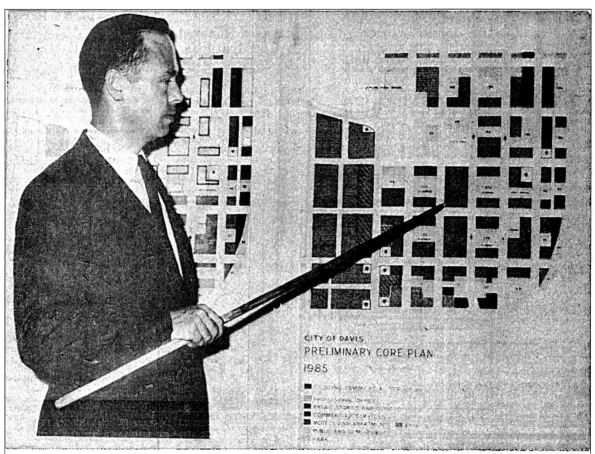

CITY PLANNER John Blayney, of Livingston and Blayney, points to a map which envisions the "core area" of the City of Davis as it can and may be in 1985 ,if definite planning is done and carried out, step by step.

A capacity crowd of citizens gathered in city hall Tuesday night to hear the planning firm's preliminary report and recommendations on a core area survey which is costing a little more than $25,000 from equal contributions from the city and the state and federal governments.

The map shows existing commercial structures, professional offices, retail stores and offices, commercial services, motels and apartments, public and semi-public buildings and parks, and off-street parking lots as they would be in 1985 if the plan is carried out.

The pointer's end is on the intersection of E and 3rd streets, almost exact center of the core area under consideration. Third street, East-West, is designated as a mall-type "parade" probably for exclusive bicycle and pedestrian use and leading into the heart of the core area from the University campus.

(Harry Low Photo)

5. 1. May 18, 1961, *Davis Enterprise* photograph and caption reporting a plan for constructing a Davis downtown to be named the "Core Area."

5.2. 1945 Sanborn "footprint" map of the old downtown and adjacent Davis (First to Fifth, B to G streets). Buildings with black footprints were no longer there in January, 2000 (Lofland, 2000: 7). (The Terminal Building was, of course, still there. In the lower right, a white arrow points to it.)

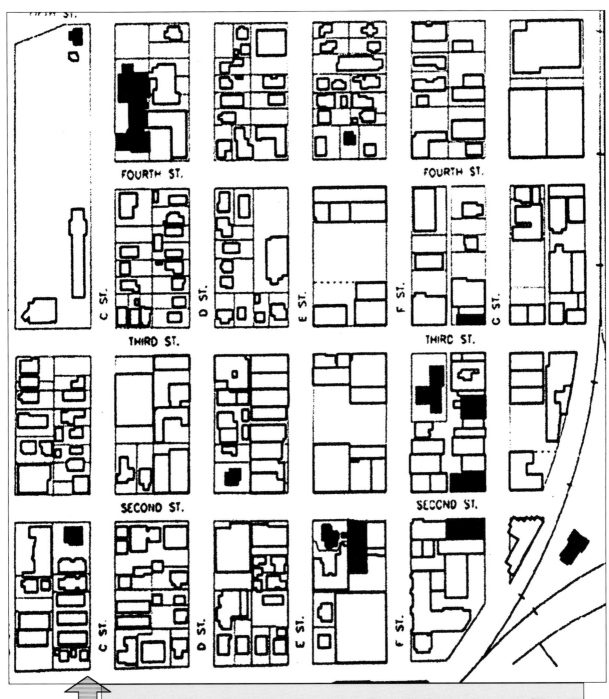

5.3. 2000 map of the same area as shown in Fig. 5.2 (First to Fifth, B to G), showing the footprints of the buildings that replaced those existing in 1945. (This map is reproduced from City of Davis, 2001: 25. (The footprints in black are "Designated Historical Resources.")

2) DEMOLISHING PRE-WAR DAVIS

If one is going to build a new downtown (aka Core Area) consisting of Corbusier-style high-rises surrounded by large parking lots (which is what the plan showed in its schematics), then one has to get rid of the old town. And this Davis did—with seeming vengeance.

Curious about just how thorough the demolitionists of the 1950s-70s had been, in January, 2000 I used the 1945 Sanborn fire insurance map of Davis to count how many of those 1945 buildings were standing in 2000.

In 1945, the entire town had, by my count, 583 buildings (excluding garages and such). In December of 2000, I went lot-to-lot with the twelve sheets of the Sanborn map in hand and I counted 330 buildings as still there, a survival rate of 57% (Lofland 2001, 7).

However, the survival rates of the four areas of this pre-war town were quite different. If we define the "downtown" as the twenty-four blocks bounded by First and Fifth and B and G, 86 of the 233 buildings existing in 1945 had survived to 2000, a survival rate of 37%.

Fig. 5.2 shows the 1945 Sanborn map for the downtown as just defined. **The buildings with footprints in black—147 of them—no longer existed or were moved outside the downtown by the year 2000.** Notice that fourteen of the twenty-four blocks were either substantially or totally cleared for new construction. **Stated most simply, about half of the downtown area was cleared and some two-thirds of the buildings were removed.**

In order to appreciate just how fundamentally Davis people constructed a new downtown, one needs to compare the 1945 footprint map in Fig. 5.2 with the footprint map of the same area drawn in 2000. The 2000 footprint map is shown in Fig. 5.3. The major contrasts are that in 2000:
> (1) there were many fewer buildings than in 1945,
> (2) the many fewer buildings were much larger than before, and
> (3) large areas were left open and surfaced to become parking lots.

The maps reproduced in Figs. 5.2 and 5.3 provide accurate overview summaries of the downtown/Core Area transformation, but they fail to capture the "grit and crunch" of this dramatic change. Let me therefore try to provide at least a glimpse of these aspects of the process.

While pursuing this research, Debbie Davis, editor of the *Davis Enterprise*, gave me 83 huge bound volumes of the *Davis Enterprise* spanning late 1966 to 1983. Around the same time, a clutch of original *Davis Enterprises* covering much of the period from the late 1950s through 1966 were donated to the Hattie Weber Museum of Davis, named the Hubert Heitman Collection, and were available to me for reading and scanning.

Reading these papers, I encountered dozens of stories on, and pictures of, the demolition of old buildings and the construction of new ones. It is not practical or useful here to reproduce this mass of pictures and stories, but I do want to provide a few, particularly of the demolitions, in order to convey the sense of the period—the grit and crunch of it. These few, representative episodes of demolition are given in Figures 5.4 though 5.11. Since each has a revealing caption from the period, each speaks for itself.

5.4. *Davis Enterprise*, May 21, 1958.

DOWN SHE GOES!—Scenes such as this will be a commonplace sight in Davis if and when a downtown redevelopment project gets under way, clearing out old substandard buildings to make way for the "new look" in the city's central business district. Shown here is the giant wrecking crane as it started smashing and crashing an old residence at 229 F street to complete clearing the site for the construction of the Winger department store and Ben Franklin Variety store, due for completion in September. The residence, smashed to bits and its debris hauled away in huge trucks for burning, was occupied for many years by Joe Huberty, former Davis constable, and his family.   ("Ed" Cottle Photo)

REDEVELOPMENT—Another big stride toward redevelopment of the downtown area of Davis is underway as this old building, the former Henry Oeste warehouse near Fourth and H streets, falls to the giant blows of demolition machinery. Rising on the site in the immediate future will be a modern building to cost around $22,000 which will house the Nicholson Plumbing firm's operations. Miles Nicholson said he believes the old Oeste warehouse was one of the oldest structures in Davis. It was put together with square-cut nails used in the era of a past century and wreckers found the floors, of redwood, had been laid directly on sand, surviving more than three-quarters of a century without signs of termites or decay.

(Harry Low Photo)

5.5. *Davis Enterprise,* July 9, 1959.

COMING DOWN — Razing of the old Central School where many a Davisite, both young and old, studied the three R's is under way. In its place will rise an Arden-Mayfair supermarket and a row of shops. First to go is the east wing and in the top picture the destructive force of the wrecking machine is portrayed. In the bottom photo the jaws of the monster are poised to wreak their havoc.

5.6. *Davis Enterprise,* September 21, 1966.

FEW TEARS SHED — Foster's Freeze at the corner of Second and F Streets, for 17 years a favorite place for a quick sandwich and the number one spot in Davis for girl watching was demolished early today. Clay Quessenberry, owner of the property will erect a modern two story building on the site. Shown operating the bulldozer is Roy Nielsen of Nielsen's Demolition Contractors of Sacramento.
— Enterprise Photo

5.7. *Davis Enterprise,* July 24, 1967.

JUNK YARD——If you think you have ever had your yard piled with junk, take a careful look at this competitor. This F street house has trash blocking the door of the front porch. Litterbugs do not live here. The house is one of the last homes on the site of the new E-F Street parking lot between 3rd and 4th Streets.
—Enterprise Photo

5.8. *Davis Enterprise,* December 14, 1967.

5.9. *Davis Enterprise* July 22, 1970.

STEEL AGAINST WOOD — Downtown Davis is taking on a new look these days as the bulldozers moved in yesterday and started the demolition of old residences on E street to make way for the new Bank of America building.

ENTERPRISE PHOTO

Historic warehouse crumbles

5.10. *Davis Enterprise,* July 13, 1972

Demolition began Wednesday of an historic grain warehouse that has been standing at the intersection of Fourth Street and the Southern Pacific Railroad tracks here since 1908.

The building—or what's left of it—is owned by Raymond Donnell, who operated a business out of it from 1923 to 1967, a 45-year period Donnell thinks might be a record for businessmen in Davis.

Donnell bought the building in 1923 from its original owners, Walter and Jennie Read, who used the place for grain storage and almond hulling. Donnell turned it into a feed business, storing and selling grain to the many livestock owners in the area.

"When you've been in one spot for 45 years you do get attached to it," Donnell commented ruefully. "But you can't live forever, I couldn't carry on, business changed and it's just one of those things."

Demolition of the building will be completed in mid-August.

HISTORICAL RUINS are all that's left of a 66-year-old grain warehouse now in the process of being demolished by building contractor Jack G. Hayes. Owned by long-time Davis businessman Raymond Donnell, the building has been standing since 1908 and was used by Donnell from 1923 until 1967. New building codes have declared the structure unsafe, and because remodelling the place is too expensive Donnell is having it torn down. Pictured helping demolish the place is Joel Vance, one of the workmen put on the job by contractor Hayes.

ENTERPRISE PHOTO

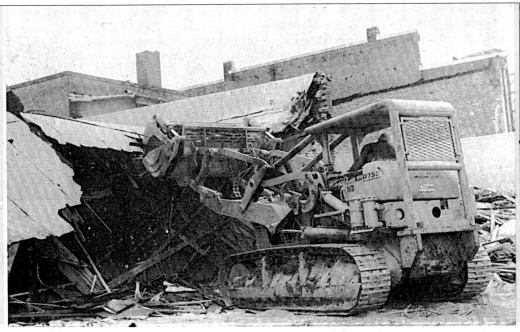

DIME STORE DEMOLISHED

THE CAPITOL Wrecking and Building Co. of West Sacramento bit into the old Riley's Five and Ten building at 233-35 G St. this morning, and by nightfall today the structure should be gone. Chief Building Official Doran Maxwell estimates the venerable landmark is 50-70 years old. There are currently no specific plans to replace the structure, owned by Warren Real Estate and Jim Adams of the Adams Construction Co. Adams told the **Enterprise** this morning they had tenants for, and plans for a new building nearly approved when the City Council slapped a development freeze on the whole block four months ago. Since then the tenants have left, and the plans are obsolete. The freeze was lifeted Feb. 20 and now a new building depends on what new tenants want, said Adams.

ENTERPRISE PHOTO

5.11 *Davis Enterprise,* March 1, 1973.

WRECKED BUILDING

A WORKER peers down at the ruins of the partially demolished Davis Shoe Shop, 231 G St. The California Building Wrecking Co. of West Sacramento began demolition Friday to make way for a new two-story commercial building on the site. The remainder of the old shoe repair shop will be levelled when local rains cease. The new building will be built this Spring by Davis realtor Robert Warren and contractor James Adams.

Enterprise photo

5.12. *Davis Enterprise, April 1, 1974.*

5.13. *Davis Enterprise*, June 22, 1979. Notice that the second and third caption columns are reversed.

Enterprise Photo

The Davis Fire Department is deliberately burning a Davis home at 423 F St. so firefighters can

firefighters were scheduled to burn the house on Thursday, today and Saturday.

gain experience. But don't worry because the house was condemned and uninhabited.

Enterprise Photo

Bulldozer clears debris at site of Al Hatton's Chevron-Standard, Russell Boulevard and B Street.

So long, Al Hatton

Davis landmark razed

Al Hatton's Chevron-Standard station bit the dust Tuesday. But Hatton, who had known of the impending doom for the past year, wasn't getting too sentimental.

"I appreciate all the business over the years. It's been a good life," he said Tuesday.

Hatton has peddled gas on the corner of Russell Boulevard and B Street for the past 25 years.

There has been a gas station on that corner for at least the last 50 years.

But Tuesday marked the end of an era as wreckers leveled out the last vestiges of a familiar Davis landmark.

Hatton said Chevron-Standard decided to give up

its lease with the owner of the land, who resides in San Jose.

He wasn't sure why. "Standard's closing a lot of its small stations," said Hatton.

It used to be a rest stop on the old Highway 40, between Sacramento and San Francisco. Hatton recalls when a restaurant was located on the site and when Highway 99W ran past as well.

There's not much to say now, said Hatton, the apparent victim of corporate change.

He said he's going to relax this month, and then beginning next year he'll start looking around for something else to do.

5.14 *Davis Enterprise*, December 19, 1979.

3) G STREET AND THE TERMINAL BUILDING

While developers were spiritedly tearing down residences and constructing commercial buildings in the new Core Area, Davis' original "Main Street" (named Olive in 1868 and changed to G in the early 1920s) was going into decline. And, with it, the Terminal Building at the center of the original town at Second and G.

After World War II, G Street became an embarrassment to local elites. In his 1959 farewell speech to the Chamber of Commerce, departing city manager Frank Fargo admonished the assembled business leaders, "You must clean up G Street, make it look more modern." The news report on this luncheon continued:

> One guest in the audience said, "G Street now looks like the backdrop for a western TV show." Another said, "Why not an editorial about our business section called "Gunfight at the Bar B Saloon" (*Davis Enterprise*, January 15, 1959).

Fargo further proclaimed: "You need to get your redevelopment plan going. It is vital. New businesses won't move into an area that is so run down."

In a speech to the Davis Area chamber of commerce in January, 1961, planning consultant Lawrence Livingston declared, "the downtown Davis appearance is not too attractive . . . ." Davis lacks "the special character of a college town center" (*Davis Enterprise*, January 19, 1961). The February, 1961 report of the Core Area Citizen's Advisory Committee characterized the "business district" as "presently drab and uninviting" (*Davis Enterprise*, February 2, 1961). In the "semi-final 'do or die'" report of the planners to citizens on July 31 of this same year, the vision was presented as a stark contrast with the "admittedly drab and uninviting appearance" of the downtown (Woodward, 1961).

Subsequent redevelopment actions in the key 200 block of G Street included tearing down most of the buildings on its east side, just north of the Terminal Building. Figure 5.15 shows that east side of G circa 1945. Only one of the ten buildings pictured in that photograph was still standing in 2001. (The Terminal Building is on the right.)

Fig. 5.15. East side of G Street, circa 1945. (Excerpt from Eastman B-2123.)

In addition, about half the buildings on the west side of G were demolished (Fig. 5.2). (Two of those demolitions are pictured in Fig. 5.9 and 5.10). This, though, was not enough to turn things around.

In 1973, downtown property owners announced what the *Enterprise* headlined as a "bold plan to pep up G Street." Actions included new facades, which the *Enterprise* described as "a facelift to dying G Street" in the hope of "a revival of the old shopping district" (October 13, 1973). Basic change was elusive, however. As late as 1982, a merchant left a G Street location because "the whole street has become tacky" (Joan Callaway, Centering Gallery, 231 G, *Davis Enterprise*, July 23, 1982). There was, in particular, concern over the recent opening of a video game arcade.

This is to say, the decline seen in the Terminal Building in the decades after World War II was part of the general sense of out-of-dateness and blight imputed to the entire G Street area in which it was situated.

The Terminal Building was owned jointly by George Tingus and James Belenis until Tingus bought out Belenis in 1946. It was subsequently deeded, in sequence, to these people and corporate entities:

Childs and Nicolson, a general partnership, 1958
Agnes Ramsey Barr, 1965
Sarah Jane Eberle and O. J. Ramsey, 1968
Antique Bizarre, Inc, a California corporation, 1972
Milton J. Eberle and Sarah Jane Eberle, 1977
Aggie Enterprises, 1977

For the purposes of this chapter, the list of owners ends in 1977. But for the sake of foreshadowing the longer term that I will treat in the next chapter, here is the rest of the list of owners:

To Lee-Jing Chen and Chao Chen (husband and wife), Yank Wang and Liang Wang (husband and wife), Fook, Shui and Lam, Pui Kwan (husband and wife) (each of the three couples with "an undivided one-third interest"), 1984
from Fook-Shui Lam and Pui Kwan Kwok to Aggie Enterprises, 1997
from Liang Wang, individually and as widow of Yank Wang to Aggie Enterprises, 1997
from Lee-Jing Chen and Chao Chen, Trustees of the Chen Family Trust, established April 27, 1990 to Aggie Enterprises, 1997 (Fidelity National Title Insurance Company, 2001).

4) 1950s-60s DRIFT

Along with much of the rest of G Street, including the revered Anderson Bank Building, the Terminal Building appeared to "drift" without clear character or identity over much of 1950s and 1960s. However, the hotel still operated and a succession of retail entities and restaurants occupied the first floor spaces (Figs. 5.16, 5.17).

5. 16. Looking north along on G, 1951. (Eastman B-7593.)

5.17. Looking north along G, 1957. (Eastman B-9151.)

A stretch of sidewalk with no buildings was created when the structures north of the Terminal Building were demolished in the 1960s in order to create a parking lot in front of Davis Lumber. As an amenity, the sidewalk area was slightly widened and a fountain and other landscaping added in order to create what was named "the G Street Plaza."

Perhaps the most prominent and persistent early use of this Plaza was the vigil held there for 302 weeks, from March, 1967 to January, 1973, the end of the Vietnam war (*Davis Enterprise*, January 24, 1973). For whatever reasons, the *Enterprise* published a fair number of pictures of this vigil. We can see the Terminal Building in several of them, serving as a backdrop and itself a silent witness to a profound American struggle. The first of these 302 events—and showing the Building—is pictured in Fig. 5.18.

In the 1967 picture reproduced in Fig. 5.18, we see that the ugly "town and country" style shade structure has been added to the western façade of the building. Oddly, City records contain documents on many modifications to the building, but no there is no record of this one. Perhaps no permit was ever taken out, or it was lost, both quite possible in that free-wheeling period. In whatever event, the best guess is that the shade structure was put there in about 1960.

5) END OF AN ERA

James Belenis, one of the original partners who built and operated the Terminal Building, died in 1959, suggesting that an era had ended. (Fig. 5.19).

Fig. 5. 18. Davis residents conduct a vigil for peace in Vietnam on the G Street Plaza by the Terminal Building. (*Davis Enterprise*, March 16, 1967.)

WE'RE THINKING ABOUT VIET-NAM WON'T YOU JOIN US?

PEACE WATCH — Housewife, student, professional man, bearded and clean shaven, they stood in the G street plaza at noon Wednesday to silently protest the war in Vietnam.   In the top picture Eric Gustafson, coordinator of the vigil, is interviewed by a radio newsman. The hour-long vigil was orderly and did not interfere with the noon hour routine.

6) NEW SEVENTIES IDENTITIES AND
THE ANTIQUE BIZARRE ERA

As the area west of G Street was being built anew in the 1960s-70s using "modern" or even "futuristic" conceptions, G Street itself was moving toward a "funky," "hip," and rather "low rent" working-people identity that moved beyond blight embarrassment. E Street and its environments centered on middle class institutions such as banks and mortgage companies, while G Street was gravitating to alternative and working-class culture.

Signal in this was the opening of the Natural Food Works in 1971 (Fig. 5. 20). One of the earliest organic food stores in the United States, it operated in the northern-most G Street space of the Terminal Building until evicted by demolition in 2000. (Relocated to 624 Fourth Street, it acquired the distinction of being one of the longest operating retailers in Davis. It was rivaled only by the very early Davis Lumber and Hardware [which arguably died when it rejected its Davis name and became Ace Hardware in the late 1990s], by Carousel Stationery, and by deLuna Jewelers.)

At about the same time, the then-owners of the Terminal Building seemed to catch the new spirit of the immediate area and of the times by opening a slightly "alternative" eating and drinking establishment named "The Antique Bizarre." Over the decade of the 1970s, it would be a combination working-class hangout and young-band performance venue. Known as the "A.B." to its many fans and habitués, it became a kind of legendary place. At the celebration of the building held on the G Street Plaza, June 11, 2000, invited and open mike speakers alike spoke frequently and fondly of their experiences in and memories of the A.B. era. (This event is depicted in Chapter 9.)

James Belenis, Well Known Davis Restaurateur, Dies

Many friends and relatives in Davis this week mourned the death of James Belenis, 69, a resident and business man here for 46 years and closely associated with the growth of the community from a village to its present size and importance.

Mr. Belenis, ill with a heart ailment, had been under care in the Woodland Clinic hospital for several weeks before death came Sunday night, Sept. 20, 1959.

Trisagion (Rosary) was said Tuesday night at the Davis Funeral Chapel and at 1 p.m. Wednesday a short service was held for local friends at the chapel followed by funeral rites in the Greek Orthodox Church at Alhambra and F streets in Sacramento. Interment followed in East Lawn cemetery, in that city.

Born in Greece in 1889, James Belenis, at the tender age of 16 came by himself to the United States and found a job as a candy maker in Quincy, Mass. When war broke out between Greece and Turkey, he returned to his native land to fight under the Greek flag, returning to the U.S. following the war's end.

In 1919 he came to Davis and soon was associated with George Tingus in building the structure at 2nd and G streets where the two men operated the Terminal Cafe, later adding a second story for hotel rooms. In 1946 he opened the 2nd street restaurant known as Phil's Grill, later adding the annex known as the Brandin' Iron.

He retired in 1956 from active operation of his restaurant business, turning it over to his son, George J. Belenis. But, always a builder and planner at heart, the father was not content with idle retirement and at the time of his last illness he was having built the Bel-Arms apartments at 1st and C streets. That enterprise is due for completion about October 1 and will stand as a memorial to the Greek immigrant boy who

JAMES BELENIS

came to America and carved out a successful career for himself.

Mr. Belenis was a charter member of the Davis Chamber of Commerce and was a member of the Greek Orthodox Church and the Greek fraternity, Order of Ahepa.

Immediate surviving relatives include the widow, Mrs. Stella Belenis, residing at the family residence, 619 East 8th street, Davis; children, Miss Peggy Belenis, George J. and Nick D. Belenis all of Davis; daughters Mrs. Bessie Konaris of San Francisco, Mrs. Helen Gaines of Stockton, Mrs. Evelyn Jouganatos of Sacramento and Mrs. Cally Anagnos of Lodi; eight grandsons and two nephews, James Belenis of Quincy, Mass., and Phil Belenis of Minneapolis, Minn.

Pallbearers were John Shokos, George Tingus, both of Davis, James Kareofelas and Jim Pappas of Woodland, George Skinas of San Francisco and George Triphon of Sacramento.

5.19. End of an Era. Obituary of one of the builders of the Terminal Building, *Davis Enterprise*, September 24, 1959.

5.20. *Davis Enterprise*, November 17, 1971. Just a few months after this photograph was taken, Bob Black would be elected to the Davis City Council in a sea change in Davis politics and serve as the Mayor of Davis in 1976-78.

PROPRIETOR Bob Black points out the wide variety of nuts and beans which his natural foods store sells in bulk. As can be seen, his store makes maximum use of a limited amount of space and has everything from "crunchy" pecan granola to wide-mouth jars.

ENTERPRISE PHOTO

The images presented in Figures 5. 21 through 5. 34 have been selected with the aim of evoking a sense of the spirit of the A.B. era. It is notable, I think, that most of these images are reporters' stories and photographers' pictures from the pages of the *Davis Enterprise*. Many of these are poignant and even touching. The fact that a local newspaper created them speaks well for the community sensitivity of the journalism of the period—and the judgement of *Enterprise* editors.

WEDNESDAY, AUGUST 1, 1973   THE DAVIS ENTERPRISE, DAVIS, CALIF.   PAGE 7

ANTIQUE BIZARRE'S most loyal and dedicated fan, Joe Irwin, is pictured on far right with the championship team. B league city softball champions are (left to right) Lee Sessars, Ed Cornado, Bill Maloney, Specer Spece, Mitch Mitchell, Ed Boosembark, Jim Willot, Paul Mc-Donagh, Bernie Phipps, Terry Maple and Gary Mitchell (6). Failing to make it were Peter 'Babe' Barton, team's leading home run hitter and the Dodge boys.

5.21. The report accompanying this *Enterprise* photograph asks how was "a loosely organized bunch of drunks" transformed into a "highly coordinated, fast-driving, hard hitting group of drunks?" (August 1, 1973).

5.22. *Davis Enterprise,* September 26, 1973. We might assume that the major historical errors with which this ad is shot through is intentional irony and flamboyance.

Get it on . . . Sleep it off
ALL IN THE SAME BUILDING

When hostelries were a must for the weary traveler . . . your Hotel Aggies was serving the public. Opened in 1890, the Hotel Aggie has seen the roaring days of the gold rush . . . the disappearance of the horse and buggy . . . the increasing popularity of the automobile and the establishment of the ultimate in travel . . . the jet plane . . . then came the dune buggy on the moon. And we are still here . . Come relax with us . . . at the Aggie . . . refresh yourself at the Antique Bizarre. We are ready to serve your needs. Few establishments are so closely connected with Davis . . .

..Bob Yohn, manager of the Antique Bizarre, says: Beer, wine, live entertainment and movies...
..A family Day on Sunday, at reduced rates: $1.25 on a large pizza, 75 cents off on a medium-size pizza and 50 cents off on a small pizza.
.. We are open from 11:30 a.m. to 2 a.m.
..We serve breakfasts, omelettes, spaghetti, steaks, sandwiches, hamburgers.
..Our specialty is the Antique Bizarre: A sourdough garlic bun, with one third pound of hamberger, a strip of bacon, and a slab of sharp cheddar cheese.
..HORSE BOARDING: At the (AB) Please call 756-2948.

THE HOTEL AGGIE and
The ANTIQUE BIZARRE

Second and G Streets In Davis Since 1890 **Davis, California**

5.23. The March 15, 1976 *Davis Enterprise* featured the hotel portion of the Terminal Building, which had now been renamed the Hotel Aggie/Aggie Hotel.

PAGE 4   THE DAVIS ENTERPRISE, DAVIS, CALIF.   MONDAY, MARCH 15, 1976

Hotel Aggie - Davis landmark

By G.L. SILVERMAN

The Hotel Aggie looks like the kind of place an unsuccessful traveling salesman might use for a flop, but some visiting professors wouldn't stay anyplace else.

The decor is of the linoleum-and-metal-bedstead style, without even those lousy motel watercolor reproductions to break the monotony. Still, several harried mothers dreamily think of it as an escape-hatch paradise where they can stare quietly at the bare walls for 24 hours, away from the hassles of home life when they've had-it-up-to-here.

It's warm in the winter and warmer in summer. The noise of the jukebox, country-western singers and clientele of the Antique Bizarre downstairs wafts upwards into some of the rooms until 2 a.m. Yet long-term residents consider this interesting and lively, a plus.

The location at Second and G Streets catches the sights and sounds of boozy action from bars on two other corners in addition to drinking spots up the street. Trains screech into the depot across the parking lot. Hotel Aggie guests, however, point to the convenient location. Almost anything a person might want, they explain, is only a few steps away.

Home away from home

To some it's home, a roost they return to after they mess up elsewhere. For others it's their first contact with Davis. When they reminisce about it later, they nod seriously and tell you they were comfortable there. They convey the feeling that they would never shell out for a posh motel as long as the Hotel Aggie stands.

It's inexpensive, ideal for visiting relatives who never seem to complain about the far from luxurious accommodations, no matter what they've been used to in their travels. The most unlikely types have said they appreciate the "typical northern California" flavor, loose and tinged with an aura of the old west. There is a get-down atmosphere that gets to folks, even though the bathrooms and showers are down the hall.

Foreigners intrigued

Most of the people who stay in the 22 rentable rooms (there are also two much-coveted apartments) are transients, including those waiting to catch a train. Many are students or newly-arrived residents who remain until they find the right apartment or roomie. Owners Milt and Jane Eberle say a lot of foreign students are especially pleased with the hotel. To some of them, the appointments are de luxe.

One from the Middle East thought it remarkable that the small hotel-size bar of soap was left in his room. When he checked out, he asked if he could take the remainder of the little bar with him, for friends at home. Eberle presented him with four extras, and the fellow was beside himself with delight.

A public service

There are rarely many vacancies, although the Eberles always find room for people brought to the hotel by the police, STEAC or the Salvation Army.

"They're mostly people who are down on their luck," Eberle explained. "One night the police sent a woman whose boyfriend dumped her on the highway." The shaken woman was not only housed but given coffee and solace by the managers.

Another time, a man who was stuck here on Christmas day looked in vain for a restaurant that was open. Sensitive to his plight, the managers shared their Christmas dinner.

Miss Dora

The present manager, Dora Donham, will retire in July and nobody can imagine the place without here. "Miss Dora," as everyone calls her, ran the hotel with Jessie Burns for almost 15 years, until "Miss Jessie" retired. They remained fast friends and have high hopes of traveling together now they both will have the time.

It's obvious to anybody who has stayed in the hotel for more than a day that Miss Dora deserves a rest from her everlasting rounds of cleaning, managing, waking people up and mothering.

Missy Rush, 18, now a cook at the Antique Bizarre, shared a room with co-worker Cheri Eberle (a daughter of the owners) for over two months, during which time Miss Dora was "just like a mom" to her. "I felt protected there," she said.

The sweet motherly qualities of Miss Dora's personality are tempered by the kind of gimlet eye most commonly seen on hardened house dicks. She has a perpetual twinkle, one guest noted, but you'd hate to be the one to disappoint her by unseemly conduct.

Hard cases melt into sheepish kids before Miss Dora. One man said, "I always felt embarassed whenever I went up the stairs if I wasn't actually living there."

Toeing the invisible line

Miss Dora never deliberately snoops; it's just that nothing gets by her. She gives the impression that you can go to hell in your own way, if that's your pleasure, but don't get sloppy and annoy anybody else. Her own patience and kindness have made life easier for a lot of lonely people.

Although she's nobody's judge, people respect her and value her good opinion. "Whenever I took a girl up to my room," remembered a young man who was once a tenant, "even though it was just to sit and talk, I felt I had to introduce her to Miss Dora. Then it was okay. I didn't feel right otherwise."

When people find out about Miss Dora's imminent retirement, they immediately look dazed and ask, "What's gonna happen? Who they gonna get instead? Who COULD they get instead?"

The Eberles shake their heads in a gesture implying that Miss Dora is irreplaceable, and also that the Lord will provide a passable substitute. After all, the hotel has been a landmark in its present location since 1927. It has to keep going or, many folks insist, the town would collapse along with their Aunt Hester who has put up at the hotel for the past umpteen years.

Down by the station

Originally called the Terminal Hotel, it was built for the convenience of train travelers who had to stop overnight in Davis. George Tingus and James Belenis were partners in the enterprise when Davis was "quite a railroad center," said Mr. Tingus' wife Bess, with "as many as 18 trains coming through Davis every day."

Her husband George came here when there were only about 1,000 people. He had a restaurant below the hotel, called the Terminal Cafe, and the building looked about the same even then.

Mr. Tingus recounted that it was a home-type hotel. Both he and Jim Belenis gave it their personal attention. They were always on duty and the food was home-cooked. The university used to hold meetings there; so did various service organizations.

In addition to the corner restaurant, there were two other stores in the building: Barthel's Butcher Shop and Mrs. Irwin's gift shop. The restaurant had a beer bar, off to one side, with a special entrance.

Living history

The continuity of the names involved, down to this day, is reassuring to those with a feeling for history and tradition. James Belenis' son, George, is well-known here as the restauranteur "Mr. B." George's brother, Nick, is at Mr. B's Brandin' Iron along with his sister Peggy.

The Tingus' son, Jim, has a Davis men's store, and another son, John, is nearby in Sacramento, production manager for an advertising firm. George Tingus, himself, has been "more or less retired," according to his wife, but he's kept his hand in for the past six years by cooking for the Theta Xi fraternity.

George Tingus and James Belenis ran the hotel and restaurant themselves until Tingus bought Belenis out in 1943. Somewhere along the line, the name changed to Hotel Aggie, and the ownership changed hands in 1948.

Pleasure in people

According to Jane Eberle, the building was bought from Tingus by Nicholson (a plumber) and Chiles (more local history). Then Agnes Ramsey Barr acquired it from them. Mrs. Eberle inherited it from her mother in 1966.

Jane Eberle minimizes the headaches inherent in any such operation, attributing the pleasure she gets from it to both customers and the managers. "The people have been darned easy to get along with," Mrs. Eberle said. "And the operation is small enough so you can get to know them. It's a 24-hour-a-day, seven-day-a-week business, but Dora and Jessie have been just great. It's made the whole thing fun."

And fun it has been, old-timers say, from the dormitory camaraderie of some years to the shenanigans of others. The simplicity and coziness of the hotel is touted by employes as well as owners.

Fast pitch

Late on a chilly afternoon last year, a man with the unmistakable gait of one who has spent most of his life on a horse rolled into the Antique Bizarre and inquired about a place to spend the night. Milt Eberle and the day bartender, Renee Burgoin, gave the poor fellow a pitch for the Hotel Aggie that had him swiveling his head from one to the other like a spectator at a rapid tennis match.

"Why not stay upstairs?" Eberle suggested. "Good beds, clean sheets, steam heat, and cheap."

"You won't have far to drag yourself after you get drunk in here," Ms. Bourgoin mentioned with a cynicism born of years of careful observation. "Stumble up the stairs in no time at all."

"Free music. You can hear the band in your room, easy," Eberle went on.

"Free coffee, too, down here or in the hall upstairs. Good grub. You'll love it," Ms. Bourgoin added.

Eberle put the clincher on it. "Where else," he demanded, spreading his arms wide to encompass the whole town, "could you get clean towels and a sweet little old lady to pat your fanny on your way to bed?"

Dazzled, the cowboy marched dutifully out and signed in.

5.24, Photo 1, captioned: "Miss Dora never deliberately snoops; it's just that nothing gets by her."

5.25. Photo 2, captioned: "Bare walls and simple decor satisfy most patrons who find the Aggie an inexpensive home or stopover between different homes and trains. Many like its old northern California flavor."

5.26, Photo 3, captioned: "Miss Dora . . . the proprietress of the Hotel Aggie will be retiring in July and many will miss her."

5.27. *Davis Enterprise,* August 26, 1976. Dedication of the Davis Arch Mural painted on the north wall of the Terminal Building.

Photo by Karen Froyland

Mural dedicated

The new mural depicting the Davis arches that graced the Second and G streets intersection from 1916 to the late 1920s was dedicated today by the Chamber of Commerce which sponsored the project. Painted on the north side of the Hotel Aggie Building on G Street just a few feet north of where the arches originally stood, the mural was described by Chamber President Al Smith as a result of cooperation between the city, UC Davis, and private citizens, representing a new sprit of unity in Davis. Shown standing in front of the mural during today's ceremonies attended by some 75 people, are Mayor Pro Tem Tom Tomasi; Karen Fox, chairman of the chamber's culture and recreation committee which organized the project; the artist, Terry Buckendorff; and Smith.

Unique Antique Bizarre

DAVIS—The Antique Bizarre is an old fashion family restaurant with something for everyone. Live entertainment is featured nightly. Relics of the past are on display for quiet relaxation. Chess, checkers, cribbage and pool are available for a greater challenge.

There are 25 wine cocktails from which to choose, along with a selection of beer including Anchor Steam Beer. When the hunger pangs strike— try a pizza, sandwich or some homemade onion rings.

However you look at it—The Antique Bizarre is the place to be for good old fashion relaxation.

5.28. March 4, 1977 advertisement, *Davis Enterprise*.

This week the
Antique Bizarre
is featuring
Food, Fun, and...

Thurs.—Scott VanLinge
Fri.—Sibling Rivalry
Sat.—Burgundy Bound
Sun.—Quiet Night
Mon.—Auditions
Tues.—Yolo Causeway
Wed.—Randy Fry

Corner of G & 2nd   756-7718

5.29. March 4, 1977, *Davis Enterprise* advertisement showing an active band schedule.

5.28. March, 15, 1978 *Davis Enterprise* story on a popular bartender leaving the A.B.

WEDNESDAY, MARCH 15, 1978

The Antique's loss is antiquity's gain

By G.L. SILVERMAN

Every person who's spent any time at all in conversation with Antique Bizarre daytime bartender Renee Isaacs always wondered, "How long is she going to work here, for crying out loud?"

The answer is 10 years. Isaacs left Davis' landmark tavern Tuesday to work as an archeological aide for the state of California.

This may seem a strange leap for a bartender, especially one with a BA in art from UC Davis. But Isaacs also studied anthropology and did two semesters of field work on two different sites in this valley.

In addition, she worked one summer with Earl Swanson and Jack Fitzwater of Idaho State University in "salvage work" for that state (excavating a site quickly to remove evidence for preservation; often done before heavy highway equipment devastates the site in the process of road building).

She spent another summer on the Olympic seacoast in Washington, working on an Ozette site for Washington State University. She did illustrations for the department of anthropology here and at Idaho State, and she was a medical illustrator for both UCD and the San Francisco Medical School.

"And then," Isaacs laughs, "I did 10 years of graduate work at the Antique Bizarre for my honorary degree in psychology!"

That degree might be a joke, but her informal qualifications for it aren't. In addition to dispensing beer and wine, Isaacs has provided a sympathetic ear and hard advice for bar "regulars," most of whom were on record as being in love with her.

One of the more familiar sights in town was a lineup of guys perched on barstools, gazing at her like a corral full of sick calves. When Renee Bourgoin married former Enterprise photographer Paul Isaacs, the lovelorn moans echoed dismally all through town.

Even tourists weren't immune.

The story is told of a typical camera-breasted seersucker husband who stopped in for a beer one hot day. He perched on a barstool, with his eagle-eyed wife next to him, and did a double-take as he glanced at the picture of the nude hanging over the bar.

His reaction was commonplace, providing much entertainment for the regulars, because the lady in the picture is a redhead, bearing a slight resemblance to Isaacs.

The customer's eyes kept shifting furtively back and forth from the painting to Renee Isaacs. Finally, when his wife went to visit another section of the tavern, the tourist turned to a regular and whispered, "Is that picture of HER?"

"Why'n't you ast her?" was the amused reply. But by the time the wife returned, the gentleman still hadn't screwed up enough courage.

Actually, says Isaacs, "That painting was done by the mother of Nick Frisch, who managed the Antique before I came." She worked with Frisch for a spell, and now he's taking her place behind the bar.

And the model for that painting? If it isn't Renee Isaacs, who is it?

Now she can tell: "The one who posed for it was Nick's father!"

All in the family, indeed.

By this time, Isaacs is glad to leave, although she admits to mixed emotions:

"I'll miss the regulars, but I'm looking forward more than I can say to being outdoors. Besides, for the past 10 years, my vista has extended to the other side of G St. and no farther. It's going to be broader now."

She's also anxious to learn more about archeology, especially the historical aspect.

Certainly none of her customer-friends begrudge her the experience and change. But everybody feels the same way she does: "I'm happy and sad."

Renee Bourgoin Isaacs

Photo by Karen Froyland

5.31. *Davis Enterprise* January 5, 1979 report on the A.B. becoming a key young performer venue.

Davis Enterprise—Weekend

Live acts center at Antique Bizarre

The Antique Bizarre has been serving an important role in the development and showcasing of local musicians for the past decade. But with the demise of Cassady's, the Antique takes on much greater importance as the primary, and almost only, music spot in town.

Offering live music Tuesday through Saturday nights, the Antique has been building the quality of its entertainment continually for the past two years, Michelle Keller says.

Keller, who does the booking, points to the wide variety off quality bands that have been performing there in recent months.

Each of several rock bands have something different to offer, she says.

One of the Antique's longest running acts, Cold Shot, also happens to be one of the best bands in town, if not the very best.

Cold Shot plays a variety of blues and country as well as a very heavy dose of vintage rock from the '50s and early '60s.

Section 8, formerly Causeway, plays more contemporary rock out of the late '60s and the present decade.

And its not unusual to find the Yolo 3, composed of the heart of Sacramento's premier rock band, the Skins, playing at the Antique during an off night for the parent band.

A night of the Yolo 3's rhythm and blues, truck driving and country music, and rock standards never fails to pack the house, Keller says.

For original rock, Johnny Flash was building a strong following before their breakup, Keller says. But as usually happens when one act departs, another comes to takes it's place, and Keller says the Suspects will be booked several times in February.

The Suspects, Davis' only New Wave band, concentrates almost exclusively on material written by the band.

On another front, one of Sacramento's purest, and most experienced blues stylists, Nate Shiner, brings his current band into the Antique several times a month.

Section Eight, one of many Davis rock 'n'roll bands, provides live entertainment at the Antique Bizarre, now the only remaining Davis nightclub where the live music can be heard.

music

Antique Bizarre endures as other night spots fade

By CRAIG CHILDRESS

Some people say the place should be condemned. Other claim that it's the only building left in Davis with real character. Despite the differences in opinion, the Antique Bizarre remains the only nightclub in Davis to feature live music and dancing.

While nightclubs such as Cassadys, The Columbian, and Bobby McGees have come and gone, the doors of the Antique Bizarre have always remained open.

"We've always been able to offer live music without having a door charge," says Bob Dunham, owner of the Antique. "Clubs such as Cassadys hired musicians from the Bay Area, thus forcing them to charge at the door to cover expenses."

The Antique hires almost exclusively local talent. "Some of the best musicians in Northern California live within a fifty mile radius of Davis," claims Dunham.

While Cassadys was charging a six dollar cover charge to see Norton Buffalo, customers in the Antique were seeing local harmonica players like Mark Miller (formerly of Powder River) and David Gage (of Section 8) for free. "Miller and Gage could easily blow the socks off Buffalo," claims Dunham.

Also contributing to the longevity of the Antique Bizarre is its unique rustic atmosphere. "Many people are turned off by the sterile environment of the disco clubs," says Dunham. "Who wants to stare at a DJ enclosed in a plastic box? I feel like I'd have to put on rubber gloves and a mask just to talk to him."

The Antique Bizarre is anything but "sterile." Antiques and just plain "junk" hang from the ceilings and walls. Ice tongs, rusted hay hooks, kerosene lamps, and worn-out farming tools find a home there.

"Most of our decor is old western," says Dunham. And with a cast-iron pig oiler used for a door stop and a five foot by eight foot painting of a nude woman hung behind the bar, there is little doubt that the Antique has captured the old western flavor.

The nude woman was painted by the bartender's mother (who used her husband as a model). "We get a lot of art students in here commenting on the painting," says Dunham. "Apparently they've never seen breasts that defy the law of gravity."

Bob Dunham, manager of the Antique Bizarre, says the popular nightspot satisfies a wide range of customers, from "jazz - intellectuals" to country-western fans.

The Antique Bizarre's clientele is as diverse as the decor. "I've got PhD's and plumbers sitting at the same table discussing almost anything under the sun," says Dunham.

Different types of music attract different types of crowds. On nights when country music is featured the Antique gets a more serious older crowd, as compared to the weekends when the place is hoppin' with rock n' roll bands and college students.

And then there is the jazz crowd, often referred to as the "Chablis drinkers" or the "intellectuals." The jazz lovers come simply to enjoy fine music and a good glass of wine.

Unfortunately not all the Antique Bizarre's clientele are as easy going as the Chablis drinkers. In the past the Antique has been the hot spot for some of the worst barroom brawls in Davis.

Prior to the change of ownership in 1976, a group of motorcyclists rode their bikes through the front door, through the bar and out the back entrance. "An experience that the eighty-year old building will hopefully never see

again," says Dunham.

During the past three years Dunham has been trying hard to change the rowdy image of the Antique.

"Getting rid of the pool table was a definite step in the right direction," says Dunham. "When people drink they start taking the game far too seriously."

To help clean the air Dunham has posted a Persona Non Grata: a list of the more rowdy individuals who are no longer allowed service in the Antique Bizarre.

Although the Antique Bizarre has become notably calmer since Bob Dunham took charge in 1976, it still has its fair share of problems. "Anytime people bring their troubles to the bar, you're going to have problems," says Dunham. But despite the occasional disturbances, the Antique still manages to have the place packed at least three nights a week.

The Antique Bizarre features live music Tuesday through Saturday weekly, from 9:00 p.m. to 1:00 a.m. It is located at the corner of 2nd and G Streets in Davis.

Davis Enterprise—Weekend

Page 4

The Davis Enterprise

ESTABLISHED IN 1897   301 G STREET, DAVIS, CALIFORNIA 95616   **15 CENTS**   **WEDNESDAY, FEBRUARY 25, 1981**

26 PAGES

Antique Bizarre: landmark dies

By ROBERT STERLING

Elegies for a dying downtown Davis bar are being sung this week. In the dimly-lit beer hall at 200 G St. the band is playing, the dancers are dancing, the drinkers are drinking.

Some play cards in the cardroom like they always have, but this week many are listening — intently, pensively — to the flickering strains of music, song, folklore.

Periodically, between sets, there will be a "remembrance," someone will get up to speak.

It's a wake of sorts, tributes to a longtime friend. But the religion here is rock and roll, the church house is filled with thick smoke, and the hallelujahs ringing out are to the glory of good times.

Sometime early Sunday morning the Antique Bizarre's swinging stead.

"I don't know how it got that name," said Jane Eberle, who inherited the building from her mother, Agnes Ramsey Barr in 1966.

"Two fellows from I think San Mateo opened the place up as the 'Antique Bizarre.' There was sawdust on the floor, peanuts, beer — the basic motif that it has now," said Eberle.

Current business operators are Bob and Kay Dunham, who took over in 1976. The owner of the building is Davis resident Lee Chen, who has plans of renovating the entire complex and one day converting the now-vacant hotel into office space.

"It's going to be like leaving home," said Dunham, drawing a glass of Anchor Steam beer for a patron. He squints and surveys his place. The past five years have been "rewarding, hectic, traumatic," he said. But now it's time to move on.

When Dunham, a retired Air Force man from Broderick, took over in '76 "there was a lot of plastic in here," which he duly replaced with his "antiques."

He strolled through the musty saloon this week, relating the anecdotes he knows behind the shrub hoe, buck saws, Civil War-era saddle, coal oil stoves, seed planters, wagon wheels, old skis, old beer cans, hay hooks, canteens, gopher traps, beaver trap lines, wine openers, the gold miners' pan now used as a wall clock, old broken radios, mirrors and more, as visitors know.

Then there's the life-size painting of the reclining nude woman behind the bar. It was painted, said Dunham, by the 67-year-old mother of former bartender Nick Frich. The story goes (and others will attest) that the bartender's mother used her 71-year-old husband as the model.

"Well look at it," said Dunham in awe. "She defies the law of gravity!"

UC Davis law student Corey Brown and UCD student and bartender Melissa Calhoun have been rallying folks to the A.B.'s cause. They met with the Romeros Tuesday and they held the recent evening meeting of concerned citizens.

The place has got character," said Brown. "It's someplace special, there's a lot of life here. It seems to represent Davis' beginnings, there's a feel for Western feelings. The woodwork, the things all over the walls and ceiling, they all have individual meaning."

A small kitchen was removed last year to make room for the crowds packing the place, and the former billiards area was glassed in and converted to a card room in an effort to deter some of the pool-playing ne'er-do-wells.

Ron Goldberg has been playing guitar at the A.B. since 1975, and he played his last solo gig there Monday. Three people there were in attendance when Goldberg played his first show six years earlier. He will play again Friday with the band Moonshine.

He recalls days when members of several different local bands would "jam all night . . . those were the interesting times."

He's seen a dozen dancers doing "what looked like the can-can" on top of the bar. He's heard tell of the time a motorcycle gang toured the place on their bikes, or the time "a pretty loony guy" took an ax to the bar.

Although there have been "some acts of violence," said Goldberg, "I'm certainly saddened to see it go."

It it was Thursday, that meant Cold Shot was playing at the A.B. The group's bassist, Richard Urbino, still plays with the group and started at the A.B. when Cold Shot was a folk duo in '75.

"It's pretty crummy it's closing," said Urbino. "Clubs have come and gone in Davis, but the A.B. was just always there, it evolved. It never tried to do anything fancy. It just presented local entertainment, with never a cover charge."

5. 33. The *Davis Enterprise* editor thought the closing of the Antique Bizarre in February, 1981 merited the top story front page headline.

The bottom column to the left continues on the next page. At the bottom of that column, the story continues in the second column from the bottom on this page.

billboard door will squeak shut for good and the late-night revelers will bid the saloon adieu.

Next month the A.B. will become the La Fogata Mexican restaurant.

Is the esteemed clientele sentimental? Nah...well, maybe.

"Save The Antique Bizarre" leaflets were being circulated through the packed house last weekend. Nearly 20 dedicated patrons, beers in hand, gathered for their own town hall discussion in the dark tavern earlier this week.

Two hundred petitions welcoming new owners Joaquin and Linda

"The place has got character. It's someplace special, there's a lot of life here. It seems to represent Davis' beginnings, there's a feel for Western feelings.

Romero and urging them "to keep the unique atmosphere and continue the live music" have been printed.

But based on encouraging discussions with the Romeros Tuesday, organizers of the drive to preserve what they call "a symbol of Davis and the place to take out-of-town friends," have decided to hold off circulating the petitions and to wait and see what the Romeros' plans are.

Meanwhile, indeed, a wake has been scheduled for Saturday at 10 a.m. at 200 G St.

Of course, the place wasn't always the A.B.

Longtime Davis residents may remember Jim DeFazio's Deboes pizza parlor in the '50s and early '60s, or before that George Tingus' Terminal Hotel, bar and restaurant.

Tingus, who celebrated his 89th birthday this week and is now a cook for the Theta Xi fraternity, bought the site in 1922 and along with partner Jim Belenis ran the show beginning in 1926.

Davis resident Warren Westgate has photos of an old Davis Post Office at "200 G St." taken during the 1890s, and other shots showing the old Bank of Davis nearby.

The place was sold in 1948 and became the Hotel Aggie. Deboes ran out of business around 1967 and the Antique Bizarre was born in its

Photo by Ken Browning

Quaffing a beer

This week marks the last waltz for Davis' Antique Bizarre at Second and G streets. It has been purchased by the owners of the La Fogata Mexican restaurant in Woodland. A wake is planned at the A.B. Saturday at 10 a.m. and owner Bob Dunham said that "something special" may be planned Saturday night.

5. 34. This photograph accompanied the February 25, 1981 *Enterprise* report of the A.B. closing.

Column continuing from the bottom column of the previous page. At the bottom of this column, the story continues in the second column from the bottom of the page on the previous page.

7) THE LAST OWNERSHIP BEGINS

Lee Jing Chen and Chao Chen (Lee Chen and Grace Chen) were involved in acquiring the building in June, 1977 (Fidelity National Title Insurance Company, 2000). When properties such as the Terminal Building changed ownership in Davis, a resale inspection was required along with a new Certificate of Occupancy. Copies of inspection reports and letters in the City's files on the building suggested that the inspection was difficult to pass and the certificate was not easily forthcoming.

The Chens put the building on the resale market in 1978, but then withdrew it. At this point the hotel portion of the building was no longer operated, although the apartments in the rear were apparently rented, as were the retail spaces along G Street.

With the turning of the decade of the 1980s, the Terminal Building entered a new period of slow decline, a further phase of what some observers of older buildings such as this have called "demolition by neglect."

But before we turn to that final phase, let us look at the degree to which and the ways in which there were historic preservationist reactions to what we have seen about the 1950s-70s.

8) LOCAL HISTORY AND PRESERVATION: FRAGILE FORCES IN DAVIS

At the time of the Terminal's demolition in 2000, organized local history and preservation interests had existed in Davis since 1963—some 37 years. Surveying this sweep, I think we would have to say that these forces were most of the time rather fragile and, sometimes, marginal.

The dominant public mood, though, was not one of active hostility. Instead, it seemed more often one of masked skepticism, apathy, and foot-dragging, with occasional and grudging support, along with flashes of mass enthusiasm. Indeed, the conflict and campaign of 1999 and 2000 concerning the Terminal's fate, may have been one of the higher points in both zeal and animosity, although it was certainly far from the first moment of high preservationist drama in Davis history.

In addition, we need to bear in mind that demolish-and-rebuild was the cry of the day across the country during the 1950s, '60s and '70s and Davis was simply typical in its demolitionist ardor and only unusual in the manner in which it constructed a new downtown. As with the rest of the country, concern that perhaps people were going too far and too fast was not well articulated before the late 1960s.

Within this dominant public mood, the focus and shape of local history and preservation forces shifted and changed over those 37 years. By my reckoning, these shifts and changes divided into five periods, with differing emphases and levels of mobilization. In overview, these were:

1. 1963-68: Local History Research
2. 1969-77: Struggle
3. 1978-87: Crisis and the New Professionals
4. 1988-94: Percolating Quiescence
5. 1995-02: Resurgence and Reaction

The first two of these five periods were in the demolitionist 1950s-70s and I discuss them in this Chapter. The third period bridged the 1950s-70s and the contrasting 1980s-90s. Because the third period ended in the 1980s, I will treat it in the next chapter, along with the fourth and fifth periods.

I recognize that I am oversimplifying in stating periods that appear to have clear boundaries and that give the appearance of being tight compartments of time. Obviously, the reality is much more overlapping and imprecise. Nonetheless, there were clusters of changes over theses decades captured by this oversimplification. I have elected to pay the price of oversimplification in order to achieve a degree of clarity.

In addition, this is not an exhaustive inventory of local history and preservation activities. I include only those that I judge to be of major import or of a charming character even if minor. I apologize to everyone offended by my having left out their favorite activity, event, or person.

FIRST PERIOD, 1963-68: LOCAL HISTORY RESEARCH. In the six or so years of the initial period, there were three main kinds of actions and activities.

1. The 1963-68 "Commission." Organized local history and preservation activity in Davis can be dated from March 18, 1963, when then-Mayor Norman Woodbury personally convened and chaired a meeting of a quasi-official citizen's "commission." It had the charge of assembling Davis history, but it had neither staff nor legal powers, and met in the homes of its members rather than in City quarters. Although its official title was the Davis Historical Landmarks Commission, it was not, in the ways just mentioned, like other commissions.

This group's picture was taken in January, 1968 and is reproduced in Fig. 5. 35. Inspecting it, we can see the members are, for the most part, rather older. One key exception is the woman fourth from the left in the photo, who is Joann Leach Larkey. In her mid-thirties in the early 1960s, she was the daughter of a well-known UCD professor, a graduate of UC Berkeley, and married to a local physician.

2. An Archive and a Book, *Davisville '68*. Educated, intelligent, and energetic, Mrs. Larkey, assisted by many people, led the local history effort. Among other things, this effort resulted in an archive of photographs and other documents (now housed in the Yolo County Archives) and in the book *Davisville '68*, which has endured as the indispensable chronicle of early Davis history (Larkey, 1969).

The labor for researching and writing this book was entirely volunteer. The 2,000 copy printing was subsidized in part by a loan from the City Council of some $9,000 (which was finally paid off in 1975). (For perspective on local history as a type of social enterprise—of which the Davis instance is fairly typical—see Kammen, 1996; Russo, 1988; Parker, 1943.)

Also of special note in Fig. 5.35, the man standing second from the left is John Weber Brinley. Mr. Brinley was the grandson of George Augustus Weber, a gentleman who opened a saloon at the southwest corner of Second and G not long after Davis was founded in 1868 and, about 1880, built a mansion at the northeast corner of Second and E streets. Present at the founding of Davis, Mr. Weber was a first-generation pioneer.

Mr. Brinley's father, Al Green (Sam) Brinley, came to Davis in 1912 as the telegrapher of the Southern Pacific station and subsequently married into the Weber family. He inherited the Weber properties and acquired yet others after he retired from the railroad in 1947 and established Brinley's Real Estate and Insurance Office (Larkey, 1969, 222-3). His son, John Weber Brinley, inherited these holdings and he was a major Davis landlord of commercial buildings (an enterprise carried on by his son, John K. Brinley).

I digress on the Weber-Brinley family because of the clear way in which these four men tightly encapsulate the entire span of Davis history. The fourth of them, John K., was, in 2000, only the fourth generation since the founding of the town—and John K. was barely in his fifties.

This information is background to understanding that Sam and John Weber Brinley, both affable and popular, had, together, lived through a great deal of Davis history and knew virtually everyone. John Weber Brinley, in particular, was instrumental in encouraging Davis "old timers" to cooperate with this citizen history group.

One irony is that while Mr. Brinley was working so effectively in collecting Davis history, he was himself demolishing early Davis buildings. These included even the historic mansion his grandfather, George Weber, had built at the northeast corner of Second and E. (Today, the commercial building at that corner is called The Brinley Building. The mansion previously on the site is pictured in Larkey, 1969: 222; Lofland and Haig, 2000: 25.)

In addition, members of this "Commission" began developing a list of "landmark structures," which might be seen as a kind of muted or backdoor resistance to the demolitions going on so energetically around them. So far as I can determine, however, this group never engaged in any public opposition to demolition.

3. The 1968 Davis Centennial. One of the most important early actions of this quasi-commission was to determine and to assert that 1968 would be the "centennial" of Davis' founding. Fortunately for the production of "history-events," both the University of California and the local public school district also claimed 1968 as their respective centennial years. So, schemes for celebrating Davis' history could be and were coordinated with and augmented by these other centennials in the same year.

5.35. Davis Historical Landmarks Commission, *Davis Enterprise,* January 18, 1968.

FACT FINDERS — Members of the Davis Historical Landmarks Commission and members of pioneer families of the Davis area got together last night at city hall to help identify old photographs from Davis' past in preparation for a centennial publication of the city's history. Shown are commission members (front row, from left) Katherine Campbell, Thelma Dietrich, Vere Asbill, Violet Gordon, John Rogers, Narcissa Pena, and (back row, from left) June Dolcini, Delpha Williamson, Joann Larkey, Chelso Maghetti, Gary Rowe and John Brinley.
—Enterprise Photo

A Centennial Committee was organized by the Davis Area Chamber of Commerce (not the City of Davis). Its Co-chairs were John Weber Brinley and Joann Larkey. The climax event, among many other celebrations over the year, was a luncheon attended by about 500 people in UC Davis' Freeborn Hall on Saturday, June 1, 1968. It was designed to honor "decendants of pioneer families," as well as "past city officials and businessmen" (*Davis Enterprise*, June 3, 1968).

Also relevant, by the mid-1960s, history/preservationist sentiments were quickening across the nation. These stirrings were expressed perhaps most importantly in the United States National Historic Preservation Act of 1966, which began the serious involvement of the federal government in preservation matters (Murtagh, 1977: Ch. 5).

SECOND PERIOD, 1969-77: STRUGGLE. The 1966 Preservation Act created the expectation, if not the requirement, that any upstanding local government needed a preservation commission.

The Davis Historical Landmarks Commission, 1969. Apparently wanting to be au courant, in late 1968 the Davis City Council created a true preservation commission, which met the first time on March 6, 1969. At that time, such commissions existed in about thirty of the some 500 California municipalities and counties (National Trust for Historic Preservation, 1976). Most of these commissions were only a few years old. So, Davis was an early joiner of a new trend. (By the year 2000, virtually all California jurisdictions had some form of an official preservation program.)

The previous "Commission" continued a kind of shadow existence with a bank account in the name of The Davis Historical Society. It finally disbanded in 1975, when John Weber Brinley closed the account with a check for $2,571.25 written to the City trust account of the new commission (Haig Collection, Box 5).

The new Commission began to develop a list of "historical landmarks," "primarily composed of structures around a hundred years old," which was then designated as such by the City Council (Taylor 1980, 5). In 1973, the City Council gave thirteen of these landmarks some protection by allowing delay of demolitions. The list grew gradually in subsequent years. Over the next ten years, the Council enacted a patchwork of three ordinances designed to designate "landmarks" and perhaps delay demolitions (Ordinance number 651 in 1973, number 722 in 1974, and number 882 in 1977).

First Preservation Campaigns. Many buildings were still being torn down with no adverse comment or protest, but at least three of them now began to attract preservationist attention.

1. Murmuring: 417 G Street, 1973. An especially striking Victorian with wooden ornamentation of the "Chalet" type at 417 G was demolished in 1973, but with public expressions of regret that seemingly no way could be found to save it.

2. The First Grassroots Campaign: Second Street Houses, 1975. In 1975, prolific local developer and builder Jim Adams fielded a plan to tear down all the heritage homes along the south side of Second Street between C and D streets and to replace them with a block-long commercial complex. A UC Davis undergraduate and artist, Julie Partansky, lived in one of the to-be-demolished homes. Personally subject to eviction, she sparked the first grassroots campaign for preservation (as distinct from the more establishment effort to save the Dresbach-Hunt Boyer mansion). In Fig. 5. 36, she is shown sitting in front of her threatened home.

This campaign is of special interest because it marks the debut of Ms. Partansky in Davis political life. After her house was demolished, she moved to a cottage on a graveled alley on D Street and then to a like-situated cottage on E Street. For the next fifteen years she lived in that neighborhood—now called the Old North—quietly and participated only on occasion in Davis politics. But then, in 1991, Davis Demolitionists again came calling at her door—almost literally, not just metaphorically. It was a fateful moment because her encounter with them subsequently changed Davis history—as will be explained in the next chapter.

3. The Dresbach-Hunt-Boyer Mansion, Late 1970s. In the late nineteenth century, a number of fair-sized mansions had been built on Second between B and F streets. By the early 1970s, only one of them remained. At the southeast corner of Second and E, it would come to be called "the Hunt-Boyer" (but formally named the Dresbach-Hunt-Boyer). Built in 1875, this "last remaining" status appears to have sparked the first major effort to preserve a threatened heritage building in Davis.

This effort first took the form of a City Council decision to float a bond issue to save the building in connection with a new city hall on the site. This scheme failed at the ballot box in November of 1976 by a vote of 54% in favor, but with two-thirds required for adoption.

The owner of the mansion had taken out a demolition permit, but also said he was willing to sell the building and property for $250,000. The Council acted to stall the demolition in the hope of another solution. A campaign called SAVE (for Save a Victorian Establishment) began to raise the money from private sources. Although led by and donated to by well-known Davis residents (including UCD Chancellor Emil Mrak and John Weber Brinley), the effort could come up with only $26,772. The matter dragged on and the building was finally "saved" in 1978 when a partnership of developers met the owner's price and made preservation possible by building a complex of shops (called "Mansion Square") behind the house (*Davis Enterprise*, May 30, 1978; December 21, 1979)

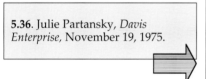

5.36. Julie Partansky, *Davis Enterprise*, November 19, 1975.

Julie Partansky lounges in front of her house at 412 Second St. Miss Partansky has taken on City Hall and the Bank of Dixon in a crusade to save old homes on First and Second streets.

Subway I, 1973. A fourth episode in this period was not clearly a preservation campaign, but would foreshadow two, more preservation-like, episodes over the next decades.

South of the First and E streets intersection there was an automobile road under the railroad tracks. Called the "subway," or The Richards Boulevard Underpass, it was built in 1917. As the decades went by, developer forces increasingly regarded it as an obstruction to full car-oriented development of the downtown. They called for widening it to four or more lanes.

By the end of the twentieth century, the City Council would have made three efforts to widen it: 1973, 1988 and 1997. I will call these Subway I, II, and III. Each effort failed.

Voter failure to approve the widening plans was not necessarily a preservationist act. Often, indeed, such failures are not. Voters simply did not want to pay more taxes. Such was importantly the case in these three instances.

Even so, if we review the pro and con reasons stated in the campaigns, we see preservationist themes. There was at least the theme of preserving Davis as a "small town" place with a "real" downtown. (In Subway III, however, there was interest in preserving the Subway **itself** as a historic structure.)

Be these preservation ambiguities as they may, the Subway I (1973) bond proposal failed nearly 2 to 1 (62 to 38% with 9,541 people voting).

First Owner Resistance to Designation, 1973. Mrs. Iva M. Bruhn of 305 E Street appears to have the distinction of being the first of a series of owners who would oppose listing their properties as a "landmark" or a "historical resource." In a letter to the City Council dated October 28, 1974, Mrs. Bruhn declared "there are numerous sites in town where historical places have been and torn down. [Sic] There is nothing to show that they or mine are a historical place" (Haig Collection, Box 3). She also had an attorney write the City Council expressing her view. Her house at 305 E was dropped from the list of possible designated resources.

The U.S. Bicentennial, 1976. Davis local history buffs and preservationists organized to celebrate the U. S. Bicentennial. They also used the occasion to elaborate at least two local history angles.

First, a "see Davis history on your bike" route was mapped out and printed in a leaflet showing where to ride and what to see. Revised and refined several times, this would become a standard history-promotion item. Second, and as previously reported, the Chamber of Commerce organized the painting of history murals on buildings, one of which was the Arch Mural on the north wall of Terminal Building (shown being dedicated in Fig. 5.27).

Davis' Three National Register Entries, Late 1970s. The United States National Register of Historic Places, begun in 1966, had, in 2002, nearly 75,000 listings.

Four of them were within the Davis city limits. Three of the four were nominated for (and given) that distinction in 1976-79, a period when preservation in Davis was struggling and not especially assertive or successful. How did these achievements occur in such an inauspicious period?

It happened because the Federal process allowed individuals to make nominations to the National Register. Local government participation and approval could be helpful, but was not required. And that is what happened in Davis. Three enterprising and knowledgeable individuals carried out the process with little involvement in (or by) official Davis preservation circles and government. Thus:

- A student intern named Judy Bond at the State Office of Historic Preservation prepared and processed the case for the Dresbach-Hunt-Boyer Mansion at 604 Second Street and it was approved for the National Register on September 13, 1976. At that time the building was threatened with demolition and registration was seen as an effort to "legitimize . . claims that the . . . structure is truly of historical significance" (*Davis Enterprise*, September 13, 1976).
- The case for the Southern Pacific Railroad Station, Second and H streets, was developed and carried through by a person whose role and identity no one I have asked can now recall: Robert M. Wood. It was approved on November 7, 1976. Indeed, Mr. Wood must be counted among Davis' truly unsung and unknown preservation heroes.
- The owner-occupant of the Joshua B. Tufts House at 434 J Street, Valerie Jones, brought about the listing of her own home on September 6, 1979 (*Davis Enterprise*, November 23, 1979). (The sources of the names of the above nominators are the respective nomination forms, which are on file with the City of Davis Cultural Services Manager and the Keeper of the National Register of Historic Places.)

9) TRANSITION

At the turn of the decade from the 1970s to the 1980s, the Terminal Building was no longer functioning as a hotel or boarding house, although the retail spaces were rented. And, it was continuing to decline.

In the next chapter, we will see how the Terminal Building owner's demolition plans collided with preservationist forces. This seemed to have produced something of a stalemate or stand-off that would not be broken for about a decade and a half.

6

NEGLECT DECADES, 1980s-90s

Over the 1980s-90s, the Terminal Building continued its slow decline. In contrast, the immediate G Street area began a slow but solid rise. Indeed, the improvements in the vicinity of the Terminal Building made its own creeping blight all the more evident. For better or worse, and with the exception of the 1984 episode described in this chapter, no one appeared to have put much pressure on the building's owners to improve their property.

As mentioned, the reason I divide the five post-war decades into the 1950s-70s versus the 1980s-90s is that the number and rate of demolitions dropped significantly from the 1950s-70s to the 1980s-90s. One obvious reason for this decline was that by 1980 almost two thirds of the older structures in the "new" downtown had already been removed. (Eighty-six of the 233 buildings there in 1945—37%—survived to the year 2000 [Lofland, 2000:7]). One-hundred percent of the buildings (or close to it) in some Core Area blocks were gone (Fig. 5.2).

In addition, policies of the more liberal Councils of the 1970s-80s began to encourage "adaptive reuse" of older buildings rather than demolition. Such use became, indeed, the line of least resistance among developers, who seemed, on the whole, more interested in getting-on with projects within the prevailing rules than in bucking them and "making statements." (William Kopper---Council member 1976-84, Mayor, 1982-84---spearheaded these adaptive reuse policies. Small world aside: Kopper was also a long-time friend and the political mentor of Julie Partansky. With Partansky, he had been a key figure in the 1975 campaign to save the Second Street houses [described in section 8, of Chapter 5, "The First Grassroots Campaign"].)

I think our understanding of the eventual fate of the Terminal Building is advanced by examining two aspects of these 1980s-90s decline decades. One, we need to bring forward and to conclude the depiction of local history and preservation activity begun in the last chapter. This aspect of the context will help us understand why the Terminal Building merely stood there in slow decay for so long. Two, in 1984, there was a (failed) effort to designate the Terminal Building a historical resource. We need to understand this failure and its consequences.

In the last section of this chapter, I will draw together (1) episodes of owners resisting preservation and (2) instances of citizen campaigns for preservation. A compact portrait of these will provide a context in which to place the struggle of these two forces that is the subject of the five chapters comprising Part II of this book.

1) THE THIRD, FOURTH, AND FIFTH PERIODS OF LOCAL HISTORY AND PRESERVATION

Recapitulating from the previous chapter, I divide Davis local history and preservationist activity into five periods, which are:

1. 1963–68: Local History Research
2. 1969–77: Struggle
3. 1978–87: Crisis and the New Professionals
4. 1988–94: Percolating Quiescence
5. 1995–02: Resurgence and Reaction

The first two of these were described in the last section of the last chapter. Let us now look at the third, fourth and fifth periods.

THIRD PERIOD, 1978-87: CRISIS AND THE NEW PROFESSIONALS. The third period featured significant influences from outside Davis along with some distinctive indigenous happenings.

Three External Changes Affecting Davis Preservation. In the later 1970s, the world outside Davis was changing in three ways that brought about changes in Davis preservation activities.

1. Proposition 13 Budget Trauma, Late 1970s. In June, 1978, the California electorate adopted a constitutional amendment that sharply curbed property taxes accruing to local governments. This, and subsequent state legislation restricting tax revenues even more, sent shock waves of spending cuts through local governments. (Bizarrely, at the Davis City Council meeting of June 21, 1978, two members voted to "stop supplying pens and pencils to . . . City employees." The motion failed with two members against and one absent.)

Already at or near the bottom of lists of spending priorities, City of Davis preservation spending was virtually stopped. Specifically, the single part-time city staff person who worked with the Commission, William H. Taylor, Jr., was reassigned to other duties. (In Fig. 6.1, he is shown at work.) He continued to help the Commission on his own time, but, in frustration, gave this up in August, 1979. In a memo to the City Manager, Taylor described the Davis preservation situation:

> I think it is . . . accurate to say that there is a lack of substantive support for Historical Preservation/Restoration/Education from the City Council, the Planning Commission, the community, etc. (to differing degrees certainly). This observation is not meant to be judgmental, I'm just stating what I believe to be the current reality. . . . The present "voluntary" framework, combined with what I have seen other communities accomplish, makes the frustrations of the current arrangement unacceptable to me. It is with regret that I rescind my former offer of voluntary service to the Davis Historical and Landmarks Commission (Haig Collection, Box 2).

This event provoked members of the Commission to speak "mutinously of their lowly stature in the city [and they] made plans to take their grievances to the City Council . . . . The commission currently has no quarters, no storage space, no regular meeting place and no city aide to help with its work" (*Davis Enterprise*, September 12, 1979). Among other indignities, the December 18, 1979 meeting was cancelled for "lack of a meeting place." In the *Davis Enterprise* of January 23, 1980, a reporter observed, "No other commission in the city raises money to pay for itself, but the funds used by the Historical and Landmarks Commission come from publication sales and donations raised by the commission."

2. Professional Preservationists Emerge, Late '70s–Early '80s. One of the effects of the National Historic Preservation Act of 1966—and subsequent amplifying legislation at both national and state levels—was to begin to create a new kind of occupation: the professional preservationist. Part architect, part historian, part lawyer, part developer, part bureaucrat, this new kind of job specialized in assessing the "whats" and "whys" of "historic resources"—the new, central concept of this occupation. (Because preservation was so heavily volunteer before professionalization, some of these new professionals have referred to themselves with ironic humor as "preservationists-for-hire.")

Enterprise photo

Bill Taylor, digging through trenches by hand, unearthed a crockery beer bottle Friday. The archeology team found remnants from old Davisville, most of them dating back to the turn of the century.

6.1. William H. Taylor, Jr., referred to in many city documents in the impersonal abstract as "the Administrative Assistant II," pictured in the *Davis Enterprise* of April 28, 1975. He is at 231 G Street, the site of the demolished building seen in Fig. 5.10.

In 1975, this kind of poking around at demolition sites was considered just fine. However, more recent preservationist practice requires that professional archeologists do this job.

Even so, and as we shall see in Part III, the excavation of the Terminal Building site in 2000 did not rate the presence of City staff, "Administrative Assistant II" or not.

Training programs for this verbal-intensive specialty were only starting. Therefore, many early practitioners were not formally trained in the topic. Instead, they were self-taught migrants from disciplines that overlapped preservation. And, as with other new professions, preservation attracted young people rather than older occupation-changers (Lee, 2002).

Such was the case for the two preservationists who chaired the Commission in the early 1980s and who had much influence on the course of Davis preservation. This influence included a ground-up consolidation and systematization of the old patchwork of ordinances, including a change in the very name of the commission. A term like "landmark" had come to seem quaint and antique. One had, instead, in the new national nomenclature, "historical resources." So also, in the new ordinance of 1984, the commission went from the Davis Historical Landmarks Commission to the Historical Resources Management Commission (HRMC).

The first of these new, young professionals was Robin Datel (Fig. 6.2), a native of Stockton, California who graduated from UC Davis in 1976 and was a "historic preservation specialist" in the California Office of Historic Preservation in the mid-1970s. In 1983, she earned a Ph.D. in geography at the University of Minnesota. Her specialty was the geography of historical preservation ("why places are preserved") and she published important research on that topic (e.g. Datel, 1985; Datel and Dingemans, 1988).

Following her as Commission Chair was Stephen Mikesell (Fig. 6.3), B. A., Harvard University, who had done graduate work in history at UC Davis before going to work for the State of California Office of Historic Preservation, the place of his employment while he served on the Davis HRMC.

PAGE 12   THE DAVIS ENTERPRISE, DAVIS, CALIF.   THURSDAY, JANUARY 13, 1983

Photo by Cindy O'Dell

Datel

Remembering

Members of the Class of '28 enjoy some happy memories of their school days during a ceremony to place a commemorative plaque at the base of a deodar tree that the class — the first to graduate from high school in Davis — planted in front of school (now Davis City Hall) 55 years ago.

Historical Landmarks Commission Chairman Steve Mikesell, second from left, holds the plaque while class members, from left, Mike Luft, Ruth Hanson Reynolds, Lucille McBride, Fern Elliott Weston, Bob Howard and Thelma Hoag Winters look on.

6.2. Robin Datel, *Davis Enterprise* photo in the Question-Of-The-Day column, May 13, 1983.

6.3. Stephen Miksell, second from the left, *Davis Enterprise*, January 13, 1983.

Commission composition was also changing in other ways. The early commissioners were "old Davis" in the sense that they were born in the town, or had lived there a long time. For them, local history and preservation often had a genealogical slant. History and preservation were in part about one's family and one's own personal past.

In the later 1970s, these features were changing. Neither Datel or Mikesell were born in Davis and neither had lived there very long. Both were young. (Datel was twenty-eight when she became commission chair.) These two features were now also seen in yet other new members of the Commission. For these immigrant, younger people, there was no genealogical slant or possible element of a quest for personal "roots." Instead, this was a new kind of cosmopolitanism in which one could be interested in local dead strangers because one was broadly interested in the past, had an appreciation of it, and wanted to learn from it.

3. "Cultural Resources" Survey, 1979-80. By the later 1970s federal and regional government programs were financially encouraging local governments to perform a "survey of cultural resources." This was a fancy name for hiring one of the new professional preservation consultants to orchestrate a listing of, mostly, a jurisdiction's older buildings (those 50 years or more old) thought possibly to possess historical significance.

In Davis, this took the form of contracting, in 1978, with the recently-formed Sacramento firm of Historic Environment Consultants. Specifically, this was Paula Boghosian, another young preservationist in this new occupation. She trained and supervised a volunteer corps of almost two dozen Davis surveyors. The surveyors, members of the Commission, and Ms. Boghosian filled out the official historical resource forms on 140 Davis and Davis-area structures. (The one for the Terminal Building is reproduced in Fig. 6.3.) Ms. Boghosian put these forms in final order and added considerable text on the larger and broader historical context of Davis.

As a physical object, the survey was a hefty tome of 450 letter-sized, comb-bound pages (Historic Environments Consultants, 1980). Something like 50 photocopies were made of it (and additional copies were prohibited as an economy measure by the then Assistant City Manager). Presented to the public in June, 1980, the inventory was a wide net that captured all structures that were plausibly historical (*Davis Enterprise*, April 18, 1979). In doing this, it set the stage for isolating an "elite" class of structures that were of special import.

The survey cost $9,000 and was possible despite post-Prop 13 tight budgets because the Sacramento Regional Planning Commission funded $4,000, which was matched by $3,500 from the Commission's Historic Trust Fund and $1,500 from the city's General Fund (Taylor 1981, 4). (For several years, the Chamber of Commerce sponsored an antique show and other fund-raising activities, which, together with receipts from the Larkey book, gave the HMRC a modest account on which it could draw.) (This regional-local matching grant arrangement is yet another example of how the level and form of local preservation was importantly influenced by outside agencies.)

Survey-Spurred Further Changes. The 1980 survey was the starting point for and the basis of a new era in Davis preservation. In addition to the three externally-stimulated changes just enumerated, there were two further changes based on, and made possible by, the existence of the survey.

1. A New Historic Preservation Code, 1984. As part of her contract, Paula Boghosian made a list of recommended changes in the existing patchwork of preservation ordinances and wrote suggestions for the elements of a consolidated and extended replacement. Her recommendations were informed by her knowledge of professional preservationist practices at the federal level and across the country. Although Datel and Mikesell were involved in the rewrite, they were working off Boghosian's recommendations.

But getting the new ordinance adopted was not easy. It went through the usual public hearings, where it encountered accusations of being too "coercive" and "heavy-handed." It was revised to meet these objections. In October, 1982, it went to the City Attorney for a final review. But, this person did nothing with it for almost a year. In exasperation, then Commission Chair Mikesell wrote the Mayor on September 9, 1983 pleading for action:

> The written and verbal requests of the Commission have produced no tangible results. It seems to me that a reasonable review period has long been exceeded and that the City attorney has simply assigned a low priority to this task (Haig Collection, Box 4).

With this prodding, the new ordinance was "sprung," and finally adopted by a 4-1 Council vote on February 22, 1984 (with minimal attention from the public, Robin Datel reports).

2. Re-Certifying "Landmarks" as "Historical Resources," Mid-1980s. A listing of 140 structures in an "inventory" raises the question of which ones might be more important or more historic. How could one identify more important structures? The Federal program called the National Register of Historic Places was dedicated to answering exactly this question and had developed four criteria of significance (Chapter 1, Fig. 1.1) that local preservationists could also use. A structure that met at least one criterion was significant. And, preservation professionals were, of course, the people trained to determine whether a structure met a criterion or not.

6.4. Survey form for the Terminal Building in the City of Davis Cultural Resources Inventory, 1980.

Datel and Mikesell also played important roles here. In order to make a structure a historical resource, someone had to (1) write a ten or so page document to be presented to the City Council that (2) asserted in some historical detail that a given structure met at least one of the criteria of significance. This in turn required doing some historical research. Datel and Mikesell were educated in doing such work and were adept at it. As well, they provided leadership for other members of their commissions in performing these tasks (Datel Files, 1980-86).

The first structures written up and put forth for the status of "designated historical resource" (a new phrase and category in the 1984 ordinance) were simply taken from old-timer lists of

"Landmarks." That is, the consolidated historic resource ordinance of 1984 involved, as a first matter, a re-certification as "historic resources" what were previously termed "landmarks."

Between 1984 and 2002, this process of the City Council voting to make a structure a "designated historical resource" would be successfully completed 34 times for properties within or near the 1917 city incorporation boundaries (Fig. 6. 6 lists all of them). (Technically, it was 35 times because 623 Seventh was done twice). Thirty-four designations over 19 years averages to about two a year. This, though, is wildly misleading. The actual number of designations in a given year is given in Fig. 6.5. There we see that almost half of the 34 (16) took place in the first year—and all these were simply re-certified "landmarks." Then the number drops off sharply, becoming zero in 1988 and remaining zero for a full decade.

6.5. Number of "1917 City" Historical Resource Designations By Year, 1984-2002					
Year	Number of Designations	Year	Number of Designations	Year	Number of Designations
'84	16	'88	0	'98	7
'85	2	'89	0	'99	1
'86	7	'90	0	'00	0
'87	1	'91	0	'01	0
		'92	0	'02	0
		'93	0		
		'94	0		
		'95	0		
		'96	0		
		'97	0		
	26		0		8

Of great pertinence to understanding the Terminal matter: **the Terminal Building was not one of the structures designated a landmark prior to the re-certification in 1984.** Instead, it appeared on lists of possible landmark structures and was in the cultural resources inventory, but had not been finally included on any landmark list.

At the point of re-certifying the landmarks as historical resources, it was added to the list. As I will describe in more detail in a moment, its nomination appears to have been accelerated in this way because the owner announced in early 1984 that he was going to demolish the building. It was in reaction to this threat that the Commission then included it in the first batch later in 1984, rather than waiting until the next years when it moved to a fresh set of structures.

Other Aspects of the 1978-87 Period. Several additional aspects of the 1978-87 period of crisis and professionalization are notable.

1. Second Printing of *Davisville '68*, 1980. The first printing of 2,000 copies of *Davisville '68* was almost all sold by the late 1970s. In 1980, the City Council authorized a second printing of 1,500 copies for a printing cost of $7,800.

2. Adaptive Reuse Begins. Although not necessarily "preservationist" in a strict sense of complying with what preservationists call "the Secretary's Standards," in the late 1970s (and especially in 1979) and continuing into the 1980s, a number of projects developed "adaptive reuse" alternatives to "scrape-off" demolition. Facilitated by zoning changes in the mid-1970s that encouraged converting residences into commercial structures rather than demolishing them, the following were among the larger of these new re-use projects:

- I have already mentioned incorporating the Dresbach-Hunt-Boyer mansion into the larger Mansion Square shopping complex at Second and E.
- With partners, Richard Berteaux converted two older houses at 125-137 E Street into commercial structures, added other buildings behind them, and integrated the set into a complex named Orange Court. Done in stages over several years, it was formally completed in April, 1979.
- Park Place at 216-224-228 D Street "combined [five] old houses and outbuildings with new construction . . . to house a complex of specialty shops, a restaurant and . . . [a] real estate office" (*Davis Enterprise*, March 24, 1978, November 2 and December 31, 1979)
- After several unsuccessful efforts to site a new and larger city hall, the school district's leaving its high school building at Russell and B opened the way for the City to purchase, rehabilitate, and open it as the new City Hall in May of 1981.
- Saunders Place at the northeast corner of Fourth and D streets was a complex of buildings reconstructed as the kind of faux Victorian structures that make some preservationists cringe. But they were charming to the eyes of others (as to, for example, the eyes of the *Davis Enterprise* on May 4, 1984).
- What might be called the Carrere-Harby complex, completed in 1982, consisted of the two converted houses at the Southeast corner of Fourth and D. The Carrere home was moved there from the Wells Fargo Bank site rather than demolished (*Davis Enterprise*, July 30, 1980, December 24, 1982).

3. The Old High School Becomes City Hall, 1981. The rapid growth of Davis meant the rapid growth of Davis government. The number of City staff greatly exceeded space available to accommodate them at the little city hall at Third and F streets. After a long and tortured search for a site and funding, the old high school at Fifth and B, as noted just above, was bought from the school district and rehabilitated. With this, the City of Davis itself went into the historic preservation business.

4. The Avenue of the Trees Protest, 1984. This period saw the first major episode of public outcry against anti-preservationist **City of Davis** actions.

The City arborist and supporting "experts"—with the City Council going along—decided, in 1984, that a significant proportion (75 of about 260, the *Enterprise* reported) of the Black Walnut trees in the Davis "Avenue of the Trees" had reached the end of their "useful lives." They should be cut down (*Davis Enterprise*, May 15, 1984).

This declaration led to numerous and packed public protest meetings and the marshalling of equally credible experts opposed to the cuttings and who testified that the trees were nowhere near the end of their useful lives and could be maintained.

At the time of the publication of this book only a few of those trees had been cut down. So, you know what happened.

FOURTH PERIOD, 1988-94: PERCOLATING QUIESCENCE. The later 1980s and early 1990s were years of relative quiescence, at least with regard to the HMRC, which seemed to have moved into a "caretaker" mode. Further, looking over the Commission minutes of these years, one sees more than a few meetings disbanded for "lack of a quorum" and meetings canceled for "lack of items."

This, though, does not mean the period was without preservation and local history episodes and brouhaha. In fact, it was rather rich in these ways.

The City Council Preserves Buildings. In acquiring the old high school and converting it into a city hall, the City started down the historic preservation road. In this period they traveled down it quite some distance.

1. Southern Pacific Station Rehabilitation, 1980s. The Southern Pacific Railroad divested itself of passenger facilities in the late 1970s and in that process the City of Davis came to own the 1913 "Mission-style" station at the intersection of Second and H streets. In work extending a decade, a million and a half (or more) dollars were spent on "restoring" or otherwise re-doing the building and its environs.

6.6. City of Davis Designated Historical Resources, 2002. An * (asterisk) means an "Outstanding" as opposed to a mere "Historical" Resource.

There are 38 rather than 34 structures on this list because four are in the wider Davis area rather in or near the 1917 incorporating city limits of Davis.

*Davis Subway (Richards Underpass) (Ord. 2003, 9/29/99)

221 First Street - A.J. Plant House (Ord. 1343, 1/8/86)

616 First Street - Boy Scout Cabin (Ord. 1282)

209 Second Street - Barovetto Home (Ord. 1363, 4/9/86)

209 1/2 Second Street - Barovetto Tank House (Ord. 1363, 4/9/86)

505 Second Street - H.J. Hamel House (Ord. 1291, 11/14/84) (National Register)

*604 Second Street - Dresbach-Hunt-Boyer Home (Ord. 1282, 7/25/84)

*616 Second Street - Varsity Theatre (Ord. 1930, 2/25/98)

716, 718, 720, 722, 724, 726 Second Street - Brinley Block (Ord. 1291)

*840 Second Street - Southern Pacific Station/Davis Junction (Ord. 1282) (National Register)

232 Third Street - Eggleston Home (Ord. 1410, 1/7/87)

923 Third Street - The Montgomery House (Ordinance 1928, 2/25/98)

619 Fourth Street - First Presbyterian Manse (Ord. 1295)

*623 Seventh Street - Anderson-Hamel House (Ord. 1355, 2/19/86) (Ord. 1929 2/25/98)

310 A Street - Asbill-Grieve House (Ord. 1364, 4/9/86)

232 B Street - Jacobson-Wilson House (Ord. 1295, 11/28/84)

337 B Street - McDonald House (Ord. 1360, 3/12/86)

137 C Street - Clancy House (Ord. 1334, 12/4/85)

*412 C Street - Davis Community Church (Ord. 1282)

445 C Street - Old Davis Library (Ord. 1282)

602 D Street - the Grady House (Ord. 1954, 7/15/98)

648 D Street - (Ord. 1954, 7/15/98)

616 E Street - (Ord. 1954, 7/15/98)

*226 F Street - Old Davis City Hall (Ord. 1282)

513 F Street - (Ord. 1954, 7/15/98)

619 F Street - (Ord. 1954, 7/15/98)

*203 G Street - Anderson Bank Building (Ord. 1282)

225 G Street - Masonic Lodge (Ord. 1291)

301 G Street - Bank of Yolo (Ord. 1291)

*320 I Street - Williams-Drummond-Rorvick House (Ord. 1282)

*334 I Street - Schmeiser House (Ord. 1335, 12/4/85)

405 J Street - McBride Home (Ord. 1402, 12/3/86)

*434 J Street - Joshua B. Tufts-Longview-Jones Home (Ord. 1282)

*1140 Los Robles - Werner-Hamel House (Ord. 1282)

*820 Pole Line Rd. - Davis Cemetery (Ord. 1282)

*Russell Boulevard, West of Arthur Street - Avenue of the Trees (Ord. 1282)

*23 Russell Boulevard - Davis City Offices (Ord. 1282)

*2727 Russell Boulevard - LaRue-Romani Home (Ord.1282)

In view of the poverty the City so commonly pled about almost everything, one could ask how such a large project was possible. The answer is that staff were adroit grant writers and that the state or federal government paid 85 percent or more (but plus or minus fifteen percent still represented a lot of City loose change) (*Davis Enterprise*, May 29, 1988).

The work was done in phases, the first major one of which was completed, in the official reckoning, on Saturday, June 4, 1988. There was an elaborate dedication ceremony that day, along with a downtown "street faire" and other celebration activities.

Work on the SP station was commonly spoken of as a "transportation enhancement" matter (as a "multi-modal" facility) rather than as a preservation effort. Even so, such a "saving" of the SP station had major preservationist import and meaning. Indeed, one might claim it was one of the two or three most important preservation events in Davis history.

2. From Old Library to Part-Time Museum, Late 1980s-Early 1990s. In the late 1970s, City officials began to conceive the properties at and near the southwest corner of First and F streets as a site for a multi-story parking structure. A building constructed in 1911 as Davis' first public library stood on one of them. The library function was transferred to a new building (on Fourteenth Street) in 1968. The structure at 117 F fell into relative disuse. Officials began to think about demolition.

But, in the early 1980s, Phyllis Haig, descendant of Davis pioneers and a major figure in Davis historical and preservationist matters, proposed a different future: A Davis history museum. Backed by the Historical Commission and other groups, she campaigned to save the building at that location or to move it.

Petitioned almost continuously by Haig and others over several years, the City Council finally agreed to keep the building as a City-owned structure, but not entirely as a museum. Instead, it would become a Parks and Recreation meeting facility that would also function, part-time, as a museum.

The building was moved four blocks northwest to Central Park (445 C) in August of 1988. Rehabilitated, it was made the Museum of Davis (although only partially used as that) in 1991.

Subsequently (see below), the building was formally named the Hattie Weber Museum of Davis in honor of Harriet Elisha Weber (1872-1961), who ran the public library in Davis from 1910 to 1953. (Those who think "small world," will appreciate knowing she was a daughter of George Augustus Weber and an aunt of John Weber Brinley.)

6.7. Phyllis Haig, *Davis Enterprise*, May 10, 1979.

Enterprise Phot

Phyllis Haig, assistant chairman of the Davis Landmarks Commission, fears the old Davis Library building might fall victim to downtown expansion.

At this time, the City contracted with "The Library Club"—a group whose membership was restricted to female descendents of Davis pioneers—to run the Museum. This contract provided that the Club would operate a museum in exchange for being allowed to use the building for club meetings. (The contract did not involve the exchange of any money and could be canceled by either party at any time.)

3. Varsity Theater Leased and Renovated, Early 1990s. Deciding the "Streamline Moderne" Varsity Theater on Second Street was obsolete for showing motion pictures, the owners closed it in September, 1990. As part of a then-new economic development strategy for the downtown, the City took a 25-year lease on it and, with significant cost overruns, spent more than $800,000 renovating it.

Orchestrated by then-Mayor David Rosenberg, more than $400,000 of these costs were raised from developer contributions. (For example, one developer pledged $240,000, which was $800 for each house he built.) Asked why almost all the donations were from developers, Mayor Rosenberg (ever the deadpan comic) opined, "Money comes from developers because they are civic-minded" (*Davis Enterprise*, October 1, 1991).

4. Dresbach-Hunt-Boyer Purchased, 1994. When the Dresbach-Hunt-Boyer mansion was "saved" through redevelopment as "Mansion Square" in 1978, the lot was split, leaving the mansion on its own small plot. In 1994, its owner decided to sell it. Saying that it was desperate for more office space, the City bought it.

Other City Preservation Activities. In addition to getting into the historic rehabilitation business, the City engaged in some other activities.

The 75th Anniversary of Davis Incorporation, 1992. In mid-1991, the HMRC and city staff began planning the City's 75th Anniversary of incorporation. Consisting of a year-long series of events, the actual "birthday party" was held outdoors in Central Park on the blessedly balmy day of Saturday, March 28. (The vote to incorporate took place on March 20, 1917.)

Among other performances in the seven-hour long celebration, Mayor Maynard Skinner arrived at noon on a "Highwheel bicycle followed by Skydance Skydivers descending into the park." Not to be overshadowed, Council Member David Rosenberg rode about on a rented horse. In a ceremony at 1:00 p.m., the meeting-museum building was formally declared the Hattie Weber Museum of Davis.

One of the more striking aspects of the 75th Anniversary was the amount of attention given to it in the pages of the *Davis Enterprise*. In addition to abundant coverage in ordinary stories, the paper developed and printed a two-part insert, called "Remembering Our Heritage," containing a great many stories on aspects of Davis history (*Davis Enterprise*, March 22 and 23, 1992). Separate from this, there was a six part series on "Davis historic homes," as well as assorted other history stories over the year.

The Second Davis History Book. In 1988, the idea that Davis needed an updated book of history that reflected the new environmental and liberal Davis of the recent period found favor among members of the City Council. A request for proposals was issued, revised after being criticized as too narrow in conception, and then reissued. Providing a stipend of $10,000, to be taken largely from the Davis History Trust Fund, an author was selected.

The writer began interviewing people for the history. Soon, word began circulating that this would-be historian lectured interviewees more than interviewed them and spent too much time giving her personal opinions on many topics, including her negative views of current Council members. The critical reaction was so wide and strong that the author resigned. A second author was recruited. But he posed a different kind of problem. He went years over the deadline to deliver the manuscript. Under the threat of having to return the portion of the stipend he had already been paid, he turned in a draft of his book in 1998. Quite well done but narrowly focused on only a few public policies, it generated almost no public reaction or interest when the draft was put on the City's web site. It never proceeded to hardcopy publication.

Citizen Campaigns. Some of the percolating aspects of this period's relative quiescence took the form of citizen resistance to City anti-preservation initiatives.

A "Defended Neighborhood:" Old East Davis, 1988. In the mid-1980s, the City Council began to think that perhaps it was time to redevelop the area bounded by the railroad, L Street, Second Street, and Fifth Street with apartment buildings at much, much greater than existing population density.

This area happened also to contain a number of the oldest homes in Davis and residents attached to those homes and the neighborhood. They regarded the contemplated redevelopment as a threat. They thereupon invented the term "Old East Davis" and formed an association with that name. This area thus become Davis' first (in sociological jargon) "defended neighborhood," an area that is spurred into creating an identity for itself and organizing its residents because of external threats (Suttles, 1972: Ch. 2, "The Defended Neighborhood").

For whatever reasons, the plan the Council floated never moved forward. In the year 2002, Old East Davis still looked very much like it did in the mid-1980s. (And, there was a continuing Old East Davis Association, which is described below.)

Subway II, 1988. In 1988, the Council tried a second time to achieve approval for a bond to widen the Subway. But, the effort was overshadowed by a concurrent controversy and public vote on the issue of building a freeway overpass at one rather than another location in east Davis. The citizenry was almost evenly divided on the two overpass locations, which aroused high emotions and intense campaigning on both sides. The consequence was rather little attention to the Subway bond either for or against. It achieved 60% approval in the November balloting, but failed because two-thirds was required.

Alley Paving Protest, 1991-92. The City of Davis Department of Public Works continuously works on a list of "capital improvement projects," a set of year-after-year construction changes in and upgrades to the City's physical infrastructure. One of those projects, that hardly anyone reviewed or paid attention to, was the cement paving of the six gravel-surfaced alleys in the Old North neighborhood. Moving up a notch in the list each year, this activity was scheduled to happen in 1992.

After she was evicted from her to-be-demolished home on Second Street, Julie Partansky had moved four blocks north and lived in a cottage on one of those six alleys. In mid-1991, she learned of the impending paving of her and the other five alleys.

With the help of dozens of residents in the neighborhood, she organized "stop the paving" petitions to the City Council. Under this citizen pressure and with Public Works Department surveys that showed most Old North people opposed paving, the City Council mostly relented. The alley between G and F streets in the 500 block, which had the most commercial presence and traffic, would be paved. The other five were re-graded and re-graveled (*Davis Enterprise*, January 9, 1992).

What makes this episode of interest here is that Partansky enlisted the HMRC in the struggle. She and the Commission made "historical resource" arguments for not paving. That is, gravel alleys were a part of the historical integrity of the Old North. While the concept of "integrity" had previously been applied to buildings, application to a feature of a neighborhood was new. And, it opened the way to thinking about a "conservation district" later in the 1990s. (Some people of course tried to discredit this line of thinking by charging that Partansky and the HMRC believed that one should preserve "historic potholes." No one ever made such an argument, but it made a good "Davis is wacky" story in the *National Inquirer*.)

Paving or not paving was a major topic of public attention in the last months of 1991 and the early months of 1992. Julie was clearly the major spokesperson for and the leader of the anti-pavers. Based on this, people urged her to run for City Council in the election to be held in June, 1992. She did and she won. (Another small world aside: William Kopper was one of the key people encouraging her to run and who worked in her campaign.)

FIFTH PERIOD: RESURGENCE AND REACTION, 1995–2002. In the early 1990s, John Meyer, the new City Manager appointed in 1990, reorganized the Davis City government. Shuffling the departmental homes of various activities, the HRMC was moved from the Planning Department, with a planner as Commission staff, to the Parks and Recreation Department, with two liberal-arts-trained people assigned (each part-time) as Commission Staff.

The HMRC Moves Upscale. In this new home, the HMRC was given a new and different identity. It was now a high-tone "cultural service," rather than a low-tone and gritty land-use restriction. As if to stress the point, the Civic Arts Commission was put beside the HRMC in the City's organizational chart. The staff person in charge was titled the "Cultural Services Manager"(as opposed to the less sacred and blunt "planner").

The importance of this change is that the two young staff with HMRC responsibilities—Sophia Pagoulatos and Esther Polito—were trained in aspects of the arts, particularly in art history, not in planning or in preservation. However, they were sophisticated and cosmopolitan about cultural matters, believed in preservation, and were hard workers who learned quickly.

Becomes a Certified Local Government. They began to educate themselves about preservation at the state and federal level and learned that there was a new a program for historical commissions called the Certified Local Government (CLG). This federal-state effort provided incentives to local governments to undertake preservation activities, especially "surveys of cultural resources." A local jurisdiction agreed to appoint commissioners of certain qualifications and specialties and to require a number of hours of training per year in exchange for which it was preferentially eligible for preservation-related grants. (CLG membership would cost the City $600 a year for the required training of commissioners.)

Pagoulatos and Polito worked-up the idea of joining. It was subsequently supported and sponsored by the HRMC, the Head of the Department of Parks and Recreation, and the City Manager, John Meyer. (Meyer was himself a preservation supporter and the owner-occupant of a house he seemed happy to see become a "historic resource" in 1998 [Fig. 6.6, 616 E Street]).

So sponsored, the City Council unanimously approved application for CLG membership on February 9, 1995. Julie Partansky, who was one of the strongest supporters of preservation ever elected to the Council, was in the third year of her first term. The then-Mayor, David Rosenberg, was also a preservationist. (We will meet both of them again in the chapters of Part II.)

<u>**Three Major Official Actions.**</u> CLG membership opened the door to a resurgence of preservationist activities. Here are what I think to have been the three most important of these.

1. The Second Cultural Resources Survey, 1996. The HMRC and its staff right away parlayed their CLG preferential eligibility for funding into a $15,000 grant for a consultant to conduct an update of the 1980 survey of cultural resources. By "right away," I mean the Council unanimously approved application for the grant on May 24, 1995, less than three months after approving an application for GLC membership.

This second survey fielded some two dozen volunteer surveyors and was conducted and completed in 1996. It produced a document about as fat the first one but in fact much longer because the type was much smaller. This time it was titled *City of Davis Cultural Resources Inventory and Context Statement* (Architectural Resources Group, 1996).

The list of possibly historical structures was longer than that of 1980. The enumeration reached farther from the original center of the town at Second and G streets and now included, in particular, many homes in the "Old North" area, the twelve blocks bounded by Fifth, Seventh, B, and the railroad tracks. And it included all the houses in the area called "College Park."

2. Eight New Designations. This expanded enumeration provided the basis for renewed effort to "designate" "historical resources." Guided by the expertise of a new set of technically-trained Commissioners, a fresh list of properties on which to work up "nominations" was created.

This fresh list importantly consisted of residences rather than other types of buildings. As one can see in Figs. 6.5 and 6.6 there would eventually be eight new designations, seven in 1998 and one in 1999. Six of the eight were residences. One of the other two was the Richards Underpass and the other was the Varsity Theater, a structure considered obsolete for its original use.

Of importance, I think, there were no ordinary commercial buildings (the Varsity Theater being obsolete). The one commercial structure that the HMRC actually moved to the nomination phase—the Terminal Building—was turned down by the Council—a subject I examine in detail in Part II of this volume.

But there was a phase previous to nomination. This was the phase in which Commissioners asked themselves if it made sense to try to work-up a nomination. One major reason it would not make sense would be an owner's already known opposition to preservation, combined with the importance of the owner's business in Davis. Indeed, at least one key building on G Street never got near the point of nomination because Commissioners were well aware of this owner's virtual hate of preservation.

Also at this time, Commissioners desired to nominate the Catholic Church at Fifth and C streets. Told of this desire, the owner said it did not want designation. Litigation and legislation pending in California regarding religious structures also clouded what was possible. Time passed and the matter was not taken up again.

3. Conservation District Design Guidelines, 2001. Aside from issues of preservation, guidelines for design of new construction in the Core Area had been an issue for many years. Indeed, the matters of "design review" and "design guidelines" had become so contentious and seemingly subjective that one Council even abolished what was called the Design Review Commission. Deciding to ignore the problem did not, though, make it go away.

Hanging out there as a sore that became acutely inflamed on occasion, this long-standing problem of what to do about design opened the way for the HRMC to broach a modest solution.

Perhaps one only needed design guidelines that applied to the "traditional" part of Davis (the 1917 incorporating area, the blocks bounded by A and L and First and Seventh streets).

The path in this direction had already been opened in the Davis *Core Area Specific Plan* of 1996. That plan stipulated that "any design guidelines developed for the City shall contain special guidelines for the Core Area that will take into account its uniqueness and architectural heritage" (City of Davis, 1996: 14).

Applying and extending that requirement, the HMRC, the Planning Commission, and staff joined in developing a plan to hire a "Design Guidelines consultant" who would conduct a series of public meetings to determine citizen desires and write up a draft booklet of guidelines. The "budget adjustment" for this was $40,000. Again with the support of the City Manager and other key city staff, the Council unanimously approved the measure on April 4, 1999. At this time, Julie Partansky was the mayor.

Of key importance, the plan called for the creation of a "conservation district," **not** a "preservation district" or a "historic district." The idea was to create a zoning "overlay" area, not to engage in entirely new zoning. This was done, HRMC members and staff said clearly, because they doubted people in Davis would accept something as strong as a preservation or historic district. (These distinctions among districts are described in Terrell, 1996: 9-10.)

Bruce Race of RACESTUDIO was awarded the contract. He orchestrated public meetings to elicit resident views of their respective areas and worked with City planner Ken Hiatt and others to produce a draft. This draft was then the subject of several more public meetings.

I was a participant in this process and I attended almost all the public meetings. I was especially interested in the degree to which and ways in which there was public opposition to the Guidelines. To my surprise, I observed or knew of no one who publicly opposed them in principle and called for the adoption of no guidelines. Instead, what little public opposition there was related to changes in particular provisions. The strongest form of this selective opposition came from architects who feared that their creative talents would be stifled by a strict reading of the guidelines. But, this was not opposition to the Guidelines per se. (And, architects were assured they would not be stifled.)

On the other side, residents who came to the meetings—perhaps two hundred people over all the meetings—were quite enthusiastic and evidenced considerable pride about living in "traditional Davis."

But still, the very absence of wholesale opposition to the Guidelines in principle made me nervous. This was because in a number of private conversations I sensed people did not much like the idea of the constraints of the Guidelines, but felt reluctant to say so. In the People's Republic of Liberal Davis, it was not "politically correct" to be against historic preservation. I therefore worried that there was a dammed up reservoir of anti-preservationist sentiment that a catalytic event might release. (The outcome of the Davis City Council election of March, 2002 and events following from it suggested that my fears were not baseless.)

 Be that as it may, three Council members were not allowed to vote because they owned property in the "1917 city." Using a random draw to allow one of these three to vote in order to achieve the possibility of a majority (Greenwald winning), the Guidelines were adopted by a unanimous vote of that three on August 1, 2001. (One of these three said, though, that she did not really like the Guidelines, but would not stand in the way of what seemed to be a well-negotiated plan that was arrived at democratically.)

Subway III, 1996-97. The above describes Davis preservationist activity dominated by government. But preservation also had other sources and actors; namely, grassroots citizen action. The 1995-2002 period had important such citizen-based episodes.

Recall that the City Council of 1973 wanted to widen the Richards Underpass, but the bond to execute the plan was defeated (**Subway I, 1973,** Chapter 5, section 8)). Then, in **Subway II, 1988,** a second bond issue failed with 60% voting in favor, but two thirds needed for adoption.

In a three to two vote, the Council of 1996 decided to try a third time to widen the Subway, but by other than bond financing. But, the two dissenting Council members—Julie Partansky and Stan Forbes—sparked a citizen referendum to overturn the plan. Vigorous campaigning by an coalition called SMART (Save Money and Reduce Traffic) triumphed in a special election held in March, 1997 (44% yes, 56% no).

As I said before, while there was a preservationist element in this contest, anti-tax sentiment was also likely a strong force. Nonetheless, preservationist values were also clearly visible in the campaign. (In addition, Julie Partansky stresses that the sheer, massive scale of the proposed replacement underpass worked against passage. Opponents developed an in-scale photographic mock-up of how the replacement tunnel would look at that location. According to her, its massiveness startled many people and turned them against the project.)

Old East Davis Celebrations, 1998- —. Starting in 1998, each Fall the Old East Davis Association held a day-long "Old East Davis Neighborhood Celebration." Several streets were blocked off, bands performed, walking and house tours were conducted, a history contest held, ceremonies celebrated, the year's Grand Marshal (an old-time resident) spoke about the neighborhood, dignitaries welcomed everyone, and, in general, a good time was had by all.

The consciously sponsored atmosphere was that of a party, but the underlying message was dead serious: We are organized and ready to respond to threats to our neighborhood. As it had developed in Davis and in the United States in general, historic preservation had become, in major respects, a government program. But in Old East Davis we saw historic preservation of a different kind with a different basis: grassroots residents acting on their own for their own neighborhood interests. Such indigenous initiative was so rare that one could not but be inspired when one encountered an authentic instance of it.

Terminal Building Demolition, 2000. For the sake of contextual clarity, I roster here the event that this book is about. The event itself and aftermath are treated in Parts II and III.

An Aside: The City as the Major Figure in Historic Buildings. Given the City of Davis' reluctance to spend money on local history and preservation, it is ironic that, by the year 2000, it had nonetheless wound up being a major owner or controller of Davis historic buildings. These were: (1) the Old Davis High School remodeled into a City Hall (late 1970s); (2) the Southern Pacific Rail station (1980s); (3) the old library remodeled into a meeting-room/museum (1980s-90s); (4) the Dresbach-Hunt-Boyer Mansion (1994); (5) the long-term lease on and remodel of the Varsity Theater (1990s); (6) The old City Hall, originally the only building the City owned; and, (7) the Boy Scout Cabin, on which the City had a lease with an option to buy the land from UC Davis, giving it operational if not "on paper" ownership.

As of finishing this book in early 2003, it was still too soon to perceive with any clarity the end of the fifth period of Davis local history and preservation and the start of a sixth one.

2) THE FAILED 1984 EFFORT TO DESIGNATE THE TERMINAL BUILDING

Against the local history and preservation background and context sketched in this and the last chapter, we come to the 1984 failed effort to designate the Terminal Building a historical resource.

Recall from the previous chapter that in 1977 it had been acquired by the Chens and a shifting series of ancillary owners and corporate entities (Chapter 5, sections 3, 7, and 9). Electing not to bring the hotel portion up to code, that use had stopped, but the apartments and retail spaces were still rented.

OWNER'S DEMOLITION PLAN. Matters drifted in the late 1970s and early 1980s. Then, in 1983-84, the owners embarked on a plan to demolish the building and to put a four story box in its place (as shown in Fig. 6. 12). Apparently not opposed by the Planning Department, Lee Chen brought this scheme to the attention of the City Council on January, 25, 1984 (Fig. 6.8).

As it happened, other developers were also starting to float ideas for four story buildings in the downtown. Davis had no buildings of such a height—or hardly any that were even three stories. The prospect of a sudden set of tall structures precipitated a City Council move to freeze development of that sort until the likely consequences of such changes could be thought through. So, the Chen plan got an initial chilly reception for other than historic preservation reasons.

But there was also negative preservationist response. Mayor Bill Kopper was quoted and re-quoted as declaring at the January 25th meeting, "It would be a public outrage if that building were torn down" (Fig. 6.8). Apparently surprised by Kopper's response and others like it, Chen said he would "not tear the building down at this time" (Fig. 6.8).

DEBATE. Three months of public debate on demolishing the Terminal Building ensued. In Fig. 6.9 we see side-by-side pro and con letters published in the *Enterprise* on January 31. Later that week, one of the two builders and original owners of the building—George Tingus, who was now 91 years of age—weighed in with a letter urging preservation (Fig. 6.10).

Responding to these and additional opinions, *Enterprise* reporter Mike Fitch composed an overview piece that appeared on February 3rd (Fig. 6.12). Of particular note, drawings of Chen's proposed building accompanied the article.

The next week saw additional pro and con letters (Fig. 6.13). The pro-preservation letter penned by Dennis Dingemans offered especially sophisticated arguments. Its sophistication is perhaps made more understandable by knowing that Mr. Dingemans earned a Ph. D. in geography at UC Berkeley in 1975 and was a UC Davis faculty member, whose scholarly specialties included the subject of historic preservation (e.g. Datel and Dingemans, 1988). In addition, he was the spouse of Robin Datel. The sentiments expressed in the second letter, by Gale Sosnick, would be reiterated by her numerous times in diverse public venues over subsequent decades.

The last item in this little flurry was an opinion piece by Stephen Mikesell published in the *Enterprise* on February 10 (Fig. 6.14). As a preservation professional, Mikesell tried carefully to separate issues that were often tangled together but logically separate.

DEMOLITION PERMIT WITHDRAWN. Although Lee Chen had said on January 25 that he would not tear down the Terminal Building, he did not withdraw his application for a demolition permit until early April. The *Enterprise* hailed this as "saving" the building in a front page story on April 4th (Fig 6.15).

THE HRMC MOVES. Recall that the City Council adopted a new and "modernized" historic preservation ordinance on February 22 of this same year (section 1, this chapter). This change required that the old "landmarks" be re-certified as "historical resources." The Landmarks Commission, now renamed the Historical Resources Management Commission, had set about this task of re-certification when the Terminal Building was suddenly threatened.

Responding to this threat, at its meeting of May 29 the HRMC added the Terminal Building to its list of structures to be considered for historical resource designation. As would also happen when the building was again presented for designation in 1999, Lee Chen was unable to be present. The hearing was postponed to June 26. The *Enterprise* story reproduced in Fig. 6.16 describes the events of the May 29th meeting, which set the stage for June 26th.

No minutes of the June 26th meeting seem to have survived, so we must rely on two newspaper accounts of it (Figs. 6.17 and 6.18). The cast of leading participants in the meeting were the familiar ones: Chen, Mikesell, Dingemans, Sosnick. One interesting change is that Lee Chen was now represented by an attorney. This was Joan Poulos, a member of the famous liberal trio who changed the direction of Davis government in the election of 1972 and who was the first woman mayor of Davis (Fitch, 1998; Lofland, 2001: 16-17).

I note that only five of the seven members of the Commission were present and one of them voted against the designation. So, unlike the second time the time the building would be considered for designation, this approval was rather tepid.

THE COUNCIL VOTES NO. Thusly supported by the HRMC, the case went before the City Council on July 18, 1984. The official City account of what happened is reproduced in Fig. 6.19. Designation failed on a two to three vote.

The two news accounts are different enough in emphasis to justify reproducing both here, as Figs. 6.20 and 6.21. Two themes broached by Lee Chen and Joan Poulos are amusingly ironic. First, Mr. Chen asserts that "we should think about the future of Davis, not the past" (Fig. 6.21). In 1984, the Davis powers-that-were had already torn down or moved away almost two-thirds of the older buildings in the downtown area and replaced them with rather futuristic structures. That massive, future-oriented fact suggests that people in Davis were thinking about the future rather more than Mr. Chen wanted to give them credit.

Second, Ms. Poulos made a telling point when she declared that "any cultural value the building may have had has long since been forgotten" (Fig. 6.21). I think a fair-minded observer would have to agree with her that, in 1984, the state of popular historical knowledge and appreciation of Davis history was not great. Indeed, the now-city was entering the fourth decade of explosive growth (Fig. 1.3). The great bulk of the then-current residents had not lived in Davis very long. Understandably, their knowledge of Davis history was scant or zero.

In addition, there were hardly any efforts at this time to promote public understanding of Davis history. The "cultural value" of most **everything** historically Davis had "long since been forgotten." Even more and to repeat: most then-residents of Davis, being new to the town, **never knew such "cultural value" in the first place.**

City wants old hotel preserved

By Teri Robinson
Staff writer

First steps were taken last night to prevent the demolition of the Aggie Hotel building and to prevent the construction of extra tall buildings in the downtown area.

Developer Lee Chen has proposed to tear down the Aggie Hotel, which is located on the northeast corner of Second and G streets, and put up a four-story office/retail building. This plan, so closely following that of two other multi-story buildings, has the city planning staff concerned and prompted last night's discussion.

"It would be a public outrage if that building were torn down," said Mayor Bill Kopper at last night's city council meeting. The building is not technically an historical landmark, but it is on a list of 100 city buildings that are historically significant. It also sports a mural of the Davis Arch.

The council requested the city staff to prepare an ordinance that would make the commercial area south of Third Street a "study zone" for four months. That would stop all building in the area until the council can decide what kind of construction should be allowed. Public hearings will be held on the proposed ordinance before the

See HOTEL, Back Page

6.8. *Davis Enterprise,* January 26, 1984. This story does not actually report that the "City" wanted an "old hotel preserved." At best, it only reports the reality that one member of the City Council did not want to tear down the Terminal Building.

Hotel

Continued from Page 1

council takes any action.

The study zone would not prevent Chen from tearing down the building, but it would prevent him from building on the vacant site. The council learned last night that it had little control over demolitions of non-historical buildings.

Chen told the council that he would not tear the building down at this time.

The council also asked the staff to recommend measures to restrict building height in the downtown area and to ensure that adequate parking accompany new or expanded structures.

Currently, there are no height restrictions on buildings in the commercial area. Also, owners of property within existing parking assessment districts are not required to supply more parking spaces when they enlarge their businesses. These businesses have already paid to provide parking lots in the downtown area.

Chen's proposed building would have created a demand for 83 new parking spaced, city staff anticipated, but it would have been required to supply none.

Changing the parking regulations for existing parking districts was opposed by Davis businessman Paul Garritson. "You have no legal right to change the rules on the first parking district," Garritson said to the council. "People have always had the idea they could add to their structures without adding more parking."

The council rejected a request by the city staff for a comprehensive study of the entire downtown area. There appears to be a trend toward tall buildings, said Senior Planner Tom Lumbrazo, which will place special demands on city services and possibly change the character of the area.

A three-story commercial/residential building has been approved for Third and B, Central Park Plaza, and a four-story movie/office building is planned for Fifth and G Street.

Lumbrazo recommended that no further building permits be issued until a consultant be hired to review the possible effects and suggest new city policies or ordinances to regulate them.

Though environmental impact reports are done on each large project, that is an "incremental approach," said Community Development Director Fred Howell last night. The study would take a broader, more comprehensive view of the situation.

Councilmember Ann Evans suggested that the study be one task of the recently approved Davis 2000 Committee, a group which will recommend programs and policies for the next 20 years and which will examine the implications of various future population levels in Davis.

"A consultant cannot know what we want the character of the core to be," said Evans. Chen told the council that he had been led to believe by the city staff that there would not be a problem with his proposal. It does not violate any city ordinance, he pointed out.

He said the structure he proposes would fit in well with the surrounding structures. "We would like to do as much as possible for the city."

It would be very costly to simply renovate the structure, he also said, because the walls would have to be reinforced to bring them up to current earthquake standards.

LETTERS TO THE EDITOR

Is the Aggie Hotel really worth saving?

Following is a copy of a letter I have sent to the City Council concerning the proposed destruction of the old Aggie Hotel which was brought up at a recent council meeting and reported in The Enterprise.

I hope there will be an uprising of objection and alternative suggestions by the citizens of Davis. I have been here only four years, but it was the spirit and the civic pride in its roots that attracted me to this community.

I fear greedy real estate developers swallowing up all the old buildings and all the vacant spaces left in Davis. If we don't get vocal about it, the Core Area will be filled in with huge, badly designed buildings worse than some of those along Second Street, and the traffic will be even worse than it is now. Moreover, it appears we will have a glut of office space if the developers are left to their own devices.

The attractiveness of Davis has already been marred. Let us not ruin the rest of it by default. The developers need control and guidance from the citizens who love and appreciate the Davis chaaracter and history, and are concerned for its future, based on its traditions and customs.

Dear Council Members,

It appears that the wily developers have pulled the wool over the eyes of the city officials and once again we are in danger of losing the ambience of Davis that was nearly decimated a few years ago.

The ill-advised Central Park Plaza is too far along to stop, and the city will find, eventually, what a mistake we have made. It is not, however, too late to stop the tearing down of the old Aggie Hotel, and possibly it is not too late to modify the plans for the property at Fifth and G.

Before taking the word of Mr. Chen that restoring the Aggie Hotel building would be too costly (to whom and for what reason?) I suggest that a careful study be made to see if the building could be restored, or if it is possible to impose strict design and structural requirements on the developer to retain the north wall, including it in the new struc-

ture, and to make the new design conform as much as possible to the original.

The usual argument of the developers is that they need to make a "reasonable" profit on their investment. But when their needs conflict with the needs of the community, someone has to ask which is more important, the laissez faire desires of the developer, or the long-range welfare of the community.

If the plans made for the renovation of the train depot are still in order, and a schedule for this construction has been confirmed, it appears to me that a cooperative planning of the two sites, the depot and the hotel, in the Core Area. With the Greyhound depot transferred to the Amtrak station, more visitors will get their first view of Davis in this part of the town. It could be made into an attractive entrance into the city, and introduce visitors and new residents to the business area in a positive way. In addition, if the Aggie Hotel could again become a functioning hostelry, it would help relieve the accommodation congestion that occurs during the times UCD has special events, and provide another alternative, convenient to transportation, for business and vacation guests.

I agree with the mayor that we cannot let the mural be destroyed. It is not only, as he said, something paid for by the city, but it is a dramatic reminder to all Davis residents of the heritage of this unique community. To destroy that mural would be to destroy a part of the heart and spirit of Davis that we all enjoy.

If the developer persists in his intention to destroy the entire building, isn't there a chance that the citizens of Davis can join together to force an alternative decision by the council and the Planning Commission?
Margaret Milligan
Davis

The real issue

I was amused to read that Mayor Bill Kopper expects "a public

Letters to the editor

outrage" if the old Aggie Hotel building at Second and G is torn down. Personally, I've always felt that that building was one of the most unaesthetic and slum-like structures in the entire city.

But really, my opinion of the building's looks is beside the point. And so is Mayor Kopper's. The central issue is that Lee Chen, and not the mayor or I, is the owner of that building.

Let's take an analogous situation. Suppose Old Mr. Smith owns a Model T. He's been driving it around Davis for 50 years. But repairs on the old car are becoming more and more expensive. Finally, he decides to junk it and buy himself a new Porsche.

"No, Mr. Smith," says the City Council. "That old Model T is part of our city's historical heritage. It would cause a public outrage if you junked it. You may not replace it with a new car."

Surely the injustice in such a council decree is self-evident. So what difference is there between Mr. Smith's old car and Lee Chen's old building? Is not the principle the same?

Those people who want to see the old Aggie Hotel building preserved have the option of raising the money and offering to buy the building from Mr. Chen. For people to pay for what they want is fair and just; to force Mr. Chen to bear the cost is not.
William S. Statler
Davis

6.9. *Davis Enterprise,* January 3, 1984.

6.10. *Davis Enterprise*, February 2, 1984.

Save the hotel

In 1924 I was the original owner and developer of the property on the corner of Second and G streets (currently the Aggie Hotel).

As a cornerstone of the original downtown Davis business area, and one of its few remaining landmarks, I strongly urge the City Council and Planning Commission to recognize its historical signficance and not allow the building to be demolished.

The future direction of the downtown Core Area is in the hands of the citizens of Davis, they have the duty to preserve a little bit of the past for future generations. I sincerely hope the citizens of Davis do not allow development of this type to change the "personality" of our town forever.

George J. Tingus and family
Davis

6.11. Photograph of the Terminal Building printed in the *Davis Enterprise*, February 22, 1984.

Debate may decide Aggie Hotel fate

Historic site or eyesore?

By MIKE FITCH

To some residents, the building is a historic landmark, a vital link to the community's past.

To others, it is an eyesore, a slum-like structure that should be torn down and replaced with something new, something more efficient.

The Davis City Council ultimately may be asked to decide who is right and who is wrong about the two-story structure which has rested at the northeast corner of Second and G streets since 1925. In the meantime, the debate continues about what should be done with the structure.

For decades, the building housed visitors to Davis, provided newcomers with a resting place while they looked for permanent accommodations and offered a refuge for transients and others down on their luck.

At first, it was known as the Terminal Hotel and Cafe and served primarily as an overnight resting place for train travelers from the nearby Southern Pacific Depot.

Later, the building housed the Aggie Hotel and the Antique Bizarre, a bar and restaurant which long was one of the city's weekend hot spots. The two businesses closed several years ago, but the memories remain.

Covering the north end of the building is another reminder of the city's heritage, a mural based on a 1919 photograph of Second Street.

The building, its past and its future were thrust into the limelight recently when Lee Chen, its owner, applied to the city for permission to build a new four-story structure on the site.

The application has polarized those who hold opposing views about the issue. Supporters charge that developers are willing to throw away the city's heritage because of their devotion to profits.

"It appears that the wily developers have pulled the wool over the eyes of the city officials and once again we are in danger or losing the ambience of Davis that was nearly decimated a few years ago," says one local resident, Margaret Milligan, in a letter to the council.

Several years ago, the community was divided over a similar issue: what to do with the Hunt-Boyer Mansion, a historic structure which sits at Second and E streets. In that case, a compromise solution was worked out that allowed the mansion to remain at its traditional location and owners to construct a shopping center, Mansion Square, at the rear of the site.

Those who oppose sentiments such as those expressed by Milligan question whether the building is worth saving.

"Personally, I've always felt that building was one of the most unaesthetic and slum-like buildings stuctures in the entire city," said William Statler in a recent letter to The Enterprise.

Chen does not want to be cast as the villain in the controversy, saying he has looked into restoring the

NATURAL FOODS   FLORIST

Photo by Ken Browning

What to do?

The old Aggie Hotel building, which displays a mural of the old Davis arch on its north wall, is the focus of a debate between

structure, but has learned that restoration may be too costly to be feasible.

According to Chen, an initial study indicates restoration of the building would cost between $70 and $75 per square foot. A new structure would cost only about $60 per square foot. He also believes restoring the building for office use will be difficult since the north wall has no windows.

Chen said he closed the hotel in 1979 because it wasn't very profitable and caused too many headaches.

He says the new building being proposed will benefit Davis and its business community and stresses its features are being designed to blend in with surrounding buildings.

Faced with strong opposition to his plans, Chen says he may withdraw his application for the new project.

"We are thinking about it, whether we should withdraw it or continue," he said this morning, indicating he plans to decide within a week or so.

Chen also indicated he may hold on to the property for several years and then decide what to do with it or may seek less expensive estimates for restoring the building.

If Chen does not withdraw the application, the City Council probably will decide the fate of the project. At a meeting on Jan. 25, Chen's plans met a cool reception, particularly from Mayor Bill Kopper.

Said Kopper during the meeting, "I think there would be a public outrage if that building was torn down."

During a telephone conversation this week, the mayor stressed that such buildings should be retained so that residents can maintain a sense of history.

He admitted, however, "If I owned the building, I would probably feel the way Mr. Chen feels."

Kopper, Chen and others have indicated that some kind of compromise can be reached which will meet the owner's financial needs, but still allow the community to retain the building.

In the meantime, the council is considering the possibility of placing much of the downtown area in a study zone, a move which would postpone development of properties such as the Aggie Hotel site until issues raised by Chen's projects and a couple of others can be resolved.

citizens who want to preserve the structure as a landmark and those who want to see a larger office and retail building in its place.

Below, artist's sketches depict the exterior of owner Lee Chen's proposed new building.

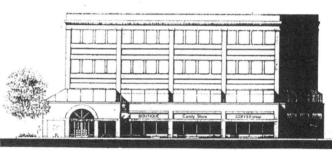

BOUTIQUE   Candy Store   COFFEE shop

SOUTH ELEVATION

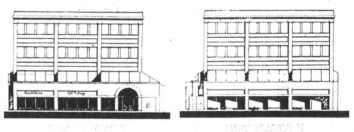

BookStore   Gift shop

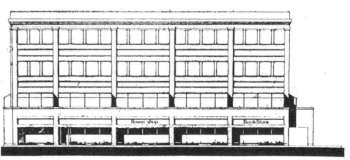

flower shop   BookStore

NORTH ELEVATION

6.12. *Davis Enterprise*, February 3, 1984.

6.13. *Davis Enterprise*, February 7, 1984.

Letters to the editor

Save building

It was not a pleasure to read that the owner claims that the Hotel Aggie "is old and deteriorating and shouldn't be there" or to hear a citizen (Paul X) at City Council declare that the building "is a piece of junk and should be torn down."

The news that this familiar place might be removed was strangely disconcerting to me when I first heard it, but after reflection I now better realize why I think it is worthwhile to pause and consider alternatives that woul save the Hotel Aggie building.

As a piece of architecture, it is an ordinary Main Street building, but as part of the recent past it has meaning and value for me. That it is possible to grow attached to a town's familiar businesses was well shown when I saw the closing of Lee's Drugs bring tears to many last-time shoppers there.

I was not one that got emotional over Lee's but the Hotel Aggie building houses many pleasant personal memories for me and, I suspect, for other citizens of our town.

When I first came here to teach part-time in 1972, overnight room upstairs were just $3.50 and you rented them from two delightful characters that exhibited a strong sense of proprietorship. J.B. Jackson, noted commentator on the ordinary landscapes of American small towns, was delighted to stay there when he visited UCD in 1975.

Downstairs, at the Antique Bizarre, town met gown and faculty met students, duplicating nicely the informal setting of Jimmy's at Chicago and LaVal's at Berkeley. Many nights during 1973-74 when my father visited me here we would finish the day with a slow walk downtown to the Antique.

Finding the hotel's Natural Food Works seemed a rare and comforting link to the Bay Area's counterculture. Next door was the Davis Florist where I am a loyal customer for bouquets that celebrated my wedding and many other lesser events. I invite the residents of Davis to consider the memories they have of events in this venerable old landmark.

Personal memories are not, even in the aggregate, the main reason why I think the city should nudge the owners toward rehabilitation and away from replacement of the Hotel Aggie building. The Aggie is the anchor of Davis' remaining "Main Street" environment.

Scholars of America's cities have discovered that the Main Street districts of small towns are powerful and positive symbols, conveying meaning and value to Americans who, overwhelmingly, prefer to live in a small town setting (albiet one that is conveniently close to a metropolis). Only the New England Village is an equivalent icon of what is good about our national urban experience.

The "Main Street" imagery of Davis is already severely damaged by the parking lot that cuts out part of eastern G Street, but the Hotel Aggie is a vital and effective reminder that Davis once had the archtypical block length of shoulder-to-shoulder commercial buildings.

As one of to remaining corners of a four-hotel intersection, the Aggie is also a railroad hotel that reminds us of the depot's role in our town's more ancient history. "Davisville '68" and the Davis "Cultural Resources Inventory," both available at the library, do a good job of illustrating the importance of G Street and the Hotel Aggie intersection as the historic center of our town's economic and social life.

Finally, we might all benefit from knowing a few facts about the economics of "rehabilitation versus replacement" at the Hotel Aggie site. The Yolo County tax rolls (public record data) indicate that the building and land carried a value of $178,593 in 1983 and surely cost less than that in 1977 when the property was last assessed for (or changed hands to) the current owners.

The lower floor commercial space occupies a bit less than 4,000 square feet (it is 53 by 75 feet) and the two currently rented apartments occupy a bit less than 1,500 square feet (they are 53 by 28 feet). Thus, even without renting the upper floors and even without getting premium downtown rents, the rental of this 5,000 square feet of space must provide an adequate return on an investment of less than $200,000.

Despite the apparent positive cash flow, and despite the apparent lack of any structural problems that would limit the long future of the building, the owners have not been maintaining the Aggie Hotel with the care that a highly visible Main Street property (or any property) deserves. I have watched for years as the only second floor window shutters break loose and tilt and drop without repairs (only 8 of the 14 now remain).

I conclude that the owners have been "disinvesting" and acting like slumlords. By skimping on normal exterior maintenance during the past 10 years the owners have failed to be good citizens or good neighbors to the rest of Main Street. A rehabilitated Hotel Aggie would do much to compensate for those years of neglect to one of our town's landmarks.

Dennis Dingemans
Davis

'New's not bad'

Thank you Enterprise for showing us the alternative to the old Aggie Hotel. All old buildings are not beautiful; all new buildings are not ugly. I happen to think that Mr. Chen's building is more handsome.

Mr. Chen's building also offers economic advantages. The entire first floor will be devoted to retail space, which will contribute to a healthier Core Area. So will offices/apartments above. High density is a sound city-planning principle.

The Aggie Hotel is not one of the 14 historical buildings that the Historical Commission designated for saving. The lease for the mural expired in 1981, and the agreement explicitly said that the mural could be demolished. (I don't know why a painting of a structure that is ugly is worth looking at.)

Let us not be carried away by nostalgia.

Gale Sosnick
Davis

Aggie Hotel worth saving as historic gateway

Opinion

By STEPHEN MIKESELL

(EDITOR'S NOTE: Stephen Mikesell, a Davis resident, is chairman of the Historical and Landmarks Commission.)

I think the Hotel Aggie should be saved, for its own sake and the sake of downtown.

The corner of Second and G streets was historically the gateway to Davis. This is illustrated in the mural on the north wall of the hotel and can be seen in the four major-historical structures that anchor that corner: the Terminal Hotel (Hotel Aggie), the Anderson Bank (Barney's Records), the Brinley Block (the Paragon Restaurant) and the Southern Pacific Depot complex.

This corner is all that remains of the traditional "Main Street" of Davis. If we lose the hotel, we lose a large part of our Main Street and the character of downtown.

The hotel is important in its visual context and for its long history of service to the community.

George Tingus, scion of a proud local family, remembers the building for the restaurant and hotel he ran in the 1920s.

My own memories of the place have to do with Anchor Steam on tap at the Antique Bizarre, while waiting for the Coast Starlight to Portland. A public house in service for more than half a century will gather such memories about it. No surprise that a large public opposes its demolition.

The issue of saving the hotel can be discussed on its own merit and should not be confused with the larger issue of growth in the central Core. I happen to believe we should not resist the tendency toward density in commercial development that accompanies population growth. The question is where dense development should take place. What is right for Fifth and G streets may not be right for Second and G streets and vice versa.

Neither should we cloud the issue with talk of inviolable property rights. The very notion of planning presumes that property rights are partially constrained by community prerogatives.

Davis, like many other California cities, includes design review as well as zoning in its planning process, effectively dividing the city into zones of compatible activities and architectural design. The hotel issue is before the City Council not only because citizens oppose demolition, but also because the proposed four-story replacement structure is so out of scale and incompatible with adjoining structures.

The Hotel Aggie issue can be resolved well or it can be resolved poorly.

In the worst case, the property owner could demolish the hotel and the City Council could deny the new project, leaving the lot vacant and everyone the poorer.

In the best case, the city and the applicant could work together to devise a plan that would provide adequate economic return to the owner while preserving what should be preserved of the old hotel.

This alternative — adaptive reuse of an historic building — is not novel. The charm of cities from San Francisco to Nevada City is attributable to the success of adaptive reuse projects there.

Let's try for the best case. Let the property owner avail himself of the talents and ideas of the city — of the City Council, city staff, Historical and Landmarks Commission, Design Review Commission. Let the city define the boundaries of an acceptable project and advise the property owner of the financial and design advantages of a reuse project.

I am convinced that this alternative is superior to any other alternative raised to date and will prove entirely satisfactory to everyone concerned with the Hotel Aggie issue.

NEW FACE?   WRECKING BALL?

a.starr

6.14, *Davis Enterprise.* February 10, 1984.

G STREET SITE

Hotel Aggie saved

By MIKE FITCH

The building that once housed the Hotel Aggie and Antique Bizarre and a mural located on the north end of the building apparently have escaped destruction.

Lee Chen, the owner of the building, has withdrawn an application that asked for city permission to demolish the structure and replace it with a four-story commercial building. The building is located on the northeast corner of Second and G streets.

"I don't think I can fight the city," Chen said this morning, alluding to the controversy his project has encountered.

Chen said he plans to keep the property for a couple of years and then perhaps come forward with a revised development. The hotel and Antique Bizarre, a bar and restaurant, were closed in about 1979. A restaurant, health food store and photography studio currently are located in the building, which was built in 1925.

The mural depicts Second Street as it looked in 1919.

Chen also indicated he did not expect his development plans to create much controversy.

"If I had known we would have that much problem I wouldn't have submitted an application at all," he said.

Chen's plans to destroy the building created considerable opposition from residents who feel the structure is a historic landmark that should be saved.

City Acting Planning Director Tom Lumbrazo announced the withdrawal of the project during a meeting of the Davis Planning Commission Tuesday. The announcement was made during a discussion of the project and other high-rise developments proposed for the Core Area.

In part, Chen's plan created controversy because initially the four-story building could have been built without providing any on-site parking. The reason: it is located in a parking district and traditionally the city has not required on-site parking for developments located in downtown parking districts.

Since then, the commission and City Council have adopted a measure that requires downtown commercial projects with more than two stories to obtain conditional use permits. City officials hope to counter parking and other problems through conditions in the permits.

During Tuesday's meeting, commissioners unanimously approved a set of guidelines for judging whether high-rise projects should receive permits.

One guideline indicates buildings should have no more than five stories and shouldn't rise more than 70 feet above ground level.

Another guideline indicates high-rise projects located in parking districts should have to provide on-site parking based only on the square footage of the structures located above the first two floors. Lumbrazo indicated the guideline makes sense because the parking exemption for developments in the parking districts was based on the assumption that downtown structures would have one or two stories.

6.15. *Davis Enterprise,* April 4, 1984.

HISTORIC STATUS

Hotel decision delayed

Outstanding historic resources cannot be demolished; the proposed destruction of a historic resource can be delayed up to a year.

The Davis Historical Resources Management Commission decided Tuesday the Davis Cemetery and seven local buildings should be protected as historic landmarks, but delayed consideration of the Hotel Aggie.

Lee Chen, owner of the hotel building, had requested that discussion of the building be postponed, because he was unable to attend Tuesday's meeting. The matter is now scheduled for the commission's June 26 meeting.

The hotel closed several years ago, but the building still is generally referred to as the Hotel Aggie. It is located on the northeast corner of Second and G streets.

The commissioners agreed to designate the cemetery and seven buildings as outstanding historic resources. Included among the seven are the Southern Pacific Depot; the Dresbach-Hunt-Boyer home at 604 Second St.; the LaRue-Romani home at 2020 Russell Blvd.; and the Williams-Drummond-Rorvick house at 320 I St.

Others are the Anderson Bank Building, 203 G St.; the Joshua B. Tufts-Longview-Jones house at 434 J St.; and the Werner-Hamel house at 1140 Los Robles St.

Commissioners decided the Davis Boy Scout Cabin, a building located on the southeast corner of First Street and Richards Boulevard, should be classified as a historic resource.

All of the buildings except the Hotel Aggie had been protected under old city historic preservation regulations, but had to be redesignated under a new two-tier system.

Outstanding historic resources cannot be demolished. The proposed destruction of a historic resource can be delayed up to a year while city officials and the property owner seek to work out some compromise.

The commission designated Russell Boulevard and four buildings protected under the old system as outstanding resources at an earlier meeting and decided the Downtown Recreation Building should be a historic resource.

6.16. *Davis Enterprise,* May 30, 1984.

Hotel Aggie gets historical designation

By Brian Fies
Staff writer

Davis' Aggie Hotel has gained "Historical Resource" status, despite several architects and its owner calling it everything from an eyesore to a safety hazard.

The Davis Historical Resources Management Commission held a public hearing Tuesday night regarding the Second and G Street building.

Owner Lee Chen, represented by attorney Joan Poulos, urged denial of Historic Resource classification, saying it would stand in the way of his plans to construct another building on the site, and that the former hotel didn't deserve the label.

"When I bought the building seven years ago, I really did think about renovating it," Chen said.

"The city planning department told me not to touch a thing unless I was doing massive renovation or it would all come down like a house made of matchsticks."

Chen said installing fire sprinklers and bringing the building up to earthquake protection standards would cost as much as a new building.

"If I could find a way to save it that was architecturally and financially feasible I would do it," Chen told the commission. "I don't want to spend $2 million on a new building. If you have an idea what I can do with it, let me know."

Commission chairman Steve Mikesell repeatedly stressed that Historical Resource status does not prevent renovation or even demolition. It only calls for a more careful review beforehand.

Arguments for the designation centered around the hotel's history more than its architecture.

Dennis Dingemans, a member of the Design Review Commission who spoke as a private citizen, defended its value to the community.

"Its primary importance is that it is a railroad terminal hotel of a type that appeared in many small towns all across America," Dingemans said. "It's one of the most important buildings in Davis in the way that it anchors the traditional Main Street.

"We have a building at least minimally attractive, and it could be very attractive if appropriately maintained," Dingemans continued. "It's a valuable reminder that we pride ourselves on being a small town."

Opponents of the designation attacked the building as having no architectural merit.

"It's an eyesore, there's no getting around it," said architect and Planning Commission member Javier Chavez, also speaking as a private citizen.

"It does not conjure up any ideas of history," he said. "I don't see how it would contribute to the social or cultural attributes of the community to preserve that building.["...]

6.17. *Woodland Daily Democrat,* June 27, 1984.

6.18. *Davis Enterprise,* June 27, 1984.

Hotel Aggie may become historic landmark

By MIKE FITCH

The Davis Historical Resources Management Commission decided Tuesday the Hotel Aggie should be protected as a local historical landmark. The commission's recommendation will be forwarded to the City Council for consideration.

Even if the building is designated as an historical resource, it could be demolished or altered, but only after a lengthy city review. The building became the center of controversy early this year when its owner, Lee Chen, submitted plans to the city for demolishing the building and replacing it with a four-story commercial project.

The Hotel Aggie is located on the northeast corner of Second and G streets. Built in 1925, it originally housed the Terminal Hotel, a hometown-style facility that served primarily as a stopover for railroad travelers.

In recent years, the building has been best known as the site of the Hotel Aggie and the Antique Bizarre, a restaurant and bar. Both businesses closed several years ago.

Lee Chen, the owner, and several others argued against designating the building as an historical resource during a public hearing, generally saying it is not significant architecturally and is not important as a symbol of the city's past.

Chen stressed that he has looked into renovating the building, but found renovation would be too expensive, in part because the walls would have to be reinforced with steel so the building could meet state earthquake standards.

In the past, Chen has argued that the new building would be an attractive addition to the downtown area. He also has said the upstairs of the current building is not well suited for offices because the north wall has no windows. That wall is covered by a mural that depicts early Davis.

Chen has withdrawn his project application because of the controversy it generated.

Commissioners indicated they don't want to place an economic burden on Chen by deciding the building should be an historical resource, saying they would be willing to work with him on a renovation project that could be economically feasible.

Commissioners indicated, for example, Chen perhaps could be allowed to add extra business space at the rear of the building, perhaps by adding a third story on the rear.

As he was leaving the meeting, Chen said he was willing to consider such renovation schemes.

During the public hearing, Gale Sosnick, a member of the Design Review Commission, told the historical commission it should carefully choose buildings for protection and shouldn't decide to designate them as landmarks because of mere sentimentality.

"I don't think that's a valid reason for keeping buildings," she said.

Dennis Dingemans, chairman of the Design Review Commission, differed with his colleague, saying the building is the second largest in the downtown area and is a significant reminder of the community's past.

Said Dingemans, "I think it would be quite attractive if it was properly maintained by its owners."

Commissioner Robert Pipkin cast the sole negative vote.

The city has a two-tier system for designating historical landmarks. The regulations governing historical resources are less strict than those for outstanding historical resources.

During the meeting, the commission chose new officers, selecting Robin Datel to replace Steve Mikesell as chairperson and naming Valerie Olsen to serve as vice chairperon.

Consideration of
Historical Commission
Action to Designate
Hotel Aggie a Historical
Resource

Opposing the recommendation was D. Anderson; C. Cunningham,
Chamber of Commerce representative; J. Poulos, attorney
representing property owner; L. Chin, property owner.

Supporting the recommendation to designate the Hotel Aggie as a
historical resource was S. Mikesell, Historical Resources
Management Commission representative.

D. Rosenberg moved to designate the Hotel Aggie as a historical
resource, seconded by T. Tomasi, but failed by the following
vote:

AYES: Rosenberg, Tomasi.

NOES: Adler, Taggart, Evans.

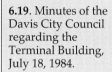

6.19. Minutes of the Davis City Council regarding the Terminal Building, July 18, 1984.

No landmark status for Hotel Aggie site

By MIKE FITCH

The Davis City Council decided Wednesday the Hotel Aggie should not be protected as a local historic resource, possibly paving the way for the building to be demolished and replaced with a new strucuture.

On a 2-3 vote, the council declined to designate the Hotel Aggie, a building that sits on the northeast corner of Second and G streets, as a historic resource. Councilmen Tom Tomasi and Dave Rosenberg cast the two votes to protect the structure.

The Historical Resources Management Commission had recommended that the building be designated, but several speakers, including the owner of the structure, lobbied against that recommendation. They stressed that the building is not architecturally significant and is somewhat ugly.

If the council had decided to protect the building, the owner, Lee Chen, could not have demolished or significantly altered it without a review by the commission.

The fate of the building and a mural of early Davis that adorns its north wall emerged as an issue several months ago when Chen submitted an application to the city for permission to demolish the building and replace it with a four-story commercial project.

Chen said this morning he may submit a new development plan to the city, but must discuss that possibility with his architect and attorney first. The owner indicated he will work with the city to design an acceptable project before officially submitting an application and said the new project may call for a structure with fewer than four stories.

6.20. *Davis Enterprise*, July 19, 1984.

Hotel doesn't qualify as historical landmark

By Brian Fies
Staff writer

Davis' City Council has decided that the Hotel Aggie, old that it may be, does not have what it takes to be an historical resource.

The council was acting on an Historical Resource Management Commission recommendation that the building be designated an historical resource based on two criteria:

● It found that the hotel "exemplifies or reflects valued elements of the city's cultural, social, economic, political, aesthetic, engineering, archeological or architectural history" and;

● The hotel "reflects significant geographical patterns, including those associated with different eras of settlement and growth, particularly transportation modes," namely the railroad.

Hotel Aggie owner Lee Chen has long opposed the designation, saying that the building is difficult to use for commercial purposes as it is, and that naming it an historical resource would frustrate any efforts to renovate or replace it.

"The point is that we should think about the future of Davis, not the past," said Chen. "At some point Davis has got to change and decide that it wants the core area to be vital and thriving."

Historical Resource Commission chairman Steve Mikesell said that the commission had wrestled with the issue in a long and open public hearing.

"No one's making a case that it's a handsome building," said Mikesell, "though I think it could look much better with renovation.

"We are not forever mandating that the property never be demolished," he continued. "The applicant would only have to come back to us beforehand."

Attorney Joan Poulos represented Chen, saying that three architects have found that the building has no design merit. She suggested that any cultural value the building may have had has long since been forgotten.

Adler suggested that the Historical Commission's concern would be better directed elsewhere.

"If you care about the railroad, we're already spending a lot of money to save the train station and the area around it," Adler said. "There used to be a nice little park back there with walkways and gaslights — if you want to preserve something, make it something worthwhile and not an eyesore."

Councilman Tom Tomasi said that he didn't particularly care what happened to the project, but that he was willing to take the advice of the commission.

"They put in their expertise, that's why they're there," Tomasi said. "I'd like to follow their guidance."

Tomasi voted in the minority with Dave Rosenberg to make the Hotel Aggie an historical resource. Adler, Debbie Taggart and Ann Evans voted against it.

6.21. *Woodland Daily Democrat*, July 19, 1984.

3) PRESERVATION RESISTANCE AND CAMPAIGNING IN OVERVIEW

The (1) resistance to preservation and the (2) campaigning for preservation we will see in the next chapters regarding the Terminal Building are better understood by viewing each of them as events in their respective series of such events.

Both these series have, for the most part, already been described in this and the previous chapter. But in that narrative, they are intertwined with other kinds of local history and historic preservation matters. Therefore, each is difficult to see.

In order to display each series as clearly as possible, I want to bring together only instances of preservation resistance (Fig. 6.22) and pro-preservation campaigning (Fig. 6.23). Having already described most of these episodes, short-title references to them will suffice. (Though a few of them do not appear in the foregoing narrative, this is not a problem for the generalizations to be offered below.)

Let me be clear that these two series are **not** rosters of land-use changes and new constructions in general. Such lists would be vastly longer than the ones we consider here. Instead, we are concerned **only** with episodes that generated either (1) **resistance to preservation** or (2) **campaigning for preservation**. Phrased differently, these are instances of **dispute over preservation**. As such, each list is a very small sub-set of all land-use changes and constructions over the five decades (or a little more) of the 1950s-1990s.

This understood, what do we see in Figs 6.22 and 6.23? **First**, there would appear to have been only a few more than a dozen episodes of either resistance to preservation or campaigning for it.

Second, viewed in the context of the large number of demolitions and related changes that took place in Davis over the 1950s-90s, this is a notably low rate of disputation. It perhaps bespeaks a very low level of preservation consciousness in, especially, the early decades after World War II.

Third, the number of preservation contentions increased over the decades. There were apparently none in the 1950s and 1960s and only a few in the 1970s. But this changed in the 1980s and 1990s.

Fourth, the scale of the "unit" acting in preservation contentions became larger over time. In the beginning, the acting unit was likely to be an individual. More recently, the "unit" was more likely a group, such as a neighborhood association or an emergent citizen network or coalition.

Fifth, the sheer number of participants in resistance or advocacy episodes increased over time (expected, in part, from large increases in the population of Davis).

Sixth, the City of Davis was increasingly a presence either as a resister to preservation or as a promoter of it.

6. 22. INSTANCES OF RESISTANCE TO PRESERVATION, 1950-2001

1974.   Owner of 305 E Street successfully opposes landmark designation.

Owner of the Schmeiser Mansion, 334 I Street, successfully opposes landmark designation but the decision is reversed by the 1986 City Council.

The Boy Scout Cabin land owner (UC Davis) and the user (the Davis Rotary Club) successfully oppose landmark designation, but the decision is reversed by the 1984 City Council.

Owner successfully opposes designating the Dresbach-Hunt-Boyer mansion a landmark, but the decision is reversed by the 1984 City Council.

1984.   Owner successfully opposes designating the Terminal Building a historical resource.

Owner of 403 G successfully opposes designating that home a historical resource (an especially ironic event because of one of the owners conspicuous involvement in local history).

City of Davis plans to cut down a substantial portion of the Avenue of the Trees (unsuccessful).

1985.   Owners unsuccessfully oppose designation of 137 C a historical resource.

1986.   Owner resists designating the McBride home, 405 J Street, a historical resource (unsuccessful).

Late 1980s-Early 1990s.   City of Davis plans to demolish the Old Library building at 117 F (unsuccessful).

1991-1992. City of Davis plans to pave all six Old North Davis alleys and is one-sixth successful in doing so.

1998.   The owner of the church buildings at Fifth and C streets successfully aborts a HRMC designation plan.

1998-2001. Owners of 328-336 A Street propose an out-of-scale building and redesign it twice, eventually achieving City approval for construction.

2000.   Owner plan to demolish the Terminal Building is successful.

City plan, joint with the Pacific Gas and Electric Company, to cut down substantial numbers of City street trees beneath overhead electric wires is stopped.

2001.   The owner of 238 G Street successfully stops a HRMC plan to make a "preservation appreciation" award for recent restoration work on that building

6. 23. CAMPAIGNS FOR PRESERVATION, 1950-2001

<u>1975.</u>   Campaign to save homes on Second between C and D is unsuccessful.

<u>Late 1970s</u>. Campaigns to save the Dresbach-Hunt-Boyer are eventually successful.

<u>1984.</u>   Campaign to designate the Terminal Building a historical resource fails.

<u>1984.</u>   Campaign to save the Avenue of the Trees from major removal of Black Walnuts is successful.

<u>1986-87.</u> Citizen efforts to stabilize the University-Rice area for single family housing, resulting in Ordinance 1415 (February 4, 1987) is successful.

<u>1988.</u>   Formation of the Old East Davis Association in response to City Council consideration of major redevelopment plans for that area seems to stop those plans.

<u>Late 1980s-Early 1990s.</u> Campaign to preserve the Old Library building is successful.

<u>1991-92.</u> Campaign to stop paving of the six Old North Davis alleys is five-sixths successful.

<u>1996.</u>   Campaign to save 239 J Street is unsuccessful.

<u>1998-2001.</u> University-Rice area residents partially successful in opposing proposed out-of-scale building for 326-338 A Street.

<u>1999-2000.</u> Campaign to in some fashion "save" the Terminal Building is unsuccessful.

<u>1999-2000.</u> Campaign to stop the City-PG&E plan to cut down City street trees under overhead electric lines in the 1917 city limits is successful (in the short run, anyway).

<u>2000-01.</u> City plan to develop and implement design guidelines for a "conservation district" is successful.

These six generalizations about the history of historic preservation in Davis bring us to the case of the Terminal Building. As we shall see in the five chapters of Part II, features of the Terminal Building case were consistent with these six trends and not a statistical "fluke."

Instead, that case expressed these six large and long-term movements. If the past is taken as the best predictor of the future, then we should predict more and bigger episodes like the one centered on the Terminal Building.

II

PRESERVATION FAILURES
TWO YEARS, 1999—2000

As explained in the Introduction, the story of the Terminal Building's 1999-2000 journey to demolition divides into **four** major forms of "preservation failure."

• Chapter 7 focuses on preservation failure in the form of not achieving Davis City Council designation as a historical resource. This process of **designation failure** played out over a period of some seven months from February to September of 1999.

• In a second period running roughly from September, 1999 through June of 2000, preservationist effort was importantly devoted to getting a professional "feasibility study" of the building. This effort and its lack of success are described in Chapter 8, where it is captioned **feasibility study failure**.

➔ Although "preservation failure" is the main story, not everything was a failure. Among other preservationist actions, a celebration of the Terminal Building was held on the G Street plaza next to it on June 11, 2000. This event was an inspiring, **celebration success**, even though it obviously did not save the building. Nonetheless, it was a special moment in the campaign, in historic preservation in Davis history, and in citizen action more generally. As such, it deserves to be placed in the historical record. I try to do this in Chapter 9.

• As it became increasingly clear that the entire building was not going to escape demolition, attention turned to saving at least its west facade and perhaps the Arch Mural on the northern wall. This "facadectomy" campaign was most active from mid-June through mid-September, 2000. It is addressed in Chapter 10 and labeled **facadectomy failure**.

• The building's story had the twist that its rear part was smashed down on September 18, but the Arch Mural and main facade were left standing while the demolition contractor salvaged brick. This pause created space for a campaign for a freeze on demolition while alternatives were considered. This effort failed and eleven days later, on September 28, the entire building was reduced to rubble. This **freeze failure** is the subject of Chapter 11.

DESIGNATION FAILURE

The failure of designation in 1984 largely ended the Terminal Building matter for the next some fifteen years. The owners made no further public moves to do anything with their property.

As reported in the last chapter, the HRMC went into a period of relative quiescence. After a flurry of designations in the four years of 1984-87, there were no significant efforts to make more of them for the full decade of 1988-97 (Fig. 6.5).

But in the later 1990s, the Certified Local Government program, its funding possibilities, and changing membership on the HRMC began a new, more activist period (Chapter 6, section 1). Along with new nominations of residences, the case of the Terminal Building was resurrected.

1) THE TWO PHASES OF DESIGNATION FAILURE

The process of this second designation failure divides into a first period in which it was before the HMRC (February–June 1999) and a second period in which it was before the Davis City Council (June–September, 1999).

By law, a property nominated by a commission to be a historical resource had to be considered by a City Council within 90 days after that commission's nomination. But in this case, by consent of all the parties, the date of Council consideration was extended and the hearing took place on September 15, 1999.

2) AN IRONY OF NOMINATION

Ironically, the beginning of the end for the building may have been initiated (or at least spurred) by the HRMC. When this commission again started the process of historic designation, the owners had done little with the building for some fifteen years. Seemingly indecisive, they might have remained so. Without the new HRMC spur, the Terminal Building might still be there in all its declining glory. (However, at least one person who was a member of the HRMC at this time believed that the commission started the designation process in response to hearing that owners had decided to move ahead with demolition.)

3) THE HMRC PROCESS

The designation process began with the HRMC instructing staff (Esther Polito) to prepare a preliminary evaluation of the possibility of nominating the building. This document is reproduced in Fig. 7.1. As shown in Fig. 7. 2, the Commission voted unanimously to nominate it for designation.

This action set the notification process in motion. One part of this process was to tell the owners a public hearing on the nomination would be held, which was done in a letter dated March 22, 1999 (Fig. 7.3.).

In an undated reply, the owners ask that the building not be nominated. They also say that "our dream in owning this property has always been to replace the existing Hotel with a structure more responsive to the potential of the site." This statement is of interest because, in 1984, one of the owners reported that he had considered rehabilitation rather than replacement (Fig. 6.17, June 27, 1984). And, as the months went on, he would from time to time declare his continued interest in this possibility.

The owners also contracted with SKY Engineering to evaluate the structure. Its report is shown in Fig. 7.5. It presents a decidedly negative view.

Esther Polito proceeded to prepare the nomination document. The first page of it is shown in Fig. 7.6. The entire document was some two dozen pages long and consisted of staff text, documents and graphics otherwise presented in this or other chapters.

The public hearing was held on June 21. The Chen's attended with their architect of the time, Maria Ogrydizak. There were apparently no members of the public present to speak either for or against the nomination. In addition, the Commission received only one written communication on the matter. This was a letter from the owner of the adjacent Davis Ace Hardware (previously the historic Davis Lumber and Hardware) opposing designation and advocating demolition (Fig. 7.8). This is to say, this topic had not yet aroused public interest one way or the other.

In Fig. 7.7 we have Esther Polito's exceptionally detailed and helpful account of the pro and con conversation on whether to designate. As such, it speaks for itself. After much back and forth, the Commission voted 7-0 to designate the hotel.

4) THE COUNCIL PROCESS

This vote led to the next step, the preparation of a proposal to the City Council recommending designation. The cover page of this document appears as Fig. 7.11.

Although a modest degree of uncertainty was reported in a *Davis Enterprise* article of September 14 (Fig. 7.10), preservationist-minded Davisites expected the Council easily to make the designation.

As a consequence, they neglected individual lobbying with Council members and only minimally mobilized to have people at the Council hearing. At that hearing on September 15, they were shocked to discover they had misjudged the situation. The HRMC suffered the rebuke of a 4-1 negative vote. The contrast with the HRMC's 7-0 vote the other way was remarkable.

An account of the matter as given in the Council's Minutes appears in Fig. 7.13. And, Fig. 7.14 provides a fuller account from the *Davis Enterprise*.

The membership of this Council is shown in Fig. 7.12. Notice that the Julie Partansky we met so prominently in the last two chapters as a leader of two preservation campaigns is now the Mayor (seated, center, Fig. 7.12). The men on either end were by reputation supporters of preservation. Despite being a rare Davis Republican on the Council, Stan Forbes, on the left, had teamed with Partansky to spearhead the successful Subway III campaign described in the last chapter. So, the defections of him and Wagstaff—a quintessential Davis liberal—was surprising, to use a very mild term.

Staff Report

Date: February 3, 1999

TO: The Historical Resources Management Commission

FROM: Esther Polito, Cultural Services Manager

SUBJECT: Prospective Nomination of The Terminal Hotel for considertion as a City of Davis Historic Resource: Draft staff report describing applicability of criteria in support of nomination

<u>Recommendation</u>
That the Commission consider whether to nominate the Terminal Hotel, 200, 202, 204 G St. as a City of Davis Historic Resource. If nominated, two public hearings will be held on the merits of the nomination, first at the Commission level for recommendation on whether to designate, and then at the City Council level for approval or denial of the recommendation. The following finding will need to be met to ultimately recommend designation:

Findings:
1. That the property located at 200, 202 & 204 G St. qualifies for designation under criterion (a) of Zoning Ordinance Section 29-145.10 in that... "It exemplifies or reflects valued elements of the city's cultural, social, economic, political, aesthetic, engineering, archaeological, or architectural history."

2. That the property located at 200, 202 & 204 G St. qualifies for designation under criterion (c) of Zoning Ordinance Section 29-145.10 in that... "It reflects significant geographical patterns, including those associated with different eras of settlement and growth, particular transportation modes, or distinctive examples of park or community planning."

The following sections of this staff report have been prepared at the Commission's request in order consider whether this property should be placed in nomination. The report should not be considered final; it is included as background information only at this point. If the nomination is approved, the report will then be finalized and sent to the building owner together with a letter describing the designation process.

---

page 2

<u>Background and Analysis</u>

1. Location:
Property is lot 70-252-04 of the Core Area and zoned C-C: Central Commercial

Applicant: City of Davis
Historical Resources Management Commission
23 Russell Boulevard
Davis, CA 95616

Owner: Chen Tr., et al   Grace Chin
P.O. Box 2094   333 Mills Drive
El Macero, CA 95618   Davis CA 95616

2. Description of the Property:
The building occupies a prominent corner site in the center of the city's commercial area and in close proximity to three important City of Davis Historic Resources: the train station (an Outstanding Historic Resource) the Brinley Bock on the southeast corner of Second and G, a Historic Resource, and the Anderson Bank Building on the northeast corner, a n Outstanding Historic Resource. The Terminal Hotel building is a two story flat-roofed brick and masonry building that has been modified sometime after 1953 by the addition of a rustic wooden gallery with exposed rafters covering the sidewalk at the ground level (see photo from Eastman Collection, attached). The siding is stucco. The overall composition of the building is symmetrical. The doors are wood with lights. Storefront modifications that have been undertaken have not been thoroughly researched as this point. On the north side of the building facing a parking lot is a mural of G Street before the destruction of its Mission Revival welcoming arch.

The second story interior, which has been vacant for many year, consists of a central corridor with doors opening off the hallway. The building is in extremely poor physical condition.

3. Application of Criteria for Designation
Originally known as the Terminal Hotel, this building was constructed in 1925 by George Tingus and James Belinis. The current importance of the Terminal Hotel lies with its cultural contributions to the city and its link to the train as an important mode of transportation rather than its architectural values. Although much altered, it does contribute in scale and form to the few early downtown Davis structures remaining. It relates to the corner structures, the Anderson Building and the Masonic Hall down and across the Street.

1. Summary of information supporting Criterion (a)

---

page 3

The Terminal Hotel was constructed during one of Davis' first growth movements, when the first City Council prepared and adopted the 1927 Davis City Plan, and when the expanding University Farm set in motion their 1925 building plan. The Hotel was built during a time when a number of city improvements were being made in Davis, such as: sewer systems, street gravelling, and street lights. The then new Transcontinental Highway ran by First, B and Russell Boulevard. Originally a home-type hotel designed to accommodate lodgers, serve food and act as a meeting place for University people and various service organizations, the Terminal Hotel also housed a Butcher Shop and gift shop. The "Terminal Cafe" purportedly offered a beer bar, off to one side, with a special entrance. The Hotel offered lodgers, farmers and University people a place to dine and socialize, as well as sleep.

From the 1860's on, hotels in Davisville accommodated transients, settlers, farmers, and eventually people associated with the University. The Terminal Hotel was unique in that it was a particularly convenient place for the University Farm "commuter" students and teachers to lodge. By the time the Hotel was constructed, the University Farm was 12 years old and growing. When in 1922 a four-year degree program was instituted, Davisville saw an influx of people needing food, lodging and places to congregate. When the Terminal Hotel was built, G Street was a busy "Main Street", a place where train travelers strolled, enterprising farmers did business and University people stopped on their way to and from campus.

The Hotel continued its ministration at least through the 1970's when the Davis Enterprise reported on the retirement of its 15 year manager, "Miss Dora". By then called the Hotel Aggie, the Hotel apparently had always found room for people brought there by the police, STEAC or the Salvation Army. "Old timers" remembered the atmosphere as a comfortable environment that fostered a "dormitory camaraderie". (The Davis Enterprise, Monday, March 15, 1976)

<u>2. Summary of Information supporting Criterion (c)</u>
The history of the Terminal Hotel is as linked to the train as it is to the City of Davis. As much as 1868 Davisville was originally planned in alignment with the first train depot, the 1925 Terminal Hotel was built in close proximity to the second train depot. At the time the hotel was built as many as 18 trains a day were passing through Davis. Originally known as the Terminal Hotel, it served as an overnight stop for train travelers who were delayed at the Southern Pacific Depot nearby. Davisville had been chosen for the university's farm campus in part because it was near the train.

The Terminal Hotel weathered the Depression, and it stood during the 1940's when, despite the manpower shortage, the railroad operated through a volunteer effort plan that won national recognition. The population in Davis boomed when UC Davis became a general university in 1959, but because of the increasing emphasis upon travel by car, the train became a less important way to reach the campus. However, the Terminal Hotel

---

page 4

building still stands in close proximity to the recently restored train depot, which is now an Amtrak station.

4. Environmental Review
The application is exempt from environmental review under section 15378 of the State CEQA Guidelines. Action on these applications does not have the potential for directly or ultimately resulting in a physical change to the environment.

5. General Plan Conformance:
The proposed designation as an historical resource is in conformance with the General Plan.

6. The Adjacent Zoning And Land Use Includes:
North - zoned C-C; central commercial
South - zoned C-C; central commercial
East   - building backs up to railroad tracks. N/E of tracks is C-S
West   - zoned C-C; central commercial

7. Summary of Significant Planning and Building Records
The permits and changes recorded in this section reflect information found in the Planning and Building microfiche files. Minor changes related to interior renovations are not included, as well as any changes not recorded in the city files.

1955 - Building permit obtained for partition and remodel.
1956 - Permit for construction of store building obtained.
1962 - Building permit obtained for restaurant remodel.
1965 - Building permit obtained for restaurant remodel.
1967 - Building permit obtained for restaurant remodel (plumbing and heating only).
1971 - Conditional use permit obtained allowing dancing at "Antique Bizarre". City council comments: "this will bring life into the downtown."
1977 - Rear addition approved.
1978 - Building permit obtained to repair $2000 fire damage.
1981 - Building permit obtained for restaurant remodel.
1987 - Building permit obtained to move entrance door back to original location
1995 - Permit issued for commercial addition/alteration (electrical).

Attachments:
Nomination Form to be completed
1980 & 1996 City of Davis Cultural Resources Inventory pages
Eastman Collection studio photo dated 1953
Davis Enterprise article "Hotel Aggie - Davis Landmark" dated March 15, 1976
Relevant pages from 1933 & 1953 Sanborn Maps
P:\COMMISN\HISTRES\CHRON\200G.DOC

7.1. February 3, 1999 staff report recommending that the HMRC consider whether to nominate the Terminal Building a City of Davis Historic Resource.

7. Historical Resources Nomination for Terminal Hotel: 200 G Street Esther introduced the item by reviewing her draft report on the building's history and asking for comments. Several minor suggestions were made which will be incorporated. Gerald Hobrecht then commented that the property appears to meet the criteria and he would support its nomination. Jeanette Schulz added that the building, although altered, still denotes a sense of time and place. The building's poor condition was briefly discussed.

7.2. This excerpt from the HRMC's March 15 minutes reports a unanimous vote to consider the building for designation.

Action   Wendy Nelson moved, and Jeanette Schulz seconded, a motion to nominate the Terminal Hotel, 200 G Street, to be considered for designation as a City of Davis Historical Resource and to schedule a public hearing after discussing the nomination with the property owner.

Motion passed unanimously.

Davis
California

March 22, 1999

Chen, TR et al
P.O. Box 2094
El Macero CA 95618

Subject: Nomination of 200 G Street for consideration as a City of Davis Historical Resource

Dear Property Owner,

At their March 15 meeting, the city's Historical Resources Management Commission nominated the old Terminal Hotel, 200 G Street, for possible designation as a City of Davis "Historical Resource." According to the city's ordinance for Historical Resources Management, a copy of which is enclosed, the Commission or members of the community may nominate buildings for consideration.

The next step is a public hearing to consider the merits of the nomination. You will soon receive a copy of the notice for that public hearing and the staff report that describes the historical significance of the property. After the public hearing, the Commission can vote to recommend designation to the City Council, continue the nomination until another meeting, or vote not to recommend designation. The City Council is the decision-making body for the designation of historical resources. Their decision will be made no later than 90 days following the Commission's recommendation.

As the owner, you will want to know what the impact of historic designation will mean to your property. If a building is designated, all building permits for work on the exterior of the building must be issued an Historic Alteration permit before a building permit is approved. The process is described in Section 29-145.12 - 15 of the enclosed ordinance which I have highlighted. Roof replacement permits, provided that no structural changes are proposed, are approved administratively. Other projects are brought before the Commission's monthly meeting for approval.

Demolition approval is different for the two types of designated properties. For "Historic Resources" (the type of designation for which your property is nominated) the Commission can suspend the issuance of the permit for up to 180 days, extendible for an additional 180 days under certain circumstances. All Commission actions can be appealed to the City Council.

The State Historic Building Code offers special advantages to owners of historic properties. This alternative code protects California's architectural heritage by recognizing the unique construction problems inherent in historic environments and offering alternatives to deal with these problems.

CITY OF DAVIS

7.3. Pursuant to the HMRC action, the owner is notified.

200 G Street
Owner letter re. nomination
March 22, 1999

Owners of designated buildings can elect to have the city use the State Historic Building Code for applicable interior and exterior projects.

The staff report and public hearing notice will be mailed no later than 10 days before the public hearing. At this point, I anticipate scheduling the hearing for the May 17 Historical Resources Commission meeting. If you plan to attend and won't be available that evening, please let me know as soon as possible. Please phone me if you have any questions.

Sincerely,

Esther Polito
Cultural Services Manager

Copy: Planning and Building Department

Enclosure: Ordinance #1784, Series 1995, Ordinance Amending Sections of 29-145.5 - 29-145.22 of the Zoning Code Pertaining to Historical Resources Management

P:\COMMISN\HISTRES\DES99\200GST\OWNLET01.DOC

Attachment 1

Grace and Lee Chen
P.O. Box 2094
El Mac ero, CA 95618

Historical Resources Management Commission
City of Davis
Park and Community Services
23 Russell Boulevard
Davis, CA 95616

Subject: Nomination of 200 G Street for consideration as a City of Davis Historical Resource

Dear members of the Historical Resources Management Commission:

We, the owners of 200 G Street, request that you not designate the Aggie Hotel a City of Davis "Historical Resource". The building does not meet current code requirements and restoration would be costly as well as impractical. According to a report by SKY EGINEERING, the structure is unsound especially in a major wind storm or earthquake and additionally, much of the finish material is no longer original.

As 30-year residents of Davis, we wish to contribute to the community we have chosen as our home. Our dream in owning this property has always been to replace the existing Hotel with a structure more responsive to the potential of the site. The finances appear to finally be possible and we hope to begin within the near future. We intend to create a project which will enhance the vitality of the downtown and add to the recent successful developments at other downtown Davis locations. Our hope is to be able to do this with your support.

Sincerely,

Grace & Lee Chen
Grace and Lee Chen

7.4. Grace and Lee Chen letter to the HMRC opposing designation an historical resource (undated).

SKY ENGINEERING
2420 K Street, Suite 250
Sacramento, CA 95816
May 28, 1999

PROPERTY
ADDRESS:

200, 202, 204, 206 G STREET
DAVIS, CA 95616

SUBJECT: Structural Inspection

DEAR MS. GRACE CHEN:

Per your request, a structural inspection has been performed for the subject property. We have found the following:

PROPERTY DESCRIPTION:

This is an L-shaped two- story building with full basement located at the corner of G and Second Street in Davis. The area is about 6000 square feet each for the basement, first and second floor. The original structure was built in late 1920. Subsequently, it was remodeled. The covered walkway in front of the building and the storage area on the back of the building were added later. The exterior walls were built with un-reinforced brick. The roof diaphragm was 1X diagonal sheathing supported by 2X roof joists connected to the interior bearing walls and exterior brick walls. The second floor was built similar to the roof. The basement walls were built with concrete and brick. The first floor was built with 1X sheathing supported by 2X8 at 16" o.c. connected with 2 toe nails on each side to 6X8 beams.

This structure can be classified as type III-N or type V-N.

DAMAGE OF THE STRUCTURE:

1)   Because the floor members and connections of the floor member are inadequate, some areas of the second floor and first floor are sloped and sagging.

2)   Some areas of the roof and ceiling have water damage.

3)   Cracking on the exterior brick walls and diagonal cracks on the window openings can be found throughout the building. The arch entrance along Second Street was severely cracked. The exterior walls are out-of-plumb.

4)   The original floor is severely worn out and in most area the floor is covered

7.5. SKY Engineering report commissioned by the Chens and mentioned in their letter reproduced as Fig. 7.4. This was the source of the repeated subsequent claim that the building might blow over in a strong wind. (The improbability of this claim was made clear by the effort that had to be put into bringing the building down, as photographically documented in Part III.)

with new floor or carpet.

5)   Cracking can be found in several retaining wall locations in the basement due to inadequate reinforcements and foundation.

6)   The wood columns supporting the covered walkway are cracked.

7)   The exterior walls are separating from each other at the corners.

SAFETY OF THE BUILDING:

1)   The exterior unreinforced brick walls acting as bearing walls support the roof and floor load; the walls also acting as shear walls provide lateral resistance to the wind and earth quake load. In the Whittier Narrows; Loma Prieta and North ridge earth quake, structures similar to this building collapsed or suffered major damage.
     Because of the poor performance of this type of structure in the past earth quake, this building is unsafe in a major wind storm or earth quake.

2)   The exit on the second floor is not adequate. The current Uniform Building Code requires minimum two exits for the second floor; However, at present there is only one exit in this building. The only exit from the second floor goes through the hair salon on the first floor which makes the situation even worse. If a fire breaks out in the hair salon, all the people on the second floor will be trapped with no way out.

3)   The dead end corridor on the second floor is more than 20 feet which violates the Uniform Building Code requirements.

HISTORICAL VALUE:

The original building was built around late 1920. Subsequently, it was remodeled. The covered walkway in front of the building and the storage room on the back of the building were added later. Only the exterior walls on the second floor along G Street is the original finish. The entire wall along Second Street and on the back of the building was covered with plaster and new paint. The window openings along Second Street were either filled with new wall or otherwise revised from original. None of the doors on first floor are original. All the original windows on second floor are either broken or beyond repair. The original interior brick walls were later covered by plaster. The original ceiling on second floor is damaged.

CONCLUSION:

1)   This building is structurally unsound especially in a major wind storm or earth quake.

2)   The majority of the exterior of the building is no longer original, since this building has been remodeled and modified significantly over the year.

This information is base on a visual inspection of the building.

Please feel free to contact us if you have any question regarding this report.

Sincerely,

Ray Kwan, S.E.

7.6.
Opening
page of the
document
nominating
the
Terminal
Building as
a City of
Davis
historical
resource.

PARKS AND COMMUNITY SERVICES

23 Russell Boulevard – Davis, California 95616
530/757-5626– FAX: 530/758-0204 – TDD. 530/757-5666

Staff Report

Date: June 11, 1999

TO: The Historical Resources Management Commission

FROM: Esther Polito, Cultural Services Manager

SUBJECT: Consideration of Historical Resources application 02-99: Terminal Hotel,
also known as the Hotel Aggie, 200 G Street, nomination for designation
as a City of Davis Historical Resource.

Recommendation
1. That the Historical Resources Management Commission hold a public hearing to
consider the nomination of the Terminal Hotel, also known as the Hotel Aggie, at 200 G
Street and inclusive of 202, 204 and 206 G Street (hereafter the Terminal Hotel) for
designation as a City of Davis Historical Resource.

2. That, either immediately following the public hearing or within a period not to exceed
thirty days, the Commission make a recommendation to City Council regarding the
adoption of the following findings:

Findings:
1. That the Terminal Hotel located at 200 G St. qualifies for designation under criterion
(a) of Zoning Ordinance Section 29-145.10 in that... "It exemplifies or reflects valued
elements of the city's cultural, social, economic, political, aesthetic, engineering,
archaeological, or architectural history."

2. That the Terminal Hotel located at 200 G St. qualifies for designation under criterion
(c) of Zoning Ordinance Section 29-145.10 in that... "It reflects significant geographical
patterns, including those associated with different eras of settlement and growth,
particular transportation modes, or distinctive examples of park or community
planning."

PARKS AND COMMUNITY SERVI—

23 Russell Boulevard – Davis, California 75000
530/757-5626– FAX: 530/758-0204 – TDD: 530/757-5666

Davis
California

Historical Resources Management Commission Minutes
Hattie Weber Museum
June 21, 1999

Commissioners Present: Gerald Hobrecht (Chair)Wendy Nelson (Vice Chair),
Richard Berteaux, Vojka Dznic, Alice Eichold, Anne
Rundstrom, Jeanette Schulz, Mike White

Staff Present: Esther Polito, Cultural Services Manager
Council Liaison Present: Ken Wagstaff, Mayor Pro Tempore

Chair Hobrecht called the meeting to order at 7:05 p.m.

1. **Approval of Agenda** The agenda was approved by consensus.

2. **Approval of Minutes**
A. **May 17, 1999 minutes** Review of these minutes was continued to the June 28 meeting.
B. **June 1, 1999 minutes** Minor corrections were made.
Action Wendy Nelson moved, and Mike White seconded, approval of the May 17 1999
minutes as amended. Motion passed unanimously.

3. **Public Communications** There were no public communications.

4. **Commissioner, City Council and Staff Communication**
A. **Applications for Design Guidelines Project** Staff reported that four applications have been
received. The selection committee will meet as soon as possible to review the applications and
select finalists.

5. **Historical Resource Designations: Public Hearings on Terminal Hotel and the Davis
Subway** followed by recommendations Staff Esther Polito introduced the item with a description
of the designation process.

**A. Public Hearing: Terminal Hotel, 200 G Street, Nomination 002-99 as a City of Davis
Historical Resource**

Chair Hobrecht opened the public hearing.

Lee Chen, one of the owners of 200 G Street, addressed the Commission. He stated that, as a long
time Davis resident and UC Davis employee, he wants to do what is good for the community. He
said the Hotel portion of the building, unoccupied since 1979, cannot be used without significant

---

Page 2

code upgrades and structural modifications. He further stated he has been unable to get an estimate
for the cost of the seismic retrofitting needed to bring the building up to seismic code. In regard to
the historic context of the building, he stated that his review of the historic maps led him to
conclude that the building lost its value in the street facade when a commercial building to the
north and a dwelling to the east were demolished many years ago. Mr. Chen added that the
building has been extensively altered, resulting in a loss of its historic importance. He asked the
Commission to deny the designation so that he and the other owners can submit an alternative plan
for use of the building's site.

Commissioner Rundstrom asked Mr. Chen if there are any current plans for the site. Mr. Chen
responded that a new building plan is being developed but that the details have not yet undergone a
thorough cost analysis.

Commissioner Nelson asked whether the new building would utilize the existing facade. Mr. Chen
responded that it would not.

Commissioner Nelson asked if the engineer selected by the Chen's to evaluate the building had
experience in historic and seismic renovation.

Architect Maria Ogrydizak responded on behalf of the Chens. She said she has been engaged by
the Chens to develop building plans. She stated that the engineer was chosen specifically because
of his experience with historic buildings. She further stated her work has focused on the site's
potential rather than on historic aspects of the existing building. She explained that she has been
working on a mixed-use concept with private underground parking for residents and that the
current building cannot support an underground parking lot. She agreed with Mr. Chen that the
original building was part of a street facade that has since been demolished and that the site has lost
its integrity. She said that the site has greatly changed and that the best option would be to look at
the current multi-face opportunities the site has as an island.

Commissioner Jeanette Schulz responded to Ms. Ogrydizak, explaining that the historic value
recognizes changes over time, and that the building continues to address the street as it originally
did. She stated further that the building complements the remaining historic buildings in its
vicinity, creating as a group a historic context. She concluded by saying that, in regard to
inappropriate alterations over time, removing the wooden sidewalk gallery would eliminate the
most historically inappropriate alteration and uncover much of the building's interesting brickwork.

Ms. Ogrydizak explained that she understood the historic context, but has not focused on it in her
planning.

Commissioner Schulz asked Ms. Ogrydziak if she was aware that additions to historic buildings
can be planned on secondary facades and occasionally even on primary facades. She further
explained that the purpose of historical resource designation is not to deny demolition, but rather
to encourage the owners to take a thorough look at other options first.

Commissioner Nelson added that several periods of time are currently represented in the structure,
and that there are likely broad options for renovation that could be approved using historic design

---

7.7. Pages 1 and 2 of 5 pages of the Minutes of the HMRC regarding designation of the Terminal
Building as a historical resource. Pages 3, 4, and 5 are on the following pages.

Page 3

standards.

Ms. Ogrydziak stated that she was interested in the discussion of change over time, but that she felt the existing building severely limits the owners' opportunity to develop retail stores on all four sides, something a new building could accomplish.

Grace Chen, another of the building's owners, addressed the Commission. She stated that her tenants in the rear apartment have told her that they have had problems with drunks and other vagrants in the nearby parking lots.

Commissioner Berteaux asked the Chens if they had prepared a proposal to seek an estimate for seismic retrofit.

Mr. Chen responded that he had not recently sought estimates.

Commissioner Berteaux explained that the extensive seismic work done in California since the Loma Prieta quake has made seismic estimates easier to obtain. He suggested that the Chens contact Woodland and Winters to find out the names of the seismic contractors for the Hotel Woodland and two brick commercial structures in Winters that were recently brought up to code.

Regarding parking spaces, Commissioner Berteaux asked how many underground spaces Ms. Ogrydziak thought a new project could provide, and whether there were off-site possibilities for parking.

Ms. Ogrydziak responded, saying that one building concept being explored was to provide housing for seniors and that it would be important for elderly residents to have parking on site. Ms. Ogrydziak further stated that, while seismic upgrades and additions would be possible, her focus is on maximizing the site utilization options and benefits to the owners.

Commissioner Berteaux commented that utilizing the existing building does not preclude the improvements under consideration, with the exception of underground parking. He suggested that a significant addition could be added to the rear of the building and that a combination of old and new is, to his thinking, a most desirable combination.

Ms. Ogrydziak stated that that was a reasonable way to think about the building, but she didn't know how much leeway she had for incorporating changes to the current structure given its condition and limitations. She reiterated that she believed it would be easier to incorporate ideas into a new structure rather than focus on retaining the old.

Mr. Chen said he was concerned about the cost effectiveness of seismic upgrade and building renovation.

Commissioner Berteaux responded that the federal tax credits available for older buildings could offset a portion of rehabilitation costs, making the project more financially feasible.

Page 4

Commissioner Schulz reiterated that the Commission's role is not to design historic renovations but rather to let the owners know that there are many options available, particularly given the improvements to seismic retrofitting that that taken place over the last ten years. She also stated that principles of sustainability are worth considering, in that the resources needed to produce new building materials make recycling an old building a preferred option.

Commissioner Eichold asked if she was correct that the Chen's could develop a structure using the existing building that had opening on all four sides and concluding that the main difference between re-use of the old building and constructing a new building would be that underground parking would only work with new construction.

Mr. Chen said that he would need to calculate costs for renovation vs. new construction before he could answer.

Commissioner Schulz stated that the Chens should get cost estimates for seismic upgrades and renovations, given that demolition and excavation is also expensive. She said that a thorough economic analysis might yield a new/old combination that would retain the historic ambience, provide valuable improvements and be economically feasible.

Staff liaison Esther Polito read into the public hearing record a letter from Jennifer Anderson opposing the designation.

Chair Hobrecht closed the public hearing.

Commissioner Schulz stated that she has heard the building described as "ugly." She commented that the architecture of the hotel is from a period that responded to the complex Victorian architectural choices with simplified design. She added that the historically inappropriate shade structure over the sidewalk hides some of the subtle brick details and that, if it were removed, the building's facade would be enhanced. She said that the building complements the other commercial buildings on the block. She concluded saying that historical buildings aren't always cute, but that their contributions to our understanding of the cultural and social values of their time make them worthy of retention.

Chair Hobrecht asked whether staff has researched the building code to see what would be required to seismically upgrade the building. Staff Polito responded that that has not been done.

Commissioner Hobrecht then asked about city requirements for on-site parking.

Associate Planner Ken Hiatt, present as an observer, came forward to describe the in-lieu parking fee system and explain that the owner of a new building would be able to pay this fee rather than provide on-site parking.

Commissioner Berteaux stated that he believes that a project could be structured to be a win for the Chens and for the city, by retaining the old facade and developing a significant addition.

7. 7. Continued. Pages 3 and 4 of the HMRC minutes regarding historical designation of the Terminal Building.

Page 5

Action   Commissioner Wendy Nelson moved, and Commissioner Anne Rundstrom seconded, a motion to recommend the building at 200 G Street for designation as a City of Davis Historical Resource, based upon applicable findings and environmental review analysis set forth in the staff report dated June 11, 1999, and incorporated into these minutes below:

Findings:

1.)   That the property located at 200 G Street qualifies for designation under criterion (a) of Zoning Ordinance Section 29-145.10 in that... "It exemplifies or reflects valued elements of the city's cultural, social, economic, political, aesthetic, engineering, archaeological or architectural history," and

2.)   That the property located at 200 G Street qualifies for designation under criterion (c) of Zoning Ordinance Section 29-145.10 in that... "It reflects significant geographical patterns, including those associated with different eras of settlement and growth, particular transportation modes, or distinctive examples of park or community planning."

Environmental Review:
The recommendation is exempt from environmental review under section 15378 of the State CEQA Guidelines. Action on these recommendations does not have the potential to result, directly or ultimately, in a physical change to the environment.

Motion passed, 7, 0.

Staff Polito explained that the City Council must act to approve, approve in part or deny the recommendation within 60 days of receiving the Commission's recommendation. The Council

7.7, concluded. Page 5 of 5 of HMRC minutes regarding designation of the Terminal Building.

7.8 June 17, 1999 letter from Jennifer Anderson, President of Davis Ace Hareware (formerly Davis Lumber and Hardware), opposing designating the Terminal Building a historical resource. Aside from the Chen's letter, this was the only other letter opposing designation (or on this topic at all).

Jun-17-99 11:52A Davis Lumber & Hardware   530 758 6173

ΛCE   *Davis Ace Hardware*   P.O. Box 1527 - 240 G St.   Phone 530-758-8000
                                  Davis, CA 95617-1527   Fax   530-758-6173

June 17, 1999

JUN 17 1999

The Historical Commission
City of Davis
Davis, CA

Dear Commission,

On Monday, June 21, 1999 you will be considering two properties to add to the designated "Historical Sites" within the City of Davis.

I oppose either of them being added to the historical classification.

First the Aggie Hotel. It is an old building in terrible condition. It is not worth putting a dime into it. It would mean so much more to the community to have it redeveloped into a HIGHER AND BETTER use with a HISTORICAL architectural design on the exterior. I have walked the halls upstairs in this building. If it had been maintained and updated 40 to 60 years ago it might be worth it. But with today's building and safety standards we as a community will never get a "return on the needed investment". Please do not add this property. We need more retail space downtown – this would be a perfect place for something of significant scale.

Second, the Richards Underpass. This is the entrance to our downtown. It is not pretty, it's not special, it is not Historically significant except to a few newcomers. It's a choked up pipe that everyone complains about and no one wants to spend the money on to widen. Do not designate this location. Leave it alone. If you really want to help the community help us turn this location into a memorable entrance that will have historical significance in the future!

Sincerely,

Jennifer Anderson
President

Cc: Downtown Business Association
      Davis Area Chamber of Commerce

Former hotel site faces an uncertain fate

Owners seek city's OK to demolish, rebuild building

By Melanie Turner
Enterprise staff writer

For the second time since 1984, the Davis City Council will consider on Wednesday whether to protect the building on the northeast corner of Second and G streets by designating it as a local historic resource.

The council will conduct a public hearing on the matter at 7:50 p.m. in the Community Chambers at City Hall, 23 Russell Blvd.

Back in '84, councilmembers received a 4-1 recommendation from the Davis Historical Resource Management Commission to designate the building as a historic resource.

On Wednesday, the council will receive the same recommendation; this time it's unanimous. The recommendation is based in part on findings that the old Terminal Hotel, built in the 1920s, "exemplifies or reflects valued elements of the city's cultural, social, economic, political, aesthetic, engineering, archaeological or architectural history."

Another factor remains the same 15 years later, as well — the owners oppose the designation. Lee and Grace Chen would prefer instead to demolish the old building and construct a new one featuring retail shops on four sides, upstairs apartments and underground parking.

The Chens submitted plans for a four-story

See HOTEL, Page A4

HOTEL   From Page A1

structure in the 1980s that were denied, but this time they say "it's not going to be that drastic." Lee Chen said any news plans would conform to surrounding downtown architecture.

The building — which currently houses Natural Food Works, The Wardrobe, Hair Chalet and La Esperanza — has been significantly altered over the years.

Lee Chen argues that because of this, "there is little historical value."

The building's western facade was changed some time after 1953 with the addition of a rustic wooden gallery with exposed rafters covering the sidewalk at ground level. Underneath that facade is the original brick building front.

According to Chen, there also was a structure on the back, which has been removed, and a first-story window on Second Street that's been covered over.

Secondly, Chen argues that the building is structurally unsound and a renovation would be cost-prohibitive. He presents a report by Sky Engineering, prepared last May, which concludes that "the building is structurally unsound, especially in a major wind storm or earthquake."

Chen has not sought any estimate for a seismic upgrade.

Most importantly, argues Chen, the prominent downtown location and the close proximity to the Southern Pacific Depot make it ideal for new uses. The upstairs hotel portion, which includes 28 rooms, has not been rented for about the last 15 years, he said.

The back portion of the building is not used and could accommodate a coffee shop or cafeteria, he suggests.

"Why only use the one side? he said.

A historic resource designation could delay demolition up to 360 days.

"We just don't want that extra layer of burden to deal with," Chen added. "From an economic point of view, that place should be demolished."

The Chens have lived in Davis for 30 years.

The Historical Resource Management Commission is recommending the lower of the city's two designation categories. Demolition permits for an outstanding historic resource can be denied, while permits can be delayed but not denied for a historic resource.

The commission hopes to encourage the Chens to find out what it would take to stabilize the building, according to Esther Polito, cultural services manager.

"They'd like to see the Chens preserve at least the facade," she said.

Commissioners believe the building's facade would be improved if the historically inappropriate shade structure over the sidewalk was removed. The original building featured a simple two-story brick commercial facade.

Polito added that, in context, the grouping of the Terminal Hotel, The Paragon restaurant and adjoining buildings, the Anderson Building on the northwest corner of Second and G streets, the Masonic Hall down the street and the Southern Pacific Depot create a sense of commercial character of Davis during the 1920s and '30s.

7.10. September 14, 1999 *Davis Enterprise* report that the Davis City Council will vote on the Terminal Building as a historical resource.

7. 11. First page of the 32 page staff report recommending designation of the Terminal Building. The other pages consist, in the main, of items seen previously in this chapter and in several of the history chapters of Part I.

PARKS AND COMMUNITY SERVICES

23 Russell Boulevard – Davis, California 95616
530/757-5626– FAX: 530/758-0204 – TDD: 530/757-5666

Davis
California

C.C. AGENDA
DATE: *9-15-99*
ITEM NO: *9-A*

Staff Report and Ordinance

Date: September 8, 1999

TO: City Council

FROM: Esther Polito, Cultural Services Manager

SUBJECT: Designation of the building at 200 G Street, inclusive of 202, 204 and 206 G Street, as a City of Davis Historical Resource.

Recommendation
1. That the City Council hold a public hearing on the possible designation the building at 200 G Street, parcel number 70-252-04 inclusive of 202, 204 and 206 G Street, as a City of Davis Historical Resources as provided for by Sections 29-145.5 through 29-145.22 of the Zoning Code Pertaining to Historical Resources Management and recommended by the City of Davis Historical Resource Management Commission on June 21, 1999, and
2. That, following the public hearing, the City Council deliberate whether to introduce an ordinance to initiate the designation process for 200 G Street, based on the following findings:

Findings:
1. That the Terminal Hotel located at 200 G Street qualifies for designation under criterion (a) of Zoning Ordinance Section 29-145.10 in that… "It exemplifies or reflects valued elements of the city's cultural, social, economic, political, aesthetic, engineering, archaeological, or architectural history."

2. That the Terminal Hotel located at 200 G Street qualifies for designation under criterion (c) of Zoning Ordinance Section 29-145.10 in that… "It reflects significant geographical patterns, including those associated with different eras of settlement and growth, particular transportation modes, or distinctive examples of park or community planning."

7.12. The 4-1 Preservation Failure Davis City Council of 1999-2000. Only the Mayor—Julie Partansky, seated, center—voted for designation. The negative voters were (l. to r.) Ken Wagstaff, Sheryl Freeman, Susie Boyd, and Stan Forbes. (This is the official City of Davis photograph of this Council.)

7.13. Minutes of the September 15, 1999 Davis City Council regarding designation of the Terminal Building as an Historical Resource. The people listed below are only a portion of all those who spoke in favor.

Public Hearing: Designation of City of Davis Historical Resources

a. 200 G Street (aka Terminal Hotel).

Cultural Services Manager Polito summarized the historic background of the property located at 200 G Street known as Terminal Hotel. She reported that the Historical Resources Management Commission unanimously recommended that the property be designated as a City of Davis Historical Resource at the lowest of the city's two designation categories. She spoke about some of the structural problems associated with the building indicating that the second story has been vacant for many years.

She spoke about the mural of the Mission Revival welcoming arch on the north side of the building and the possibility of being able to save the mural if the building is demolished. She responded to questions from the City Council.

Historical Resource Management Commission Chair Nelson emphasized points that were considered by the commission for this building to be designated as historic. She stated it is not the job of the commission to determine whether the building can be saved but to consider the historic value of the building. She further stated there is funding available and encouraged the owners to consider other options than demolishing the building.

Mayor Partansky opened the public hearing.

L. Chen, owner of 200 G Street, stated the hotel portion of the building has been unoccupied since 1979 and could not be used without significant code upgrades and structural modifications. He further stated he has been unable to obtain an estimate for the cost of the seismic retrofitting needed to bring the building up to seismic code. He also added that the building has been extensively altered, resulting in a loss of its historic value. He asked that the building not be designated as historic.

Commissioner M. White spoke about the beauty, character and simplicity of the building stating that it adds to the character of the street. He asked that the

7.13, concluded.

owners review alternatives.

B. Rivers asked that the City Council look at how the City of Winters restored an old building in their community. She spoke about the style of the building.

V. Dvorak spoke about neglect of limited historical resources by the landowners claiming that it is cost prohibitive to repair or rehabilitate these buildings. She stated this appears to be a trend in Davis. She urged the Council to designate this building as historic.

S. Mikesell stated he was chair of the Historical Resources Commission 15-years ago when this issue was considered and is concerned the discussion is going in the same direction it did at that time. He urged the City Council to continue with the two-step process which is designation and project review. He stated the Council is at the step for designation and the question is does this building meet the criteria for being designated as a historic resource. He urged support for designation.

K. Pryor spoke in behalf of designation. He read a letter from N. Price supporting designation as a historic resource.

M. Johnson said even though the building looks like it is falling down, she supports designation.

P. Barker opposed designation of the building as historic stating it is not an attractive building for Davis.

G. Chen spoke about the beauty of the depot and the need to make this corner attractive in correlation with the depot.

Mayor Partansky closed the public hearing.

Following comments and questions of staff by the City Council, S. Freeman moved, seconded by S. Boyd, to decline designating the building at 200 G Street, parcel number 70-252-04 inclusive of 202, 204 and 206 G Street as a historic resource. The motion passed by the following vote:

AYES: Boyd, Forbes, Freeman, Wagstaff.

NOES: Partansky.

J. Partansky moved, seconded by K. Wagstaff, to direct staff to prepare a letter to the architect expressing the desire that she work with the Historical Resources Management Commission to assure that the design of the building fits historically with the neighborhood. The motion passed by the following vote:

AYES: Boyd, Forbes, Freeman, Wagstaff, Partansky.

NOES: None.

J. Partansky moved, seconded by S. Freeman, to direct staff to research procedures and costs associated with the preservation of the mural. The motion passed by the following vote:

AYES: Boyd, Forbes, Freeman, Wagstaff, Partansky.

-99   8

NOES: None.

City Council requested a report back on the recycling options for the demolition of the building.

7.14. September 16, 1999 *Davis Enterprise* report of the Council action on the building.

No historic protection for hotel

Site may be razed for new downtown project

By Melanie Turner
Enterprise staff writer

Despite a unanimous recommendation to designate the building on the northeast corner of Second and G streets as a historic resource, the City Council voted 4-1 Wednesday to make it easier for the building to be demolished.

A house restorationist, Mayor Julie Partansky cast the lone dissenting vote, believing the old building is not beyond restoration and the owners could get financial help only if the building had the designation.

"I find the building of a certain kind of cowboy, Old West style," she said. "It says something about the history of Davis and I appreciate that."

The two-story building — known to old-timers as either the Terminal Hotel or later, Hotel Aggie, and to the younger generation as the building with the mural of the Davis arches on the north side — was built in 1925.

Underneath a Western-style awning placed on the building in mid-century is a typical brick commercial building of its time.

The owners, Lee and Grace Chen, asked the council to deny the historic resource designation, arguing against a burdensome extra level of review that would be required before any changes are made to the facade.

They wish to construct a building with retail shops on four sides, which may require tearing down the old building and replacing it with a new one.

However, Chen said afterwards he has not ruled out saving the brick facade.

See HOTEL, Page A4

> *"I think we can welcome visitors with something much nicer than is there right now."*
>
> **Councilwoman Sheryl Freeman**

HOTEL
From Page A1

"Maybe we will end up saving parts of it. That may be cost-effective. We don't know yet," he said.

While he has not sought an estimate for a seismic upgrade, he has attempted unsuccessfully to get an estimate of the cost of renovation.

"No one can give us exact cost," Chen told the council.

He said he's been told parts of the building would have to begin to be removed before such an estimate could be made.

"I cannot have that uncertainty," he said.

The Chens are concerned that the building's physical condition could make restoration cost-prohibitive. After visually inspecting the site, Ray Kwan of Sky Engineering determined that the building is structurally unsound.

Lee Chen also argued that the building has lost its historic character, what with so many changes being made over the years.

When members of the city's Historical Resources Management Commission examined the building in its historic context, it considered that it stands in a grouping that creates a time and a place in Davis, said Esther Polito, cultural services manager.

Davis was growing and the university had established a four-year degree program by 1922. Frequent passenger train service occurred at the Southern Pacific Depot. For the many visitors, G Street was the town's commercial hub.

Today, the Terminal Hotel sits near the old depot, across the street from a designated outstanding historic resource, the Anderson Bank Building, and not far from the old brick Brinley building on Second Street.

"As a grouping, these really set the character of the commercial Main Street in the '20s and '30s," Polito said.

The Terminal Hotel was a "valuable meeting place in the city," added Polito.

The hotel qualified for a historic designation based on two criteria in the city's zoning code, including that the building exemplifies valued elements associated with the city's history and it reflects significant geographical growth patterns, including those associated with different areas of settlement and growth, particular transportation modes and community planning, she said.

The historical commission recommended that the council adopt the lower of the city's two designation categories in order to leave more options for the Chens.

Under that designation the Chens could have demolished the building if they found renovation to not be economically feasible. But demolition could be delayed up to 360 days.

Said Wendy Nelson, chair of the commission, "We certainly would encourage the Chens to at least make some attempt to renovate it. This is an important historic structure."

Nelson argued that if cities demolished all old buildings with problems, a lot would be lost.

Two council members, Ken Wagstaff and Susie Boyd, called the building "ugly."

"Why preserve that, in particular?" Wagstaff said.

He added that the building "turns its back on the train station," and he's concerned about ensuring that the downtown becomes the retail hub of the city.

Nelson countered that it could be a retail hub "with character," and an historic designation would not preclude the owners from building something welcoming and attractive on the backside.

Said one woman, "I don't think we need to rip it down to do something different on the back."

Added Commissioner Mike White, "I would hope the council could find some beauty in the simplicity of that building."

Several people spoke in support of the designation.

Steve Mikesell, who chaired the commission when it made a similar recommendation to the council 15 years ago, reminded council members that the question before them was whether the building met the historic resource criteria. Project review would come later.

The council agreed that while the Terminal Hotel once greeted great numbers of people getting off the train, the site still serves as an important gateway to the city.

"I think we can welcome visitors with something much nicer than is there right now," said Councilwoman Sheryl Freeman. "This building, to my opinion, is just too far gone."

While Councilman Stan Forbes agreed with Partansky

that the building could be restored, he argued that it's not "substantial enough of a historic resource" to give it the designation, knowing it could make things more difficult for the Chens.

He argued for replacing it with something in keeping with the street's historic flavor.

But, said Boyd, "For me it's not a fiscal issue, it's an aesthetic one. ...I want people to get off the train and see an inviting structure."

Partansky added that she is very concerned about saving the mural.

Davis Subway: In other action, the council approved, 4-1, the highest level of local historic designation for the Davis Subway, an outstanding historic designation. Also known as the Richards Boulevard underpass, it was listed in the National Register of Historic Places in May 1998.

"It really is a formality that we're going through this process," Polito told the council.

Boyd voted against the designation.

"I find it particularly ironic that we would be creating this monument to the automobile," she said.

The votes of Freeman and Boyd had always been more uncertain on preservation matters, as was their liberalism in general. So, there was less surprise about them. Boyd, in particular, was widely regarded as inconsistent in that she claimed to be a preservationist but sometimes voted the opposite. Indeed, this very evening she was the lone member of the Council to vote against endorsing the nomination of the Richards Underpass for listing on the National Register of Historic Places. In column 5 of Fig. 7.14, we read that she explained her dissenting vote as an expression of her opposition to the automobile: "I find it particularly ironic that we would be creating this monument to the automobile." The implication was that she disdained cars, but she in fact owned two of them (a family sedan and a red convertible sports car). Ironic, indeed.

5) TRANSITION

This could well have been the end of the Terminal Building as a topic and concern. But in fact, the struggle had only begun.

8

FEASIBILITY STUDY FAILURE

Naively, preservationists assumed that "of course" the building would be designated a historic resource. When that did not happen, there was, at first, a shocked silence. But then people began to respond.

1) CALLS TO RECONSIDER AND LETTERS TO THE EDITOR BEGIN

Initially, these actions were calls for the City Council to reconsider its actions. There were many of these and some of the first were made in the Council "public comment" period of September 29th, the next time the Council met after the September 15th denial (Fig. 8.1).

8.1. Text of City Council minutes of September 29, 2000 reporting citizens requesting a reconsideration of the denial action.

R. Bushman, A. Hastings and B. Rivers spoke in support of designation of the Aggie Hotel as a historic resource.

Another type of action was a "letter to the editor" of the *Davis Enterprise*. These letters started on September 28 and kept up almost as a steady drum beat to the end, a year later. The first three of them are reproduced in Fig. 8.2.

Sunday, October 3, the *Enterprise* did a further background-type story featuring the fact that the previous Wednesday citizens called on the Council to reconsider its designation denial (Fig. 8.3). This story helped to keep the concern alive.

8.2. First three of a year-long stream of letters urging preservation of the building.

THE DAVIS ENTERPRISE

▶ LETTERS

FRIDAY, OCTOBER 1, 1999

TUESDAY, SEPTEMBER 28, 1999

Please reconsider

I know that the City Council is busy and not always able to give full attention to all matters. I was disappointed when at the Sept. 15 meeting they declined to consider the nomination of the old Hotel Aggie as a historical resource.

This designation does not restrict the property owners from destroying the building but it does give the city (community) and the owners the opportunity to look at options other than total destruction. Such options could include maintaining the original facade surrounding an entirely new structure. There are several options available for consideration, some of which could bring additional benefits to the owners.

The subject building at 200 G St. has historical significance because of its location and proximity to the train depot, the Anderson Bank building on an opposite corner, the Brinley building also on an opposite corner and the Masonic building on Second Street adjacent to the Second and G streets corner.

The old Hotel Aggie building has been called many things, including "ugly". This is a very subjective term and not a basis for consideration of "historical resource."

The Historical Management Commission voted 7-0 to nominate this building as a "historical resource" according to Zoning Ordinance Section 29-145.10(c). *"It reflects significant geographical patterns, including those associated with different areas of settlement and growth, par-*ticularly transportation modes, or distinctive examples of park or community planning."

The City Council should reconsider its action and I will work to open this point of view at the next council meeting Sept. 29.

Richard Buschman, Davis

Historic status

The following is a copy of a letter to the Davis City Council:

I am concerned about attempts to revoke the historic status of the Aggie Hotel. This building dates from 1928. For many years it personified Davis for travelers on the passenger trains and the old highway which is now Olive Drive. Now it is part of a very small remnant of the historic downtown.

I have watched with sadness as Davis gradually gives up its character to development. You now have the opportunity to preserve a landmark which will continue to embody old Davis for many years after your term of office is over.

Guy Kyser, Davis

Worth preserving

I am sorely disappointed that the Davis City Council did not designate the old Hotel Aggie as a historical resource.

There is simply no other large building downtown of this time period and style. The distinct character of the city relies on such large structures; smaller buildings, even with many distinguishing features are not sufficient on their own. The presence of a large brick building close to a train station links Davis to its location and its history, since this is a feature common to old railroad towns in the Central Valley.

The loss of this building will be irreplaceable. It is important not just for its appearance but its genuine value.

I urge the City Council to reconsider this designation, and the landlord and architect not to plan on demolishing the building.

This failure to save the building is one of the most serious errors that the council has made in this decade.

Judith Dresher
Davis

8.3. *Davis Enterprise*, Sunday, October 3, 1999.

La Esperanza's building won't get city protection

By Melanie Turner
Enterprise staff writer

The fate of the old Terminal Hotel — on the northeast corner of Second and G streets and home today to four business including La Esperanza — remains solely in the hands of the building's owners.

That is despite pleas by citizens to the City Council on Wednesday to designate the brick building as a historic resource.

"That is a very important structure downtown," Richard Buschman told the council. "The city has the opportunity to maintain some small degree of control."

The council voted 4-1 on Sept. 15 to deny the unanimous recommendation of the Davis Historical Resources Management Commission to designate 200 G St. as historic.

A few citizens asked the council to reconsider the decision, but the council had no interest in doing so.

"It doesn't look like we're going to get council to reconsider this one, so take a lot of pictures, I guess," said Mayor Julie Partansky, who cast the lone no vote.

The designation forces the owner to look at alternatives to demolition, Buschman said. With a historic designation, the owners could still demolish the building with a one-year delay.

As it stands, the owners, Lee and Grace Chen, could have a demolition permit granted Monday.

But Lee Chen, reached on Friday, said he is not committed to tearing down the building's brick facade, which the commission was most interested in preserving.

"I really have no idea at this moment what we should do," he said.

See BUILDING, Page A3

BUILDING From Page A1

"The bottom line is really whether it's economically feasible."

He said he will work with the city and the commission in coming up with his final plans.

The Chens are interested in creating a three-story structure with ground-floor retail on four sides, apartments on the second floor and senior housing on the third floor.

"I will try to keep the facade if it's cost effective," Chen added.

The Chens are thinking about hiring architect Maria Ogrydziak, who designed the Davis Food Co-op project, to design the 200 G St. project.

Buschman said it's clear that 200 G St. should be designated as a historic resource, especially given its proximity to other historic buildings.

"And yet the comments I heard from the City Council had to do with whether it was too short, too tall, too ugly, too unworthy of anything but destruction," he said.

"Because it doesn't have an elegant facade doesn't make it less historic," added Audrey Hastings. "...In Davis we have to fight to save the few buildings we have."

The building is in poor physical condition and the Chens have argued that restoration would be costly as well as impractical.

The Terminal Hotel was built in 1925 when G Street was a busy main street in Davis, a place where train travelers strolled, residents and farmers did business and university people stopped on their way to and from campus.

Today, the upstairs hotel is not used.

Richard Hastings asked the council to establish a demolition-review ordinance for the downtown. He suggested the ordinance could allow a review period for all buildings over 50 years of age.

City attorney Harriet Steiner said the commission and staff could establish a historic district that could provide for additional demolition control and other additional guidelines within the district.

The Historical Resources Management Commission is working with the community to prepare design guidelines for the area bounded by the original 1917 Davis city limits, which includes the city's commercial core and three adjacent neighborhoods.

A community workshop on Davis Conservation District design guidelines is scheduled for Wednesday, Oct. 27, from 7 to 9 p.m. in the Community Chambers, 23 Russell Blvd.

8.4. The writers of these letters were both long-time Davis residents and active in public matters in various ways. Audrey Hastings was a Downtown business owner, the proprietor of Hastings' Backporch.

Please reconsider

This is the second time I am fighting to save the old Hotel Aggie at the corner of Second and G.

The first time was some years ago (I can no longer find the evidence in my growing "fight" file) when the owners first requested permission to replace the historic site. They submitted a photo of the model for building, which was published in The Enterprise. It was a tall white square-based shaft with a pagoda-like extension at the top. Not a bad-looking building, but the wrong site and the wrong design for that part of town.

We have a great historic cluster of buildings in that area, although the old fire station is almost obliterated by continuous remodeling. We need to preserve it.

I am distressed that the City Council has voted to allow the destruction of the building and its wonderful, nostalgic painting of the arches on the north wall. Please, Ken, Sheryl, Stan and Susie, reconsider. Allow the old structure to remain in its honored place, at the heart of the original Davis.

It can be renovated — Sacramento has done it, San Francisco has done it, and many other towns have honored their birth places through renovations and reconstruction. What would Los Angeles be without its original old plaza downtown?

We need to keep Davis' roots — to remember where it began — to keep its honored birthright. Please council, reconsider.

Margaret Milligan, Davis

Historic resource

We came to Davis in 1966, went to school, frequented the Antique Bizarre — a pub in the Aggie Hotel — and I know a lot of young and old people who lived there during the 1960s.

It is unfortunate that the owners of these historic buildings allow them to deteriorate, therefore giving them the excuse to demolish rather than restore. Davis fits well in this scheme of thing; money is the important issue, not the historic value.

"Ugly" is a term that has come up twice in this council's vocabulary. This simple early 20th century commercial structure did what it was supposed to do — serve as an hotel for train passengers. Because it didn't have an elegant facade doesn't make it less historic. It also contributed to the Davis commercial core in the 1920s and '30s.

Davis is way behind when it comes to saving these older structures. Every City Council we've had has not been historic preservation-friendly. When you get a unanimous recommendation from the Historical Commission you totally disregard it. Why do we have these commissions? To aid in the process of your decision-making?

I traveled extensively this summer in Minnesota and eastern Wisconsin and encountered so many towns with historic downtown districts — Port Washington, Racine, Kenosha, Cedarburg and Waukeshal. In Minnesota I visited New Ulm, a great small downtown with lots of red brick residences, and Northfield, the home of Carleton and St. Olaf Colleges; their whole downtown is historic with a grand 1870 red brick Archer House Hotel at the core. Woodland, too, has an historic downtown district.

In Davis we have to fight to save the few buildings we have. I'm very disappointed in the City Council's decision and would hope for a reconsideration in designating the Aggie Hotel as a historic resource.

Audrey Hastings
Davis

8. 5. *Davis Enterprise* letters to the editor, October 18, 1999. Robin Datel's role in preservation matters in the 1980s and more generally was described in Chapter 6.

MONDAY, OCTOBER 18, 1999

Ignoring history

The following is a copy of a letter to the Davis City Council:

I urge the four of you who voted that the Terminal Hotel is not an important historical structure — the meaning of it not being an "historical resource" — to reconsider and to change your vote.

You should reconsider and change because by your vote you supported a factually incorrect assertion of major importance; namely, that the Terminal Hotel was *not* among the most important buildings in the history of Davis.

The historical facts are clearly and without dispute the opposite. As the ample documentation provided by your Historical Commission shows, the building was a key element of the commercial landscape and Davis social life. The Historical Commission was unanimous on this point and it is a common-sense truth to everyone who knows even the slightest bit of Davis history.

But, no, you decided the historical truth was otherwise! Such a shocking rejection of fact cannot but awaken questions about credibility. I urge your reconsideration.
John Lofland
Davis

Reasons to preserve

I am adding my voice to those who are urging the City Council to designate the Hotel Aggie a historical resource. It meets several of the designation criteria stated in our local ordinance, embodying as it does elements of our social, economic and transportation history.

The building's original name, the Terminal Hotel, helps tell the story of its early function and reminds us of the importance of the railroad in the history of Davis. Together with the Southern Pacific Depot, the Anderson Bank building, the Brinley block and the Masonic Lodge, the Hotel Aggie captures what is left of the era when 18 trains a day passed through Davis and when the life of our downtown was focused on the corner of Second and G streets.

The hotel was not only an essential economic part of a railroad-oriented town, it also was important socially. It was the first home for many newly arriving UCD students and faculty through the years.

Many university and service organizations held their meetings in the Terminal Hotel, in part because the owners wanted it to be a community center. Reading through back issues of The Davis Enterprise would reveal countless meetings and events in our history that took place in the Terminal Hotel.

Our downtown is not particularly rich in historical buildings, compared, for example, to Woodland, which grew larger at an earlier time, thanks to its role as county seat and agricultural service center. We should value and preserve those we do have for several reasons.

First, such buildings do link us to our past, and helping us to understand it and honor it.

Second, such buildings make our downtown more interesting visually. Despite the alterations to the Hotel Aggie, it still has that antique texture that no modern building, however excellently designed, can have. The popularity of antique texture and its contribution to successful downtowns is well established.

Third, as Davisites we pride ourselves on recycling and using resources carefully; preservation contributes to those goals.

The case that the Hotel Aggie meets the criteria for designation is open and shut, and it was confirmed by a unanimous vote of the city's own Historical Resources Management Commission.

The property owner has made the argument that it should not be designated because it is in bad shape. That is not a valid argument. The reason that the property is in such bad shape (yes, I have been upstairs) is because the property owner has let it deteriorate. This is an old, old landlord trick used to avoid historical designation. Let's not reward it.

The building clearly deserves to be designated; once that occurs, then we can take the next step of considering its preservation. It would be worthwhile to spend a few city dollars to have an architect trained in preservation inspect the building and make recommendations.

Then we can work with the property owner and the project architect (who is on record as supporting a healthy downtown) to come up with a wonderful recycled, adaptively reused building that will both stir our memories and make a contribution to the modern townscape and economy of Davis.
Robin Datel
Davis

2) THE PLOT TAKES A NEW TURN: THE CITY ACTS

As a relatively superficial structural assessment undertaken by a firm commissioned by the owner, the City could not accept as definitive SKY Engineering's claims that the building might well blow over in a strong wind (Fig. 7.5). Neither, also, could it ignore the report.

Always skittish about liability because citizens are prone to try to pick what they see as the deep pockets of a government, City prudence demanded that the SKY Engineering claims be followed-up.

This was especially necessary because, according to Lorin Gardner, the City's Chief Building Official, the Chens had given him a copy of the SKY Engineering report (first paragraph, Fig. 8.6). That is, the Chens were making certain he knew of the report and that they knew that he knew.

Hence, Gardener's letter to "Ms. Lee Chen" dated October 22, 1999 (Fig. 8.6).

8.6. Gardner Letter to Chen, October 22, 1999.

PLANNING AND BUILDING DEPARTMENT

23 Russell Boulevard – Davis, California 95616
530/757-5610– FAX: 530/757-5660 – TDD: 530/757-5666

October 22, 1999

Ms. Lee Chen
P.O. Box 2094
El Macero, CA 95618

RE: 200 G Street, Davis, CA

Dear Ms. Lee Chen:

I have received a copy of a letter to you from Mr. Raymond Kwan, Structural Engineer from SKY Engineering, concerning your referenced property. Mr. Kwan had completed a structural inspection of your property and identified some areas that may have structural deficiencies. Mr. Kwan states that " the exterior unreinforced brick walls, acting as bearing walls, support the roof and floor loads; the walls also act as shear walls and provide lateral resistance to the wind and earthquake load". Mr. Kwan noted that "...cracking can be found in several retaining wall locations in the basement due to inadequate reinforcements and foundation"; "...floor members and connections of the floor members are inadequate"; "...the exterior walls are out of plumb". Mr. Kwan concluded that "...this building is structurally unsound" and that "... this building is unsafe in a major wind storm or earthquake."

Based on Mr. Kwan's observations and conclusion, the City of Davis must initiate an investigation of the possible inadequacies to determine the actual condition of the structure and then make a determination of what must be done with the building.

Therefore, the City asks your permission to enter the building and conduct a comprehensive inspection to determine its condition. The City will hire an experienced Engineer familiar with buildings of similar construction to conduct the investigation. The cost of this investigation will be at your expense. At this point it is difficult to guess what the outcome of the process will be. The worst results could be a conclusion that this structure must be declared a public nuisance per the California Building Code, Sec. 102 of the Uniform Code for the Abatement of Dangerous Buildings. If the danger is determined to be imminent, the structure would have to be vacated immediately and remain unoccupied until such time that repair, rehabilitation or demolition abates the building. Other outcomes are certainly possible, including a determination that the building is adequate for continued occupancy. The City has no preconceived outcome; our objective is to perform a thorough investigation to ensure appropriate actions, if deemed necessary, are taken.

Letter to Ms. Lee Chen
October 22, 1999
Page 2

Please provide within ten days of the date of this letter, written authority for the City to conduct the above-described investigation.

Sincerely,

Lorin Gardner
Chief Building Official

h:\Bldg\200G.doc (clc)

8.7. This October 25 letter from the Chuck Roe, a Davis developer and elected head of the Davis Chamber of Commerce is notable for the fact that it signals that this organization did not think the Terminal Building matter was settled.

That is, if the episode was concluded, this letter was unnecessary and could only serve further to antagonize proponents of preservation (i.e. to drive customers away from Davis businesses for no good reason).

This letter boomeranged in the sense that it sent the signal to preservationists that demolitionists did not think the struggle was over. Therefore, further effort might be successful.

MONDAY, OCTOBER 25, 1999

▶ LETTERS

The right decision

The Board of Directors of the Davis Chamber of Commerce would like to commend the Davis City Council on its recent decision to deny historical status to the Aggie Hotel building on the corner of Second and G streets.

The Historical Resources Commission is a very knowledgeable watchdog commission charged with the task of advising the council on matters of our historical resources. In this case they suggested a historical designation for the Terminal Hotel building.

It is certainly old, once served visitors arriving on the railroad and has a brick exterior. Coming from a commission charged with historical preservation, this recommendation is appropriate.

The job of the City Council is to weigh commission recommendations in the context of all the city goals and in this case the downtown. The train station neighborhood provides thousands of travelers with their most intimate look at our town and welcomes those who arrive in Davis.

Unfortunately, the old hotel is not architecturally interesting and turns its back on the station. It is easy to imagine a more creative anchor building to our most active commercial street.

Given its location, structural condition, and great potential for redevelopment, the options for the Terminal Hotel should not be restricted by a historical designation.

We congratulate Council members Boyd, Forbes, Freeman and Wagstaff for their far-sighted and courageous decision.

Chuck Roe
Chairman, Board of Directors, Davis Chamber of Commerce, Davis

Preserve the hotel

Davis doesn't have many older historic buildings. We have a few and I think we should work to keep them. I'm not in love with the aesthetics of the old Terminal Hotel but I think it should be preserved in some way.

I think the City Council overlooked this issue when they voted 4-1 to take this treasure off the Historical Resource list, against the Historic Resource Management Commission's recommendation. This means we could have something much worse.

Take a look around at some of the buildings that were allowed to be built in this town. Remember the old State Market across from Coldwell Banker? What a beautiful hunk of concrete we have now! Let's not be shortsighted because we have a busy agenda and "Oh who cares? I don't like the looks of that old building anyway."

If places like Nevada City, Grass Valley, Sutter Creek, Eureka and Old Sacramento felt this way what would they have instead?

That corner at Second and G Street has other buildings that are part of an older historic block and removing one piece of history will make a significant impact on that area.

I think our council members should rethink this issue and work to preserve the integrity of the first paved street in Davis. Please voice your opinion to our City Council members.

Sandy Weaver, Davis

8.8. In this November 1 *Enterprise* letter Lee Chen follows in the footsteps of Chuck Roe (Fig. 8.7) in suggesting that the Terminal Building matter might not be over, at least in his avowed desire "to hear constructive suggestions, especially how we can deal with this issue. . . ."

However, read from the vantage point of knowing what actually happened, this letter might be also be viewed as a sugar-coated declaration of a demolition plan.

MONDAY, NOVEMBER 1, 1999

▶ LETTERS

● ●

Let's work together

Our ex-city mayor, Vigfus Asmundson, once told me that the golden rule in dealing with the Davis public is "keep silent and keep smiling." But when you are accused of "playing tricks" and "neglecting" your own personal property, I am sorry, but I have to break that rule.

There is no reason for us to play "tricks" to let the Terminal Hotel building at Second and G streets deteriorate in order to tear it down. We can tear it down without playing "tricks" because the city previously voted against preservation.

The main purpose for any owner to own a commercial building is to generate a profit. A "neglected" or vacant building will not produce any income. There is no incentive for us to neglect our own building. In addition, my wife operates a beauty salon within the building. I do not think she will be able to tolerate a "neglected" building.

It is not necessary for us to tear down the building. We are against the designation of the building as a historical resource, because we would like to have other options. As most of you know, the City Council has voted twice against preserving the Hotel Aggie Building, once 15 years ago, and again in September of this year. But this does not mean we cannot work together, without any name calling. We would like to hear constructive suggestions, especially how we can deal with this issue and in a manner that makes financial sense.

We have lived in Davis for 30 years. We love the city of Davis like most of you do. We want to maintain its special character. We are not villains. We call all resolve this matter without attacking personal integrity.

Lee Chen
Davis

Dignity of process

I write to dispute the claim that the Terminal Hotel in not an historically important building (an historical resource) for the two reasons that it "is not architecturally interesting and turns its back on the station" (the wording in an Oct. 25 letter to the editor).

Applying such reasoning, we would need to conclude that Civil War battlefields, World War II Japanese internment camps, and civil rights movement sites are not historically significant if they lack architectural interest or are inconveniently located. Such reasoning is clearly absurd.

Instead, in these three examples and in the case of the Terminal Hotel, historical significance derives from what happened in the locations and their relevance to larger contexts and not from physical appearance or place in space.

Since no one disputes the historical significance of the Terminal Hotel, there is no reason not officially to signal its import in Davis history (i.e., to bestow the label "historical resource"). Indeed, intellectual integrity requires it. It is surely ironic for a community conceiving itself as a pre-eminent university city to make a major claim in its official, government history that everyone knows is not true.

Designation as an "historical resource" does not "save" the Terminal Hotel from major alterations or demolition. Instead, it simply creates a period of deliberation on what will happen. Demolition can be the outcome (perhaps because of lack of architectural interest and openness to the train station). So be it.

But, if demolition or some such is to be the outcome, let us undertake an orderly and methodical assessment that honors the building's historical significance. To do otherwise is to deny it the dignity of due process. Sadly, at this time, rather than giving it a fair trial in which it is acquitted or convicted, we are embarked on a rush-to-judgment lynching.

We in Davis rightly pride ourselves on our sense of fair play and thoughtfulness. Let us apply these points of pride to the case of the Terminal Hotel as much as we do to other matters.

John Lofland
Davis

8.9. Taking up Mr. Chen's expression of interest in "constructive suggestions," the day after his November 1 *Enterprise* letter (Fig. 8.8), I sent him the letter reproduced at the right advocating a "facadectomy" solution. The attachments to this letter were published as an op-ed in the *Davis Enterperprise* on June 11, 2000 (Fig. 9.1) and they are therefore not also reproduced here.

I did not receive even an acknowledgement of receipt from Mr. Chen. But, in a phone conversation with Mayor Ken Wagstaff on May 31, 2000 (seven months later) I was asked if I had spoken with the Chens about facadectomy. I told the Mayor about this November 2nd letter and expressed my sense that Chen was less than gracious publicly to solicit suggestions and then not even to acknowledge receipt of one, much less to respond to its substance.

A few minutes after I hung up the phone with the Mayor, I got a call from Lee Chen.

I report what he said at the May 31, 2000 point in the narrative (Fig. 8.30).

John Lofland
523 E Street
Davis, California 95616

530-758-5258
fax 530-752-0783
jflofland@ucdavis.edu

November 2, 1999

Lee Chen
P. O. Box 2094
El Macero, CA 95618

Dear Mr. Chen:

I am responding to the Davis Enterprise letter of November 1 in which you say that "we would like to hear constructive suggestions" regarding the future of the Terminal Hotel.

I think I have a constructive suggestion that is expressed in the form of an op-ed article I have proposed to the Davis Enterprise. I enclose a copy of it here for your consideration. As of today, I do not know if the Enterprise will use it or not, but the idea can be considered whether or not it appears in the Enterprise.

Since writing this "facadectomy" suggestion, I have discovered a picture of the Hotel in near its original condition and come to the realization that the building looks very much like the two on the other two corners. That is, we see it as "ugly" because so many terrible things have been done to it since about 1945. If all the junk were taken off its façade, it would be an excellent complement to the Brinley Bock building and the Anderson building on the other two corners.

Should you want to explore these suggestions further, I would be happy to meet with you and/or other people you may desire.

Cordially,

John Lofland

Enc: nine page draft of an op-ed item
Photo of G Street Looking North

8.10.. Thanksgiving eve, 1999, the Chens took out a permit to demolish the Terminal Building. This was two weeks in advance of when the City would receive the structural evaluation report it had commissioned in October (Figs. 8.6 and 8.11).

CITY OF DAVIS
BUILDING INSPECTION DIVISION
23 Russell Blvd. Davis, CA 95616
757-5659 - For Scheduling Permit Inspections
757-5610 - For Inspectors

IMPORTANT: Always use the permit number below when requesting inspections or information concerning this permit.

PERMIT

LICENSED CONTRACTOR DECLARATION
I hereby affirm under penalty of perjury that I am licensed under provisions of Chapter 9 (commencing with Section 7000) of division 3 of the Business and Professions Code, and my license is in full force and effect.

License No. 66290　Lic. Class C-21-61

Contractor　Date 11/24/99

OWNER-BUILDER DECLARATION
I hereby affirm under penalty of perjury that I am exempt from the Contractors License Law for the following reason (Sec. 7031.5, Business and Professions Code: Any city or county which requires a permit to construct, alter, improve, demolish, or repair any structure, prior to its issuance, also requires the applicant for such permit to file a signed statement that he or she is licensed pursuant to the provisions of the Contractors License Law. (Chapter 9 (commencing with Section 7000) of Division 3 of the Business and Professions Code) or that he or she is exempt therefrom and the basis for the alleged exemption. Any violation of Section 7031.5 by any applicant for a permit subjects the applicant to a civil penalty of not more than five hundred dollars ($500).):

☐ I, as owner of the property, or my employees with wages as their sole compensation, will do the work, and the structure is not intended or offered for sale (Sec. 7044, Business and Professions Code: The Contractors License Law does not apply to an owner of property who builds or improves thereon, and who does such work himself or herself or through is or her own employees, provided that such improvements are not intended or offered for sale. If, however, the building or improvement is sold within one year of completion, the owner-builder will have the burden of proving that he or she did not build or improve for the purpose of sale.).

☐ I, as owner of the property, am exclusively contracting with licensed contractors to construct the project (Sec. 7044, Business and Professions Code: The Contractors License Law does not apply to an owner of property who builds or improves thereon, and who contracts for such projects with a contractor(s) licensed pursuant to the Contractors License Law).

☐ I am exempt under Sec. _____ B.& P.C. for this reason _____

Owner _____　Date 11/24/99

WORKERS' COMPENSATION DECLARATION
I HEREBY AFFIRM UNDER PENALTY OF PERJURY one of the following declarations:

☐ I HAVE AND WILL MAINTAIN A CERTIFICATE OF CONSENT TO SELF-INSURE FOR WORKERS' COMPENSATION, as provided for by Section 3700 of the Labor Code, for the performance of the work for which this permit is issued.

☐ I HAVE AND WILL MAINTAIN WORKERS' COMPENSATION INSURANCE, as required by Section 3700 of the Labor Code, for the performance of the work for which this permit is issued. My workers' compensation insurance carrier and policy number are:

Carrier Villenova Insurance　Policy Number WC2-120 9946

This section need not be completed if the permit is for one hundred dollars ($100) or less.

☐ I CERTIFY THAT IN THE PERFORMANCE OF THE WORK FOR WHICH THIS PERMIT IS ISSUED, I shall not employ any person in any manner so as to become subject of the workers' compensation laws of California, and agree that if I should become subject to the workers' compensation provisions of Section 3700 of the Labor Code, I shall forthwith comply with these provisions.

Applicants Signature _____　Date _____

WARNING: FAILURE TO SECURE WORKERS' COMPENSATION COVERAGE IS UNLAWFUL, AND SHALL SUBJECT AN EMPLOYER TO CRIMINAL PENALTIES AND CIVIL FINES UP TO ONE HUNDRED THOUSAND DOLLARS ($100,000), IN ADDITION TO THE COST OF COMPENSATION, DAMAGES AS PROVIDED FOR IN SECTION 3706 OF THE LABOR CODE, INTEREST, AND ATTORNEY'S FEES.

CONSTRUCTION LENDING AGENCY
I hereby affirm under penalty of perjury that there is a construction lending agency for the performance of the work for which this permit is issued (Sec. 3097, Civ. C.).

Lender's Name None

Lender's Address _____

I certify that I have read this application and state that the above information is correct. I agree to comply with all city and county ordinances and state laws relating to building construction, and hereby authorize representatives of this county to enter upon the above-mentioned property for inspection purposes.

Applicant/Agent Signature _____　Date 11/24/99

Permit Nbr:　99-　4605
Access Nbr:　92700

Print Date:　11/24/99
Job Address:　200 G STREET
Subdivision:
Parcel Nbr:　70-252-04-　-
Valuation:
　Tenant Name, Nbr:
　　DEMO BUILDING
Work Description:
　DEMOLISH NON-RESIDENTIAL BUILDING

Owner:　　CHEN TR ETAL
　　　　　P O BOX 2094
　　　　　EL MACERO CA 95618
　　　　　(530) 753-2436

Contractor:　JOHN'S HAULING
　　　　　PO BOX 1522
　　　　　DAVIS CA 95617
　　　　　(530) 753-3220

Permits:　　　　　Issued:
*DEMOLITION PERMIT COMM/INDUS 11/24/99

Fees Paid:　　100.00

Special Notes and Comments:

DEMO PERMIT FOR 200, 202, 204, AND 206 G STREET.
WORK NOT TO BEGIN UNTIL: 10 DAYS AFTER YOLO/SOLONO AIR QUALITY RECIEVES APPLICATION. 12-04-99

JOB FINAL BY: _____　DATE: _____

THIS PERMIT BECOMES NULL AND VOID if work or construction is not commenced within 180 days from date of issuance, or work is suspended or abandoned for a period of 180 days any time after work is commenced.

8.11. The "Conclusions and Recommendations" page of the McKennyKrug structural evaluation report contracted in October. Received by the City on December 9, 1999, the report *only* dealt with "life-safety" in a "seismic event."

On this score, the firm found the building was not up to FEMA standards. (Without upgrading, this was also true of virtually all brick structures built in California before World War II.)

PAGE 10

BUILDING EVALUATION REPORT
A "FIRST TIER" STRUCTURAL AND LIFE-SAFETY EVALUATION
200 G STREET BUILDING

D. CONCLUSIONS AND RECOMMENDATIONS

Appendix II (Item 2) of this report highlights aspects of this building found to be "non-complying" based on the criteria set forth in FEMA 310 *General* and General *Supplemental* Checklists. Both checklists are used because this building is deemed to be located in a region of "high" seismicity based on seismic maps incorporated into the FEMA document. (Note: these same maps are proposed to be included in the upcoming International Building Code, although that document is not yet published). This places the building at a higher level of scrutiny, even though the "Life Safety" only (LS) criterion is used. Refer to of Appendix II (Item 1) of this report, specifically pages 2-4 and 3-6.

> *Note: the establishment of a level of seismicity is a probabilistic and scientific effort undertaken by various governmental agencies using recent USGS seismic mapping efforts. The FEMA 310 criteria defines anticipated ground accelerations based on known faults and specific fault characteristics, and it is from these criteria that the high seismic characteristic of this building's site is classified. Previous UBC seismic classification groups the City of Davis in a "zone 3" area which is not the highest level of anticipated seismic activity. It is beyond the scope of this report to comment on the probabilistic likelihood of the design seismic event FEMA 310 defines.*

Of twenty-three (23) applicable issues listed in the *General* Checklist, eight (8) were found to be complying, eleven (11) non-complying and seven (7) unknown (three of the items are shared by complying and non-complying due to uncertainty). Of fifteen (15) applicable issues presented in the General *Supplemental* Checklist, five (5) were found to be complying, seven (7) non-complying and three (3) unknown. See Appendix II Item 2 for a reproduction of these checklists and the results of each applicable item.

These checklists are developed to bring attention to building components known to be crucial to a building's proper performance as it relates specifically to a design seismic event. Given the number of identified non-complying issues, this report concludes that this building, in its present condition, is not suitable to withstand the design seismic event prescribed by the FEMA document for life-safety occupancy.

Using the Uniform Code of Building Conservation as a guideline, the same various components identified in the FEMA checklists would probably be identified as in need of retrofit and rehabilitation as a result of a more thorough structural evaluation of the building. The difference in analysis and design procedure between FEMA 310 and the 1997 UCBC (for instance) is considerable, yet both are acceptable.

This building's lateral force resisting system, in general, lacks the continuity demanded of more modern structures. This is more a characteristic of this *type* of building than it is a unique characteristic of this *specific* building; the checklists emphasize those areas known to be problematic. Unreinforced masonry buildings (URM's) have been on the forefront of statewide rehabilitation efforts, especially in areas identified with high seismic activity. State law (SB 547/URM Law) has been passed for seismic "zone 4" areas, mandating an inventory and mitigation process for URM's. The City of Davis is <u>not</u> in a zone 4 category and not subject to this program. The enforcement of this law realizes that URM's known to exist in traditional high seismic regions, with some exceptions, are permitted a reasonable timeline for evaluation and rehabilitation.

Should the building's continued use be desired, it is the recommendation of this report that the building undergo a deliberate process of structural evaluation, preferably to an accepted guideline such as FEMA 310, and a mitigation program be developed within a timeline that permits such studies to be properly and reasonably developed.

****

STRUCTURAL & CIVIL
ENGINEERING

CODE REVIEW

11201 GOLD EXPRESS DR., SUITE 201
GOLD RIVER, CA 95670
PHONE (916) 852-0762
FAX (916) 852-0765

8. 12. The next day, the City Chief Building Official wrote the Chens (once again mismatching gender and form of address).

PLANNING AND BUILDING DEPARTMENT

23 Russell Boulevard – Davis, California 95616
530/757-5610– FAX: 530/757-5660 – TDD: 530/757-5666

December 10, 1999

Ms. Lee Chen
P.O. Box 2094
El Macero, CA 96618

RE: Finding of Structural Report for 200 G Street/Actions Required

Dear Ms. Lee Chen:

The City appreciates your cooperation in this matter.

I have received copies of the structural evaluation report for your property from Douglas Krug and Edwin Nicholson and have attached a copy for your use.

Based on the findings of this report, I have determined that the structure at 200 G Street is seismically unsafe. Although the danger of the building collapsing is not imminent, the existing condition dictates that it must be mitigated. You are to provide the Building Division with a mitigation plan within six months of this date with the actual mitigation completed within six months of the Division's approval of your plan. Failure to complete these actions within the established time frame would necessitate follow-up action by the City, which, in a worst case scenario, could result in limitations on the building based on the nuisance provisions of the California Building Code.

Please be aware that prior to completion of the mitigation requirements, the second floor of the structure will not be used for any type of occupancy.

Please contact Mark Wood, Assistant Building Official, or myself if you have any questions.

Sincerely,

Lorin Gardner
Chief Building Official

3) A NEW COUNCIL AND NEW HOPE

Elections for the five seat Davis City Council were held every even year. In the year 2000, three seats were open and the election was held on March 7.

Among the three incumbents with completed terms, Boyd and Forbes sought re-election and Partansky did not. Therefore, at the outset, the prospects for the Terminal Building with a new council were not promising. That is, incumbents tended to win reelection and neither of these two had supported designation.

The election shaped up as a loose coalition of three conservative democrats against an equally loose coalition of three more liberal democrats (called "progressives" in Davis). As the incumbent, Boyd was the de facto leader of the conservatives. Jerry Kaneko, a retired veterinary professor and a large owner of rental housing who had served on the Council in 1994-98 but who was defeated for reelection in 1998, was allied with her. Joe Boyd, a newcomer to Davis who was a professional organizer of educators and who had the considerable monetary support of organized labor, was also allied with her (but not related, despite their shared name).

On the more liberal/progressive side, Mike Harrington, an aviation attorney and member of "progressive" social circles was supported by Partansky and ran as her political heir. Community activists Tansey Thomas and Sue Greenwald had supporters on the left that overlapped with, but were not identical to, the Partansky progressives.

A complicating factor in this race was a local measure labeled "J" that, if adopted, would require a public confirming vote before a new development could be added outside the City's existing boundaries. Seven of the eight candidates in the race supported Measure J. Only Susie Boyd did not.

The outcome was surprising to everyone and indicated a rather divided and diverse electorate. First, Measure J was supported by the electorate 54 to 46 percent. Second, Susie Boyd ran first in the Council race, with 43%, which was in the range of the declining percent of votes recently received by first-place finishers (Lofland, 2000: 9). But, her two conservative allies trailed at fifth and seventh places in the eight-candidate field.

Third, the three "progressives" ran second, third, and fourth, with Harrington and Greenwald elected.

Fourth, incumbent Stan Forbes, a rare registered Replublication in a Davis Council race, ran a surprisingly weak sixth. Positioned as a liberal Republican who was not clearly aligned with either the Boyd or Partansky tendencies, he was the odd man out.

Future growth, its control, Measure J, and which of the candidates could best deal with these matters were the overarching topics of the campaign. The Terminal Building was not an issue and preservationists did not seek to inject it into the campaign.

However, the election results cheered preservationists. Harrington publicly supported designating and preserving the building, as did Greenwald, who was a long-time advocate of the downtown. In replacing Forbes, the preservationist side had grown at least one vote stronger (Fig. 8.13).

8.13. *Davis Enterprise* March 8, 2000 report on the City Council election held March 7, 2000. Three of the five seats were up and preservationists were heartened that two of the three newly elected members were preservation-minded. As Pam Gunnell puts it in the story to the right, "we now have a progressive majority . . . "

8.14. The official photograph of the 2000 Council visually displayed distribution of sentiment on the Terminal Building.

The anti-preservationist members are seated on the left and right ends: Sheryl Freeman (left) and Susie Boyd (right).

The pro-preservationists are standing and flank the swing-vote mayor, who is seated in the middle.

Standing to the left: Michael J. Harrington. Standing to the right: Sue Greenwald.

Seated in the middle: Ken Wagstaff.

Harrington, Greenwald fill council seats

By Melanie Turner
Enterprise staff writer

Just after midnight, as final Davis City Council election results became clear, the mood was jubilant at three separate parties for Susie Boyd, Michael Harrington and Sue Greenwald.

Capturing 18.5, 14.5 and 13.5 percent of the vote, respectively, these three will fill the three open seats on the Davis City Council, joining Councilwoman Sheryl Freeman and incoming Mayor Ken Wagstaff.

The new council members will be sworn in on April 5. The current council meets twice more, on March 15 and 22. Top vote-getter Boyd will take over as mayor in 2002.

A total of 19,062 of 30,103 registered Davis voters — 63.3 percent — flocked to the polls Tuesday. That's more than the statewide turnout of 51 percent. During the last presidential primary, 42 percent of voters turned out statewide.

As the final results were tallied, 30 to 40 Greenwald supporters, celebrating at the home of supporter Heather Caswell in South Davis, shouted with glee. Greenwald immediately gathered them together to thank them for their hard work and ask for their continued support. She then danced happily with a friend.

"I really credit this to a team effort," she said.

This marked Greenwald's third try for a council seat. She received 5,965 votes, behind Harrington's 6,379 and Susie Boyd's 8,175.

The race for second and third place was tough to call for much of the night. In the end, there were just 620 votes separating third and sixth place — 1.4 percentage points — indicative of the tight field.

Behind Greenwald were Tansey Thomas with 5,595 votes, or 12.7 percent; Jerry Kaneko with 5,532 votes, or 12.5 percent; and incumbent Stan Forbes with 5,354 votes, or 12.1 percent.

Newcomers Joe Boyd and Peter Carroll finished with 5,051 votes (11.4 percent) and 1,902 votes (4.3 percent), respectively.

Greenwald's campaign manager Pam Gunnell was elated.

"It bodes well for the future of Davis," she said. "I'm incredibly happy that we now have a progressive majority on the council. That's the key. And with a progressive majority, we can do unbelievable things. It's exciting."

8. 15. After a visit from at least one of the Chens (mentioned in the first sentence, below), Mr. Gardner appeared in this letter to believe it was prudent for him to repeat in writing what he had already written to her/him/them the previous December (Fig. 8.12). This seemingly redundant and therefore unnecessary action might be interpreted as a concern regarding clarity of communication. (This aspect loomed larger as matters went along.)

PLANNING AND BUILDING DEPARTMENT
23 Russell Boulevard – Davis, California 95616
916/757-5610 – FAX: 916/758-0204 – TDD: 916/757-5666

March 23, 2000

Ms. Lee Chen
P.O. Box 2094
El Macero, CA 96618

RE: Structural Report for 200 G Street/Actions Required

Dear Ms. Lee Chen:

I enjoyed our conversation yesterday when you were in. Please consider this letter as a reminder of the action required by you prior to the tenth of June 2000. The City appreciates your cooperation in this matter.

On December 10, 1999, you were sent a structural evaluation report on your property at 200 G Street. Based on the findings, I determined that the structure is seismically unsafe and that the existing conditions must be mitigated. You are to provide the Building Division with a mitigation plan within six months, June 10, 2000, and with the actual mitigation completed within six months of the Division's approval of your plan. Failure to complete these actions within the established time frames would necessitate follow-up action by the City, which, in a worst case scenario, could result in limitations on the building based on the nuisance provisions of the California Building Code.

Please advise us of the progress that has been made by contacting Mark Wood, Assistant Building Official, or myself.

Sincerely,

Lorin Gardner
Chief Building Official

8. 16. Letter to Lorin Gardner from Grace Ghen dated April 3, 2000.

April 3, 2000

Lorin Gardner, Chief Building Official
City of Davis Building Department
23 Russell Blvd.
Davis, California 95616

RE: Structural Report for 200 G Street

Dear Mr. Gardner:

Thank you for your letter of March 23, 2000. With respect to the structural evaluation report dated December 10, 1999, I understand that I am to provide you with a mitigation plan prior to June 10, 2000. I will make a decision regarding this issue within the next two months.

At this time, I am still weighing my options (and costs) with respect to any action I might take. Should I decide to postpone the seismic upgrade work, it will be to undertake an alternative route to develop the property and to provide a safer building in the longer term.

Thank you for your patience and understanding in this matter.

Sincerely,

Grace Chen

4) CITIZEN ACTION STARTS IN ERNEST

The question of the structural condition of the building and how now to proceed had brought matters to something of a standstill in March and April of 2000.

But the lull began to end when two of the business owners renting shop space in the Terminal Building started to react to the uncertainly of their circumstances. Specifically, Heather Caswell, owner of The Wardrobe, a women's clothing store, and core member of a citizen's group named Save Davis, initiated a series of actions.

C.C. AGENDA

DATE: 4-26-00

ITEM NO: 12

DATE: 4/19/00

TO: Davis City Council

FROM: Heather Caswell, owner, The Wardrobe
Rose Anne DeCristoforo, owner, Natural Food Works
204, & 206 G St
Davis, Ca. 95616

SUBJECT: Terminal Hotel

As we enter the 21st Century, a new chapter in Davis' history has begun, and we are all a part of it. What exciting opportunities lie ahead.

In our opinion, it is up to the City Council to lead our community through the challenges we face. As dedicated downtown business owners, and as active members of the community, we urge the city council to take responsibility for the fate of the Terminal Hotel.

As you are aware, last year the owners of the Terminal Hotel were granted a demolition permit. At that time, much information was lacking, especially related to costs involved in building a new structure vs. restoring the existing one.

Even though they have paid for a second engineer's report, required by the city, the owners are at a standstill. But, with more information available, including the exorbitant costs of demolition and building a new structure, the owners are willing to re-examine their options.

After much investigating, and review of similar projects with historical experts, we feel confident the city could create a powerful and positive outcome for the landlord, the merchants and the downtown by working more closely with the parties involved in this project.

Downtown design workshops, held in the past six months, have provided much more information related to our city's design concepts. The workshops revealed an overwhelming interest in preserving our downtown's character and, implicitly, preserving our historical buildings.

Similarly, the Davis Downtown Business Association has applied for membership in the California Main Street program. This program, which is dedicated to preserving America's downtowns, operates on the proven principle that historic, traditionally designed central business districts provide strong economic health. The DDBA has shown support for, and great interest in, following the Main Street guidelines for historical preservation.

We propose that the City Council direct city staff to issue redevelopment funds in order to finance a professional historical evaluation of the Terminal Hotel. This action would provide the owners with critical information related to costs of preservation. This would be a step toward a healthier downtown.

The Terminal Hotel is the most recent heritage building in our downtown to face a challenging fate. Though we try not to be attached to the outcome, we feel that, with more time, more money, and more information, we can help create a more successful downtown.

We encourage the city council to represent the best interests of the community. Let's honor the Terminal Hotel's history so that we all in turn can honor ourselves and our future.

Respectfully submitted,

Heather Caswell   *Rose Anne DeCristoforo,*

Heather Caswell   Rose Anne DeCristoforo,
for The Wardrobe   *for Natural Food Works*

---

8. 17. In this April 19, 2000 public letter to the Council, two Terminal Building business owners call for a professional assessment of how the building might be redeveloped.

8.18. Save Davis leaflet on half a sheet of yellow paper circulated in Downtown businesses in April, 2000.

Did you know that the Terminal Hotel's fate may be terminal?

Currently downtown Davis is in a challenging position. In the fall of 1999 the city granted a demolition permit to the owners of the Old Aggie Hotel (Natural Food Works, The Wardrobe, La Esperanza tenants). The Historical Commission had voted unanimously to designate this heritage building into a historic landmark. Meanwhile Davis is soon to become a Califorinia Main Street City who's primary ethic is preservation. With new city council members on board there seems to be a new sentiment for greater appreciation of our historic resources.

We already know that Sue Greenwald and Mike Harrington are interested in preserving the Terminal Hotel. We are encouraging the Mayor, Ken Wagstaff to join this effort. Please help by calling or emailing Ken Wagstaff.

Ask the City to require more time to determine the best outcome for the building and all concerned.
Ask to sponsor the Terminal Hotel on the meeting agenda for a public hearing.
Write a letter to the editor requesting that we preserve this building.

Ken Wagstaff: phone: 758-3722, fax: 758-0534, email: kjwag@dcn.davis.ca.us

Davis Enterprise: editor@davis.com

8.19. Heather Caswell took the lead in involving outside-Davis professionals in providing assessments of the Terminal Building

Here we see a fax of a letter to her from a San Francisco architect who specialized in feasibility studies of older commercial buildings.

Caswell duplicated and distributed many documents of this kind to anyone interested.

A campaign for a feasibility study had now begun.

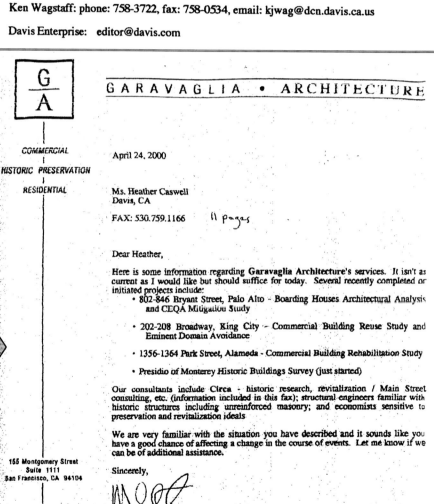

GARAVAGLIA • ARCHITECTURE

COMMERCIAL
HISTORIC PRESERVATION
RESIDENTIAL

April 24, 2000

Ms. Heather Caswell
Davis, CA

FAX: 530.759.1166   11 pages

Dear Heather,

Here is some information regarding **Garavaglia Architecture's** services. It isn't as current as I would like but should suffice for today. Several recently completed or initiated projects include:

• 802-846 Bryant Street, Palo Alto - Boarding Houses Architectural Analysis and CEQA Mitigation Study

• 202-208 Broadway, King City - Commercial Building Reuse Study and Eminent Domain Avoidance

• 1356-1364 Park Street, Alameda - Commercial Building Rehabilitation Study

• Presidio of Monterey Historic Buildings Survey (just started)

Our consultants include Circa - historic research, revitalization / Main Street consulting, etc. (information included in this fax); structural engineers familiar with historic structures including unreinforced masonry; and economists sensitive to preservation and revitalization ideals

We are very familiar with the situation you have described and it sounds like you have a good chance of affecting a change in the course of events. Let me know if we can be of additional assistance.

Sincerely,

Michael A. Garavaglia, A.I.A.
Principal, Garavaglia Architecture

155 Montgomery Street
Suite 1111
San Francisco, CA 94104

415.391.9633
Fax 415.391.9847
mike@garavaglia.com
www.garavaglia.com

MICHAEL A. GARAVAGLIA, A.I.A.
PRINCIPAL

8.20. The reality of the uncertainty of the future of the Terminal Building was finally starting to hit home. Even the venerable (and very cautious) Yolo County Historical Society finally took a stand in early May (prodded by Heather Caswell's personal appearance before and appeal to its Board).

Yolo County Historical Society

Post Office Box 1447   Woodland, California 95776

11 May 2000

Davis City Council
Davis City Hall
23 Russell Blvd
Davis, CA 95616

Dear Council Members,

The Board of Directors of the Yolo County Historical Society voted at its May 8th meeting to express support for the preservation of an historic resource, the Aggie (Terminal) Hotel, and to urge the City of Davis to preserve it as an integral part of down town.

Sincerely yours,

BJ Ford, President

cc. Davis Planning Commission
    Davis Historic Resources Commission

8.21. Also in May, it came to light that City Council member Susie Boyd was circumspectly working to bring about demolition. In this note circulated to various parties, Boyd promoted the views of a demolition-disposed Woodland architect named Bill McCandliss.

May 17, 2000

Telephone conversation with Architect Bill McCandliss re: Terminal Hotel

Impractical to save just the wall because it is an unreinforced masonry building.

A study could determine a range of reasons for and against..
I have done a lot of preservation (including the Hotel Woodland)
The building could be saved. The question is whether it warrants being saved.
> **It has no architectural significance.**
> **It is not a great building.**
> **It does not have significant architectural detail.**
> **It has not been the scene of historical events.**

It would cost as much to save as to build a new one.

There was a similar vacant building in Merced. A $20,000.00 study was done to determine whether to save. Outcome: costs to save or to build a new building were virtually the same.

"My personal feeling about that corner—a new building would be better".

8.22. At long last, there was a City response to the call for a feasibility study. Unfortunately, it was only a promise to consider it.

REDEVELOPMENT AGENCY
23 Russell Boulevard – Davis, California 95616
916/757-5610 – FAX: 916/758-0204 – TDD: 916/757-5666

May 18, 2000

Heather Caswell
Owner, the Wardrobe
206 G Street
Davis CA 95616

Rose Ann DeCristoforo
Owner, Natural Food Works
204 G Street
Davis CA 95616

RE: Terminal Hotel Building, 200 G Street

Dear Heather and Rose Ann:

Your letter to the Redevelopment Agency Board of April , 2000, has been referred to me for response. Thank you for writing, and Heather, thank you for taking the time to meet with me last Tuesday. I appreciate your willingness to devote personal time for the betterment of the downtown and the Davis community.

Your idea of commissioning a feasibility study of preserving the Terminal Hotel is an interesting one that has caught the attention of city staff and decisionmakers. Mayor Ken Wagstaff has begun a series of meetings with city staff and the building's owner to investigate this possibility. He is also exploring the option of requesting the Redevelopment Agency Board authorize some limited financial assistance to this study. I believe the building owner has had preliminary conversations with a local architect experienced in both historic preservation and new construction, with the goal of identifying alternatives that work best for the site and the city.

We will continue to work with the property owner in exploring options for the building and the site. If this item is scheduled for a future Redevelopment Agency agenda, I will be sure to send you a copy of any staff report. Again, thank you for your interest in the health of downtown Davis and the community as a whole.

Sincerely,

Katherine Hess
Planning and Redevelopment Administrator, AICP

C: Bill Emlen, Planning Director
     Esther Polito, Cultural Resources Manager

8.23. *Davis Enterprise*, May 24, 2000. Mr. Barnes was the editor of a Davis "alternative" newspaper named *The Flatlander* that was far to the left of the *Davis Enterprise*.

Save the hotel

The Terminal Hotel is a building that is worth putting public money into for the sake of our downtown's spirit. This is a building worth saving!

Martin Barnes

Davis

8.24. *Davis Enterprise* letters, May 25, 2000.

THURSDAY, MAY 25, 2000

Save our heritage

I recently learned that the Terminal Hotel located on G Street is scheduled for demolition in the near future. This building was unanimously designated a historical landmark by the Historical Commission.

The architectural richness of that part of downtown is one of the things that makes Davis special, not to mention the unique Davis business establishments (La Esperanza, Natural Food Works and The Wardrobe) that are tenants.

The cost for bringing the building up to current earthquake standards is minimal. Clearly it is a case of a developer wanting to tear down a historical landmark in the hopes of rebuilding and moving in higher-rent chain store tenants.

It is my hope that a city with a consciousness for history, art and culture will not allow this process to go forward. I appeal to Ken Wagstaff and the City Council to stop this demolition of an integral part of Davis heritage.

Jon Fenske

Davis

A citizen's appeal

The following is a copy of a letter to Mayor Ken Wagstaff:

This is to request that you do all you can to prevent the demolition of the Old Aggie Hotel. Davis is rapidly developing new surrounding growth areas but it would be a terrible shame to lose, from the Core Area, the flavor of the original Davis. We've restored the train station, and it would seem fitting to keep the Old Aggie Hotel as a part of that era and decor.

Please, vote to preserve this building and encourage the owners to pursue other alternatives. I also encourage you to support the use of city redevelopment funds for the purpose of saving the hotel as a landmark. It would certainly be a nice legacy for you as mayor.

Thank you and good luck.

Donna Turcot, Davis

5) THE OWNERS REACT

At the time of the designation hearing before the HRMC, the Chens were being advised by Davis architect Maria Ogrydziak. Well known for her daring post-modern structures, her relation with the owners apparently did not gell. As the May 17 note by Susie Boyd (Fig. 8.21) intimates, an architect named Bill McCandless from the nearby city of Woodland appeared to have entered the picture in May.

He made his involvement public in a letter to Mayor Wagstaff dated May 25, 2000. It is reproduced below as Fig. 8.25. At least three aspects of this document might engage our attention.

First, we see that public copies were sent to Grace Chen, Susie Boyd, and Heather Caswell. Together with the Mayor, this would seem to be Mr. McCandless' conception of the four major players in this drama as of May 25. Curiously, Lee Chen was not on this list. Even more puzzling, Susie Boyd was, although she had no more official relation to this matter than the three members of the Council who were not listed. But, her listing obviously implied that she was on the short list of key players.

Second, in this letter McCandless clearly favored demolition. His view was based on several surmises about the economics of the matter for which he presented no data. Instead, he tacitly assumed the kind of data that would be provided by a feasibility study, which did not in fact exist.

Third, he did not mention that in situations of this kind a feasibility study was the "of course" and ordinary course of action. It was a puzzling omission for someone who was a professional in matters of this sort.

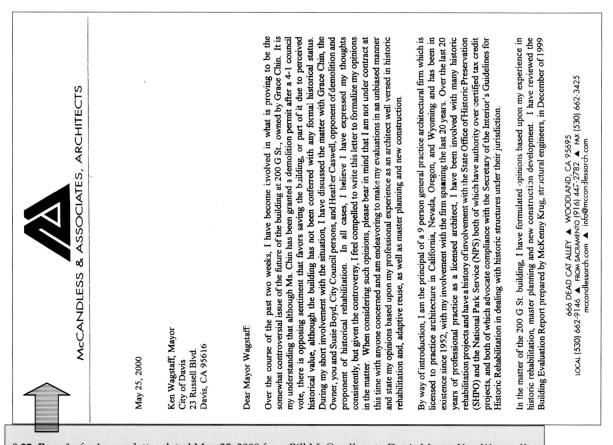

8.25. Page 1 of a 4 page letter dated May 25, 2000 from Bill McCandless to Davis Mayor Ken Wagstaff.

Aside from expense feasibility issues, the implications of renovation verses demolition/new construction to City of Davis downtown planning issues and the streetscape in general should also be of prime consideration. As the building currently exists all original storefronts face the G St. side with secondary windows and entry to apartments elevated ½ story above the street facing 2nd St. The H St. side which faces the train depot is the back side of the original building and presents a back alley look. If the building is to be retained and rehabilitated as an historic building according to Secretary of the Interior's standards, the potential for site development could be severely restricted by rehabilitation efforts. If the building is to be rehabilitated under the standards, tearing down any part of the original building to open all 3 street sides as storefronts would be non-compliant. However, if the building is to be rehabilitated independent of any state certified process, partial building rehab/partial demolition-new construction scenarios would be possible, although they would present some added costs. If the building is to be demolished, obviously new construction would present a variety of options for building design which could feature primary street frontage on G St., 2nd St. and H St. without the inhibitive features present in the existing building which presents a front face to only one street.

Also worthy of consideration in this matter are the property owner's desires and entitlements. To date, Grace Chin has faced building repair or condemnation and has chosen, for development potential purposes, to pursue demolition and new construction. Her stated vision for the site is to construct a new mixed use building with commercial/retail space below and residential use above which will feature a design with 3 prominent street elevations to maximize street frontage potential. Of her particular interest is to have a building that presents a pleasing welcoming face to the train depot rather than a back alley look as the existing building currently does. Ms. Chin has been granted a demolition permit and has subsequently made arrangements to have her tenants vacate the building by mid-July when she intends to demolish the building and as has been expressed to her, she will be well within her rights to do so.

The final and perhaps most important issue I would like to touch on is that of historic significance. The existing building can be characterized as a low style transitory hotel which most likely serviced traveling salesmen and/or interim workers during the early part of the 20th century. As such, there is no doubt that the building has a particular history as all old buildings do. Architecturally speaking, however, the building is devoid of much character and its' structural configuration is not conducive to redevelopment without major alterations which may or may not be acceptable under the Secretary of the Interior's Standards for Rehabilitation. The building at this time has not been conferred with historic status and has in fact been denied such status by the City of Davis, if the building was to be conferred with historic status by the City of Davis, the City would be responsible for negotiations with the owner to establish partial or total building rehabilitation and how such efforts would be accomplished. Of all issues involved, the question of historic significance is the most sensitive as aesthetic value (which in and of itself subjective) and historic importance must be evaluated on their own merits. It is my understanding that the City is actively pursuing implementation of the California Main Street Program which focuses on revitalizing downtown areas by using volunteers at a local level to make improvements on everything from window displays to existing building facades. Naturally under such a program, historic preservation efforts can be a key component; likewise, new development should be considered crucial to revitalization efforts and not necessarily be discounted as insensitive or invasive in the context of the existing urban fabric.

In conclusion, it is my considered opinion as a proponent of both historic rehabilitation and new

and am basing some of my opinions on the results of that study as well as my inspection of the building itself.

As I have stated to all concerned from the outset of my involvement, this building could be rehabilitated, as a state and federally reviewed tax credit project, or as a private non-reviewed project. On the other hand, the building could also be demolished and replaced with new construction. In order to evaluate these two options, a number of issues should be considered in either case, which for the purpose of this letter have been distilled to the following: feasibility and expense; implications to City of Davis downtown planning and streetscape; owner's rights and desires and historic and architectural significance.

Having reviewed the Building Evaluation and Report, and visited the site, the condition of the building is obviously directly related to feasibility and expense issues regarding saving the structure or any part thereof. As is the case with most unreinforced masonry (URM) multi-story structures, the building suffers from inherent inability to withstand seismic loading due to the lack of any reinforcement within the walls, and the "soft story" conditions present at the ground level. "Soft story" is the term that refers to a condition where most of a ground level wall plane is comprised of building openings (door/windows) where most of the wall above is solid. In a significant seismic event this condition contributes greatly to building collapse. As is also the case with URM buildings of this vintage, floor and roof structures are not mechanically fastened to the walls and are instead held in place by gravity. This creates an "out of plane" condition in which the walls tend to move out and separate from the floor and roof structures in a seismic event. This building has a few added structural disadvantages to those typically found in URM buildings. The roof structure is very sub-standard as it is comprised of 2 x 4 framing members at 24" on center and has been suffering from sagging and dry rot. Also, there is a significant amount of wall linear footage that is constructed of hollow clay units rather than brick; hollow clay units perform significantly worse than unreinforced masonry, compounding seismic stability problems. The building also features a non-original sidewalk roof cover structure which is unsafe by current standards and aesthetically inappropriate. And finally, the building's "L" shaped configuration contributes to increased lateral loading implications in a seismic event due to differential movement in each wing of the "L" as the building has been declared unsafe by the City, the structure needs to be demolished or upgraded for life safety reasons. If the existing building or any part thereof is to be upgraded, improvements must be made to meet the requirements of the Uniform Code for Building Conservation (UCBC, 1997).

With regard to feasibility and expense issues, the bottom line comparison is between the cost of rehabilitation verses the cost of new construction. This building requires remedies for all structural items mentioned above, as well as a host of other rehabilitation expenses including new electrical service wiring, plumbing and mechanical system, fire protection and replacement of non-original (also structurally sub-standard) street canopy cover. New construction, requires most of the same components. In my experience, rehabilitation of a structure of this size and condition can be as expensive and sometimes more expensive that new construction. I am currently completing a rehabilitation project converting a 1920's high school into a County Administration Center for Del Norte County and rehabilitation costs are running approximately $130/sf, which is well within the range of new construction costs for that kind of facility. Incidentally, that particular structure is poured concrete, which has a much greater inherent structural value than unreinforced masonry.

8.25, continued, pages 2 (bottom) and 3 (top) of a 4 page letter from McCandless to Wagstaff dated May 25, 2000 (pages in the original letter were unnumbered).

development within the urban fabric that unless there is reason significant enough within the buildings' past as a presence in downtown Davis to confer the building with historic status and mandate rehabilitation, the existing buildings' present condition, lack of aesthetic appeal, and limited development potential all point to demolition and redevelopment as the most viable use of the site under the present conditions. This is also consistent with the City's position to date with regards to this building, and the owner's present plans. I would suggest however that it would be wise to enter into discussion with the owner regarding new building development to assure that her vision is consistent with City planning goals and efforts. Naturally, the design review and planning process will help to nurture redevelopment in the best interests of the community. Should the City, however choose to recognize the building as in some way being historically significant, and worthy of saving in whole or in part, the City should be prepared to commit with reason to such a position and also be prepared to work with the owner to facilitate the implications of that commitment as economic feasibility may be at issue, depending upon the extent of rehabilitation required.

Although this brief dissertation is by no means a formal study, I hope it has been somewhat informative. It is not by any means my place to decide the fate of the existing building and the future for this potentially important site, I hope my thoughts will help to assist those involved with their decision to stand by current commitments or develop new ones in a fair and reasonable manner. Should you wish to discuss any aspect of my considerations or have any other questions please feel free to contact me.

Respectfully Submitted,

Bill McCandless, AIA

WHM/gs

cc: Grace Chin
       Susie Boyd
       Heather Caswell

8.25, concluded. Page 4 of 4 pages, letter from McCandless to Mayor Wagstaff dated May 25, 2000 (pages in the original letter are unnumbered).

The pace of action further quickened when, at the Davis City Council meeting of May 31, new member Michael Harrington sought an update on the Terminal Building situation. As shown in Fig. 8.26, he managed to get three votes in support of a status report to be given on June 6.

b. Request for Status Report on the Terminal (aka Aggie Hotel) be Agendized.

Following discussion, M. Harrington moved, seconded by S. Greenwald, to agendize a status report on the Terminal Hotel (aka Aggie Hotel) for the June 6, 2000 agenda. The motion passed by the following vote:

AYES: Greenwald, Harrington, Wagstaff.

NOES: Boyd, Freeman.

8.26. Minutes of the Davis City Council Meeting of May 31, 2000 showing the vote on scheduling a status report on the Terminal Building.

Preservationists viewed this "status report" now scheduled for June 6th as an opportunity for the "new" City Council elected in March (1) to reconsider its action not to designate the building a historical resource and (2) to move forward with a feasibility study.

One part of preservationist strategy was to rebut the expert opinion of architect McCandless with experts of their own. San Francisco preservationist architect Michael Garavaglia was a key participant in this rebuttal. At the invitation of Heather Caswell, he traveled to Davis, talked with Grace Chen, and toured the building. He faxed his much more positive view to Council member Harrington (Fig. 8.27), who provided it to the Council at the May 31ˢᵗ meeting at which he asked for a status report on the building.

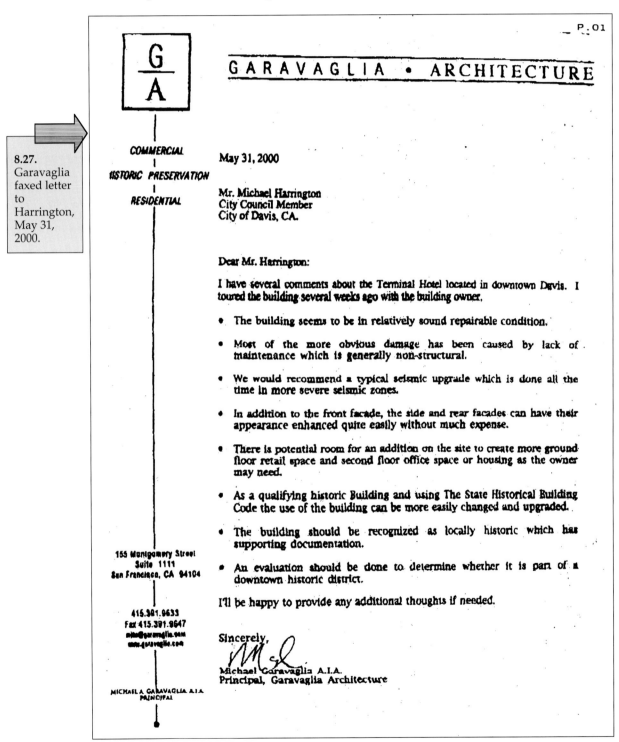

8.27. Garavaglia faxed letter to Harrington, May 31, 2000.

_ P. 01

GARAVAGLIA • ARCHITECTURE

COMMERCIAL

HISTORIC PRESERVATION

RESIDENTIAL

May 31, 2000

Mr. Michael Harrington
City Council Member
City of Davis, CA.

Dear Mr. Harrington:

I have several comments about the Terminal Hotel located in downtown Davis. I toured the building several weeks ago with the building owner.

- The building seems to be in relatively sound repairable condition.

- Most of the more obvious damage has been caused by lack of maintenance which is generally non-structural.

- We would recommend a typical seismic upgrade which is done all the time in more severe seismic zones.

- In addition to the front facade, the side and rear facades can have their appearance enhanced quite easily without much expense.

- There is potential room for an addition on the site to create more ground floor retail space and second floor office space or housing as the owner may need.

- As a qualifying historic Building and using The State Historical Building Code the use of the building can be more easily changed and upgraded.

- The building should be recognized as locally historic which has supporting documentation.

- An evaluation should be done to determine whether it is part of a downtown historic district.

I'll be happy to provide any additional thoughts if needed.

Sincerely,

Michael Garavaglia A.I.A.
Principal, Garavaglia Architecture

155 Montgomery Street
Suite 1111
San Francisco, CA 94104

415.391.9633
Fax 415.391.9647
mike@garavaglia.com
www.garavaglia.com

MICHAEL A. GARAVAGLIA A.I.A.
PRINCIPAL

8. 28. Along another strategic track, the preservationists were gearing up to appeal to the public-at-large with a celebration of Davis history in general and the Terminal Building in particular at the plaza next to the building on Sunday, June 11ᵗʰ. This is the first *Davis Enterprise* announcement of this event. (Because of its importance, this event is described in Chapter 9.)

8.29. Letter to the Editor, *Davis Enterprise*, May 31, 2000.

Repair and restore

The closest thing Davis has to the Statue of Liberty is the (Aggie) Terminal Hotel.

They didn't consider tearing down the statue. Instead, its safety and structural failings were solved by repair and restoration. We should do as well for our historic local point of entry.

Henry E. Bennett, Davis

WEDNESDAY, MAY 31, 2000

Davisites celebrate Terminal Hotel

Enterprise staff

Local residents are invited to join historians and storytellers to celebrate Davis' 1920 heritage and the history of the Terminal Hotel building in downtown Davis on Sunday, June 11, from 1 to 4 p.m.

The event will be held on the G Street Plaza in the 200 block of G Street, adjacent to the former Terminal Hotel. The building, now home to several locally owned businesses, once housed the Terminal Cafe, which was the major social gathering place in Davis during the 1920s.

By a 4-1 vote last September, the Davis City Council rejected a bid to declare the building a historic resource. The building's owners are considering demolishing it and constructing a new facility with retail shops on all four sides.

Attendees are encouraged to wear period clothing. Backstreet Jazz will play music from the '20s beginning at 1 p.m. Refreshments will be available.

A special commemoration of the Terminal Hotel, moderated by Yolo County Supervisor Dave Rosenberg, will begin at 3 p.m. Local residents are invited to share memories of their experiences with the hotel during a special open mike period.

Presenters include historical storyteller Jean Jackman, Davis Enterprise columnist Gerald Heffernon and other local historians and leaders.

The event is sponsored by The Wardrobe, Natural Food Works and La Esperanza, and partially funded by the Davis Downtown Business Association. For more information, call Heather Caswell at The Wardrobe. 756-1128.

Wednesday, May 31 and the days just before and after it were action-filled. At the same time the preservationists were taking action, Mayor Wagstaff was meeting and talking once more with the Chens. Lee Chen memorialized one of these meetings in his letter to the Mayor dated May 31st (Fig. 8.30).

As I read it, the letter in Fig. 8.30 seemed clearly to state that he, Chen, had no plans to save any part of the building.

Curiously, this same day I received the phone call from Mr. Chen that I described earlier (regarding Fig. 8.9) as resulting from the public relations advice Wagstaff was giving him.

On the phone with me at about 5:00 p. m., Mr. Chen was friendly and gracious and I heard him say he was most definitely interested in the possibility of a "facadectomy" of the building's west wall. The only question was the financing and he hoped that City might be able to help.

In addition, he expressed the belief that the Arch Mural on the north wall could be removed and therefore saved.

With these hopeful messages, our conversation concluded. Obviously, however, his letter reproduced as Fig. 8.30, said something different than what he said to me, as did the slight revision of it published as a Letter to the Editor in the *Enterprise* the next day (Fig. 8.31).

AGGIE ENTERPRISES, INC.
P.O. BOX 2094
EL MACERO, CA 95618

May 31, 2000

Mr. Ken Wagstaff, Mayor
City of Davis
Davis, CA 95161

Dear Mr. Mayor:

Thank you for meetings with us to discuss the plan for the Aggie Hotel Building at the Second and G Streets.

As we stated in the City Council meeting last year, we would try to save the building as long as it was cost effective. We have talked to Mr. McCandless, the architectural firm which restored the Woodland Hotel. According to his opinion, it is not feasible to save any part of the building to make it economically worthwhile. We thought it might be possible to save the west wing of the building (the side faces G Street), but in order to do that we have to demolish the rest of the building by hand to preserve the wall. It will be too costly.

We understand your concern regarding the future plan of the building. We are in preliminary discussion with an architect and hope to have a design rendering in the near future. The new building will emphasize its orientation which will serve as a main entrance from the Train Depot, with a "open arms" design. We realize that people are sensitive to the size, the shape, the color and material of the new building, especially its compatibility to its historical surroundings. Therefore, we will discuss the plan with planning and cultural resources staff , and the members of the Historical Commission, to have their input regarding the building's design.

Let me reassure you again, we will try the best we can to work with the City of Davis to produce a project of which all of us , the City, the citizens and us, can be proud.

Sincerely yours,

Lee Chen

8.30. Lee Chen Letter to Mayor Ken Wagstaff, May 31, 2000.

8.31. Chen *Davis Enterprise* letter to the editor published Thursday, June 1, 2000.

LETTERS

Building's future

The mayor has asked us about the status of our building at Second and G streets, the Terminal Hotel, also known as the Hotel Aggie. We wanted to share our response as several persons have also asked.

An official study has shown that the building is not seismically safe. We have been ordered to correct the safety problems. That means retrofit to earthquake standards or demolition. Either way, we have been forced to ask our tenants to move out, for their own safety. We have a permit to demolish the building by the end of July.

As we stated at the City Council meeting last year, we would try to save the building as long as it was cost-effective. We have talked to Mr. McCandless, whose architectural firm restored the Hotel Woodland. According to his opinion, it is not feasible to save any part of the building to make it economically worthwhile.

We thought it might be possible to save the west wing of the building, the side facing G Street, but in order to do that we have to demolish the rest of the building by hand to preserve the wall. It will be too costly.

We understand everyone's concern regarding the future plan of the building. We are in preliminary discussion with an architect and homo to have a design rendering in the near future. The new building will emphasize its orientation, which will serve as a main entrance from the train depot, with an "open arms" design.

We realize that people are sensitive to the size, the shape, the color and material of the new building, especially its compatibility to its historical surroundings. Therefore, we will discuss the plan with planning and cultural resources staff, and the members of the Historical Commission, to have their input regarding the building's design.

Let me reassure you again, we will try the best we can to work with the city of Davis to produce a project of which all of us — the city, the citizens and us — can be proud.

Lee Chen
Davis

8.32. Letter to the Editor, *Davis Enterprise*, June 1, 2000.

We must speak up

We care very much for both the downtown and the historic heritage of Davis. When a building designated by the city's Historical Commission as a historic landmark is threatened with demolition, we must speak up!

We urge the mayor and city staff to help the owners of the Old Aggie Hotel with bringing the building up to safety code.

Craig and Darien Blomberg
Davis

The Council's request for a June 6th "status report" on the Terminal Building meant that a member of the City's staff had to assemble an account of the situation. This task was assigned to Esther Polito. Her report, submitted to the City Manager on June 1, 2000, is reproduced as Fig. 8.33.

Memorandum

June 1, 2000

TO: City Manager John Meyer

VIA: Jeanie Hippler, Parks and Community Services Director

FROM: Esther Polito, Cultural Services Manager

SUBJECT: Status Report on the Terminal Hotel, also known as the Hotel Aggie, 200 G Street

At the Council's request, I am providing an outline of recent activities regarding the Terminal Hotel and the status of the owners' current plans for the building.

In summary, the City Council held a public hearing last September to consider designating the building as an historical resource. Building owners Grace and Lee Chen described the building's structural problems and explained their wish as owners to replace the old building with a new structure. Following the hearing, historical designation was denied.

Additional structural evaluation was requested by the city and completed in December. The Chens received a demolition permit in November that originally expired in May and was recently extended until July 31, 2000.

At this time, the owners favor demolition over seismic stabilization. Tenants have been given until July 15 to vacate their stores. A demolition contractor has been hired and asbestos abatement preparatory to demolition has begun. Grace Chen confirmed to staff as recently as Tuesday, May 30, that she expects the building to be demolished by the end of July. In a letter dated May 31, Lee Chen describes their plans for a new building (attachment 5 to this report).

It is relevant to note that the issuance of a demolition permit is a ministerial action in the City of Davis for all structures except designated historical resources. No environmental analysis is needed.

The building has three retail tenants: La Esperanza, The Wardrobe and Natural Food Works. The owner of La Esperanza has decided to close her restaurant, concentrating her efforts on her other Davis location in University Mall. She has stated that she would be interested in returning to the site if space is available in the future. Owners of The Wardrobe and Natural Food Works are both still looking for suitable locations. There is also one residential tenant whose plans have not been confirmed by staff.

8.33. Staff "Status Report" on the Terminal Building, June 1, 2000. It consisted of 3 pages, one of which is above and the other two of which are on the next page.

City Council Memorandum, June 1, 2000
SUBJECT: Status Report on the Terminal Hotel, also known as the Hotel Aggie, 200 G Street
Page 2 of 3

Outline of Recent Actions:

- **Historical Resources Management Commission Public Hearing (June 21, 1999):** HRMC held public hearing re: designating the structure an historic resource. The Chens attended with Architect Maria Ogrydziak. They described plans to demolish building and replace it with three-story structure and submitted a letter from Sky Engineering dated May 28, 1999, describing significant safety concerns. The Commission recommended designation at the lower level of historical resource, which would ultimately delay demolition a maximum of 360 days.

- **City Council Public Hearing on designation recommendation (Sept 15, 1999):** City Council held public hearing. A motion to deny designation was approved by a vote of 4 to 1 (Partansky opposed).

- **Demolition Permit issued (Nov. 1999):** The Chens hired a demolition contractor and received demolition permit on Nov. 24, 1999 (original expiration date May 23, 2000).

- **Further structural evaluation required by city (November 1999):** City's Chief Building Official required the Chens to have additional engineering evaluation done to determine safety to occupants. Engineering Evaluation by McKenny Krug Structural Engineers received December 9, 1999, verified significant seismic stability concerns.

- **Plan to stabilize building required by city:** The Chief Building Official required that the Chens develop a plan to mitigate seismic stability problems by June 10. Alternative to stabilizing building by June 10 is vacating the building until stabilization is complete.

- **Occupancy Extension and Demolition Permit Extension (April/May):** The Chens requested an extension on occupancy until July 15, 2000, to allow tenants to complete term of lease. Tenants noticed that last day of occupancy is July 15. Demolition permit extended until July 31.

- **Asbestos Abatement (April/May):** Demolition contractor began asbestos abatement in basement and second story, preparatory to demolition. First story asbestos abatement is to be completed after tenants vacate.

- **Review and letter by Architect Michael Garavaglia (April/May):** At urging of retail tenants, the Chens and tenants met with Michael Garavaglia, a preservation architect active in California Main Street program. Purpose of meeting was to discuss feasibility of rehabilitating the building. Garavaglia submitted letter to tenant Heather Caswell dated May 3 outlining two optional approaches to completing a feasibility study.

- **Review and letter by Architect Bill McCandless (May):** The Chens discussed feasibility options with Bill McCandless, Woodland architect with historic preservation experience. McCandless wrote letter to Mayor Wagstaff on May 25 describing rehabilitation difficulties and outlining choices, including a summary statement that the current state of building and

---

City Council Memorandum, June 1, 2000
SUBJECT: Status Report on the Terminal Hotel, also known as the Hotel Aggie, 200 G Street
Page 3 of 3

the decision of the city not to confer historic status appear to point towards demolition and redevelopment.

- **Second letter from Michael Garavaglia (May 31):** In a letter to Councilmember Harrington dated May 31, Garavaglia provided brief comments supporting the feasibility of building rehabilitation.

- **Status Letter from Lee Chen (May 31):** In a letter to Mayor Wagstaff dated May 31, Mr. Chen describes their study of rehabilitation options and their conclusion to redevelop the site with a new building with an "open arms" design that will be compatible with its historical surroundings. The Chens confirm that they will continue to consult with staff and members of the Historical Commission on compatibility and design issues.

Outline of Future Actions:

- **June 7:** Davis Downtown Business Association board to discuss taking a position on encouraging further feasibility study of rehabilitation versus redevelopment.

- **June 11:** Community members led by tenants have planned a celebration of the building's history. The event is partially funded by the Davis Downtown Business Association.

- **July 15:** Last day of occupancy.

- **End of July:** Demolition likely as per Grace Chen in conversation with me on May 30.

- **Plans for replacement structure:** The Chens have indicated a desire to begin planning for a new building in the near future. Economic analysis and project scoping need to be done.

- **Status of mural:** Council had previously requested that staff advise on whether the large Davis Arches mural located on the building's north wall could be saved. Based on several informal discussions with art conservators, I believe that the costs for saving this mural would be prohibitive. However, the artist, Terry Buckendorf, has indicated an interest in repainting the mural at a new location. Staff is currently working to identify possible sites. The artist will be visiting Davis in June and will check out options at that time. In the meantime, I have contracted with Axiom Photography to photo-document both the mural and the building.

Attachments:
1. Photos of Terminal Hotel
2. City Council Staff Report dated Sept. 8, 1999 and HRMC minutes dated June 21, 1999
3. Letters from Chief Building Official and Engineering Reports
4. Letters from Architects Garavaglia and McCandless
5. Letter from Lee Chen dated May 31, 2000
6. Press Release for June 11 Celebration

\\CHDRIVEDATA\APCS\COMMISN\HSTRESRDES99\2000GST\Terminal hotel Memo to CC.doc

Wayne Tilcock/Enterprise photo

HISTORIC? The two-story brick building at Second and G streets known as the Terminal Hotel was built in 1925. A Western-style awning was added in the 1950s. Below, a photo provided by John Lofland shows the building as it looked in about 1940.

Support mounts for restoration of Terminal Hotel

By Melanie Turner
Enterprise staff writer

Community members have voiced concerns about the old brick building on the northeast corner of Second and G streets ever since the Davis City Council voted last fall against designating the building historic.

The action increased the possibility that the building could be demolished.

In fact, things have been heating up since the building owners, Lee and Grace Chen, took out a demolition permit from the city and notified the building tenants — La Esperanza, The Wardrobe and Natural Food Works — to vacate after their leases expire on July 15.

Grace Chen operates a hair

■ LOOKING BACK: The heritage and history of the Terminal Hotel will be celebrated at a public party Sunday, June 11. **Page A12**

salon in the building as well.

The notice to vacate, however, is mandated by the city's efforts to meet safety standards, according to Lee Chen.

After a seismic evaluation of the building was conducted, the city's chief building official, Lorin Gardner, ordered the Chens to make the building seismically safe. That means a retrofit, or demolition.

The Chens' permit runs out at

See HOTEL, Back page

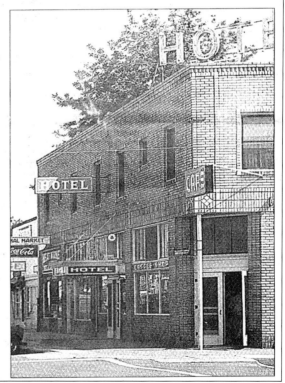

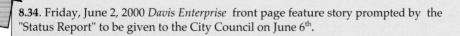

8.34. Friday, June 2, 2000 *Davis Enterprise* front page feature story prompted by the "Status Report" to be given to the City Council on June 6th.

Locals invited to join historians at Terminal Hotel

Enterprise staff

Local residents are invited to join historians and storytellers to celebrate Davis' 1920 heritage and the history of the Terminal Hotel building in downtown Davis on Sunday, June 11, from 1 to 4 p.m.

The event will be held on the G Street Plaza in the 200 block of G Street, adjacent to the former Terminal Hotel. The building, now home to several locally owned businesses, once housed the Terminal Cafe, which was the major social gathering place in Davis during the 1920s.

By a 4-1 vote last September, the Davis City Council rejected a bid to declare the building a historic resource. The building's owners are considering demolishing it and constructing a new facility with retail shops on all four sides.

Attendees are encouraged to wear period clothing. Backstreet Jazz will play music from the '20s beginning at 1 p.m. Refreshments will be available.

A special commemoration of the Terminal Hotel, moderated by Yolo County Supervisor Dave Rosenberg, will begin at 3 p.m. Local residents are invited to share memories of their experiences with the hotel during a special open mike period.

Presenters include historical storyteller Jean Jackman, Davis Enterprise columnist Gerald Heffernon and other local historians and leaders.

Historical exhibits, prepared by Phyllis Haig and John Lofland of the Hattie Weber Museum, will be on display. Exhibit items include restaurant menus, photographs and press reports of key events that have taken place at the Terminal Cafe and Terminal Hotel.

The event is sponsored by The Wardrobe, Natural Food Works and La Esperanza, and partially funded by the Davis Downtown Business Association. Admission is free and all activities are open to the public.

For more information, call Heather Caswell at The Wardrobe, 756-1128.

HOTEL   From Page A1

the end of July, according to Gardner.

Last September's 4-1 council vote was cast despite a unanimous recommendation by the Historical Resources Management Commission to designate the building as historic — the second such recommendation. Then-Mayor Julie Partansky cast the dissenting vote.

Heather Caswell, owner of The Wardrobe, wants to see the building restored. She hopes to persuade the new council to take a greater interest in the building's fate.

"It has not been approached with importance, in my opinion," Caswell said.

On Wednesday, Councilman Michael Harrington convinced his colleagues to place the matter on next week's council agenda for discussion. The council meets on Tuesday next week.

Caswell also has requested that the Davis Downtown Business Association recommend to the council that the city fund a feasibility study in order to determine the costs associated with restoration and other alternatives to demolition.

Laura Cole-Rowe, executive director of the DDBA, confirmed that Caswell has made that request of the DDBA board. Grace Chen is scheduled to appear before the board on Wednesday, when a decision will be made on Caswell's request.

The two-story building, also known as the Terminal Hotel, was built in 1925. Underneath a Western-style awning placed on the building in the 1950s is a typical brick commercial building of its time.

To meet a state requirement, the Chens have been removing asbestos from the unoccupied upstairs. Asbestos must be removed prior to demolition.

About 15 years ago, the Yolo County Health Department condemned the upstairs and it has been unoccupied since. Before that time, the Chens operated a hotel upstairs.

Members of the Davis Historical Resources Management Commission said the building is especially historically valuable because it stands among other buildings of its time that create a time and place in Davis.

The Terminal Hotel sits near the Southern Pacific Depot, and across the street from a designated outstanding historic resource, the Anderson Bank building, and from the brick Brinley building on Second Street.

"It's almost a matched set," said John Lofland, who has authored a couple of books about Davis history. "We're very fortunate to have a set of these."

He added, "If people just had the vision, there's a unique opportunity to create this '20s commercial center."

The council encouraged the Chens to look into the possibility of saving the building or the facade. If neither proved possible for the Chens, a new building would replace the old.

The Chens have owned the building for 20 years. They first came to Davis 34 years ago. Grace Chen said she wants to do what is "best for the city."

They hope to create a welcoming entrance on the side of the building facing the depot.

"The main reason for me wanting to take this building down is Davis is growing. Everybody comes to the depot," Grace Chen said.

She said while the tenants must vacate — at the very least in order for seismic work to be done — they will be her "first priority" when she finds leases for the new building.

"La Esperanza has already expressed an interest to me to save a space," she said.

"As far as I know, no one has an alternative and everyone has had a strong interest in returning to that location," Caswell said.

Caswell said Save Davis and its membership of hundreds — a group of people with a mission to maintain and preserve Davis' "identity and individuality" — fully backs her efforts to see the building restored.

"We want a fair, non-biased evaluation to look at the cost of demolishing versus the cost of keeping it historic," she said.

Said Lofland, "There's a big shift going on in this town and in lots of towns" as cities are more carefully considering the fate of old buildings.

"Virtually any building can be saved," he said. "It's a question of how much you want to spend."

The Chens are concerned that the building's physical condition could make restoration cost-prohibitive.

Michael Garavaglia, principal architect for Garavaglia Architecture in San Francisco, viewed the building at Caswell's request.

He believes it has historic value and could be restored. Said Garavaglia, "Yes, it's homely. But that doesn't mean it's not historic."

He said it's difficult to estimate the cost of renovation, compared to the cost of building new, until more analysis is done.

A feasibility study, at a cost of $5,000 to $10,000, would be necessary to provide that information, he added.

Bill McCandless of Wirth & McCandless Architects in Woodland, viewed the building about two weeks ago at the Chens' request.

In a letter to the mayor drafted last week, McCandless writes, "In my experience, rehabilitation of a structure of this size and condition can be expensive and sometimes more expensive than new construction."

He concluded that unless historic status mandated rehabilitation, "the existing building's present condition, lack of aesthetic appeal and limited development potential all point to demolition and redevelopment as the most viable use of the site under present conditions."

Lee Chen said Mayor Ken Wagstaff has suggested to him the council may consider paying for a feasibility study. "If that's the case, I do not oppose it," Chen said.

THE DAVIS ENTERPRISE

A7

OP-ED

SUNDAY, JUNE 4, 2000

10 reasons
to think again about the Terminal Hotel's future

**By Heather Caswell
and John Lofland**

The future of the Terminal Hotel building is uncertain, to put it mildly. Indeed, its future may even be nonexistent because it is apparently scheduled for demolition by the end of July. We are close to but have not quite reached the point of no return.

We believe we have arrived at this perilous situation by a process of drift and inattention. We have had neither the public discussion, the education, nor the deliberation appropriate to a building as historically and economically important as the Terminal Hotel.

We therefore propose that, as a community, we pause and turn our attention to the building for the purpose of thinking through the purpose of thinking through — really for the first time in a serious way — its future. For those who doubt this need, we point to 10 ways in which public education and deliberation on the issues and possibilities have not been adequate.

Leading expert and lay sentiment alike condemned the building as, in the words of an exhibit at the museum: "ugly and obsolete — a Victorian eyesore, dark, ornate, oppressive. The building deteriorated over the 1950s and 1960s. Plans were laid to demolish."

The exhibit text continues: "But tastes were changing. Victorian buildings were being re-evaluated." The upshot is that in our time the National Building Museum is widely regarded as a magnificent, almost spiritual structure, a breathtaking example of the Victorian aesthetic and its beauty. Indeed, a great many people have seen images of the building and admired it without knowing it: The main hall of the Presidential Inaugural is always held there.

This little story highlights two key points. One is familiar: Beauty is a judgment that varies with place and date. Ugly now can be beauty later, and vice versa.

Two, the rejection of Victorianism and its replacement by various forms of modernism is exact-

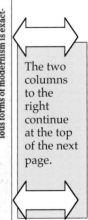

FAR LEFT: the Terminal Hotel, circa 1940.
LEFT: the intersection of Second and G streets, ringed by brick buildings and the Southern Pacific Depot. **BELOW LEFT:** The 200, block of G Street in the 1940s.

Courtesy photos

Hear stories of Davis' past

People desiring to know more about the Terminal Hotel and historic Davis will want to attend the events and view the exhibits that will be at the G Street mini-plaza just north of the building on Sunday, June 11, from 1 to 4 p.m.

At 3 p.m., Yolo County Supervisor Dave Rosenberg will kick off a fast-paced set of three-minute stories on the building. The dozen or so tellers of these three-minute accounts will include Jean Jackman on early Davis hotels and artist Gerald Heffernon on the studio he once had in the building.

8.35. Heather Caswell and John Lofland Op-Ed article in the Sunday, June 4th *Davis Enterprise.*

The two columns to the right continue at the top of the next page.

1. Upgrading cost assessments not yet done. It is standard practice in cases of buildings like the Terminal Hotel to have an appropriate engineering firm evaluate in dollars-and-cents terms how much it will cost to achieve various degrees of upgrading. Achieving seismic safety is the lowest degree of such upgrading (and a virtually standard procedure for brick buildings built before World War II). Even this most basic cost assessment has not been performed.

Without such dollar estimates, it is not possible to think rationally about how best to proceed. We call on the owners, the city and other interested parties to get on with cost assessments for seismic and higher levels of upgrading.

2. Inadequate public education on the actual appearance of the building. Some people think the building is ugly — and they are right about what is most conspicuous there now. This is because it has been massively overlaid with elements that make it ugly.

The "town-and-country-like" shade overhang on its west wall and corner is a much later and plainly horrible add-on. Its south wall is of a pleasing brick pattern, but it has been covered with stucco, and — as bad — several windows in that wall have been covered over.

Some sense of what the building originally looked like — and the state to which it could be restored — can be gathered from the accompanying photograph, taken about 1940, of its G Street front and southwest corner entrance.

3. Lack of understanding of aesthetic eras and of modern, commercial brick architecture. Some feel the building is ugly even in its original condition. This perception reminds of us of the fact that many early 20th century Americans did not like the 1880s-constructed building that is now the National Building Museum in Washington, D.C.

ly what we see in the Terminal Hotel building. The collective American sense of what was beautiful in buildings moved from ornate and curving opulence to clean, linear sparseness. Partly inspired by the linearity of mass production, architecture of straight and bold lines replaced structures of intricate form.

The commercial brick genre exhibited by the Terminal Hotel (built in 1924) expresses this anti-Victorian sentiment. It is not simply a building, it is a considered statement of what its builders thought pleasing and attractive.

Therefore, the claim of an Enterprise letter-writer some months ago that the building "is not architecturally interesting" merely says that this architecture is not interesting to the writer. In contrast, we find it quite interesting — as does a legion of other Davis residents and a great many architectural experts.

4. Lack of perception that there are three matching buildings at Second and G. What is more, the building was intentionally designed to complement what we today call the Anderson Bank building, which is directly across the street at the northwest corner of Second and G (and built in 1914).

The Davis Enterprise lead story of Aug. 1, 1924, reporting that a contract has been let for its construction tells us: "The walls will be of brick, faced with pressed brick somewhat similar to the outside finish of the Bank of Davis (Anderson Bank) building."

Photograph Number Two shows this similarity very clearly.

Four years later (1928) a third commercial brick building was constructed at Second and G. On the southwest corner, we now call it the Brinley Block building and it, also, is in the commercial brick style of the era. Coming later, it goes further in using the color and arrangement of bricks in the facade to create an interesting pattern that is at the same

time not overly-intricate.

5. Lack of appreciation that the Second and G area contains a set of four classic buildings that define historic Davis. In pre-World War II Davis, there was no fourth building at the fourth corner of Second and G. Instead, there was an open, plaza-like space for loading and unloading freight on a loading dock. This openness means that the Southern Pacific Depot occupied the fourth corner of this rectangle/square. Getting off the train, one could immediately see the entire Second and G area and thus be invited into the town.

Sadly, the removal of the side tracks and the loading dock and the construction of the buildings now at and near the southeast corner of Second and G have functioned to turn the city's back on the train station. This was, of course, physically and symbolically appropriate. People in Davis and elsewhere did, in fact, turn their backs on the train.

These facts make it especially ironic and ignorant for some people to claim that the Terminal Hotel is not a worthy building because it "turns its back on the station" (the phrase used in an Enterprise letter some months ago). The truth is the reverse: Davis physically and in other ways turned its back on the station. (Only recently have there been small second

thoughts on having done this.)

6. Failure to think comprehensively about the Second and G area. Taken together, these four buildings form a coherent set of commercial structures that define the Main Street period of Davis history — the 1910s-1940s. The four of them created what was the historic center of Davis before the demise of train travel.

Rather than a lemon of which we must rid ourselves, the need to do something about the Terminal Hotel building should spur us to think positively about possibilities for capitalizing on and enhancing this entire historic center of Davis at Second and G.

Indeed, the enormous investment in historic authenticity already made in the train station would be severely compromised and under-leveraged if we do less than restore and enhance the Terminal Hotel building and, thus, the entire area.

The resources are there. The important question is, instead, Do we have the vision and the will to do something creative with these resources?

7. The lack of appreciation for the strong possibility that the mural of the arch on the building cannot be saved. A series of reports have assured people that the mural of the Davis Arch on the north wall of the building is detachable and can be removed and relocated. This possibility presumably helps to accommodate people to the building's possible demolition.

However, the current best assessment is that the mural is not detachable and therefore cannot be saved.

8. Demolition violates the spirit if not the letter of the new General Plan. Policy HIS 1.4 of the new plan says that the city shall "preserve historic features of the core area and historic districts." Removing a major downtown historic building is obviously contrary to this policy.

9. Demolition violates the spirit if not the letter of the California Main Street Program. We are all appropriately proud that Davis is about to become a member of the prestigious California Main Street Program, a program that develops strategies of economic revitalization of downtowns. One key ethic of this program is historic preservation, especially in the form of capitalizing on a downtown's "historic buildings and human-scale commercial architecture." Removing a major commercial, historic structure obviously violates this ethic.

10. The 1998-2000 council's startling lack of serious deliberation and stunning disregard of the professional assessment of its Historical Commis- sion. We believe that the 1998-2000 City Council failed in its responsibility to provide informed and deliberative leadership in making a decision on a public policy when, in September 1999, it denied historical resource status to the Terminal Hotel building.

Rejecting the unanimous positive vote of its Historical Management Resources Commission and the ample historical documentation provided by the commission and others, the council majority substituted personal preferences in prettiness for objective criteria in evaluating historical resources.

As one of us has written previously, since no informed person disputes the historical significance of the Terminal Hotel building, there is no legitimate reason not officially to signal its import in Davis history (i.e., to bestow the label "historical resource"). Indeed, intellectual integrity requires it.

It is surely ironic for a community conceiving itself as a pre-eminent university city to make a major claim in its official, government history that all knowledgeable people know is false.

We call on the new council to think again about what was done — and to correct this mistake.

In conclusion, we believe these 10 considerations provide more than sufficient reasons to begin a new, serious phase of thinking about the future of the Terminal Hotel building, together with its Second and G context. Perhaps eventually, the Terminal Hotel building can become a universally acclaimed treasured Davis landmark.

— Heather Caswell owns and operates The Wardrobe, a women's apparel shop in the Terminal Hotel building, and was a member of the Civic Arts Commission that helped develop the cultural element of the General Plan. John Lofland is the co-author of "Davis, California, 1910s-1940s," and the author of "Old North Davis."

LOCAL

THE DAVIS ENTERPRISE

TUESDAY, JUNE 6, 2000

▶ **BRIEFLY**

. . . .

Gather for Terminal Hotel celebration

Local residents are invited to join historians and story-tellers to celebrate Davis' 1920 heritage and the history of the Terminal Hotel building, from 1 to 4 p.m. Sunday.

The event will be held at Davis' G Street Plaza, in the 200 block of G Street, adjacent to the former Terminal Hotel. The building, now home to several locally owned businesses, once housed the Terminal Cafe, which was the major social gathering place in Davis during the 1920s.

By a 4-1 vote last September, the Davis City Council rejected a bid to declare the building a historic resource. The building's owners are considering demolishing it and constructing a new facility with retail shops on all four sides.

Attendees are encouraged to wear period clothing. Back-street Jazz will play music from the '20s beginning at 1 p.m. Refreshments will be available, and local residents are invited to share memories of their experiences with the hotel during a special open mike period.

Historical exhibits will be on display: restaurant menus, photographs and press reports of key events that have taken place at the Terminal Cafe and Terminal Hotel.

For further information, call 756-1128.

8.36. Tuesday, June 6, *Davis Enterprise* notice of the upcoming Terminal Building Celebration.

CALIFORNIA PRESERVATION FOUNDATION

Oakland, California 94612

510-763-0972
510-763-4724 fax

www.californiapreservation.org

June 6, 2000

Honorable Ken Wagstaff
City Councilmembers
City of Davis
23 Russell Blvd.
Davis, CA

Re: The Terminal Hotel

Honorable Mayor, Councilmembers:

I am writing on behalf of the California Preservation Foundation (CPF), California's only statewide non-profit historic preservation membership organization, regarding the proposed demolition of the Terminal Hotel. Incorporated in 1976, CPF's mission is to ensure that California's rich and diverse historic resources are identified, protected and celebrated for their history and role in California's economy, environment and quality of life.

Throughout the state, communities are taking advantage of their historic resources to create unique and vital downtown spaces. The Terminal Hotel, along with the other historic buildings at Second and G, form the core of historic downtown Davis and offer a great opportunity to take advantage of the economic and community benefits which historic preservation offers. The significance of the hotel is well-documented, as confirmed by the Historical Management Resources Commission in recommending historic resource status, and there is strong community support for efforts to retain the building.

We understand that the City of Davis has submitted an application for designation as a Main Street Community. As you know, Main Street is a highly successful downtown revitalization program which relies on a basic four step approach. One of the basic tenets of the program is that capitalizing on the historic character of downtown is a key ingredient in creating a lively, pedestrian oriented downtown.

In light of the commitment to historic preservation which the Council has made, both in terms of the Main Street application and the General Plan policy to preserve the historic features of the downtown, it seems shortsighted to allow demolition of this key property without an objective analysis of feasibility of retrofit and reuse. The hotel and the historic area of which it is a part would greatly benefit from an approach which seeks to preserve the important historic features as part of an overall revitalization program.

We urge you to carefully consider the possibilities for retention and reuse of the Terminal Hotel, and the contributions which it could make to the success of Davis' Main Street efforts.

Thank you for the opportunity to comment. Any correspondence should be directed to the California Preservation Foundation, 1611 Telegraph Avenue, Suite 820, Oakland, California 94612-2145.

Very truly yours,

Carolyn Douthat, Esq.
Chair
Advocacy Committee

8.37. June 6, 2000 letter to the City Council from a California Preservation Foundation official urging a feasibility study of the Terminal Building.

8.38.. Bob
Dunning,
*Davis
Enterprise,
June 6,
2000.*

NEWS TUESDAY, JUNE 6, 2000

Bob Dunning
THE WARY I

HYSTERICAL LANDMARK ...
I for one find the current hysteria about the future of the old Terminal Hotel completely inappropriate in a town where owl killers are still on the loose ... I mean, we really do need to prioritize our causes lest we spend too much time on one and not enough on another ...

Still, if the people protesting really feel strongly about this, they ought to put their money where their mouths are and pony up whatever is necessary to preserve what is truly an historic structure ... why this burden should fall to the property owners is unclear ...

Still, it's nice to know there will be a group of Terminal Hotel "storytellers" — most of them newcomers — gathering on G Street this Sunday to tell us everything we ever wanted to know about this brick building ...

Of course, it's only a nouveau old-timer who calls this structure the Terminal Hotel ... mid-range old-timers have always called it the Hotel Aggie, whether it housed Deebo's — Davis' first pizza parlor — or the legendary "A-B" (also known as the Antique Bizarre) ... the building itself is beautiful, but that fake western front has to go ...

No matter how this one works out, it's going to be interesting a hundred years from now when historians try to categorize the architectural style of the Year 2000 ... they'll have to conclude there was *no* architectural style in this era because all historic buildings had to be preserved and all new buildings had to at least mimic the style of the old buildings ...

Which is fine with me ... after all, my humble East Davis hovel is now old enough to qualify as an historic structure, which means some city funds may soon be flowing my way to upgrade — I mean *preserve* — the bathroom ...

6) THE JUNE 6th "STATUS REPORT" TO COUNCIL

Preservationists hoped that the "status report" appearance of the Terminal Building matter before the City Council might open the door to new actions.

The two new members—Greenwald and Harrington—were known to be sympathetic to new initiatives and Boyd and Freeman were known to be against any further Council action.

Wagstaff had voted no in the original denial of designation, but he had a solid reputation as a progressive and as someone who was thoughtful and open to rethinking courses of action. No one really knew the degree to which he might entertain a new initiative, but his open-mindedness on other matters in the past made preservationists hopeful.

As I describe in the chapter on sources and methods that follows Chapter 15, I asked all the principle participants in the Terminal matter to read this book in draft. Mr. Wagstaff did so and responded to the above report of preservationist hopefulness that he at no point reconsidered his position and anyone who thought he might was in error.

This is an important piece of information. It suggests that preservationists were poorly informed and not especially skilled in gathering relevant information on how a person in power might act. Apparently, none of them had sounded out Wagstaff thoroughly enough to know that they were wasting their time in turning out in force at this June 6th Council meeting. Nothing was going to change. And, as can be seen in Fig. 8.39, Wagstaff did not, in fact, change his vote or support any other initiative

Also pertinent to understanding preservationists' lack of accurate information on Wagstaff's views, during the Terminal campaign a rumor was circulating with regard to the relation of his family to the owners of the Terminal Building. The rumor expressed concern that there was a personal bond between the two families that might influence his actions in favor of the owners on the Terminal matter.

I heard this rumor independently from six varied people, most of whom did not know one another well, and each of them had heard it from people other than the other five who told it to me. As is true of rumor as a generic phenomenon, some of those who related it to me did not necessary believe it was true.

Mr. Wagstaff only learned this rumor existed when he read my report in the draft of this book. He has written to me that he is insulted that any such story about him would circulate and that he believes that the rumor is an assault on his integrity.

The facts of the matter are, in his words: "Until I joined the Council I did not know the Chens . . . [in the sense of] . . . a close friendship or business relationship."

I have termed this report a "rumor" because it is clearly an instance of that phenomenon: "an unverified report circulating in a community," or "hearsay not based on definite knowledge" (phrases quoted from the Random House and the Oxford English dictionaries).

This is of course far from the first time that an unfounded, negative story has circulated about a public figure. Indeed, social science studies of rumor routinely give examples of them (e.g. Allport and Goodman, 1946; Rosnow and Fine; 1976, Koenig, 1985; Shibutani, 1966).

Those studies also help us understand how and why stories of this sort arise. Key stimulating factors, according to students of rumor, are ambiguity and uncertainty as to the meaning and implications of important events. Ambiguity and uncertainty are themselves stimulated by what has been summed up as the "three Cs" of conflict, crisis and catastrophe. Significant forms of these include, of course, war, sharp economic downturns, and "tensions between major segments of domestic populations" (Kocnig, 1985: 4). It is well-established that such situations are rife with rumors. (The so-called "basic law" of rumor is that "the amount of rumor in circulation will vary with the importance of the subject to the individuals concerned *times* the ambiguity of the evidence pertaining to the topic at issue" [Allport and Postman, 1946: 34].)

The dynamic at work is that of people trying to make sense of events that trouble them, that they do not understand, and on which they can get little definitive information. When something is puzzling and official, written sources of information on it are silent (or untrustworthy), people try to make sense of events based on whatever bits of information are at hand. In the famous phrase of rumor expert Tomatsu Shibutani, rumor is **improved news** (Shibutani, 1966, 1968).

In the case of this rumor, ambiguity and puzzlement may have been prompted by what some people thought was Wagstaff's inexplicable behavior. He had a strong and positive reputation as a deliberative person and as a supporter of preservation. But, he did not support designating the hotel a historical resource and was, in the view of some, unhelpful on the Terminal matter in other respects. To pro-Terminal Building people this failure to "see the light," so to speak, was a puzzle (a puzzle not presented by Susie Boyd, for example). A preservationist could anguish, "How could such a good guy—our guy—not be with us?"

The rumor of a compromising relationship provided an answer—not the only possible answer and not the right answer, but an answer.

Status Report on Recent Events Related to the Terminal Hotel (aka Aggie Hotel).

Cultural Services Manager Polito, outlined the recent activities regarding the Terminal Hotel and the status of the owners' current plans for the building including an overview of past events. She stated the property owners requested a scoping meeting with staff and their architect.

Lee Chen, property owner, stated they would like to build a project that would be compatible to the surrounding historic area. He outlined some thoughts about how the building could be designed to have an attractive opening facing the depot. He said they do not have costs or a design at this time.

Grace Chen said they would like to fix the building indicating that she has been working for fifteen years to find a project. She stressed the need to use an architect they choose for compatible working relationship.

Fourteen citizens, including members of the Historic Resources Commission and tenants of the building, relating suggestions and expressing feelings about the building.

Following discussion S. Boyd moved, seconded by S. Freeman, to reaffirm City Council's previous action to not grant historic preservation status to the building and asked that the property owners work with staff to preserve whatever historic features of the building that is possible. The motion passed by the following vote:

AYES: Boyd, Freeman, Wagstaff.

NOES: Greenwald, Harrington.

Following further discussion, S. Greenwald moved, seconded by S. Freeman, to reissue the demolition permit and waive the fee for the permit. The motion passed by the following vote:

AYES: Boyd, Freeman, Greenwald, Harrington, Wagstaff.

NOES: None.

8.39. June 6, 2000 Minutes of the Davis City Council Status Report on the Terminal Building.

City to Chens: Work with us on hotel

But gives go-ahead for demolition

By Melanie Turner
Enterprise staff writer

Grace Chen told the Davis City Council on Tuesday she has a dream of creating a building at the northeast corner of Davis Second and G streets in downtown Davis that acts as a welcoming entrance to visitors arriving at the train station.

The Chens have taken out a demolition permit for the former Terminal Hotel building at Second and G and plan to build a new structure, while working to save as much of the old facade as possible, they say.

But others in the community say while they don't physically own that building, they do feel some sense of ownership.

"We own not the physical parts of the building, but the visual, meaningful parts of the building," said Jeanette Schulz, vice chairwoman of the Historical Resources Management Commission. "My concern is, how will we know we're Davis if we cut ourselves off from where we've been?"

"It is the last remaining building of its type in the city," said Wendy Nelson, chairwoman of the historical commission.

The commission recommended last June that the council designate the building as historic. The council denied that request last September, on a 4-1 vote.

On Tuesday, after a discussion that lasted nearly three hours, the council voted 3-2 to reaffirm an action it took last year giving the Chens the go-ahead with their demolition permit.

The motion also included an extension of the demolition permit and a request that the city work with the Chens to try to reuse some portion of the old building.

Councilwoman Susie Boyd, who made the motion, said it's not an economic issue for her, but one of aesthetics.

Boyd was joined in the majority by Mayor Ken Wagstaff and Councilwoman Sheryl Freeman. Councilman Mike Harrington and Councilwoman Sue Greenwald voted no.

Wagstaff said he believes the Chens when they say they want to do what is

See HOTEL, Page A4

8. 40. Wednesday, June 7th *Davis Enterprise* account of the Terminal Building "status report" session before the Davis City Council on June 6th.

The account continues onto the next page.

HOTEL From Page A1

best for the city.

Roughly a dozen people spoke on the matter during an informational item intended to bring the council up to speed on past events related to the building. The matter was placed on the agenda at Harrington's request.

Members of the public expressed mixed feelings.

"The building is falling apart," said Lois Baer, a friend of the Chens.

"That building has been my home for 16 years," said the owner of La Esperanza, Geneva Ayala. "I hate to see it go, but that's the way it is. It is begging to be put to rest."

But Jim Leonard, a Davis resident since 1950, said the city should have a downtown anchor, something that connects the city to its past.

"We have a strong upswell of support to keep this building downtown," said Dick Livingston, a 25-year member of the State Historical Resources Board.

Grace Chen invited members of the community to come see for themselves the building's poor condition.

Her friend, Margaret Ong, said people should be grateful for the mere fact that the Chens are willing to work with the community.

"I am amazed that my friends have persevered," she said of the pressure the Chens have been under. Grace Chen said the controversy has been affecting her health.

Grace Chen and her husband Lee have lived in Davis for 34 years. For 20 years, they have owned the two-story brick build-

ing, built in 1925. It is also known as the Terminal Hotel, or Hotel Aggie.

For the last 15 years the upstairs portion of the old hotel has been condemned. And now, after a seismic evaluation of the building was conducted, the city ordered the Chens to make the building seismically safe. That means a retrofit, or demolition.

At this point, the building's tenants — La Esperanza, The Wardrobe and Natural Food Works — have been given notice to vacate the building by July 15. A demolition permit was extended to allow tenants to stay through the expiration of their leases.

The Chens recently requested that a project scoping meeting be put together with their architect, Bill McCandless, city planners and members of the Historical Resources Management Commission, to take a look at opportunities for the site.

The Chens say they want to build something many people can be happy with.

"As I said last year, we'd like to build a project that's compatible with the historical surroundings," Lee Chen said. "We talked to our architect and learned we may be able to build a new building incorporating some of the old structure."

To what degree they could save the facade Chen said he did not know at this point.

Wagstaff and Boyd emphasized that they'd like to see the Chens' plans as soon as possible.

Heather Caswell, owner of The Wardrobe, pushed for the city to fund a feasibility study. Such a study would enable the city and the Chens to get the information

they need about the costs of renovation versus building new.

Caswell has requested that the Davis Downtown Business Association board of directors take a position on the idea of a feasibility study.

The DDBA board met this morning, Laura Cole-Rowe, executive director, said the board is sending a letter to the council explaining its general support for feasibility studies to be done in the future on projects like this.

"We felt that taking a position now after they made their decision was kind of a moot point," she said this morning.

Joyce Thorp, president of the DDBA, told the council Tuesday evening, "If the Chens were comfortable, and the city was comfortable in having a feasibility study done, I think a third architect should be brought in — someone who knows nothing about any of the reports that have preceded him."

Despite voicing support for a feasibility study during the lengthy discussion, Greenwald did not make a motion to grant one. She said the cost of such a study has been estimated by one architect at between $5,000 and $10,000.

She said afterwards, "After meeting with the Chens I hope we can then pick an architect/engineer to do the feasibility study who comes to it without strong biases."

8.40. Concluded.

CITY OF DAVIS
BUILDING INSPECTION DIVISION
23 Russell Blvd. Davis, CA 95616
756-4907 - For Scheduling Permit Inspections
757-5610 - For Inspectors

IMPORTANT: Always use the permit number below when requesting inspections or information concerning this permit.

PERMIT

LICENSED CONTRACTOR DECLARATION

I hereby affirm under penalty of perjury that I am licensed under provisions of Chapter 9 (commencing with Section 7000) of division 3 of the Business and Professions Code, and my license is in full force and effect.

License No. _____ Lic. Class _____

Contractor_____ Date _____

OWNER-BUILDER DECLARATION

I hereby affirm under penalty of perjury that I am exempt from the Contractors License Law for the following reason (Sec. 7031.5, Business and Professions Code: Any city or county which requires a permit to construct, alter, improve, demolish, or repair any structure, prior to its issuance, also requires the applicant for such permit to file a signed statement that he or she is licensed pursuant to the provisions of the Contractors License Law. (Chapter 9 (commencing with Section 7000) of Division 3 of the Business and Professions Code) or that he or she is exempt therefrom and the basis for the alleged exemption. Any violation of Section 7031.5 by any applicant for a permit subjects the applicant to a civil penalty of not more than five hundred dollars ($500).):

☐ I, as owner of the property, or my employees with wages as their sole compensation, will do the work, and the structure is not intended or offered for sale (Sec. 7044, Business and Professions Code: The Contractors License Law does not apply to an owner of property who builds or improves thereon, and who does such work himself or herself or through his or her own employees, provided that such improvements are not intended or offered for sale. If, however, the building or improvement is sold within one year of completion, the owner-builder will have the burden of proving that he or she did not build or improve for the purpose of sale.).

☐ I, as owner of the property, am exclusively contracting with licensed contractors to construct the project (Sec. 7044, Business and Professions Code: The Contractors License Law does not apply to an owner of property who builds or improves thereon, and who contracts for such projects with a contractor(s) licensed pursuant to the Contractors License Law.).

☐ I am exempt under Sec. _____ B.& P.C. for this reason _____

Owner_____ Date _____

WORKERS' COMPENSATION DECLARATION

I HEREBY AFFIRM UNDER PENALTY OF PERJURY one of the following declarations:

☐ I HAVE AND WILL MAINTAIN A CERTIFICATE OF CONSENT TO SELF-INSURE FOR WORKERS' COMPENSATION, as provided for by Section 3700 of the Labor Code, for the performance of the work for which this permit is issued.

☐ I HAVE AND WILL MAINTAIN WORKERS' COMPENSATION INSURANCE, as required by Section 3700 of the Labor Code, for the performance of the work for which this permit is issued. My workers' compensation insurance carrier and policy number are:

Carrier _____ Policy Number _____

This section need not be completed if the permit is for one hundred dollars ($100) or less.

☐ I CERTIFY THAT IN THE PERFORMANCE OF THE WORK FOR WHICH THIS PERMIT IS ISSUED, I shall not employ any person in any manner so as to become subject to the workers' compensation laws of California, and agree that if I should become subject to the workers' compensation provisions of Section 3700 of the Labor Code, I shall forthwith comply with these provisions.

Applicants Signature _____ Date _____

WARNING: FAILURE TO SECURE WORKERS' COMPENSATION COVERAGE IS UNLAWFUL, AND SHALL SUBJECT AN EMPLOYER TO CRIMINAL PENALTIES AND CIVIL FINES UP TO ONE HUNDRED THOUSAND DOLLARS ($100,000). IN ADDITION TO THE COST OF COMPENSATION, DAMAGES AS PROVIDED FOR IN SECTION 3706 OF THE LABOR CODE, INTEREST, AND ATTORNEY'S FEES.

CONSTRUCTION LENDING AGENCY

I hereby affirm under penalty of perjury that there is a construction lending agency for the performance of the work for which this permit is issued (Sed. 3097, Civ. C.).

Lender's Name _____

Lender's Address _____

I certify that I have read this application and state that the above information is correct. I agree to comply with all city and county ordinances and state laws relating to building construction, and by authorize representatives of this county to enter upon the above-mentioned property for action purposes.

Applicant/Agent Signature _____ Date _____

```
Permit Nbr:        00-   6604
Access Nbr:              116186

Print Date:     9/29/00
Job Address:  200 G STREET
Subdivision:
Parcel Nbr:   70-252-04-    -
Valuation:              5000
  Tenant Name, Nbr:
      DEMO BUILDING
Work Description:
  DEMOLISH NON-RESIDENTIAL BUILDING

  Owner:        CHEN TR ETAL
                P O BOX 2094
                EL MACERO CA 95618

  Contractor:   JOHN'S HAULING
                PO BOX 1522
                DAVIS CA 95617
                (530) 753-3220

Permits:                      Issued:
*DEMOLITION PERMIT COMM/INDUS 6/07/00

Fees Paid:       .00
```

⬆

```
Special Notes and Comments:

DEMO PERMIT FOR 200, 202, 204, AND 206
G STREET.
```

JOB FINAL BY: _____ DATE: _____

THIS PERMIT BECOMES NULL AND VOID if work or construction is not commenced within 180 days from date of issuance, or work is suspended or abandoned for a period of 180 days any time after work is commenced.

8.41. The next day, June 7th, the Chens drew a new and extended-time demolition permit. (The black arrow points to the new issue date.)

A6

THE DAVIS ENTERPRISE

WEDNESDAY, JUNE 7, 2000

FORUM

 LETTERS

Tear down history

I don't understand why people are so surprised and upset about the prospect of tearing down the Aggie Hotel. Don't you realize this is America? We're the country who tears down our history.

In Europe they have structures that are thousands of years old. In America we marvel and are amazed at structures less than a hundred years old. Dumping a bunch of money into restoring old buildings is not the American way at all. But tearing them down and putting up strip malls? A lot of wealthy people (and wannabe wealthy people) call that progress ... often times they call it the American Dream.

I mean, why should we care about stupid old buildings when there's so much money to be made? Demolish away!

Ned Sykes
Davis

8.42. Letter to the Editor from Ned Sykes, native Davisite and frequent commentator on public affairs.

8.43. More commentary by *Davis Enterprise* columnist Bob Dunning, June 9, 2000.

THE DAVIS ENTERPRISE **NEWS** FRIDAY, JUNE 9, 2000

No evidence for this latest charge of racism

FALSE CHARGES ... one individual testifying about the Terminal Hotel fight — he says tear it down — claims this whole fiasco wouldn't be happening to the property-owing Chen family but for a nasty strain of racism in this town ... now, with all due respect to racists everywhere, to terminate or not to terminate the Terminal Hotel has nothing at all to do with the race of the owners ... and making such a charge without foundation does the whole town a disservice ...

Yes, we have racism in Davis ... yes, there is racism everywhere ... yes, many people are much too fanatical for my blood when it comes to preserving this sagging brick building ... but I haven't seen a shred of evidence that any of them are racists ... the individual making the charge should apologize to everyone involved ...

MAD AS HELL ... activist Jean

Jackman took to the city microphone shortly after the allegations of racism (see above) were greeted with a chorus of boos and told the one making the charges that "He'd better lose that racist talk real fast" ... amen to that, Jean ...

Bob Dunning
THE WARY I

EVEN MORE TERMINAL NEWS ... one speaker at Tuesday's council meeting claimed that "A strong wind could bring that building down," referring, of course, to the Terminal Hotel ... since strong winds blow generally from the north around here, Rio Vista has been warned to watch out for flying bricks, not to mention hyperbole ...

STRONG TESTIMONY ... the

high point of Tuesday's meeting, at least for me, came when Sunny Shine hinted the reason for the Terminal Hotel's potential demolition was because we are "afraid of the past" ... wow, was Jerome C. Davis really *that* bad? ...

The lovely Sunny, who certainly brightens my day, said it would be a shame to "build a building that doesn't mean anything" ... in other words, by definition, a new building can't be meaningful ... which means the Terminal Hotel, when it opened for the first time, was also a meaningless building ...

HISTORICAL OR HYSTERICAL?
... folks in Rome, Athens and Cairo are chuckling over the historic designation of a building built in 1924 A.D. ... heck, I have a dining room table older than that
...

— Reach Bob Dunning by e-mail at dunning@davisenterprise.com.

A6
THE DAVIS ENTERPRISE
FRIDAY, JUNE 9, 2000
FORUM

▶ **LETTERS**
....

Historical wealth

I am sad that the City Council has given the go-ahead for demolition of the Terminal Hotel building at Second and G streets, despite the recommendations of our own Historical Resources Management Commission and the urging of many Davis citizens to preserve this historic building, this piece of our community's history.

On opening my mailbox today, I received a wonderful postcard-invitation that pictures Second and G streets in Davis in what I imagine must be the 1940s. The Terminal Hotel building is in the foreground. The postcard announces a celebration of the building to take place there this Sunday from 1 to 4 p.m.

What an enchanting idea, to gather together to see historic photos of the hotel from the Hattie Weber Museum, to hear collected stories of this landmark and our history. Could this experience of our historical wealth move our policy-makers to reconsider? I hope so.

Once it is gone, we can never retrieve it.
Elaine Fingerett
Davis

8.44. Letter to the Editor of the *Davis Enterprise*, Friday, June 9. The picture on the promotional postcard referred to in this letter is the same picture that appears on the verso page of the title page leaf. The text on the postcard appears just below, as Figure 8.45.

A 1920's Festival of Historic Davis and Celebration of the Terminal Hotel Building

Residents are invited to join local historians and storytellers to celebrate Davis' 1920's heritage and the history of Terminal Hotel building on Sunday, June 11 from 1 – 4 p.m.

The event will be located in the G Street Plaza on the 200 block of G Street, between Second and Third streets, adjacent to the former Terminal Hotel, now home to several locally owned businesses. The Terminal Hotel … … was the major social gathering place of Davis, during the 1920's.

Event-goers are encouraged to wear period clothing. Backstreet Jazz will play music from the 1920's beginning at 1 p.m. Refreshments will be available at the event.

A special commemoration of the Terminal Hotel, moderated by Yolo County Supervisor Dave Rosenberg, will begin at 3 p.m. Local residents are invited to share memories of their experiences with the Terminal Hotel during a special open mike period. Presenters include historical storyteller Jean Jackman, local Davis Enterprise columnist Gerald Heffernon and other local historians and leaders.

Historical exhibits, prepared by Phyllis Haig and John Lofland of the Hattie Weber Museum of Davis, will be on display at the event. Exhibit items include restaurant menus, photographs and press reports of key events that have taken place at the Terminal Café and the Terminal Hotel.

This event is sponsored by the Wardrobe, Natural Food Works, La Esperanza and partially funded by the Davis Downtown Business Association. For further information on the event, please call Heather Caswell at the Wardrobe, 756-1128.

Davis Research

8.45. Text on the address side of the postcard referred to by Elaine Fingerett in Fig. 8.44. About a thousand of these cards were printed, placed in stacks at checkout counters in Downtown stores, and mailed. Printed on stiff glossy stock measuring 8 1/2 by 5 1/2 inches, the card proved to be a popular keepsake item and was difficult to keep in stores.

Hotel celebration set Sunday

Enterprise staff

Local residents are invited to join historians and storytellers to celebrate Davis' 1920 heritage and the history of the Terminal Hotel building in downtown Davis on Sunday from 1 to 4 p.m.

The event will be held on the G Street Plaza in the 200 block of G Street, adjacent to the former Terminal Hotel. The building, now home to several locally owned businesses, once housed the Terminal Cafe, which was the major social gathering place in Davis during the 1920s.

This week, the Davis City Council affirmed its decision last fall to allow the owners, Grace and Lee Chen, to demolish the building while preserving as much of it as possible. The Chens hope to build a new facility with retail shops on all four sides.

Attendees are encouraged to wear period clothing. Backstreet Jazz will play music from the '20s beginning at 1 p.m. Refreshments will be available.

A special commemoration of the Terminal Hotel, moderated by Yolo County Supervisor Dave Rosenberg, will begin at 3 p.m. A dozen or so presenters each will offer a three-minute story about the hotel.

They include Jean Jackman, author of "Down Home Tales of Davis," speaking about early days at Second and G; Phyllis Haig, curator of the Hattie Weber Museum, talking about the Terminal Cafe; Davis City Councilman Mike Harrington, remembering student evenings in the late '70s; Former Mayor Julie Partansky, discussing environmental ethics; Audrey Hastings of Hastings' Back Porch, sharing memories of hotel residents; and Jeanette Schulz of the Davis Historical Resources Commission, speaking on modernism and Victorianism.

Local residents are invited to share memories of their experiences with the hotel during a special open mike period.

Historical exhibits, prepared by Haig and John Lofland, an author and local historian, will be on display. Exhibit items include restaurant menus, photographs and press reports of key events that have taken place at the Terminal Cafe and Terminal Hotel.

In addition, attendees are invited to take a look at The Wardrobe's window display, which features a 1920s theme in honor of the building.

"It kind of says thank you and goodbye," says Wardrobe owner Heather Caswell.

The event is sponsored by The Wardrobe, Natural Food Works and La Esperanza, and partially funded by the Davis Downtown Business Association. For more information, call Heather Caswell at The Wardrobe, 756-1128.

8.46. Friday, June 9th *Davis Enterprise* announcement of the celebration of Terminal Building history to be held on the G Street Plaza next to the building on Sunday, June 11th.

7) THE SITUATION

On the eve of the G Street plaza event, preservationists were in the situation of having experienced two forms of preservation failure: designation (the previous chapter) and not obtaining a feasibility study (this chapter).

Both could still **conceivably** be reversed—but neither change was very likely.

There remained, however, still the possibility of saving part of the building in some fashion. In the chapter after the next one, I report how this possibility played out.

9

CELEBRATION SUCCESS

June days in the Sacramento Valley can be very hot and/or have the dreaded, dry and grit-bearing "north wind." Organizers of outdoor events therefore routinely worry whether the weather will favor or hinder. The celebration of Sunday, June 11th "lucked out." The sun was out but the temperature was mild and the wind was quiet.

As seen in Fig. 5.18 and other photographs, the sidewalk just north of the Terminal Building had been widened and landscaped. It was named the "G Street Plaza." Celebration lead organizer Heather Caswell and her associates selected the site as the symbolically and logistically best location to hold the event.

As an event focused on the downtown, the gathering was eligible for (and got) sponsorship by the Davis Downtown Business Association (DDBA). This was important in several ways, not least of which was the free use of several dozen plastic chairs and two shade structures the DDBA employed in other of its promotional activities. Because the DDBA was a quasi-official extension of the city government, organizers had, in turn, free use of City of Davis portable stage units and the otherwise locked City electrical outlets at the Plaza.

The above and other forms of official assistance signal that the citizens involved in the campaign to save the Terminal Building may not have been politically dominant in Davis, but they were not outsiders either. If it is not otherwise obvious in other chapters, these forms of assistance tell us that the debate over the Terminal Building was very much carried on in the mainstream of Davis political life.

1) LAIMA DRUSKIS AND SUNNY SHINE PHOTOGRAPHY

The diverse and variously involved people making up the Terminal Building campaign included two who liked to take photographs and who each assumed the role of event photographer. They were Laima Druskis and Sunny Shine. Between them, they took several rolls of film. I am extremely appreciative of their making those pictures available to me for use in this chapter and I am sorry that because of constraints of space I can only use a small portion.

2) THE OVERALL PLAN

The overall plan of the event was to create a Sunday afternoon of "hanging out" and light entertainment that would climax with an hour of fast-paced speaking **honoring** the Terminal Building and recognizing its role and significance in the community. The event would run some three hours between 1:00 and 4:00 p.m. (And, it was hoped that, in turn, the fact of the event would encourage public-at-large sentiment in the direction of saving the building in some manner.)

Because the Building was constructed in the 1920s and symbolized that period, Caswell and her circle of organizers decided to make "the 1920s" the theme of the event. Two "Twenties" aspects were quite conspicuous.

THE BACKSTREET JAZZ QUARTET. First, a local band, the Backstreet Jazz Quartet, specialized in playing music of the 1920s. The group played in part pro bono and in part paid with DDBA event promotional funds and private donations. They can be seen in several of the following photographs, but particularly in Fig. 9.2.

The fast, upbeat, and amplified music they made was a key factor in creating a festive atmosphere in the 200 block of G Street. They performed an impressively varied repertoire of jazz compositions enhanced by the excellent performance of vocalist Heidi Bekebrede.

1920s-STYLE CLOTHES. Second, in much of the publicity for the event, people were encouraged to celebrate Davis history by wearing 1920s-style clothes. To my surprise, many people actually showed up in at least some semblance of such attire. Therefore, in looking at the following photos do not jump to the conclusion that Davis people dressed oddly in 2000. They were simply trying to appear to be wearing 1920s fashions.

In addition, Heather Caswell did more than operate a women's apparel shop at The Wardrobe. She was also fond of costumes of various kinds and had a stock that she rented out—with access to more on special occasions such as this. She personally undertook to costume a number of people.

3) THE EVENT'S TEMPLATES AND SOURCES

No undertaking is simply made-up or invented *de novo*. Instead, each is molded on and/or borrows from previous undertakings. Such was the case with this gathering.

It drew its features from two main templates for "doing" events. (1) As an aspect of her apparel business, Heather Caswell had previously organized fashion shows and costume parties, as well as having produced theater. She applied portions of these templates to this event in such features as helium-filled balloons, banners written in 1920s style fonts, poetry readings, a popcorn concession, a lemonade stand, and a snow cone concession. I have already mentioned the specialized band with a jazz singer and the 1920s costumes. These source-templates brought an emotional tenor of **upbeat celebration** to the event.

(2) A second template, to which I was disposed, was the political or protest rally. The core feature here is the parade of speakers from constituencies stressing the themes of the campaign. Classic at such events is the table of the campaign's literature. At this event, Yolo County Historical Society publications table filled this role (Fig. 9.12). Exhibits of salient icons are also common. In this case, the icon exhibit was composed of enlarged newspaper reports of aspects of the Terminal Hotel and Cafe through the decades (Fig. 9.6.). (These news stories were seen in chapters 3 through 6, above.)

Contrasting with the first kind of template, the emotional tenor of the rally tends to anger or **indignation**. This, also, was seen, especially toward the end of the event. Overall, though, this gathering amalgamated elements of both kinds of templates, that of the celebration or party and that of the protest rally.

4) THE CROWDS

No one kept a count of the turnout, but my guess, based on having been present and on a study of the photos, is that between one and two hundred people were on the scene at various times over the three hours. Estimating attendance is particularly tricky because people arrived and left at various times throughout the afternoon. Many seemed to have "passed though" or visited rather than to have been there the three hours or a major portion of it.

5) THE THREE-MINUTE SPEAKERS

Advised by several people, I organized the 3:00-4:00 p.m. speaker session. Having attended hundreds of political rallies as a citizen and as a sociological analyst, I approached this task with the strong belief that the bane of rallies—the runaway, undisciplined activist who vastly exceeds her or his allotted time—had to be avoided here.

I therefore built the hour around the theme of telling "three-minute stories." At the point of inviting each speaker, I made "three minutes only" a major point. At the event and before speaking, I further admonished each on this matter. The Master of Ceremonies, David Rosenberg, supported the three-minute rule and built it in at the start as a form of humor. In various photos, one can see he is carrying a cane. In his welcoming introduction, he humorously explained that speakers who exceeded their time would be given the hook (holding up the hooked cane), just as in old time Vaudeville, and pulled off the stage. Indeed, I kept time and signaled Rosenberg when a speaker went over. One did to the degree that Rosenberg started (humorously) to use the hook, whereupon that speaker stopped. Otherwise, speakers were reasonably self-disciplined.

Figures 9.16 through 9.27. present pictures of the speakers, an identifying affiliation, and the titles of their topics. They are shown in the sequence in which they spoke at the event. As one can see, the topics were ordered chronologically, running from the early days of Davis to the present. The progression was also from historical to political or policy. The first eight addressed the history of the hotel. The last four were contemporary and policy-oriented.

The speakers themselves were almost all well known or fairly well known and long-time Davis residents. Scanning Figures 9.16 through 27, the reader can see that these are the names of people encountered in previous chapters as participants in Davis local history and preservation matters.

Each of the three-minute talks were, for varying reasons, contributions to Davis history in themselves and worthy of preserving. Fortunately, they were videotaped (and broadcast) by Davis local access Channel 5 (Davis Community Television) and a copy of that tape is available in the archives of the Hattie Weber Museum of Davis (Fransway, 2000).

6) THE SPECIALLY INVITED WHO DECLINED

As every organizer knows, not everyone invited to speak on a particular day at a specific time is available. Nor, can all those one specially invites mange to attend. Such was the case with this list of speakers and some specially invited guests (who it was hoped would elect on the spot to speak). Among speakers invited, Mayor Ken Wagstaff declined, saying he would be away from Davis that day. Among honored guests who one hoped might speak, Terminal Building owners Grace Chen and Lee Chen likewise declined with the explanation that they would not be in Davis.

7) THE MASTER OF CEREMONIES, DAVID ROSENBERG

For several reasons, the campaigners were extremely fortunate to have David Rosenberg consent to act as the master of ceremonies.

First, his presence in this high-profile role endowed the affair with mainstream import and legitimacy. He had served three terms on the Davis City Council, twice as Mayor, and was, at this time, a Yolo County Supervisor. He had been an associate of California Governor Gray Davis since the days they both served in the Governor Jerry Brown administration and Davis had recently appointed him Commissioner of the California State Lottery, as his director of intergovernmental relations, and as a senior advisor.

Second, Rosenberg clearly loved to emcee events because he did so with some regularity for a variety of groups. As one can infer, groups asked him to do this not simply because he was rather prominent, but because he was entertaining. He was clever with both good and bad jokes, at ease, and quick on his feet with an audience. On this day, he was, in fact, at the top of his game.

Third, we have met Mr. Rosenberg before in this saga. (1) In the early 1980s, he was a member of the HRMC, the only person ever elected to the City Council who had so served. More than almost all Davis political figures, he was both familiar with and supportive of historic preservation. (2) He was no newcomer to the topic of the Terminal Building. He was in the first months of his first term as a City Council member when its nomination for designation arrived there in 1984 (Ch. 6, section 2). The designation failed on a 3-2 vote with Rosenberg joining with the fabled citizen-politician Tom Tomasi in voting yes.

He was so popular as an emcee that he could not accept all such requests. He did in this case, I surmise, because he was a supporter of the cause at hand. In addition, he and Heather Caswell had worked together with success on previous political matters.

9.1. Looking southwest across the G Street Plaza just after 3:00 p.m. Jean Jackman, back to us in the middle right, is speaking. The Backstreet Jazz Band is behind her, under the canvas shade structure. David Rosenberg is on the right, in a white jacket, his back to us. (S. Shine.)

9.2. The Backstreet Jazz Quartet. (S. Shine.)

9.3. poetry reading by Alyssa Nielsen. (S. Shine.)

9.4. Good jazz music inspired a number of people to dance, some quite well, as shown by Brad Powell and Doreen Pichotti. (S. Shine.)

9.5. "Hanging out" on the G Street Plaza. The exhibit of news accounts of events at the Terminal Hotel and Cafe is seen in the upper right. (S. Shine.)

9.6. The starting point of the exhibit on the Terminal Building. (L. Druskis.)

9.7. Boy tending the lemonade stand. (L. Druskis.)

9.8. Sign announcing the event that stood on the sidewalk outside the Wardrobe. Moved to the G Street Plaza. It is also seen in Fig. 10.2.. (S. Shine.)

9.9. Davis Lumber (aka Ace Hardware) sold a wineglass etched with an image of the Davis Arch. Sunny Shine and Laura Cole-Rowe bought a number of them, added their own decorations and sold them at this event. The proceeds went to help defray the celebration's expenses. (S. Shine.)

9.10. If one was going to dress up in1920s costume, then one should have one's picture taken. (S. Shine.)

9.11. They may appear to be drinking wine, but their glasses are empty. They are only hawking fund-raising wine glasses. (L. Druskis.)

9.12. The display table of the Yolo County Historical Society. As can be seen, that Society has a rather extensive publication program. (S. Shine.)

9.13. Another view of the literature table of the Yolo County Historical Society, this one featuring then City Council Member Susie Boyd (on the left). (L. Druskis.)

9.14. Preservation is not all old people. (S. Shine.)

9.15. At 3:00 p.m., Davis Rosenberg started to warm up the crowd for the "three-minute stories." (L. Druskis.)

9.16. "Early Davis at Second and G." Jean Jackman, author, *Down Home Tales of Davis*. (L. Druskis.)

9.17. "Modernism Rejects Victorianism," Jeanette Shulz, Historical Resources Management Commission. (S. Shine.)

9.18. "The Terminal Cafe," Phyllis Haig, Hattie Weber Museum of Davis. (S. Shine.)

9. 19. "My Art Studio at the Aggie Hotel," Gerald Heffersnon, artist and columnist. (S. Shine.)

9. 20. "Memories of Hotel Residents," Audrey Hastings, Hastings' Back Porch. (S. Shine.)

9. 21. "Student Evenings in the Late '70s," Michael Harrington, Davis City Council. (S. Shine.)

9.22. "Ministering at the Aggie Hotel," Rev. John Pamperin, Street Minister. (S. Shine.)

9.23. "Experiences at the Aggie Hotel," Mike White, Historical Resources Management Commission. (S. Shine.)

9.24. "The Building, the Commission, the Council," Wendy Nelson, Chair, Historical Resources Management Commission. (S. Shine.)

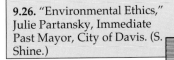

9.25. "Rehabilitating the Building," Richard Hastings, State Park Archeologist. (S. Shine.)

9.26. "Environmental Ethics," Julie Partansky, Immediate Past Mayor, City of Davis. (S. Shine.)

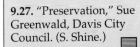

9.27. "Preservation," Sue Greenwald, Davis City Council. (S. Shine.)

"My Art Studio at the Aggie Hotel," Gerald Heffernon's Remarks at the Celebration of The Terminal Building, Davis G Street Plaza, June 11, 2000

I'm a little upset that memories from my adult life qualify as historic recollections. I don't think of myself as being that old. But since I need notes in order to make a 3 minute speech about my own memories, I guess I do deserve those AARP mailings.

I first arrived in Davis in 1982, which to me seems like just last week separated by a week's worth of heavy dreaming. Being an artist, the first thing I needed was a studio. And one of the first possibilities that caught my eye were those familiar tank houses or pump houses, one of which, as you know, is the subject of its own preservation debate.

None of these was available and I started looking around for old warehouses, only to find out that Davis didn't have warehouses. Eventually, through a realtor I came across this building, the Terminal Hotel—or as I knew it then, the Aggie Hotel. I met with Lee Chen and I rented two adjoining rooms with a bathroom in between.

I really didn't give any thought to the building one way or the other, historically or aesthetically. Since I came from the Midwest, it simply seemed like a familiar old building.

Tom Deininger had his photo studio on the first floor in the space where Grace Chen now has her hair salon. I had to enter through Tom's storefront to get upstairs to my studio, which was a nice inconvenience because I was new in town and it gave me someone to say hello to.

One other renter was upstairs doing a small engineering project at odd times, but essentially I was there all by myself in this big empty upstairs.

At the time I was making photovoltaic, or solar-kinetic, sculptures so I did a lot on tinkering with mechanical things and it was a convenient location because I could run downstairs to

Davis Lumber, which had it's hardware section in the adjacent building at the time, and get little widgets and fasteners or whatever I needed. In fact it was a little too convenient since I think I made six or seven trips a day to the hardware store.

Now and then Lee Chen would pop in and look at this bizarre activity of mine and kindly suggest that maybe I should get my gadgets manufactured somewhere, but I was having so much trouble just getting the prototypes to work that mass-production never happened.

All this tinkering was hungry work so when I wanted something to eat I'd run down to the Natural Food Works and grab a pre-made alfalfa sprout sandwich or a high-density cookie with the minimum daily requirement of everything, and that would sustain me. I'd quickly be hard at work wasting time some more. It seemed like the future was everything and I didn't think much about the past. I had plenty of time to go looking for widgets and snacks.

While speculating more than working I'd occasionally poke my head out the window and I'd see the train station and the palm trees and I'd realize I wasn't in the Midwest. It was a kind of wistful realization. And then I'd hear the station master announcing that the train was coming in from Chicago, or leaving for Chicago, and I felt this connection to my past that made it a little easier to make the transition to my new home.

I think those kinds of transitions are important as we go from past to future. I think history can really only be seen in the light of change but change also needs the shadow of history to give it shape.

In fact, I've had people tell me I was history myself. But I still seem to be here, give or take a few loose bricks and some unwanted cosmetic changes.

9.28. I thought Gerald Heffernon's remarks captured the moment well and, with his permission, I present them here. When Heffernon finished, Rosenberg remarked: "Great Job. You know, you really are a great public speaker. I mean that sincerely. If you ever want to give up that column, I think you have a career in public speaking."

9.29. On the left, Susie Boyd was present at the start of the three-minute talks, acknowledged as a public official, and then departed almost immediately. (L. Druskis.)

9.30. A couple nicely outfitted in 1920s fashion. (S. Shine.)

9.31. A couple listening to the three-minute stories. (S. Shine.)

9.32. Dr. Caron Cioffi, who also read poetry. (S. Shine.)

9.33. Heather Caswell and David Rosenberg pose. (S. Shine.)

9.34. Rose Anne DeCristoforo, owner of the Natural Food Works, which was evicted from the Terminal Building. (S. Shine.)

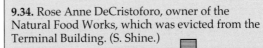

8) OPEN-MIKE SPEAKERS

The event became "open-mike" after the scheduled speakers. This period was, to me, the most enlightening and uplifting of the afternoon. No one counted or kept a record of all of them, but perhaps another dozen or more people came to the stage and spoke. I did not know most of them or even know of them. Diverse in age and gender, they recounted moments deeply meaningful in their lives associated with the building. Indeed, a tinge of catharsis of grief over lost places ran through their both accounts and the mood of the crowd. Miriam Montgomery, shown in Fig. 9.35, advocated saving the building and spoke of Del's Fix-it shop run by her and her husband just to north on G Street in the decades after World War II. The young man in Fig. 9.36 spoke about musical groups associated with the building. The gentleman in Fig. 9.37 is Clarence Berry, the retired long-time postmaster of Davis.

9.35. Open-mike speaker Mrs. Miriam Montgomery. (S. Shine.)

9.36. Open-mike speaker. (S. Shine.)

9.37. Clarence Berry. (S. Shine.)

9.38. David Rosenberg had his photograph taken in front of the soon-to-be demolished Arch Mural. (S. Shine.)

9.39. As the event broke up, various participants posed in groups before the Arch Mural. (S. Shine.)

10

FACADECTOMY FAILURE

The term "facadectomy" was originally a derisive preservationist label for saving a visually conspicuous side/facade of a building while doing away with the rest of it. This is butchery, not preservation, these preservationists declared. But, as happened with terms like "Christian" and "queer," the stigmatizing label was embraced by those to whom it was imputed and flipped from negative to positive. I use the word here in this affirmatively reversed way.

The period of important focus on facadectomy for the Terminal Building can be dated, roughly, from the publication of my advocacy of it in the *Davis Enterprise* of Sunday, June 11 (Fig. 10.1) to the demolition of the first part of the building on Monday, September 18. At the end of that Monday, the mural and the west wall still stood, but the likelihood of their preservation was now slim, at best.

The facadectomy period itself divided into three segments.

There was, **first**, a stretch of about five weeks—June 11 to July 14—in which facadectomy seemed a possibility and during which the four retail business in the building were moving out.

A **second** period began on Saturday, July 15, when all four businesses were finally gone and the Terminal building sat as a somber and empty derelict.

The penultimate act and the **third** part of the facadecomy phase began August 30, when the owners submitted a pre-application design for a new building.

1) FACADECTOMY CAT-AND-MOUSE

While facadectomy seemed a serious possibility, it was not assured. Instead, it was a rather "cat and mouse" affair over these weeks.

Its possibility was put on public display, so to speak, in my *Davis Enterprise* op-ed of June 11, 2000 (Fig. 10.1).

10 1. My "Facadectomy" Op-ed, *Davis Enterprise*, Sunday, June 11, 2000.

THE DAVIS ENTERPRISE **OP-ED** SUNDAY, JUNE 11, 2000

'Facadectomy' is one way that Terminal Hotel could be saved

By John Lofland
Special to The Enterprise

One solution to the preservation problem posed by the Terminal Hotel is to keep its facade (and hence the history it represents) and construct a new (and likely larger) building behind it on the site.

In some circles this is called a "facadectomy." Preservation purists use the term derisively because it often requires changes they think destroy historic structures. But preservationists of a pragmatic bent look on the practice more favorably, even though they may not be enthusiastic about it.

Facadectomy is not that well known, so before coming to the Terminal Hotel let me show — by means of a photograph I took recently — an example of it in process in Washington, D.C. In the picture, we see a 3 1/2-story building facade with no building behind it. Notice that the facade ~~is held up by a steel beam struc~~ture extending over the sidewalk that substitutes for the support provided by the now-absent building behind the facade. (After the new building is in place, the steel beams will, of course, come down.)

What might be the pertinence of this practice to the Terminal Hotel?

In starting to think about this, a first and prime matter to bear in mind is that facadectomy is a variable. There are many degrees and forms of it. For example, in one conservative form, the building behind the facade would be brand-new but an identically configured incarnation of the old building. The exterior of the building would show little or no change.

In contrast, at the other ends of several variables, and in one radical version, only the G Street facade would remain and a large, two- or perhaps three- or more-story building of a clearly different design would rise behind it.

The point is that the facadec-

tomy of any building can take a great many forms and degrees of preservation and change. Whether or not this method of dealing with the Terminal Hotel turned out to be a critical success or not would be a function of exactly how it was done, not simply of doing it. So, the choice of architect and the process of a plan's evolution should figure heavily in thinking and acting along facadectomy lines.

There are, of course, two other courses of action possible for the Terminal Hotel: strict preservation and level-the-ground demolition. In my view, the former is unlikely to happen, but the latter might, so let me offer two less-often heard reasons for a well-done facadectomy rather than demolition.

First, the strongest form of facadectomy would think in terms of calling attention to the fact that the Terminal Hotel is one of three 1910s-'20s business buildings at Second and G. Taken together with the Brinley Block and the Anderson Bank buildings on two of the other corners, we have an excellent physical representation of Davis' Main Street period. The three buildings form a coherent set of the commercial brick structures distinctive to that period.

In point of historical fact, this corner and these three buildings were the center of Davis prior to the eclipse of train travel.

A creatively facadectomized Terminal Hotel could centerpiece the historic character of the entire intersection and the adjacent areas — the original downtown.

Rather than a lemon of which we must rid ourselves, the need to do something about the Terminal Hotel should spur us to think positively about possibilities for capitalizing on and enhancing the historical center of Davis. (And, I urge those who dislike the building to consider: If you have a lemon, make lemonade.)

Second, with facadectomy I

ABOVE: A black-line rectangle shows the original facade of the 19th-century Atlantic Coast Line building on the corner of Pennsylvania Avenue and Sixth Street in Washington, D.C., behind which a modern commercial building has been built. **LEFT:** A steel beam structure provides support for a facade with no building behind it. After the building is in place, the steel beams will come down.

Courtesy photos

think we could avoid the divisiveness, vilification and hard feelings that would likely accompany and follow in the wake of level-to-the ground demolition.

So, with facadectomy, perhaps we can have our cake and eat it, too.

— John Lofland is a resident of Davis, the author of "Old North Davis," and, with Phyllis Haig, "Davis, California, 1910s-1940s," a photographic history published this spring. He thanks Robin Datel and Dennis Dingemans for tutoring him in "facadectomy."

Happy for the hotel

Alyssa Nielsen, left, and Caron Cioffi chat during the celebration for the Terminal Hotel on Sunday in downtown Davis.

Fond memories of hotel shared

By Jennifer Rutherford
Enterprise correspondent

On Sunday afternoon, local historians and others interested in Davis' past celebrated the history of the Terminal Hotel building, built in 1925 at Second and G streets.

The event was held at the G Street Plaza adjacent to the building, which once housed notable Davis businesses such as the Terminal Cafe and the Antique Bizarre and now is home to Natural Food Works, The Wardrobe and La Esperanza.

Last September the Davis City Council rejected a bid to declare the building a historical resource; that decision was affirmed by another council vote last week. After a recent seismic evaluation of the building,

the city ordered its owners, Grace and Lee Chen, to make the building seismically safe. The Chens have taken out a demolition permit and are considering building a new facility.

Sunday's celebration was designed to remember the building's past and discuss efforts to preserve it.

About a third of the crowd wore period clothing in the spirit of the 1920s. Backstreet

Jazz played 1920s music, and a few attendees enjoyed some swing dancing.

Books about the history of Davis and other nearby areas were for sale, and petitions were available to sign that promote reconsideration of the hotel as a city of Davis historical resource.

Elaborate Davis Arch wine glasses also were on

See HOTEL, Page A8

10.2. Monday, June 12th *Davis Enterprise* front page coverage of the previous day's celebration of Terminal Hotel and Davis history (which was also depicted in the last chapter).

HOTEL

From Page A1

sale, with proceeds going toward saving the building.

Phyllis Haig and John Lofland of the Hattie Weber Museum created a circular exhibit on the Terminal Hotel building, showing the evolution of the building through photographs, advertisements, restaurant menus and newspaper articles on the hotel and the Terminal Cafe.

Yolo County Supervisor Dave Rosenberg moderated a special commemoration of the hotel, titled "The Terminal Hotel Building: A Dozen (or so) Three-Minute Stories." Presenters were historians, city leaders and others involved in the building's past.

Jean Jackman started the reminiscences by telling about the origins of the railroad in Davis and how it helped put Davis on the map. Everything that happened in Davis had to do with the train and other businesses in the area.

"The train, the water tower, the depot and the hotel: that was the heart of this town," Jackman said.

Jeanette Shulz then gave a talk about the more modern visual aspects of the hotel. It was designed in response to the Arts and Crafts movement to be simpler and less elaborate, and was built with bricks to give it elegance.

"We must also remember that for most of us, our history involves smaller, more intimate day-to-day events," Shulz said.

Haig, curator of the Hattie Weber Museum, then related the history of the Terminal Cafe. It was the second restaurant in town and was a good meeting place for many Davis organizations.

Artist and Enterprise columnist Gerald Heffernon recalled the days when he first moved to Davis and rented a studio in the Aggie Hotel, when he could make quick trips to Davis Lumber and Natural Food Works.

"I think history can really only see in the light of change — change also needs the shadow of history to give it shape," he said.

Audrey Hastings related her memories of working with F. Hal Higgins, an Aggie Hotel resident for several years. Davis City Councilman Mike Harrington told the crowd about one memorable night he spent in the Antique Bizarre with a date and several cowboys who wanted to dance with her.

The Rev. John Pamperin talked about the role the Antique Bizarre played in the student and social movement of the 1960s and 1970s, and how the hotel also served as a homeless shelter.

SINGING FOR THE HOTEL: Heidi Bekebrede of Davis sings to the music of the Backstreet Jazz Band.

"Many people got their life back together by having a place that was cheap and seemed to be without judgment," he said.

"This building has been a part of my life for nearly 40 years," longtime Davis resident Mike White said. He has been patronizing businesses in the building since he was 19 years old and has met friends there.

Wendy Nelson, chair of the Historical Resources Management Commission, outlined the process that her committee went through when recommending that the Terminal Hotel building be classified as a historic resource and compared the criteria to the building's qualities.

State parks archaeologist Richard Hastings commented on ways to rehabilitate the building and recalled the most unforgettable wedding he ever attended in the hotel.

Former Davis Mayor Julie Par-

tansky, who was the lone vote last fall to declare the hotel a historic resource, also discussed the definitions of the words "ethic" and "environmental."

Davis City Councilwoman Sue Greenwald then spoke of her desire to preserve the building, and how she wants a feasibility study done. She also spoke of working with and giving support to the Chens, who she believes want to do what is right for the city.

"Like so many things in our lives, we don't really think about the importance of them to us until we're at risk of losing them," Greenwald said.

After the stories were over, Rosenberg invited audience members to an open mike to share their feelings and memories.

It is hoped that this celebration of local history will become an annual event.

10.3. Gerald Heffernon was the semi-official "progressive" columnist of the *Davis Enterprise*. Long-time house columnist Bob Dunning so regularly infuriated Davis liberals that the paper tried to balance him with Heffernon. While Dunning specialized in corrosive and ad hominum sneering, Heffernon provided thoughtful analysis, liberals believed. Of some import, Dunning wrote daily while Heffernon appeared only once a week. Several years in the past, Dunning and Heffernon fell into writing biting columns about each other with some regularity. The *Enterprise* editor ended these exchanges with the rule that neither could write about the other.

FORUM
TUESDAY, JUNE 13, 2000

Hold that wrecking ball, please

My tastes in architecture are catholic. I grew up in Frank Lloyd Wright country and so that idiom is ingrained in me, but my favorite architect was always Antonio Gaudi, the Spaniard whose buildings look like they were made by hallucinating swallows.

I even studied architecture briefly in Chicago but, being a curvy thinker, found I had trouble drawing the mandatory straight lines.

I like brash, radical, mold-breaking buildings and I like old, subtle, rich buildings. The point is to have both. What Davis is short of in this mix is ... both.

That's because I left out a third category: the big wad of beige out there we call housing. But forget that, and let's talk about buildings that were given at least a modicum of thought by their designers. Like the Terminal Hotel.

We don't yet know if the name "Terminal" is predictive of an end for the old and storied building or whether some form of "adaptive reuse" (a term I just learned) will preserve at least some of the original building in recognizable form.

Put aesthetics aside for a moment. The building is more decorated by its past uses than by important architectural flourishes. It has gone from a meeting place for movers and shakers in the 1920s to a home for down-and-outers and tough bars in the 1970s. More recently it has housed small retail businesses and a restaurant.

I knew that, but until last Saturday I had never really looked at the building itself with a critical eye.

Gerald Heffernon
LOOSE CANON

I don't think the Terminal Hotel building can — at least not fairly — be called ugly. True, it has receded and been made anonymous by various insults to its original character.

The building cannot even be judged in its present condition. It wears way too much makeup. But strip away the awning and the stucco and the butchered windows and what you have is a simple brick building I would call plain.

Plain can be good. Plain can be beautiful. The Shaker style, for instance, was religiously plain. Self-effacing though it was, that plain style has come to be admired for its simple beauty.

Likewise, the Terminal Hotel is trim and straight-forward. Seen in its original brick skin, it makes almost no stylistic statement, its main features being brick patterns and a pleasant rhythm of windows on the south face.

But who officially judges aesthetics in this city? The City Council voted 3-2 not to give the building historic status and, as Councilwoman Susie Boyd stated explicitly, they did it on the basis of aesthetics.

Sorry, but I don't think this or any other City Council (the big beige wad of approved housing as evidence) is qualified to judge architectural beauty and they should stay out of that area.

Furthermore, this isn't the old Kentucky Fried Chicken building we're talking about. No one is saying, "Gee, remember when they came out with Extra Crispy in that building?" The Terminal Hotel is one building that defines history for many Davisites.

John Lofland and Heather Caswell have written eloquently about the building's historic relationship to the train depot. Sunday, people gathered at a celebration of the building and spoke of more recent and peculiar memories. For these reasons alone, the Terminal Hotel deserves some degree of preservation.

First, the City Council must vote for a feasibility study. There is no reason to think that the Terminal Hotel will be more difficult to seismically retrofit than any other building built in the 1920s. The technique is well established.

Looking over the building with an "adaptive reuse" mindset, I came to the conclusion that the west-facing front and two adjoining sides (or most of them) could be substantially preserved. The east, or back, side could virtually accept an architectural insert, and with ample setbacks even a third or fourth story could work there. Considerable extra square footage would be added to the building without using a wrecking ball.

More importantly, this would make a whole new presentation to the train depot, a welcoming face offered to people arriving on the train.

IN MY BRIEFS ... What was the big rush to approve the General Plan Update EIR at 1 a.m. last Wednesday ... I mean Thursday? Sue Greenwald was right to ask for more consideration of the EIR at a later date and earlier hour, given that there is serious doubt about its adequacy.

Her point about the assumed resident-per-unit rate was also well taken. Davis assumes a 2.46 rate. Other cities in the area assume something closer to 3.0, and the statewide number is 2.9. That makes a huge difference in predicting the impacts of any given project.

Boyd's recent pattern of making pre-emptive motions was finally cut off during that debate. In the middle of the first burrowing owl discussion she stunned everyone and got the publicity by suggesting the Mace Ranch retail site be used for owl habitat.

Partway through the Terminal Hotel discussion she cut off debate by making a motion to reaffirm last year's vote in which the building was denied historical status.

But when Boyd tried the quick-vote tactic during the EIR discussion, City Attorney Harriet Steiner interrupted to say that the council first had to take public comment.

Ah, democracy can be so messy and inconvenient.

— Gerald Heffernon is a Davis resident. His column appears weekly.

10.4. Taking Lee Chen's several statements that a new building might incorporate "some of the old structure" at face value (e.g. *Enterprise*, June 6th), I once again wrote encouraging the facadectomy route.

As previously, I never received a response— not even a call pressured by the Mayor (reported above, Figs. 8.9 and 8.30).

John Lofland
523 E Street
Davis, California 95616

530-758-5258
fax 530-752-0783
jflofland@ucdavis.edu

—————————

June 14, 2000

Lee Chen
P. O. Box 2094
El Macero, CA 95618

Dear Mr. Chen:

I write to applaud Mrs. Chen and your decision further to study the possibility of preserving all or part of the Terminal Hotel Building and to wish you well in these studies.

I also want to report some new information on the building you might find interesting and useful.

The structure was apparently put up in two phases, the first in 1924 and the second in 1926-27. An August 1, 1924 *Enterprise* story (attached) says the original building is 75 by 57 feet and one story tall, but built to support a second or third story.

Two 1926 *Enterprise* reports describe adding a second story to the first building and extending it to the rear as hotel rooms and two apartments (stories attached).

I assume this means that the western portion has an unusual degree of independence from the eastern portion (i.e. the western portion once stood on its own).

These construction facts might be relevant to how one thinks through rehabilitating all or part of the structure.

For your reference, I also enclose a copy of the now-published op-ed piece I sent you in draft form in November, 1999.

Cordially,

John Lofland

Enc: *Davis Enterprise* reports August 1, 1924, November 12, 1926, December 10, 1926.
    Lofland, *Enterprise* op-ed on "facadecotomy," June 11, 2000.

Davis Downtown Business Association

P.O. Box 72497
Davis, CA 95617
(530) 756-8763
Fax (530) 756-6504

Destination
DOWN TOWN DAVIS

June 16, 2000

Davis City Council
City of Davis
23 Russell Blvd.
Davis, CA 95616

Dear Mayor Wagstaff and Council Members:

In mid-May the DDBA Board of Directors was asked to take a position whether we would support a feasibility study on the Terminal Hotel. A special board meeting was held on Wednesday, May 24 to hear from Heather Caswell, owner of The Wardrobe and tenant of the building, regarding information on the possible rehabilitation of the building. We then moved up our regularly scheduled Board meeting from June 14 to June 7, to hear from the property owner, Grace Chen, in order to render our position to the council at their June 7 meeting.

We did not know that the city council meeting had been moved from its' regularly scheduled June 7 meeting to June 6 until after we had scheduled the meeting and notices were posted. Although we did not have a formal position at the time of the city council meeting, DDBA President Joyce Thorp stated at the council meeting that she thought that the Board would lean toward supporting a feasibility study of the Terminal Hotel property.

Though the council opted **not** to pursue a feasibility study on the Terminal Hotel at this time, the DDBA Board of Directors (with the exception of Shel Givens, who abstained from voting) would like to state their position regarding any projects that involve demolition or rehabilitation of historic properties.

Most projects incorporate a feasibility study early on as a part of the normal review process **before** any ground is broken or rehabilitation begins—how can you determine a budget, financing needs, upfront costs, etc. without having a projection (feasibility) study done? Knowing the feasibility of **any** project always makes good economic sense for all parties involved. A non-biased firm or individual that has no prior connection to the project should conduct the feasibility study.

Only after a historic building goes through the feasibility process can it be determined how much it would cost to rehabilitate versus rebuilding. Comparisons of rehabilitation, rehabilitation with an addition, saving a façade with new construction behind it and a new structure are viable options that should be incorporated in a feasibility study of a historic structure. Only after knowing the actual costs of options involved in a project can a viable decision be made on that project.

June 16, 2000
Davis City Council
Page 2

In the case of the Terminal Hotel (or any other future historical building that may be affected), the feasibility study provides **all parties** additional information regarding the financial ramifications of a project. Only after the study is reviewed can the business owner, property owner, City staff and historic preservationists have a clear, accurate accounting of the costs involved to rehabilitate and the possible cost gap between rehabilitation and new construction. After the study, options could be explored on funding sources, historical tax credits, grants, etc. that could bridge the gap for rehabilitation of the building if the cost of restoration is greater than demolition and new construction.

The DDBA Board of Directors advocates the Council include a feasibility study as part of any City decision making process concerning historic structures in the downtown area.

Sincerely,

Laura Cole-Rowe

Laura Cole-Rowe
Executive Director

cc: Heather Caswell
    Grace Chen
    Michael Garavaglia
    Ellen Fishman – California Main Street
    Ken Hiatt - City of Davis
    Esther Polito – City of Davis
    Davis Enterprise

Fig. 10.5. Now that it was too late, the association of businesses in the downtown (the DDBA) finally took a position favoring a professionally done feasibility study.

The DDBA was well organized, had a professional staff, was a quasi-governmental entity as a "business improvement district" supported with a tax on downtown businesses, and was, at this, time, an applicant to be a National Trust Main Street city. This combination of facts made the slowness of this response especially puzzling.

10.6.
McCandless to the Chens, June 19, 2000. This letter implies that facadectomy is still an option, but the phrase "incorporating elements" is elastic.

Notice that the phrase "feasibility investigation" rather than the professionally standardized terms feasibility study or analysis was used here.

Whatever the term, no credible work of the relevant kind was carried out (or at least not made public).

Curiously, this writer does not seem to know the name of the building on which he is working, since he calls it the "Travelers Hotel."

McCANDLESS & ASSOCIATES, ARCHITECTS

June 19, 2000

Lee and Grace Chen
44150 Country Club Dr.
El Macero, CA 95618

Dear Lee and Grace;

As per our discussion of Friday June 16, 2000, I am enclosing herewith 2 copies of our Standard Form of Agreement between Owner and Architect. We are proposing to provide design and planning services as well as project feasibility assessment and related cost estimating for the purposes of beginning the pre-application process and subsequent design review for your anticipated development at your 2nd and G St. property.

Pursuant to our meeting with City representatives last Friday, I think it would be prudent to fully explore the possibility of incorporating elements of the Travelers Hotel into any new development we are considering. The notion of retaining some presence of the original building to maintain a visual relationship to its' historic neighbors is an intriguing one worthy of investigation. As such part of our services will include further structural investigation and analysis of the existing building as a means of assessing in an informed manner the feasibilities of the several options we have discussed.

Please sign and return one copy of the agreement to our office and we will begin work. The phase of work represented by this contract is feasibility investigation and preliminary design for the purposes of presenting to the City in the form of a pre-application submission, our design proposal for your anticipated development. To properly execute this phase of work in preparation for schematic design, design development and construction documentation, we will need to work closely with you to set some design parameters and budgetary constraints; as I have already advised you, we will also be working with the City Planning department on this phase with respect to building use, occupancy, parking requirements, etc.

Thank you for selecting our firm to provide architectural services for this project. Despite initial controversy, we are certain that the resolution of this project can be rewarding to all involved. We look forward to working with you.

Sincerely,

Bill McCandless, AIA

WHM/gs

enc

666 DEAD CAT ALLEY ▲ WOODLAND, CA 95695
LOCAL (530) 662-9146 ▲ FROM SACRAMENTO (916) 447-2782 ▲ FAX (530) 662-3425
mccandlessarch.com ▲ info@mccandlessarch.com

JUN-23-00 FRI 04:12 PM   DAVIS ENTERPRISE   FAX NO. 5307566707   P. 01
JUN-23-00 FRI 1:32 PM   CITY OF DAVIS   FAX NO. 5307560377

McCANDLESS & ASSOCIATES, ARCHITECTS

10.7. The same day, McCandless reported his contract with the Chens to the City and outlined his proposed work.

This letter includes the phrase "some of these alternatives will consider saving portions of the original building."

Readers with an inquisitive turn of mind might want to keep this phrase in mind as they examine how the story develops from this point.

RECEIVED
CITY OF DAVIS
JUN 21 2000
CITY MANAGER'S OFFICE

June 19, 2000

Ken Wagstaff, Mayor
City of Davis
23 Russell Blvd.
Davis, CA 95616

Dear Mayor Wagstaff:

As of Friday June 16th, 2000, our firm was asked to provide architectural services by Lee and Grace Chen for their anticipated development at their 2nd and G St. property. As evidenced by the attached copy of our contract for services cover letter, we will initially be conducting further investigations as to the existing buildings' structural integrity for the purposes of determining project feasibility relative to a number of building design alternatives. To properly address the controversy surrounding the future of the Chen's building, the former Travelers Hotel, some of these alternatives will consider saving portions of the original structure.

As stated in the letter to the Chens, the concept of retaining elements of the original buildings' streetscape relationship to its historic neighbors is an intriguing design approach. We will be further assessing the buildings' structural condition and the feasibility of incorporating elements of the original building into the new development. It is the Chens vision to make full use of the site's potential by creating a structure that is three-sided in its presentation to the streetscape. The current buildings' storefronts relate only to G St. leaving the potential for 2nd St. and H St. exposures unrealized. The Chens desire to present a welcoming facade to the train depot is a noble one worthy of appreciation. As discussed in the meeting last Friday attended by the Chens, myself, you and several other City representatives we will be studying various options relative to reconciling the possibilities of retaining elements of the Travelers Hotel and still achieving the intent of the Chens vision for developing their site to its full potential. This is an important site for the City of Davis not only because of its past presence, but because of its potential to be a revitalized focal point in the future urban fabric of downtown Davis. Following some initial site investigation and feasibility assessment, we will be beginning the City review process by submitting pre-application information to the City Planning Dept. in the form of conceptual design drawings. It is our hope that careful consideration of all possibilities will lead to a successful project resolution that all concerned can be proud of.

666 DEAD CAT ALLEY ▲ WOODLAND, CA 95695
LOCAL (530) 662-9146 ▲ FROM SACRAMENTO (916) 447-2782 ▲ FAX (530) 662-3425
mccandlessarch.com ▲ info@mccandlessarch.com

Thank you for your concern. We look forward to working with both the Chens and the City of Davis on this important project.

Respectfully Submitted,

Bill McCandless

Bill McCandless, AIA

WHM/gs

cc   Lee & Grace Chen

A4

THE DAVIS ENTERPRISE

MONDAY, JUNE 26, 2000

FORUM

▶ **LETTERS**

Who wants 'modern'?

The following is a copy of a letter to the Davis City Council:

I am writing to protest the planned demolition of the Hotel Aggie/Terminal Hotel building. As previously noted, this building completes a trio of buildings at a historic intersection in downtown Davis.

G and Second streets in this section of downtown has always been the "downtown," and these original buildings should be preserved. Once these edifices are gone, you will *never* have them back.

Constructing a modern or even a "retro" building will diminish the feeling and the aesthetics of the present intersection. A building that is run-down is usually that way because its owners *let* it become run-down.

In recent years, many of the old buildings and storefronts have been torn down or "renovated." The small-town feel people like to boast about is just about gone. With each passing year, Davis feels more and more like any other freeway town, especially with the cluster of fast-food joints and gas stations along the I-80 exits.

The older buildings that still exist retain the character of what Davis used to be, and help to make Davis different. Without them, Davis will soon resemble just another "modern" city with "modern" buildings in this "modern" country. Once this happens, we lose our sense of history, and without history, we lost our sense of self, our sense of place.

In a world that is rapidly industrializing and absorbing American culture and materialism, all of us need to preserve our past.

Aesthetics, you say? Many people (including me) don't like concrete and steel "boxes" that proclaim to be "distinctive and welcoming." In the past, Davis has offered instances of preservation; the present City Hall and the Varsity Theater are excellent examples. The Hunt-Boyer Mansion stands as yet another example — in fact, it, too, originally was to be removed to make way for "progress."

As a resident who cares, I am willing to contribute to any fund that may be established with the purpose of preventing demolition and encouraging restoration. Remember, as the song says, "Don't it always seem to go that you don't know what you've got 'til it's gone. They paved paradise and put up a parking lot."

David S. Evans
Davis

WEDNESDAY, JUNE 21, 2000

Inconsistent action

The Davis City Council contradicted and perhaps even mocked itself last week when it (1) began financing a visitor/tourist attraction program while also (2) acting less than assertively to preserve the Terminal Hotel Building.

The self-mocking contradiction resides in the fact that people, in the words of Arthur Frommer, "travel in large part to commune with the past. ... They seek their roots in the broadest sense, (and) gain solace or inspiration from visiting the sites of earlier happenings ..."

In not actively seeking to preserve the Terminal Hotel, the council has increased the probability that the historical fabric of Davis will be deeply and irremediably torn, thus compromising one of the important reasons people might visit Davis. Absent a vibrant historical fabric, tourist attraction dollars are in significant part wasted. Consistency requires supporting or opposing *both* the visitor attraction program and Terminal Hotel preservation.

John Lofland, Davis

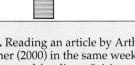

10. 8. Reading an article by Arthur Fromer (2000) in the same week the City started funding a "visitor attraction program," prompted me to write a letter to the *Enterprise* Editor printed June 21, 2000.

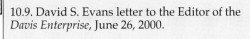

10.9. David S. Evans letter to the Editor of the *Davis Enterprise*, June 26, 2000.

2) EVICTION SADNESS

For at least two of the four evicted shops—the Natural Food Works and the Wardrobe— leaving was bitter and unwanted. The proprietors loved the building and their location. For them, this was a time of sadness. A sense of this is provided in Figs. 10.10, 10.11, 10.12 and 10. 14.

4 Davis fixtures plan to relocate

Restaurant, shops to leave Terminal Hotel

By Melanie Turner.
Enterprise staff writer

Michael Brooks/Enterprise photo

LOOKING AHEAD: Heather Caswell, owner of The Wardrobe, has plenty of packing to do as she prepares to move her store from its current site on G Street to 206 E St. after The Children's Corner closes.

Four downtown business, each of which have operated for years out of what is known as the old Terminal Hotel — the brick building on the northeast corner of Second and G streets — must move out by midnight on July 14 to make way for big changes on that corner.

Two businesses, The Wardrobe and Natural Food Works, have plans to relocate permanently in the downtown.

The other two, La Esperanza and the Hair Chalet, reportedly have not yet made immediate future plans. Grace Chen, owner of the Hair Chalet, said she does plan to reopen her salon elsewhere. A manager of La Esperanza said while the restaurant has not finalized plans to move it will continue to operate out of its other location, at 825 Russell Blvd., in the University Mall.

Owners of the 75-year-old building, Lee and Grace Chen, plan to create an expanded use of the site by building a project that features retail on at least three sides, including retail that would face the Southern Pacific Depot. The Chens' latest demolition permit expires on Dec. 4.

The Chens' efforts to bring changes to this well-traveled corner of the downtown have proved controversial as community members, historic commissioners and tenants of the building have voiced concerns over placing the building's fate solely in the owners' hands.

A year ago, the Historic Resources Management Commission made a unanimous recommendation to the City Council that the building be designated as historic, at the lowest level, recognizing even then that demolition may proceed while

See HOTEL, Page A3

10.10. *Davis Enterprise,* June 28, 2000 report on the four businesses displaced by the closure of the Terminal Building

THE DAVIS ENTERPRISE **LOCAL** WEDNESDAY, JUNE 28, 2000

HOTEL   From Page A1

stressing the building's historic significance.

But the council voted 4-1 last fall to deny the commission's request. And again last month, the council voted 3-2 to reaffirm its earlier vote giving the Chens the go-ahead. The council did request that the city work with the Chens to attempt to re-use some portion of the old building.

Since then, the Chens' demolition permit was extended through Dec. 4. And a meeting was held since the council's June 6 meeting between the Chens, Mayor Ken Wagstaff, Cultural Resources Manager Esther Polito, Historic Commission Chairwoman Wendy Nelson, Downtown Coordinator Ken Hiatt, Planning Director Bill Emlen, and the Chens' architect, Bill McCandless.

Before leaving on a trip to Spain last week, Mayor Wagstaff said he is pleased the Chens have committed again and again to not tear the building down without first sharing their plans for the site with the city. "I think that's a sign of good faith," he said.

The Chens have said they want to build something that many people can be happy with, and they aim to build a project that's compatible with its historical surroundings.

Wagstaff said it is his understanding that the architect will now lay out some design options which include saving features of the building. Polito clarified that still there is no commitment to save any portion of the building.

But Polito said those who attended the meeting agreed on the latest approach, which involves conducting a limited feasibility study that examines the cost of various designs which include saving the historical character of the building. Namely, the G Street brick facade and brick corner on Second and G.

"I don't see the point of a feasibility study that could save the whole building if the owners aren't interested in doing that," Polito said.

Polito said the latest approach is not a "demolition and new building" approach. But the understanding was that this new approach would attempt to yield a design that everyone can live with.

"It is a feasibility study of a design," rather than a more broadbased study that would look at the

Michael Brooks/Enterprise photo

CHANGES DUE: Four businesses that have operated for years out of the old Terminal Hotel, the brick building at Second and G streets, will be moving out by mid-July to make way for big changes. They are Natural Food Works, The Wardrobe, the Hair Chalet and La Esperanza. Owners of the 75-year-old building plan to create an expanded use of the site by building a project that features retail on at least three sides.

cost of saving the old building, she added. "I'm happy that the architect has recognized the importance of the building in relation to its historic neighbors," said Heather Caswell, owner of The Wardrobe. "I am hopeful that we will achieve a fair compromise."

Laura Cole-Rowe, executive director of the Davis Downtown Business Association, sent a letter to the council dated June 16, that indicates the DDBA Board of Directors "advocates the council include a feasibility study as part of any city decision making process concerning historic structures in the downtown area." The DDBA stressed that knowing the feasibility of any project makes good economic sense for all parties involved.

Meanwhile, a couple of the businesses are busily making plans to start anew in another part of the downtown.

Rose Anne DeCristoforo has owned Natural Food Works just three years, but the store itself was founded in 1971 and has operated out of 206 G St. almost all that time.

"It's a place where people

come and say, 'It's the only thing in Davis that's still the same.' " DeCristoforo said. Natural Food Works features a wood-planked floor and a large collection of culinary and medicinal herbs in bulk, as well as discounted supplementals.

The store is likely moving to a roughly 1,000-square-foot location at 624 Fourth St., where Jeff's Contemporary Crafts is now. That store is consolidating into JGlenn Gallery, at 603 Fourth St. There, the store owner hopes to add a kitchen which will feature bio-regional food, or locally grown produce and high quality food in a deli-style setting.

Caswell, owner of The Wardrobe, had originally intended to try to move back to Second and G, but has now found a new place where she intends to stay for a while, as well.

After looking into several options, The Wardrobe is moving to 206 E Street, what has been home to The Children's Corner, not far from the new E Street Plaza.

"The location is such a great location I just can't think twice," she said. "Change has been a gift

in disguise. I think a great, new location is my gift."

Caswell's new location will be about 1,300 square feet, larger than the 965-square-foot store she has now.

She says she will miss her old location, the place where she developed her "experience and character."

But she's excited about the high visibility and an "opportunity to reinvent ourselves."

She anticipates opening on Sept. 1, with a grand reopening on Nov. 11. The Wardrobe holds a "last chance" sale from Friday, June 30, to July 14.

Caswell has owned The Wardrobe for the last 12 1/2 years. Prior to her taking over the store, The Wardrobe began 10 years earlier where Sophia's Thai Kitchen is now. It began as a used clothing and consignment store and has been evolving ever since.

"The Wardrobe has found that our commitment to inspire others to discover their own individual style by exploring and expressing their uniqueness with fashion and color is as vital now as it was when we began," she added.

10.11. Moving notice in the window of the Natural Food Works, July, 200.

10.12. Moving sign in the window of the Wardrobe, July, 2000.

Consider the Chens

I read with some amusement John Lofland's June 21 letter to The Enterprise. I have resisted making any comments about the Terminal Hotel dilemma but after reading his comments, I must respond.

Having lived in Davis since 1958 I, too, appreciate what goes on in the core area of the city. But to accept the argument in Lofland's letter that one of the most important reasons for people to visit Davis (and thereby drop some tourist dollars) is to enjoy the historic fabric of Davis stretches the imagination.

The dilapidated Terminal Hotel apparently fits into that fabric of history. Ever since I moved to Davis I considered the hotel an ugly building with no possible charm or even history attached to it. Do people actually step off the train at the station and admire the hotel for its historic fabric? I doubt that very much.

The real troubling thought I have is that the Chen family, anxious to build a structure that will give them some return to their longtime investment, never seem to be included into the equation of the history enthusiasts.

Let the Chen family terminate the building and with the approval of the appropriate committees put up a structure that is designed to embrace the needs of the history enthusiasts and still be attractive and allow the Chen family finally to get a return on their investment.

Paul Stumpf, Davis

10.13. Paul Stumpf Letter to the Editor, *Davis Enterprise,* June 29, 2000.

10.14. Randy Lupka removes the Wardrobe's sign from the Terminal Building, July, 2000. (Photo by Heather Caswell.)

Heather Caswell Letter to the Editor regarding the move, *Davis Enterprise,* July 9, 2000.

OP-ED

THE DAVIS ENTERPRISE

SUNDAY, JULY 9, 2000

Wardrobe's moving

Just a reminder that The Wardrobe is moving to 206 E St. (next to the E Street Plaza). We will be temporarily closed for six weeks. The Wardrobe's last sales day will be Thursday, July 13. We are excited to be moving into our new location and plan to reopen on Sept. 1.

Also, I would like to extend my deepest gratitude to all of my dedicated staff and customers for helping The Wardrobe become what it is today. It's been a pleasure doing business in downtown Davis!

Heather Caswell, Davis

Vintage building

In the June 29 Enterprise, Paul Stumpf's descriptive comments on the Terminal Hotel such as "ugly," "no charm" and "dilapidated" are very troubling. He also states there is no "history" attached to the hotel.

His critical remarks of John Lofland's stand on preservation is also troubling. At least Mr. Lofland is working for a solution to preserving our downtown. There are actually people who do look at the hotel and see beauty in its texture, its simplicity and historic quality.

Perhaps Mr. Stumpf does not understand and appreciate towns that protect and enhance their historic downtowns. I have traveled extensively in Minnesota and Wisconsin where tourists flock to enjoy historic buildings they shop in.

One definitely comes to mind: Cedarburg, Wis., a small town just north of Milwaukee and a hundred or so miles from Chicago. Illinois license plates are quite abundant there as well as in Racine, Kenosha, Port Washington — all small towns that "cash in" on their historic downtowns.

Even downtown Woodland is now designated as an historic district. Santa Rosa has a wonderful old Railroad Square area. They have likewise restored their depot and the Railroad Hotel, a charming stone building that houses wonderful shops.

Unfortunately, the Chens and Mr. Stumpf do not consider preserving a plain brick facade building "full of Davis history" important enough. Actually, the old hotel is a very important element as one of the four anchor buildings on Second and G.

It comes down to economics. Restoration of a building made of good quality materials is more cost-effective than tearing down and building new. The city stands to gain and is for demolition as they get a much larger chunk in permit fees with a brand-new building.

Take a look down G Street, also on Second — there are many brick facade buildings that are beautiful in their texture and simplicity. Strelitzia Flower Company did a great job in restoration of their corner at Third and G. Restoration of the Cradwick Hotel in Winters was well worth the investment and it was in worse condition then the Terminal Hotel.

Let's hope the Chens work with the architect and the Historical Commission to save as much as possible to retain this simple, brick "historic" building that some of us enjoy in Davis.

A vintage building of plain design does not make it less historic. We need to preserve what precious little we have here. Once it's gone you can't bring it back.

Audrey Hastings, Davis

10.15. Audrey Hastings letter to the *Enterprise* editor, July 9th.

10.16. Bill Bossart letter to the editor, *Davis Enterprise*, July 13, 2000.

THURSDAY, JULY 13, 2000

FORUM

▶ LETTERS

More on the hotel

In many ways I think beauty is in the eye of the beholder. But in view of the attacks made against Paul Stumpf's comments concerning the Terminal Hotel, I feel compelled to add a word or two.

I arrived, it appears, a year before Professor Stumpf and taught philosophy until I retired in 1993. Sometime after my arrival, I visited a friend who had taken a room in the hotel in the hope of finishing his doctoral dissertation undisturbed.

My impression of the hotel at that time, after having spent almost three years at a student in cheap lodgings in Europe, was that it was pretty much a flophouse. I didn't visit the lodgings again for some time but I did visit the late and often lamented Antique Bizarre on the ground floor — a place where pool hall fights, amateur musicians and Little League teams happily intermingled. Why didn't the city save that location? Or the wonderful pool hall that was replaced by a pizza parlor, or Stan's Meat Market?

The second time I visited the interior of the hotel proper I went, on the invitation of a graduate student, to hear some alternative pop music. Walls had been knocked out to accommodate the various groups.

Professor Stumpf is correct in my opinion (with 40 years of teaching aesthetics and art theory); the place is ugly and I would add ruined. It is not in a neighborhood like Professor Lofland's beloved Old North Davis neighborhood, which contains, as far as I know, nothing of architectural importance, but it is a neighborhood and a pleasant one at that.

The Chens have been patient. The claim that restoration is more cost-effective than building new is addle-brained and naive. Davis has a fine restoration of its train depot and I hope the Chens will manage to provide passengers with a new welcoming terminus.

Bill Bossart
Davis

3) AN EMPTY, VANDALIZED BUILDING

In the deep summer of July and August, the building stood empty and forlorn—and became an object of vandalism. At the same time, letters to the *Enterprise* editor continued.

10.17. John Mason letter to the *Davis Enterprise* editor, July 19, 2000.

Social justice

Unless there is a miraculous intervention, the Terminal Hotel with all its aura of history will soon be destroyed and replaced by a new building with little if any history about it at all.

The hotel's being brought to the brink of this imminent death has filled me with feelings of moral disapprobation about the ugly project, feelings that have arisen in part from my conviction that the hotel's demolition, besides being unjust in itself, has over time been brought about by past injustices of city government.

Failing to perceive their duty to protect and preserve a building that is symbolic of our railroad origins, former city councils neglected to require past owners of the hotel to keep the building in reasonably good shape.

As a result of this negligence and of the passage of decades of time, it should come as no surprise to anyone that much of the building has fallen into disrepair and that some part of it is now dilapidated. Yet, in spite of this bleak assessment of the structure's condition, there are some competent architects who think that the hotel can be refurbished.

Our City Council should acknowledge that the city bears some responsibility for the poor condition of the building, a rundown state of affairs that has put the hotel's owners in the position where apparently their only option is to demolish it. To avow this responsibility would be to reopen the question of the historical status of the hotel.

There is good reason to reopen this question, for in my opinion the council's granting the hotel's owners a demolition permit was unjust. The notion of origins is central to the right conception of justice. A court's decision in a civil or criminal trial can hardly be just if it is not based on legal or constitutional origin or precedent.

The legislative nature of a city council does not exempt it from the origin requirement of justice, for a council has an obligation to the community's origins.

In the case of the hotel, our City Council has a duty to those of our ancestors who have over decades contributed the most to the economic and social life at this downtown corner.

Expressed in more specific words, the Davis City Council, in respect for these ancestors and out of a debt owed them in gratitude, ought to have granted them a representative voice in their deliberations about their fate of the hotel, a voice they could have given them by seriously considering and thoroughly discussing what some of these forefathers would have thought about the proposal to demolish the hotel.

Our council did not show them this respect and consideration and they did not grant them a representative voice. This was most unfair and for this reason their granting of the demolition permit was unjust.

Social justice is almost always achieved through the sacrifice of economic interest. Question: If the council can authorize spending millions of dollars to develop small areas of Davis, why can't the council authorize a million to help the hotel's owners refurbish their building, especially in light of the fact that the city bears some responsibility for its poor condition?

John Mason, Davis

10.18. Bob Dunning, "The Wary I" column *Davis Enterprise* , July 21, 2000.

Bob's claim that "a historian this author is not" might be applied to Bob. In a single three-dot sentence he manages to achieve two major misstatements of Davis history.

First, it is not accurate to say that the railroad "came to town." It was the reverse: the town came to the railroad. As at hundreds of other places in the 1800s, the railroad builders selected open land, laid out a grid for a town, named it, and sold lots. In this way, the railroad *created* the town.

Second, the railroad predated the Terminal Building by 56 years (1868-1924). The length of a generation is ordinarily defined as about 30 years. In that accounting, the railroad preceded the building by two generations, at most. The phrase "several generations" is, at best, an exaggeration.

FRIDAY, JULY 21, 2000

Bob Dunning
THE WARY I

HISTORY LESSON ... I was happy to see that letter to the editor taking the council to the woodshed for not preserving the Terminal Hotel, which, according to the author, is a building "symbolic of our railroad origins" ... and never mind the railroad was once a new and scary thing and

the very people who now want us to save the Terminal Hotel would have been arguing *against* the railroad back when it came to town ... but a historian this author is not ... the railroad in this town predates the Terminal Hotel by several generations ...

10.19. Going by the building on Thursday, July 27, I was struck by how lifeless it had become now that the signs of two of the shops had been taken down—especially with the removal of the Natural Food Works sign on the end of the sidewalk overhang structure.

I also noticed something else. The two plaques describing aspects of the Arch Mural were gone. (The white arrow points to one of the locations.)

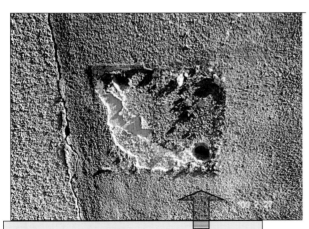

10.20. Location from which the left-hand plaque was removed from the Arch mural.

10.21. Location from which the right-hand plaque was removed from the Arch Mural.

4) THE PLOT DEEPENS

Based on statements of architect McCandless (e.g. Figs 10.6 and 10.7), saving at least a portion of the building in some reasonable form was viewed by preservationists and others as a possibility, albeit not a certainty.

This remained the prevailing view through the summer and up to Saturday, September 16th. That day, at a site-visit meeting of the Davis Planning Commission, total demolition starting Monday, September 18 was, without forewarning, announced by architect McCandless.

I inject these elements of the story out-of-order here for the purpose of providing a context for understanding the actions we will see between July 27 and September 16. The first of these actions is shown in Fig. 10.22.

10.22. On the same day I observed the mural plaques were missing (Thursday, July 27), one Stan Bowers came to Davis to take out a sidewalk-crossing permit to begin demolishing the Terminal Building.

This was a permit the City Public Works Department required in addition to the Planning and Building Department permit.

This permit did not say when the work would start. But, the contract we shall see later (Fig. 10.31), suggested that a demolition plan with a start date was in formation at this time.

A6   THE DAVIS ENTERPRISE **NEWS** FRIDAY, JULY 28, 2000

2 plaques removed from mural

By Melanie Turner
Enterprise staff writer

In what appears to be an act of vandalism, two plaques, about 8-by-10 inches in size, were removed from the mural of the Davis Arch that adorns the north wall of the Terminal Hotel. The theft reportedly took place sometime between Wednesday and Thursday afternoons.

Moira Murdock of the city's Parks and Community Services Department inspected the mural this morning, observing that the plaque removal left about a foot-long crack in the mural itself.

City Cultural Services Manager Esther Polito has called the Davis Police Department. She anticipated early this morning that the police would take a full report later in the morning.

The vandalism came at a time when officials are working together to come up with a plan to move forward with a new, appropriate design for the former Terminal Hotel building at Second and G streets that could save portions of the building.

"There is potential for saving the mural," said Polito.

Property owners Lee and Grace Chen are working with city officials and their architect in an attempt to come up with a plan for the building that many people can be happy with. The second story of the building has been condemned and hasn't been used for the past 15 years.

Polito learned from an observant Davis resident, John Pla, that the plaques were missing on Thursday. She then spoke with property owner Grace Chen, who knew nothing about it. She also spoke with the contrac-

tor in charge of the project, who said his crew did not remove the plaques. He told Polito he last saw the plaques in place sometime Wednesday.

The contractor has been conducting asbestos abatement and other work, such as removing two rear storage sheds from the property, but demolition work has not begun.

"To see (the mural) open game for vandalism and destruction really saddens me," Polito said.

She encourages any member of the public who may have seen someone remove the plaques to call the police. The plaques read: "A mural of the Davis Landmark Arch/1916-1922/Bicentennial 1976."

A spate of vandalism reportedly has been ongoing for several months at the E Street Plaza a couple of blocks away.

10.23. On July 27, I e-mailed Melanie Turner and Esther Polito that the plaques were missing. The next day's *Enterprise* carried the above report. "John Pla" is actually me. Melanie got my name wrong.

A way to save hotel?

As I read through Melanie Turner's article on Davis' new California Main Street certification this past Friday, these are the kinds of phrases that jumped to the fore: "enhance the economic, social, cultural... well-being of California's traditional commercial districts"; "improving and preserving our fabulous downtown"; "(millions) in private facade and building investment"; "traditional commercial district revitalization"; "based on a model developed by the National Trust for Historic Preservation."

And, after I read each one I practically had to say "Terminal Hotel!" aloud to make sure that the Davis City Council, Mayor Ken Wagstaff, Davis Downtown Business Association members, the Chens (Terminal Hotel owners), and all the interested parties who attended the tribute soiree last month were thinking what I was thinking.

If I'm understanding the article correctly, might this opportunity provide an avenue to obviate the impending demolition of the hotel?

It is clear that the Chens are really not in a financial position to preserve and renovate the building for the benefit of civic pride without some outside help. Those of us who got together to reminisce, tell stories, and lobby for the preservation of the structure aren't sitting on nest eggs to burn either.

I encourage the council, the DDBA and the Chens to immediately consult with the California Trade and Commerce Agency, who issued the certification, with an eye toward what this new status for our downtown might mean for this building in particular.

G Street *is* Davis' Main Street, and though Mr. Dunning may beg to differ, it is not Jack In the Box that lends it its traditional character.

I attended the tribute to the hotel for two reasons: the first because, as Sunny Shine said, "I learned to love rock and roll in that building!"

I went to the tribute with my pal Paul, who was the last in a long line of friends who rented the back apartment of the building with a tacit understanding that they provide rehearsal, recording and performance space for literally dozens of local bands, as well as artists from all over the United States, Europe and Australia. That space was the hub of the "alternative music" scene in this town for years before that term even entered the vernacular.

The second reason was because as a third-grade teacher in the Davis schools, a main thread of study that I am charged to cover in the social studies curriculum is communities and city and county history. I would rather not take my students on a field trip to see the SuperCuts space or Starbucks, with only photographs to show what their hometown used to look like. Any teacher will tell you that the real thing is far superior to a picture in any lesson.

The Terminal Hotel is an integral part of Davis' "Davisness." As a native, I've watched the town losing itself for more than three decades. On a broad boulevard in Newport News, Va., a few years back, lined with fast-food joints, auto parts stores, "no-tell motels," and discount chiropractic offices, I realized that there wasn't much evidence in sight to prove that I wasn't in Ames or Urbana or West Sacramento on the corner of Harbor and Capitol. Is that what we want for Davisville? I think not.

Has a way opened to assist the Chens in preserving an integral piece of our civic terrain? I hope so, and I wish them the best.

The word "terminal" means "situated at the end of something." Hopefully this building is situated at the end of us dismantling our own heritage.

Rusi Gustafson, Davis

10.24. Rusi Gustafson letter to the *Enterprise* editor, August 3, 2000.

10.25. John Mason letter to the *Enterprise* editor, August 11, 2000.

▶ LETTERS

A Terminal shame

During the last year, the Davis City Council has (1) refused to designate our downtown Terminal Hotel as an historical resource and (2) has issued a demolition permit to the hotel's owners. I found these actions odd; indeed, I thought they bordered upon absurdity. If ever there were in Davis a building that merits historical designation, that building would be the old Terminal Hotel. Located only 50 yards from a major junction in railroad traffic, the hotel over the decades has come to stand for the railroad heritage of old Davis.

The council's actions deserve the following appraisal. (1) Past Davis city councils did not require previous owners of the hotel to keep their building in good repair. Here it is 75 years later and much of the building because of years of neglect has fallen into disrepair. By issuing a demolition permit, the present council has washed its hands of the "dirty ugly wreck" and has swept under the rug any responsibility which the city has had in causing the poor condition of the building. We Davisites should expect the city to avow their responsibilities for this run-down state of affairs, especially in a matter as important as preserving the town's heritage as symbolized by the hotel.

(2) Two city councilpersons have argued that, if the city should prevent the owners from demolishing their building, this would violate the owner's property rights. The city attorney and the two attorney councilmen should know that the right of private ownership is not absolute but can be and is sometimes overridden by legitimate public interest. In the present case under dispute, the public interest of preserving the town's railroad heritage as represented by the hotel should override the owner's property rights. The argument from private property does not justify council's issuance of demolition permit.

(3) One main function of government is to distribute the community's social wealth in a fair and equitable manner, social wealth being understood to include such valued goods as schools, parks, clinics, open space, historic places, etc.

If in the past the Davis City Council has decided that there would be no primary schools in East Davis, this would have amounted to an unfair distribution of the community's social wealth, unfair because schools belong not just to people living in three sections of Davis but to everyone in virtue of being members of this community.

Davis' railroad heritage as symbolized by the hotel belongs to all Davisites; it is part of this city's inherited social wealth. In issuing the demolition permit, the City Council has decided otherwise: They determined that this heritage is the private possession of the hotel's owners. This reallocation of a public good is unjust because unfair: It amounts to taking away something that rightly belongs to everyone and giving it to a privileged few.

(4) The approved demolition of the hotel in unjust for the further reason that it violates the rights of the entire community. Should the people of Davis be instructed about the large contribution which the Terminal Hotel and the railroad have over the years made to this community, were they to gain understanding and appreciation of the detail of this local history, there would not be one Davis person who would consent to or approve the hotel's demolition.

This universal consensus of a community enlightened by historical knowledge shows that all of Davis have a reasonable claim upon council and the hotel owners to cease pursuing the wasteful project of demolishing the hotel. To ignore or deny this claim would consist in council violating the rights of the community.

As noted by the French Philosopher, Jean Jacques Rousseau, what the enlightened people of a community wills is always the general or public good. If we ask why so few societies have succeeded in achieving this good, the explanation lies in the tragic and disillusioning fact that governments have led the people astray, away from the true good that they will. Blinding themselves to the wisdom available in the people's government seek a private good through promoting the economic interests of small groups of myopic individuals.

The common good of the Davis community would be served by the preservation of restoration of the old Terminal Hotel. In issuing a demolition permit to the hotel's owners, the Davis City Council prefers to seek a private good. What small group of individuals stand to gain financially from the demolition of the historic building?

John Mason
Davis

An earthy alternative

Michael Brooks/Enterprise photos

Rose Anne DeCristoforo, owner of Natural Food Works, stands in front of the store's vast selection of bulk medicinal herbs. Below is the store front of the 30-year-old business's new location at 624 Fourth St. in Davis.

Store was natural before it was hip

By Melanie Turner
Enterprise staff writer

The concept of using herbs, organic foods and supplements for better health is much more mainstream than it was when Natural Food Works was founded by a group of about nine partners in 1970 on Olive Drive in Davis.

"There was a time when the whole business of using whole foods and using supplements for therapeutic purposes was extremely revolutionary," said Natural Food Works owner Rose Anne DeCristoforo.

Today, while Natural Food Works recently made its second move in its 30-year history, DeCristoforo wants to assure long-time customers that the business is alive and well at 624 Fourth St.

It's still a unique spot in the region featuring an herbal pharmacy, a wide variety of discounted supplements and things like organic produce and coffee.

Seven of the founding partners — a mix of UC Davis students, former UCD students and law students — divided up

responsibilities and went to work.

"At that time it was very counter-culture to be involved in natural foods," said De-Cristoforo, owner of the store since 1997.

Former Davis City Councilman Bob Black, now Del Norte's county counsel, was among the original founders. He estimates Natural Food

See NATURAL, Page A4

10.26. The Natural Food Works was the only one of the three evicted shops to reopen elsewhere by the end of the next month. This reopening was celebrated in this Sunday *Enterprise* story of August 27.

NATURAL   From Page A1

Works is among the top five oldest businesses in downtown Davis.

In the early years Black worked as the store's organic farmer. He tended to a one-acre plot near the Unitarian Church on Russell Boulevard where they grew produce for the store, and for a couple of organic, natural food stores in the Bay Area.

While in Berkeley once a week he'd pick up things like organic coffee in bulk, wheat flour and molasses. Today, the store still uses the same old red coffee grinder, the same big coffee jars and the same coffee distributor — Capricorn Coffee.

"I think the natural food notion was just breaking out beyond a very narrow group of people that had historically been a small segment of the population," Black said. "Initially, it attracted the hippies and the political left."

Today, organic foods are more standardized and enjoy greater public awareness.

"Just in general I think the average person is much more conscious with not wanting to ingest all the preservatives and pesticides," Black said.

The selling of vitamins and supplements helped support the rest of the store's activities, and still does today.

In 1971, the store moved to 206 G St., where it remained until its recent move within the Core Area. During big anti-war demonstrations in the 1970s, the back room of Natural Food Works served as a meeting place for people, like Black, promoting anti-war activities.

In the late '70s, Beverly Batha of Davis purchased the store and owned it for the next 20 years.

Early on, the original founders began to disperse and go their separate ways. One of the law students is now a judge in Los Angeles, according to Black. Another man, Bob Gerner, owns El Cerrito and Berkeley Natural Grocery.

While a student at UCD, Gerner, now of Pleasant Hill, was the first manager of the store. He worked for free, but the connections he made paid off as he founded Westbrae Natural Foods only months after leaving the store.

He recalls attending a California organic merchants meeting at Mt. Shasta with another of his Davis partners.

"We were a bunch of hippies up in the mountains trying to start a new industry," he recalls. "We knew we were going to be different from other stores and run things differently. We tried to agree on certain standards on what we wanted our businesses to be."

Although the business was having financial difficulties when DeCristoforo purchased the store, she says she saw it as "an opportunity to put what I know out there."

She was a journalist, covering governmental issues in Nevada, but she had a personal fascination with natural foods and herbal remedies.

"For years I was telling people about this stuff who really didn't want to know," she says.

"People who come in here really want to know."

She says the store plays the role of an intermediary, helping to make modern research available to people in search of answers.

Customer and part-time employee Deborah Williams says, "It's unique. There's nothing like it, especially the herbal pharmacy."

The herbal pharmacy — shelves of herbs in jars and a staple of the store — is more prominently displayed in the new location. People buy the herbs in bulk to create their own teas, elixirs and tonics. There are herbs used for incense, to combat immune problems, to soothe sore throats, and to better one's vision.

"Really we are our best doctors," Williams says. "We have to learn to heal ourselves."

DeCristoforo also sells vegicaps and herbs in powdered form so customers can make their own supplements, knowing the exact potency they are ingesting. Cooking herbs, such as oregano and orange peel, also are sold in bulk.

"It's the best bargain," says Williams, noting that things like nutmeg can be ground fresh and used for cooking, or, to drive away ants. "I don't like using chemicals."

Williams says she learns something new ever day working in the store. As a shopper she likes that it's small so finding what she needs is easy. And customers are encouraged to take a seat and rummage through the many nutritional books DeCristoforo keeps on hand.

Priscilla Hawkins of Davis was having various health problems, which began to fade once she came to Natural Food Works. Hawkins had lost 18 pounds and suffered from stomach problems.

She said doctors performed numerous tests and came up with nothing.

"I had been praying, 'God lead me to a person who can help me.'"

DeCristoforo suggested Hawkins could be gluten intolerant. Hawkins tried a gluten-free diet and since, she reports she's gained back 14 pounds and feels much better.

"I tell everybody, this is amazing," she says.

While DeCristoforo acknowledges she had to give up some of the nostalgia that went with the old location — customers loved the only wood-planked floor — she is optimistic that the new store will offer even more in time. She moved because the owners of the building on the northeast corner of Second and G streets, known as the Terminal Hotel, have plans to demolish some portions of the building and do a remodel. All the businesses moved out in mid-July.

DeCristoforo says while the store has undergone a big change, it still offers the types of things it's been known for all these years, like one of the best collections of culinary herbs in the Valley.

"We sell a lot of herbs so they're very fresh and high quality," she said.

The discounted supplements — buy-one-get-one-half-price — also are a big draw. While some things are still the same, DeCristoforo says Natural Food Works is still evolving. In its next phase, she plans for the store to "put the food" back in Natural Food Works by eventually adding a commercial kitchen that offers healthy foods.

5) THE PENULTIMATE ACT BEGINS

The next-to-the-last set of actions commenced the last days of August, just before the long Labor Day weekend. On Wednesday, August 30th, Grace Chen submitted a "preapplication" proposal for a new structure on the Terminal Building site. It's cover page is reproduced here as Fig. 10.27.

🚲Davis
California

RECEIVED

AUG 3 0 2000

City of Davis
Planning & Building

PLANNING APPLICATION FORM

Please complete this application thoroughly and accurately, and attach the required exhibits as indicated in the attached matrix. Please note that incomplete applications will not be accepted for processing. Contact the Planning Division at 530-757-5610 with your questions.

Application Type (Check applicable boxes)

[X] Preapplication [ ] Prezoning/Rezoning [ ] Design Review
[ ] General Plan Amendment [ ] Rezoning/Prelim. PD [ ] Minor Modification
[ ] Specific Plan Amendment [ ] Final P.D./Revision [ ] Conditional Use Permit
[ ] Zoning Ordinance Amendment [ ] Tentative Subdivision Map [ ] Public Convenience or Necessity
[ ] Variance [ ] Lot Line Adjustment [ ] Other _____

Project Description - Describe in detail. Add separate sheet if necessary.

Demolition and removal of existing building; new construction of approximately 21,000 s.f. consisting of ground floor retail (8100 s.f.), second floor service commercial/residential (6200 s.f.); third floor with partial fourth floor loft residential (7000 s.f.).

Location of project (address) *NE* 2nd & G St.   Assessors Parcel # _____

Name of Project___Chen___   Property size ___9375___ ___.22___
                                          Square Feet   Acres

Building size ___12,000___ ___21,000___   Height _____
              Existing   Proposed

Land Use ___mixed___ ___mixed___
          Existing Proposed

Applicant/Contact McCandless & Associates, Architects   Phone (daytime)___662-9146___

Address 666 Dead Cat Alley, Woodland, CA 95695

Property Owner___Aggie Enterprises___   Phone (daytime)___753-2436___

Address 44150 CountryClub Dr., El Macero, CA 95618

Property Owner's consent. I declare under penalty of perjury that I am the owner of the property involved in this application. I certify that the information furnished above and in the attached exhibits is true and correct to the best of my knowledge and belief. Property owner letter is acceptable.

Chao (grace) Chen   Aug 29, 2000
Owner's signature   Date

For office use only:
Received by MAW   Date 9/30/00   Fee Total: Deposit ___750___   Fixed _____
PA# 26-00   Application# 1-00   Project (billing) # _____

10.27. Cover page of the August 30 Chen "preapplication" for a new building on the Terminal Building site.

She also submitted a McCandless and Associates Architects sketch of a proposed new building (shown in Fig. 10.28). According to people in a position to know and whose veracity I trust, the design shown in Fig. 10.28 was created at the direction of Grace Chen, who had been inspired by the Swiss-Chateau-style ski lodges she saw on a skiing trip to Canada. (In addition, her beauty shop was called the "Hair Chalet"). She had directed McCandless to execute a design so inspired in the expectation that the people of Davis would find it pleasing.

I am told that this design met with virtually universal and strong derision as well as peals of laughter as photocopies of it began to circulate in the Planning and Building Department and in wider circles of interested parties. In these wider circles, the design was dubbed the "Swiss Lodge," the "haunted house," and other less kind appellations.

Over the Labor Day weekend, news of the negative reaction reached Grace Chen, who withdrew it when the Planning Department opened the next Tuesday, September 4. Close to tears, according to one observer, Mrs. Chen expressed her surprise and dismay that people did not like the design. All she wanted was "the right thing for Davis."

Promptly, the pitched roof sketch was replaced with a flat roof version, which is shown in Fig. 10.29. Indeed, the rapidity with which this second design appeared suggested to me that it was McCandless' original design. All he needed to do was pull it out of a file and send it to the Planning Department.

VIEW FROM SOUTHWEST

10.28. The Swiss Lodge/Haunted House initial design proposed for the Terminal Building site.

If the account of this Swiss-Chateau episode I have just given is reasonably accurate, I think it helps us understand some of the dynamics of the Terminal Building story considered as a whole. The implication of Mrs. Chen's behavior is that she had less-than-accurate perceptions and conceptions of Davis public opinion on architectural and related matters. One consequence was that she could innocently embark on a course of action to which the social responses would bring her grief.

VIEW FROM SOUTHWEST

10.29. Second sketch of a building for the Terminal Building site, quickly submitted after the first sketch was almost immediately withdrawn.

Both designs appeared not to save any of the Terminal Building. But, since the building was still there and the two designs suggested considerable conceptual fluidity, the possibility of prevailing on the Chens to reconsider remained.

One key problem was identifying who might be able to persuade the Chens to reconsider. It seemed clear that people identified with the preservationist position had little influence with them and conversations with preservationists might even be counterproductive.

One had, instead, to rely on the most-involved City representatives. These were Planning Director Bill Emlen, Downtown Coordinator Ken Hiatt, and Mayor Ken Wagstaff.

Wagstaff's position, though, was apparently moving toward total demolition, although in an e-mail he sent me on September 4 (Fig. 10.30) he seemed undecided on a specific course of action.

Exact timing was becoming important. The Chen's long ago declared they would demolish the building and they, in fact, had all the official permission they needed. The key questions were only when it would happen and how much of the building would be taken down.

In his September 4 e-mail to me (Fig. 10.30) we see that Wagstaff had asked the Chens to "delay demolition until after the public discussion." And in the next sentence he reported that the Planning Commission would have a special meeting at the site on September 16. That meeting would be, presumably, a part of and the **start** of "the public discussion."

Let me underscore Wagstaff's phrase:

"delay demolition until after the public discussion"

Keep this phrase in mind as we look at the next events.

The first of these next events was the demolition contract Stan Bowers signed with Grace Chen dated Wednesday, September 6 (Fig. 10.31). Of key importance, this contract provided that demolition would begin "on or about 9/18/00."

So: while Mayor Wagstaff desired to "delay demolition until after the public discussion," which presumably involved more than one meeting or occasion, the Chens were planning to take the building down two days after the September 16 meeting of the Planning Commission.

However, the existence of this contract and plan was known to hardly anyone at this time—this time meaning the period from September 6th to the 16th.

Instead, over this period, the key players—who included Ken Wagstaff, Bill Emlen, and Ken Haitt—still believed that the Chens would delay for at least some weeks of public discussion.

Indeed, these people met with Lee Chen on Wednesday, September 13th and it seems that they came away with the understanding of a delay until after the Planning Commission had properly considered the matter, the first session of which would be the next Saturday, September 16. **They did not realize that, for the Chens, a single session was all the public discussion necessary.**

Although the Chens had clearly decided on a total demolition of the building, they—or least their architect—apparently thought some legitimizing window-dressing of their action was nonetheless needed. This took the form of what construction estimator Bob Hart (Fig. 10.32) termed a "conceptual cost comparison" for three options for the building (Fig. 10.33).

To belabor the obvious: These cost estimates were produced two days **after** signing a contract to demolish the building starting September 18. This suggests that these estimates addressed to rehabilitation options were obtained for public relations purposes rather than for serious economic comparisons.

Although the Harrison Construction Company documents shown as Figs. 10.32 and 10.33 were produced on September 8, their existence was not made public until the Planning Commission meeting on September 16. Even then, the documents themselves were not produced. The public was only told (by McCandless) that an unnamed entity (two of them, in fact) had worked up three estimates, with the conclusion that anything but demolition was too costly. Moreover, these documents were not part of the public process. Instead, I discovered them in the City files months later.

I must also point out that the very sketchy cost treatments seen in Fig. 10.33 are by no stretch of the imagination anywhere near a feasibility study as that term in used in professional circles. As detailed in Chapter 1, valid feasibility studies consist of three parts: the physical facts of the building and construction costs; market potential income; and, financing and valuation. The document in Fig. 10.33 deals, at the very best, with only the first of these three major parts (and even that part was done in a cursory fashion).

Ken Wagstaff, 9/4/00 6:50 PM -0700, telephone call

```
X-POP3-Rcpt: jlofland@ike
X-Sender: kjwag@dcn.davis.ca.us (Unverified)
Date: Mon, 04 Sep 2000 18:50:52 -0700
To: jflofland@ucdavis.edu
From: Ken Wagstaff <kjwag@dcn.davis.ca.us>
Subject: telephone call
```

John,
Thanks for your call.
You said you didn't require a return call, but perhaps this email is a good way to reply.
I assume from your call that the Chens have finally filed their preliminary plans. They showed me a sketch earlier. They want to go beyond two stories, which will require a conditional use permit, and which will give the planning commission wide latitude v/v design.
>From your message I gather you may have forgotten my position, which is that I want the new building to fit in with its neighborhood, preserving to a reasonable degree the brickwork of the west wall. I believe that is what the Chens are doing.
The existing wall can actually be preserved (per your "facade-ectomy (sp?)" idea), which the architect has determined would be feasible to do, but at a cost of about $200,000. Chen doesn't want to pay for it, and in my opinion the city can't afford it. The alternative is to rebuild the wall to its original appearance, using as much of the original brick as possible. From an historic-fabric standpoint, many would prefer the actual original wall.
>From a structural and cost standpoint (and even an aesthetic one, given the fact that retaining the original wall might result in extra-thick and thus somewhat displeasing/non-useful windows), the architect recommends rebuilding- rather than preserving- the wall. I am still considering this question, and for that reason have asked Chen to delay demolition until after the public discussion.

A special meeting of the planning commission is scheduled for Sat Sept 16 10am.
Prior to that there will be an information item on the Sept 13 agenda of the Council.

Ken

10.30. Wagstaff e-mail to me, September 4, 2000. The "information item" mentioned in the last sentence of this e-mail apparently did not happen, for, there is nothing on the Terminal Building matter in the September 13 minutes of the City Council.

10.31. Stan Bowers' September 6th contract with Grace Chen to demolish the Terminal Building "on or about 9/18/00." The black arrow points to the date.

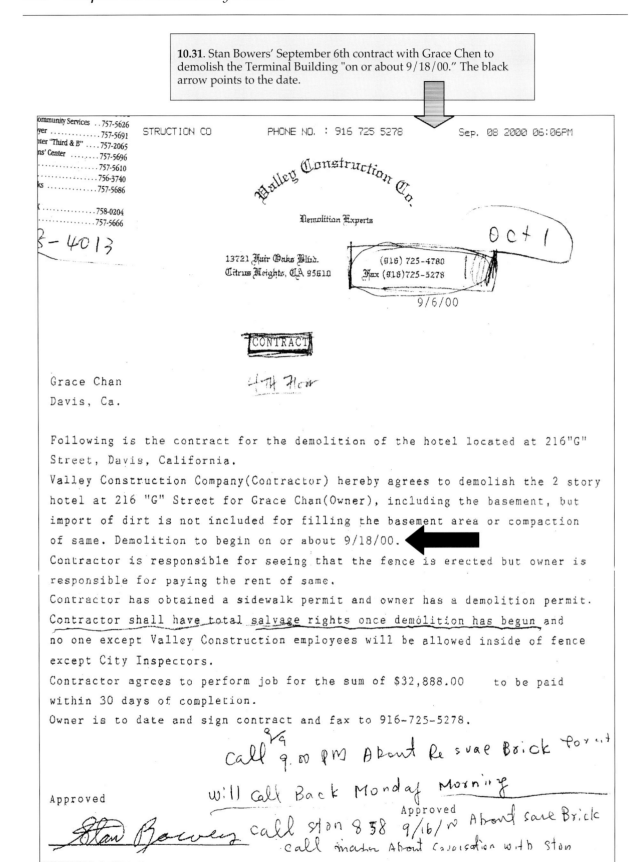

STRUCTION CO   PHONE NO. : 916 725 5278   Sep. 08 2000 06:06PM

Valley Construction Co.

Demolition Experts

13721 Fair Oaks Blvd.
Citrus Heights, CA 95610

(916) 725-4780
Fax (916)725-5278

Oct 1

9/6/00

CONTRACT

Grace Chan
Davis, Ca.

4th Floor

Following is the contract for the demolition of the hotel located at 216"G"
Street, Davis, California.

Valley Construction Company(Contractor) hereby agrees to demolish the 2 story
hotel at 216 "G" Street for Grace Chan(Owner), including the basement, but
import of dirt is not included for filling the basement area or compaction
of same. Demolition to begin on or about 9/18/00.

Contractor is responsible for seeing that the fence is erected but owner is
responsible for paying the rent of same.

Contractor has obtained a sidewalk permit and owner has a demolition permit.

Contractor shall have total salvage rights once demolition has begun and
no one except Valley Construction employees will be allowed inside of fence
except City Inspectors.

Contractor agrees to perform job for the sum of $32,888.00   to be paid
within 30 days of completion.

Owner is to date and sign contract and fax to 916-725-5278.

Call 9.00 PM About Re svae Brick for it

will call Back Monday Morning

Approved

Stan Bowers   *call Stan 858 9/16/~ About save Brick*   Approved

call master About Conversation with Stan

10.32. Bob Hart of Harrison Construction "conceptual cost comparison" sent to Bill McCandless, September 8th, 2000.

8-00 MON 8:22 AM   MCCANDLESS & ASSOCIATES   FAX NO. 5300623425

FAX NO. :   SP. 08 2000 03:24PM P1

2940 Spafford St. #100 • Davis CA 95616-5600
P O BOX 1227 • Davis CA 95617-1227
(530) 753-0373 • FAX: (530) 753-0431

September 8, 2000

Mr. Bill McCandless
McCandless & Assoc.
Via fax: (530) 662-3425

Re: Terminal Hotel

Dear Bill,

Attached is the conceptual cost comparison for the three options. As discussed all options are based on the same size building of 12,000 square feet. Option #2 will result in damage to the existing mural. Harrison Construction does not guarantee the extent of or responsibility for this damage.

Should you have questions, do not hesitate to call. I can be reached directly at 757-0877.

Sincerely,

Bob Hart

Bob Hart
Project Manager

.8-00 MON 8:22 AM MCCANDLESS & ASSOCIATES FAX NO. 5306623425 P.

ROM : FAX NO. : P. 08 2000 03:25PM P2

HARRISON CONSTRUCTION CONFIDENTIAL 9/8/00 3:13 PM

PROJECT:		TERMINAL HOTEL			
DATE:		9/8/00			
SQUARE FEET:		12,000	12,000	12,000	
NOTES:		CONCEPTUAL COST COMPARISON			
		OPTION			
		1	2	3	
ACTIVITY		REHAB EXISTING BUILDING	NEW CONST. SAVING WEST & NORTH EXT. WALLS	DEMO (E) STRUCTURE & REPLACE WITH ALL NEW CONST.	COMMENTS
OFF SITE		$18,000	$18,000	$18,000	CITY SIDEWALKS
HAZMAT ABATEMENT		$0	$0	$0	EXCLUDED
DEMOLITION		$85,000	$100,000	$35,000	TEMP SHORING REQ. FOR OPTION 1 & 2
FOUNDATION		$120,000	$84,000	$72,000	OPTION 2 INCLUDES CONNECTING (E) WALLS TO NEW FRAMING
SEISMIC RETROFIT		$100,000	$25,000	$0	
SUPER STRUCTURE		$288,000	$300,000	$288,000	WOOD FRAMED WITH STRUCTURAL STEEL COMPONENTS
EXT. CLOSURE		$100,000	$135,000	$150,000	ROOF, STORE FRONT, PLASTER, ETC
BUILDING SYSTEMS		$144,000	$144,000	$144,000	ELEVATOR, FIRE SPRINKLER, HVAC, PLUMBING, ELECT.
INTERIOR FINISHES		$240,000	$240,000	$240,000	INCLUDES BASIC INTERIOR FINISHES
SUBTOTAL COSTS		$1,095,000	$1,046,000	$947,000	
GENERAL CONDITIONS	12.00%	$131,400	$125,520	$113,640	INCLUDES PUBLIC PROTECTION & TESTING SERVICES
CONTRACTOR CONTINGENCY		$109,500	$78,450	$47,350	
GL & BUILDERS RISK	0.60%	$10,785.00	$6,276	$5,682	
PERFOR. & PAYMENT BOND	1.22%				EXCLUDED
SUBTOTAL		$1,346,685	$1,256,246	$1,113,672	
CONTRACTOR FEE	8.00%	$107,735	$100,500	$89,094	
		~$1,453,000	~$1,356,000	~$1,200,000	
		+$250,000	+$150,000		

1 OF 2

10.33.. Harrison Construction September 8th, 2000 "conceptual cost comparison" for three treatments of the Terminal Building.

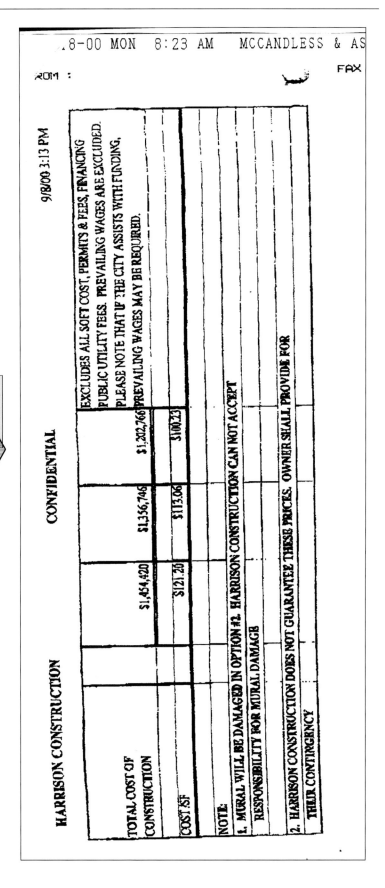

6) SEPTEMBER 16: "SURPRISE! SURPRISE!"

A crowd of some thirty people assembled at the northeast corner of Second and G streets for the Planning Commission's site visit, Saturday morning, September 16th. After preliminaries, there was a collective gasp when Woodland architect Bill McCandless made his Davis debut by announcing that the Chens had decided to commence demolition the day after tomorrow—the very next Monday. Therefore, the only purpose of this meeting was to discuss the new structure that would replace the Terminal Building. One person present recalled of the moment: "I'll never forget the looks of horror and disbelief" on the faces of many people.

It was now a public and social fact that when Lee Chen had agreed to wait for public discussion conducted by the Planning Commission, he only meant to wait for the Saturday meeting and then to proceed immediately to demolition! There would be no public discussion in the sense of multiple meetings in which various alternatives were seriously considered. This Saturday morning gathering was it.

But, the involved parties had to admit that the Chens had not promised to delay for any particular period of time or to take the public discussion seriously. Therefore, for Wagstaff, Emlen and Haitt (and everyone else) to assume otherwise was in error, albeit an understandable and natural error. That is, people assume that other people use language to mean the same things that they mean

Many people at this meeting were flabbergasted and continued to call for historical designation of the building, exploration of tax credits, a feasibility study, and the like. But the state of play was clearly a long way past for any serious talk about such matters.

In Fig. 10.34, we see Mr. McCandless at the site. Fig. 10.35 provides the official record of what happened at the meeting. The Sunday edition of the *Davis Enterprise* also provided a report, under the curious headline "Mural will be demolished" (Fig. 10.36).

10.34. Bill McCandless (center) at the Planning Commission Terminal Building site visit, September 16, 2000. The construction fence seen in the background had been placed around the building a few days before this.

10.35. Minutes of the September 16th meeting of the Planning Commission.

**MINUTES FROM PLANNING COMMISSION
SITE VISIT FOR 200 G STREET – TERMINAL HOTEL
SEPTEMBER 16, 2000**

Commissioners Present:
Emily Burstein (Vice Chairperson), Pamela Gunnell (Chairperson), Robert Hagedorn, Eileen Sarnitz, David Sandino and Mark Spencer. Wendy Nelson(Historic Resources Commission Chair)

Staff Present:
Bill Emlen, Planning and Building Director; Katherine Hess, Planning and Redevelopment Administrator; Ken Hiatt, Associate Planner/Downtown Coordinator; Cindy Norris, Associate Planner; Bob Wolcott, Senior Planner; Esther Polito, Cultural Services Manager.

Applicant:
Bill McCandless, Project Architect

10:00am   Call to Order by Pam Gunnell.
Discussion of meeting purpose and ground rules for meeting conduct.

Ken Hiatt, gave an introductory discussion of the Planning Process. That the intent is to look at the proposed building within the context of the existing site. No action will be taken as a result of the meeting, but that comment will be received to provide input to the applicant for future design work and to assist in expediting future public hearing process. Intent to discuss general concepts such as proposed uses, parking, general design.

Ken Hiatt mentioned that the Historical Resources Commission will be meeting the following Monday, September 18, 2000 at 7:30pm and will be discussing the Terminal Hotel.

The meeting was then turned over to the project architect, Bill McCanless to discuss the proposed project design and analysis conducted to date in determination of the current proposal.

McCandless mentioned that there were several objectives in mind while developing the project: Creating a vital, commercially viable focal point for the downtown; Providing an attractive face to the train station; and developing an economically viable project for the property owners.

McCanless indicated that they have had two structural reports prepared to date that have resulting to three possible scenarios with regard to rehabilitation of the structure. He indicated that these were comparable comps for a 12,000sf building 1) To rehabilitate the existing structure will cost 20% more than the cost of all new construction; 2) to save the north and west wall will cost 13% more than the cost for all new construction; 3) All new construction. He indicated that the cost differentials are in the hundreds of thousands of dollars and therefore the owners have opted to go with option 3, All new construction.

He also mentioned that the owners are in possession of a demolition permit, that has twice been issued to them.

McCanless indicated that the proposed design concept is for a larger building, approximately 21,000sf that will have up to 4 floors. The ground floor will be built to the lot area, approximately 9300sf, and will be retail space. The second floor will have service commercial and some residential with flex space. The third floor will be residential with the fourth partial residential with possibility for lots and townhouse development.

At this point questions, comments from commissioners and general public were taken and discussion provided.
The following is a partial list of some questions and comments:

Q. Are there funds available from the MainStreet program or through the City's facade improvement program?

Issue is eligibility for those funds as the building/site was not designated as a historic structure by the City Council. Also, in order to qualify for tax credit funds, the owner would not be able to alter the building. This is problematic as the upstairs is not conducive to re-use.

Q. Are there funds available from the façade program to help preserve the existing bricks for re-use?

Staff indicated that they would look into this possibility.

Q. If the building is demolished the next week, approximately how long will the site remain vacant?

Staff estimated that if the owner proceeded with the project that it would be approximately 2 years before a new building is constructed on site.

Q. Could the existing fenestration (window/opening) pattern and brick patterning be reproduced on the new building?

The architect indicated that those design elements could be reproduced. But he did note that larger plate glass on the ground floor is more conducive to retail use.

At this point there was some general discussion regarding the issue of exactly reproducing or mimicking a historic structure. That generally, it is considered to be inappropriate to replicate a historic structure to give the appearance that the new building is an older building. The architect explained that in fact the State Historic Preservation standards indicate that add-ons to historic structures should not be replication of the old, and while reminiscent should be clear that it is different.

Regarding the North/Mural Side of the building

The architect discussed the mural application, that the plaster has been applied right onto the bricks and is very difficult and expensive to try to refurbish or remove. It would be extremely difficult to take down brick by brick and then replace and repair any damage to

the mural. Esther Polito, the Cultural Services Manager, indicated that she has been in contact with the mural artist, Terry Buckendorf, who has indicated that he is interested in possibly working on a new mural for the building. Polito indicated that there has been extensive documentation of the existing mural.

When asked, the architect indicated that at this time the owners are not prepared to re-create the mural and have not been asked to do so. In response to inquiries, Polito indicated that there may be some possibility of using the Municipal Art fund, however, a project of this type may take away from other project and there would have to be public discussion of whether this is a viable use of public funds.

Q. What is the maximum size building an owner could put on this site?

Hiatt responded that an owner could put up a two-story building without a use permit, and if the building is demolished and replaced with one of the same size, that they would not have to replace or add any new parking. (Design review would be required for any new project) The theoretical maximum for the site is 40,000sf or 4 stories with a Conditional Use Permit for the height.

The group moved to the south side of the building, facing the depot.

Q. Can the City find out about the future use of the depot parking lot and Amtrak ridership?

Hiatt indicated that Anne Brunette with City staff has been working with Amtrak in this regard.

Several people raised a concern with regard to parking availability should the residential units go in. It was mentioned that in-lieu fees would be required and that the Core Area Specific Plan discourages at-grade parking. Hiatt, indicated that in one of their early proposals that the Owners had looked at underground parking, but found that it would be extremely expensive (approximately $50,000 per space) and that only a few parking spaces could be provided.

An additional issue raised while evaluating the south/depot side is the proposed building height. Wendy Nelson, the Historic Resources Commission Chair, indicated that she was concerned about the proposed 4-story height at this end. She indicated that she felt that if this building is allowed to go high, that it could start a trend toward larger heights in this area. She indicated that if the City wants to maintain the coziness, that the building should stay at a lower height in this area.

It was noted that the on G street, the Anderson Bank building, which is directly across the street from this site, is three stories tall (30 feet in height). The proposed four story sections of the new building would be 40 feet in height. On the G Street and 2nd Street sides the four-story sections have been primarily stepped back from the street front. There are sections toward the south end where the four stories are at the street front.

Some general comments and concerns were raised at this time that the City review of the proposed project should take place prior to the demolition of the existing building. That once the building comes down, the historic resource has been lost and there is no guarantee that a new structure will be built in its place. There is concern that this site will

10.35. Continued, pages 2 (bottom) and 3 (top).

• That the City formally pusue re-creation of the mural on the east wall. See if the applicant can contribute some of the cost.

Eileen Samitz:
• Concern with a 4th Floor
• Concern that residential may not be appropriate due to noise and parking issues. Maybe limit on residential. Consider noise analysis
• Focus on building commercial
• Help reduce massing of building
• Would like to see the front façade preserved or alternatively replicated.
• Would like to see a re-creation of the mural

Emily Burstein:
• Felt Pam summarized her concerns as well
• Make sure there will wall space available for a future mural
• Preserve elements of the front façade
• Willing to consider the 4th floor in trade off to underground parking (economic trade off)
• Comment that residential may in fact require less parking than retail.
• Would prefer to see a 4th floor with an open courtyard rather than a denser shorter building. Prefer more open space; interior public space.

Bob Hagedorn:
• Concern with mass and denseness on the depot side and the 4th floor. Recess 4th story from street on depot side. Don't want verticle wall 4-stories up.
• Concern with lack of parking for the residential component
• Replicate the front details and would like to see the mural reproduced

Mark Spencer:
• Make effort to save the bricks
• Agree with Emily. Open to considering a 4th floor. If go above 2-story step back from street. Not overwhelm street.
• If residential would like to see something like a rooftop garden or private open space

---

sit vacant for a long period of time. It was stated that there is some loss of trust with the owners destroying the building, before completing the public review process for a new building.

Ken Hiatt, indicated that the owners are proceeding with the demolition due to pressure received from their insurance carrier. Hiatt indicated that he would ask the owners if they could delay the demolition for a period of time.

The group was reminded that the City's leverage was removed when the City Council did not vote to designate the building a historic resource.

The project architect stated that the owners have followed through with what they were asked to do. They said they would investigate options, which they did. They have chosen to pursue one of those options.

General discussion ensued in which it was suggested that the Owners be asked to hold off on demolition in order to investigate other options, such as re-use of the brick and to clarify the City Council's understanding with the Owners.

Katherine Hess indicated that she is not sure what action the City Council could take at this time legally. There were no conditions other than life safety that were conditioned (fencing/secure the site). The item is not on the agenda and the Council can not take any action.

It was noted that currently there is a demolition ordinance in the draft process that would require an approved plan prior to issuance of a demo permit, to help prevent resulting vacant lots for long periods of time.

Planning Commission Motions:
1. The Planning Commission requested that an item be placed on the City Council agenda as an urgency item for next Wednesday (9/20/2000) that would clarify the informal understanding between the Chen's and the City Council with regard to preservation of the bricks.
2. That the Staff contact the Chen's as soon as possible and ask them to hold off on the demolition until Wednesday in order to work toward a solution to preserve the bricks.

Planning Commission Comments Regarding Building Design:
Pam Gunnell:
• Trouble supporting 4-stories. Three story seems more reasonable with the bank building across the street. If 4th floor should be recessed across from street. Don't want a verticle wall 4-stories up.
• Explore the potential to put some parking on-site. Push the envelope and not be a prisoner of parking spaces.
• Indicated that residential could be an exciting component near transportation hubs. A "lofty goal" if sensitive design.
• Would like to see the window and brick pattern on 2nd and G Street
• Place emphasis on preserving some of the brick and some of the original building components

10.35. Concluded, pages 4 (bottom) and 5 (top).

Mural will be demolished

Streetscape to go down with brick building for renovation project

By Melanie Turner
Enterprise staff writer

As early as Monday morning the large mural that has graced G Street since 1976 depicting an early Davis streetscape through the old Davis arches, along with the 75-year-old brick building that it's attached to, will be demolished.

Downtown coordinator Ken Hiatt estimates it will be two years before a replacement building is completed on the site at 200 G St.

Property owners Lee and Grace Chen plan to replace the old building on the northwest corner of Second and G streets with a new one roughly double the size of the 12,000-square-foot building that's there now. In places, the new building could be as high as four stories.

This despite unanimous recommendations by the Historic Resources Management Commission that the City Council give the building a historic designation, and despite talk of possibly saving some of the building's original character elements, such as the unique brick work on the G Street side of the building.

Known as the Terminal Hotel, having once served as a hotel for early train passengers, the building has been at the heart of controversy for months now.

The Chens took out a demolition permit about a year ago and this summer had it extended through Dec. 4. The City Council's action not to designate the building as historic opened the door for the Chens to demolish it.

Last June, the council did request the city work with the Chens to attempt to reuse some portion of the old building.

Saturday morning, the Planning Commission held a meeting outside the now empty building (four businesses moved out in mid-July) to hear the latest plans for the

See MURAL, Page A3

Wayne Tilcock/Enterprise photo

SAYING GOODBYE: A group of area residents gathers in front of the G Street mural for a last look on Saturday morning. Artist Terry Buckendorf painted the mural, which includes arches that once spanned Second Street, the old Anderson Bank building and Model T Fords.

10.36. *Davis Enterprise*, Sunday, September 15 feature write-up of the Saturday, September 16, Planning Commission on-site meeting.

MURAL From Page A1

site from the Chens' architect, Bill McCandliss, and to receive feedback from the public.

The idea behind the on-site meeting was to help the applicant address any concerns before submitting a final application for approval to the city.

Seven members of the commission were present, including Pam Gunnell, David Sandino, Eileen Samitz, Robert Hagedorn, Emily Burstein and Mark Spencer. The Chens were reportedly out of town.

McCandliss said the Chens are interested in developing a commercially viable site with ground-floor retail on at least three sides, including the side facing the train station.

In response to public concerns, McCandliss said the Chens had a couple of contractors compare the cost of three scenarios, figuring it would cost 20 percent more than building new to rehabilitate the old building, and it would cost 13 percent more to save two walls — the facade along G Street and the northern mural wall.

"We're talking hundreds of thousands of dollars," he said. "The owners have no interest in putting that kind of money into saving this building."

The concept McCandliss outlined Saturday included first-floor retail, a second floor with a combination commercial, residential and courtyard, and a third and fourth floor of residential. There would be no on-site parking. The total number of residential units proposed is from eight to 10.

While at least one member of the public said he was pleased with the direction the project was going, of the roughly 20 members of the public who turned out the majority were not happy.

"This building is way out of scale and too complex," said Margaret Milligan. "It's just going to be a horrible, horrible mess. I'm very disturbed about this."

"If you want to maintain some of the coziness that we've enjoyed (in downtown Davis), then you don't want this project," said Wendy Nelson, chairwoman of the Historic Resources Management Commission.

The commission will discuss the matter at its meeting at 7:30

Courtesy graphic

This artist's rendering shows the proposed design of the Terminal Hotel from the southwest.

p.m. Monday in the Hattie Weber Museum, 445 C St.

Dick Hastings, a member of the state Historic Buildings Safety Board, said demolishing the building Monday will do the city and the Chens a disservice since other concepts that perhaps involve saving some elements of the building will not be considered. "Everybody loses on that," he said.

Eric Nelson said once the Chens demolish the building, the property value will rise. He fears the property will go up for sale.

"That takes care of all their problems," he said. "They've got their money. They're out of here."

Some folks felt betrayed by the mayor.

"There's been a real violation of trust," said Jean Jackman. "We were assured by the mayor they would work to help save some elements of the building."

Added Heather Caswell, who found some elements of new project "quite desirable," also said there had been false promises. "I'm very disappointed with the mayor," she said.

Caswell said she was told recently by the mayor that the option to save the building facade and mural-side was still open.

The Chens have said they want something many people can be happy with, and they aim to build a project that's compatible with its historical surroundings.

About a month ago, Wagstaff said he was pleased the Chens have committed again and again to not tear the building down without first sharing their plans for the site with the city, saying, "That's a sign of good faith."

The commission voted unanimously Saturday to request the Chens delay demolition at least through Wednesday, and to ask the City Council to clarify at its Wednesday meeting what the councils' expectation has been. It is reportedly the hope of commissioners that at least the bricks could be preserved and used in the new building construction.

Wagstaff said he purposely did not attend Saturday's Planning Commission meeting since the commission will need to make its own decisions on the project design and use permit.

"I think the idea was the owner and architect were going to consider the reaction of the commission," he said.

He said the design presented

Saturday was a pre-application, opened to change.

"I originally said if it was structurally, architecturally and economically feasible to save a couple walls, it would be good to do that," he said. "The architect had qualified people review the integrity of those two walls and determined the cost of saving them to be around $200,000, assuming no damage during demolition."

He added, "I think the disappointment that people feel is the desire to keep the original wall and to keep the original fabric. If the city had the money maybe we could do that."

Wagstaff said the drawing he viewed previously illustrates an attempt by the architect to recreate the look, "in a fresh, original way," of at least the west wall of the Terminal Hotel. He also said it's been his understanding that bricks from the old could be salvaged for the new.

7) THE DRAGGED–OUT SITUATION

Our media-inspired images of demolitions prompt us to believe that because of carefully placed explosives or hefty wrecking balls structures fall rapidly and almost all-at-once (Liss, 2000). Such was not to be the case for the Terminal Building.

Instead, demolition began the next Monday, but then stopped when the east and north walls were down. The Arch Mural and much of the building were still intact. This pause lasted eleven days. During this time, some people still had some hope of saving the west wall and the Arch Mural.

The goal therefore became that of freezing demolition short of destroying those two walls. In the next chapter, I examine this final phase of the struggle—this final preservation failure.

11

FREEZE FAILURE

At the Saturday, September 16 meeting described at the end of the last chapter, the Planning Commission "voted unanimously . . . to request the Chens to delay demolition at least through Wednesday and to ask the City Council to clarify at its Wednesday meeting what its expectations had been" *(Davis Enterprise*, September 17 and Fig. 9.42).

A delay of the demolition scheduled to begin Monday morning had thus became what would be the next-to-last objective. But it also failed when, on Monday, the rear of the building was reduced to rubble. This partial demolition sparked the last, pathetic hope for a freeze of the now-underway demolition.

The eleven days of this period—September 18-28—bring us to the level of fine-grained maneuvering and even dramatic confrontations. The narrative comes down to a day-to-day pace, in contrast to the month-to-month and week-to-week gait seen previously.

1) MONDAY, SEPTEMBER 18: DEMOLITION BEGINS

In action terms, Monday, September 18 was exceptionally long. It began at 3:14 a. m. when night-owl preservationist and computer guru Alan Miller activated the Save Davis e-mail list with his assessment of the situation and a call to action (Fig. 11.1).

A copy of this e-mail apparently went to Mayor Ken Wagstaff, who replied to the person who sent it to him with the e-mail note reproduced in Fig. 11.2. Of significance, the Mayor had clearly now focused on only saving some brick from the building.

The previous day, Sunday, September 17, a large machine called an "excavator" was delivered on a flat-bed truck to the rear of the Terminal Building, offloaded, and pulled close-in to it, behind the chain-link fence. The photo in Fig. 11.3 shows it in the early light of Monday.

Also early this morning, architect McCandless apparently felt it prudent to provide City staff Ken Hiatt with a copy of the construction estimates reproduced in the last chapter as Figs. 10.32 and 10.33. The puzzle is why he waited until this day to provide the City these numbers—or why he bothered to provide them at all.

>>> Save Davis <<<,9/18/00 3:14 AM -0700,Aggie Hotel Demolition Monday: Help Save

```
X-POP3-Rcpt: jlofland@ike
Mime-Version: 1.0
X-Sender: sleeper@mail.omsoft.com (Unverified)
Date: Mon, 18 Sep 2000 03:14:41 -0700
To: <mindx@omsoft.com> (Save Davis)
From: ">>> Save Davis <<<" <mindx@omsoft.com>
Subject: Aggie Hotel Demolition Monday:  Help Save West Wall
X-Antirelay: Good relay from local net2 168.150.0.0/16
```

SATURDAY MEETING WITH ARCHITECT. A meeting on Saturday morning at
the hotel by the architect revealed a plan which calls for total
demolition of the building, with a building which 'recalls' the west
wing up front with a simplified design, a second floor courtyard, 1st
floor retail, and a 4th floor building on the SE corner. The third
floor of the west wing will be set back.

DEMOLITION MONDAY. We were all surprised to learn total demolition
will begin Monday. The entire building could be lost, including the
facade and the mural. Reason given was the Chen's insurance company
insisted that they would be dropped if they left a vacant building
downtown. The lot will be vacant for at least 2 years.

DEMOLITION EQUIPMENT IN PLACE. Over the weekend a very large
bulldozer was moved into place inside the fence behind the building.
As it will reach the 100's this whole week, expect the demolition
crew to start as early as 7am.

CONSENSUS TO SAVE WEST WALL. The general consensus of those present
at the meeting Saturday was that an effort should be made to save the
bricks of the west wall. Reportedly, they are owned now by the
demolition contractor, but could be sold back to the city or the
Chen's. Another possible solution is to preserve the sense of the
building is to have an agreement in place that the brick design and
window arrangement (with some leeway for larger 1st floor retail
windows) of the west wall be incorporated into the west building
design. They felt cooperation with the rest of the design would be
more forthcoming if the Chen's agreed to this.

To this end, the planning commission voted to look into this as a
possibility. With the demolition looming, and the Chen's reportedly
out-of-town, the mayor will attempt to be contacted to urge the
Chen's to delay demolition of the west wall until after the Historic
Commission and City Council Meetings this week.

POSSIBLE CIVIL DISOBEDIENCE TO STOP DEMOLITION. If you can, stop by
the hotel Monday morning or anytime Monday (sorry this is so late
getting out). There will be concerned citizens on site before
sunrise to make sure the demolition does not proceed to damage the
west wall. The goal is to delay the demolition long enough to have
the Historic, Planning and Council to possibly act to save the bricks
or encourage an agreement to incorporate the design. Once it's gone,
it's gone. Please show your support even for a few minutes if you
can.

MONDAY HISTORIC COMMISSION MEETING at 7:30pm--Hattie Webber Museum in
Central Park.--Aggie Hotel agenda item at about 8:00pm on the design.
Please come and show your support for saving what little we
can--bricks or the design of the west wall.

WEDNESDAY CITY COUNCIL MEETING--CITY HALL. Come show support for the
Aggie Hotel bricks of west wall design to be saved. There won't be

>>> Save Davis <<<,9/18/00 3:14 AM -0700,Aggie Hotel Demolition Monday: Help Save

an agenda item, but we can show there is support in the community by
showing up and speaking. This may be our last chance to save any
part of the hotel.

CHEN''s IN BAD FAITH? Should the Chen's proceed with this demolition
with no agreements in place to better preserve the sense of the west
wall of the building, including possibly saving the bricks, they can
expect to have a fight at every turn with any building design they
present. If they agree to sign an agreement to better preserve the
sense of the west wall, many of us would be much more willing to
support them with the rest of their proposal.

ENTERPRISE ARTICLE. An excellent article in the Enterprise Sunday
describes the Saturday meeting and the current state of affairs.

Thank you for listening.

If you have no interest in being on this email list, which is solely
devoted to Davis preservation issues, reply to this email and let us
know.

11.1. 3:14 a. m., September 18, Save Davis rallying e-mail.

11.2. Wagstaff e-mail note early Monday morning.

J-
Just happened to see your late-nite note.
Talked to Lee by phone because he remains in LA due to flight problems-
something about fog and redirected air traffic.
He will take first flight in the am.
I will meet with him upon his return.
I am still working to save the west-side brick.
K

11. 3. Valley Construction Company Excavator, Monday morning, September 18.

11.4. Cover fax of Harrison Construction estimates from McCandless to Hiatt, stamped 8:22 a.m., September 18.

SEP-18-00 MON 8:22 AM   MCCANDLESS & ASSOCIATES   FAX NO. 5306623425   P. 1

McCANDLESS & ASSOCIATES, ARCHITECTS

FAX TRANSMISSION

DATE: 9/18/00

COMPANY:

ATTENTION: Ken Hiatt

REGARDING:

FAX NUMBER:

JOB NAME/NUMBER:

FROM: Bill McCandless

THIS FAX TRANSMISSION CONSISTS OF ___ PAGES, INCLUDING THIS COVER SHEET. IF YOU RECEIVE FEWER THAN THE INDICATED NUMBER OF PAGES PLEASE CONTACT OUR OFFICE AT (530) 662-9146 OR (916) 447-2782   FAX (530) 662-3425   e-mail: info@mccandlessarch.com

COMMENTS: Ken — Attached is the cost comparison from Harrison Construction regarding 3 comparative (theoretical) scenarios:
#1 Rehab existing 12,000 sf building
2 Save North & West walls; build new 12,000 sf building behind
3 Demo existing building; build new 12,000 sf structure.
This is for your files and for discussion should it come up tonight. Thanks, Bill

666 DEAD CAT ALLEY ▲ WOODLAND, CA 95695
LOCAL (530) 662-9146 ▲ FROM SACRAMENTO (916) 447-2782 ▲ FAX (530) 662-3425
mccandlessarch.com ▲ info@mccandlessarch.com

About 10:00 a.m., 67 year-old Stan Bowers, who *was* the ironically named Valley Construction Company, arrived to begin the demolition. Talkative, with a penchant for oratory, Mr. Bowers exuberantly explained what he was about to do to the small group of protesters who assembled around him next to the building. *Davis Enterprise* photographer Allison Portello was on the scene and one of her photos, shown as Fig. 11.5, appeared in that afternoon's paper.

Farewell to a landmark

Richard Buschman holds a sign protesting the demolition of the Terminal Hotel building while Stan Bowers of Valley Construction Co. explains how his firm will bring down the building. Protesters will take their cause to the Davis Historical Resources Commission meeting today at 7:30 p.m. at the Hattie Weber Museum.

Alison Portello/
The Enterprise

Fig. 11.5. *Davis Enterprise* front page story, September 18, 2000.

The affable and acerbic Mr. Bowers liked to tell stories and spent some time entertaining the assembled with tales of protesters he had encountered at previous demolitions in various Northern California locations. These included accounts of people who chained themselves to houses and to his machines and made him an object of abusive speech.

His performance over, the elderly but agile Bowers climbed up, onto, and into his excavator and quickly smashed down rear portions of the Terminal Building, as shown in Figs 11.6 through 11.11. Because salvage of the brick was a significant component of his revenue from this demolition, he only brought down the rear south and west walls in order to get the bricks onto the ground but not to cover them up with non-brick debris.

11.6. First Strike: west sheds and parking lot wall.

11.7. Rear north wall.

11.8. South end of the rear east wall.

11.9. north end of the rear east wall.

11.10. State of the rear south wall demolition the end of Monday and through Wednesday.

11.11. State of rear west wall demolition the end of Monday and through Wednesday.

This pause to salvage bricks meant that Bowers engaged in demolition only an hour or so this Monday. He left the building in the state shown in Figs. 11.10 and 11.11. The structure would remain this way through Wednesday, September 27 as workers laboriously removed mortar from bricks and stacked them onto pallets.

In the midst of all this, Mayor Ken Wagstaff arrived to arrange with Bowers to save the brown bricks that made up the west facade of the building.

Bowers had already contracted sale of all the bricks to a brick dealer, but he agreed to hold out the brown ones—which were thought to be about a quarter of all the bricks—and to sell them to the Chens, who now said they wanted to use them in the new building.

In Fig. 11.12, we see Bowers explaining to Wagstaff and others how he will take down the street-facing walls of the building so that they will fall in and not out onto Second or G streets. In this figure, Julie Partansky is on the left. (As reported, she was Wagstaff's immediate predecessor as mayor and had elected not to run for office again.) Gerald Hefferson, back to the camera, was a well known Davis artist and a *Davis Enterprise* columnist.

Saving the Arch Mural was a matter of concern and the degree to which it might be detachable was not clear. In Fig, 11.13, we see Heffernon proposing possibilities for taking it apart in sections. (It would turn out to be inseparably melded to the wall and Bowers would smash it to bits.)

11.12. L. to r.: Julie Partansky, Gerald Heffernon, Stan Bowers, Ken Wagstaff, Ken Hiatt, mid-day, September 18, northeast corner of Second and G streets.

11.13. L to r.: Gerald Heffernon, Stan Bowers, unidentified Bowers worker, Ken Wagstaff, Julie Partansky.

Amazing to me, at least, by the end of this event-packed day, Mayor Wagstaff had composed a letter to the people of Davis on the Terminal Building situation and had it mounted on a special page of the City of Davis website. It was so large that I have had to spread it over two pages as Fig. 11.14.

On this web page we see, at the lower right, a photograph of this day's demolition. In what was surely a record of City staff speed, a picture was taken at no earlier than about 11:00 a.m. this Monday, a "spin" statement written, and a web page designed and mounted by the late afternoon. In the Davis form of the city manager system, the mayor has little real power. Therefore, the rapidity of staff in responding to his web page request was testimony to Wagstaff's personal influence.

11.14. Mayor Ken Wagstaff's September 18th especially mounted City web page explaining his actions.

Mayor's Statement on the Terminal Hotel
September 18, 2000

Our memories and emotions have been stirred as the old Terminal Hotel comes down. Due to seismic safety concerns, however, and in compliance with an order from the city's building officials, the tenants had to move out during the summer. The building has stood empty and unsafe.

Mayor Ken Wagstaff

The owners, citing insurance costs and liability concerns, wanted to demolish the building immediately. At a Council meeting in June, they agreed to delay doing so until their architect and consulting engineer determined the feasibility of incorporating some part of the old structure into the design of the new. I was particularly interested in what could be done to keep the west, or G Street wall, and the north wall, which has the Davis arch mural. I also asked that preliminary plans be submitted as soon as possible, to get an idea of what the new building would look like.

The architect has now completed the feasibility review of these things and has presented preliminary plans. On Sunday, the Enterprise published a drawing of the proposal. Unfortunately, as the architect advised the planning commission, saving these two walls will cost about $200,000. This is not feasible for the owners or the city. Further, the plaster mural cannot survive.

While this news is disappointing, other factors are more encouraging: First, I have received assurance from the demolition contractor that much of the brick from the west wall can be salvaged. I have arranged for the city to provide safe storage. The owners are willing to pay for salvaging the bricks. Their architect says he will be able to use this material in the construction and design of the new building. Second, I will seek support from my Council colleagues to work with the city staff and the artist, Terry Buckendorf, to re-create the mural,

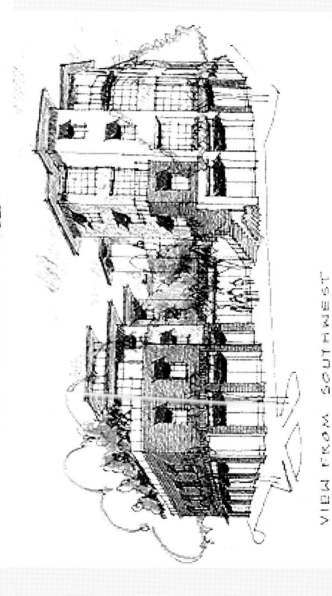

Courtesy of Eastman Collection

either on the new building or at another suitable location.

Third, we will insure that the design review process provides full opportunity or the Historical Resources Management Commission and all interested parties to participate.

As this process moves forward, I am optimistic that through the combined efforts of the owners, their architect, the city staff, the Planning Commission, and the Council, a new building will rise that will respect and evoke the history of this special site.

Mayor Ken Wagstaff

VIEW FROM SOUTHWEST

Conceptual drawing of the new building

09/20/2000 09:44 5307583722 MAYOR WAGSTAFF PAGE 01

Aggie Enterprises, Inc.
P.O. Box 2094
El Macero, CA 95618

Stan Bowers
Valley Construction Company
13721 Fair Oaks Blvd.
Citrus Heights, CA 95610

September 18, 2000

Dear Mr. Bowers,

This will confirm our previous conversation, and the conversation you had this morning with Ken Wagstaff, the Mayor of Davis, concerning the salvage of the face brick on the west side of the Terminal Hotel, 200-206 G Street in Davis, California.

Please consider this letter as an amendment to our contract with you.

You have agreed with the Mayor, as you proceed to demolish this building, to attempt as best you can to save this brick. You will clean it and stack it on pallets. We will buy it from you at $.40 (40 cents) per brick. Your estimate was that approximately 7500-10,000 bricks would be salvageable. If more than 10,000 face bricks are salvaged from the west side, we wish to purchase them also.

The mayor and we have arranged for the City of Davis to pick up the brick material and store it.

With respect to the mural on the north side, you will be contacted by Ms. Esther Polito, who will have some suggestions for keeping any segment that might survive.

Under separate cover you will receive instructions from Mr. Ken Hiatt, the City's Downtown Coordinator, about the transfer of the brick to the City. If you have any questions, please call me at 530-758-8666 or Mr Hiatt at 530-757-5610.

09/20/2000 09:44 5307583722 MAYOR WAGSTAFF PAGE 02
DELTA PROPERTIES P.02

Sincerely,

Lee Chen
Aggie Enterprises, Inc.

11. 15. Also this Monday, Lee Chen wrote to Bowers to confirm the agreement Wagstaff made with Bowers on his behalf that morning.

As chance would have it, Monday, September 18 was the third Monday of the month. This made it the regular meeting night of a group with which the reader is now well familiar—the Historical Resources Management Commission.

The concept for a building that the Chens had proposed on August 30, and then revised a few days later (Figs. 10.28 and 10.29), was on the agenda for HRMC review and comment at this meeting. (City law required this Commission to review and comment on the compatibility of all new construction proximate to existing historical resources, which were, in this case, the train station—a National Register listed structure—and three other Designated buildings at or near Second and G streets.)

One might hypothesize that the Chens planned the demolition to coincide with this meeting in order to ingratiate themselves to the HRMC——or perhaps gratuitously to antagonize it.

Or, one might theorize that they did not think about matters of this kind very much. Alternatively, they might have realized the coincidence and decided simply to take the heat.

Whatever the case (and we are unlikely ever to know the truth), neither the Chens nor their architect appeared at the meeting. This was itself an unusual act. The norm in Davis regarding the Planning and the Historical Commissions and the City Council was for the applicant and the architect to appear and to make a case for a project. Commonly, the applicant did not speak, but she or he was at least there and typically, at minimum, answered questions.

The reason for expecting such appearances was, of course, that fairness demanded that anyone who proposed a project be able to speak on its behalf. If that was not allowed or did not happen, one was missing an indispensable part of the picture.

At this HMRC meeting, Ken Hiatt, City Planner assigned to Downtown projects, explained that the Chens did not appear because they were fearful of how they would be treated. No one explained why McCandless was not there.

Be all that as it may, Mr. Hiatt (who seemed to me to be uncharateristically uneasy) described the project to the assembled Commission and residents. Photographs of this scene are reproduced as Figs. 11.16 and 11.17.

After his presentation, the floor was opened to comments from the public, which are summarized in the HMRC minutes given in Fig. 11.18. The public comment period was closed and members of the HMRC offered their observations and assessments.

As one can read directly from the minutes, the proposed new building was not received in a positive fashion. And one can wonder if *any* building proposed in this situation would have been thought of positively.

11.16. Ken Hiatt (standing, far right) explains the Chen project to the Historical Resources Management Commission at the Hattie Weber Museum of Davis the evening of September 18, 2000. On the left, we see Commissioners Wendy Nelson and Alice Eichorn.

11.17. View of Commissioners and residents attending the September 18 meeting of the HRMC. Alan Miller is shown in profile in the extreme left foreground. Council member Mike Harrington is second from the left. Commission member Mike White is next to him.

11.18. Minutes of the Historical Resources Management Commission regarding the Terminal Building and Site, September 18, 2000.

Historical Resources Management Commission Minutes
Meeting of September 18, 2000
Page 2

Commissioner Neeley, having previously recused himself on the Terminal Hotel and Design Guidelines projects due to personal conflicts, left at this time.

7. **Terminal Hotel** Introduction by Cultural Services Manager Esther Poli, reviewing responsibility of Commissioners to advise on design as per its impact on four nearby historic structures (SP Depot, Anderson Bank, Brinley Block, and Masonic Hall. Brief review of architectural features of four historic buildings. Staff presentation on conceptual project plans by Downtown Planner Ken Hiatt

HRMC questions following staff presentation:
1. Are the drawings scaled? Would the southeast tower be visible from G Street? More study is needed.
2. How many parking spaces are required? *Staff response: Estimated only based on assumptions as per use - 41 currently spaces based on parking district payments; 58 for new structure.*
3. Will bricks be re-used? *S.R. In some form, but not as re-built wall.*
4. Clarify City Council direction and whether process has been complied with. *Process reviewed.*

Comments from public:

• Dick Hastings, former member HRMC, member of State Historic Safety Building Code Committee: Difficult for staff to speak for project, architect or owner should have been present. In-lieu parking fees should be reserved as enticements for preservation, not used for new buildings. All facades of new design should be more compatible with area. Fenestration not historic character as shown, bulkheads should be used on retail windows. Mural space should be increased to size of original. Third and fourth floors should be kept to depot side of project; confirm sight lines so that they are not visible from G Street. Asbestos bags are visible on second floor behind partially demolished wall - they should be removed so that asbestos does not get placed in landfill. Visual roof planes are jarring, doesn't work well at this point. In general design needs a great deal more work to improve compatibility with area.

• Elizabeth Sherwin, Davis Enterprise: Asked for clarification re. parking   cost of underground spaces, in-lieu fees vs. required on site parking.

• Betty Rivers, Old East resident: Two buildings (east and west modules) don't mesh well. The size of the east building will make depot look like a dollhouse.

• Marilyn Underwood, Old East resident: Glass windows close to ground re excessive, bulkheads should be used. Perspective may be faulty, building will appear taller than shown. Where will residents of new building park? Current stress on Old East will be exacerbated if no deeded parking is supplied. Owners shouldn't get credit for any parking not currently being paid for.

Historical Resources Management Commission Minutes
Meeting of September 18, 2000
Page 3

• Allen Miller, 21-year resident of Davis, former Terminal Hotel renter: Impressed with project, but not delighted with fourth story, should be three story maximum. Concerned with simplification of front façade, wants to see original G Street façade replicated. Concerned about parking. Dislikes idea of more parking structures downtown, believes they will be needed if city moves in direction of not requiring on site parking. If owners decide to sell vacant lot, wants design approval transferred with site. Wants bricks numbered and mapped so they can be re-used as currently placed.

• John Lofland, Davis resident and local historian: West wall (G Street) should be recreated. Chens for pay for painting a new mural. Discussion of compatibility requires that that building is viewed in context. Architect should be required to provide context sketches showing new design with neighboring buildings. Perspective should be confirmed to ensure accuracy.

• Heather Caswell, Davis resident and business owner: Likes the idea of making the depot side of project friendlier. West side should be closer to original. Chens should be responsible for cost of new mural. New design could include arches similar to depot and Anderson Bank building.

• Audrey Hastings, Davis resident and business owner: Design is totally out of scale with building on other three corners, will dwarf them. Doesn't like mix of stucco and brick.

• Julie Sontag, Davis resident: Retail windows should go to ground, bulkheads needed. Likes courtyard. Questions viability of second floor retail. Thinks combination of brick and stucco is tacky. Roof needs simplifying - current roof design is too busy and not compatible. Generally concerned that developers are tearing the heart out of downtown.

• Robert Lideman, 27 year Davis resident: Imaginary parking spaces need imaginary cars, parking must be provided. Questioned why apartments are considered a compatible use since there are no apartments on street. Wanted to know why Chens weren't at meeting.

• Holmes Jr. High student: Parking in area is already filled, building will put too big a stress on existing spaces. Prefers a design with all bricks, no stucco. Recommends stairways are made inaccessible to skate boarders. Likes current overhang on G Street, would like to have new overhang incorporated in design as weather protection.

Public comments closed.

Chair Nelson led general discussion on appropriateness of "replication." General agreement that replication is not an historic treatment.

Commissioner Schulz: Replication seems wrong for a modern building, more effort should be placed on massing and scale compatibility. Retaining bricks not a component of historic preservation when component parts are not used in their historic context. Proposed building is not articulated well, should be built to lot line. Feels similar to Comfort Suites and KFC in South Davis. Doesn't address compatibility with Second and G corner. Upper floors should be set back. Second level retail difficult to retain. Courtyard increases need for second story retail and so is not viable. East tower overwhelms the retail storefronts beneath it. Parking is a serious concern. Much work needs to be done to make design more compatible.

Commissioner Berteaux: Invited Dick Hastings comments on Schulz's statements.

Historical Resources Management Commission Minutes
Meeting of September 18, 2000
Page 4

Dick Hastings: Generally concur. Doesn't like use of combed brick. Fenestration, rhythm and massing don't complement each other. Hesitates to give specific design direction other than be compatible, don't replicate, don't be foreign to area.

Chair Nelson: Also concurs. Rather than replicate, use more historic fenestration, dentile brick detailing. Lack of parking a significant issue that must be addressed.

General discussion about re-use of bricks followed. HRM agreement that re-use is a social rather than historic choice.

Commissioner White: Owe the public a compatible building. Dislikes southeast side, overwhelms rear. Asked about placement of courtyard.

Staff Hiatt commented that architect originally investigated having east courtyard, but moved it to south side because of street and train noise.

Commissioner Berteaux: City needs to salvage what it can from a bad situation.

Commissioner Dzinic: City was caught by surprise by demolition schedule. Owners should have made a greater effort to communicate and meet with HRMC re. compatibility issues.

Commissioner Eichold: Asked about design review process for 5th and G project.

Chair Nelson: Discussed compatibility with Design Guidelines. Page 31 speaks to two and three story buildings downtown, no mention made of 4 stories. Upscale housing is not needed. Apartments for seniors might be appropriate. Target low-income housing. Asked why the city is bargaining about height. Stay with guidelines: two stories at street edge with third story set back and include a courtyard as per guidelines.

Commissioner Rundstrom: Generally agree with comments. Four-story building is too high. Natsoulas elevator tower is out of scale, this project will be too.

Commissioner Berteaux: Site is unique with its four-sided orientation, creates special opportunity that couldn't happen elsewhere.

Chair Nelson: Needs visual interest on north wall.

Commissioner Schulz: North wall could have mural, but also could have interesting brick patterning.

Roof discussion: General discussion followed. Commissioner Eichold said the building design would require parapets to hide HVAC and other utilities. Commissioner Berteaux agreed. General consensus that horizontal rooflines need simplification and that final drawings should include all roof top mechanicals if they are visible from street.

Historical Resources Management Commission Minutes
Meeting of September 18, 2000
Page 5

Commissioner White left at this time.

Staff Hiatt asked about importance of courtyard. Commissioner Schulz responded that a courtyard serves to break up mass and the courtyard as designed seems fairly successful in reducing mass but she's was concerned that the resulting design creating too much interior focus away from street.

Ken Hiatt asked about diagonal treatment at Second and G corner. No consensus was reached. Commissioner Eichold said she thought the proposed treatment was a good echo of existing corner treatments. Commissioner Schulz didn't like the treatment as a glass wall, but felt a diagonal entryway would be appropriate.

John Lofland asked to commission to review their discussion re. replication. He requested that they consider it as an valid social choice not dependent on historical appropriateness. Some discussion followed. General agreement by HRMC that replication is a social not an historic choice. General consensus that HRMC that replication is not an issue for them although it may be for the community. Dick Hastings commented that he didn't think the rhythm of the existing second floor fenestration would fit with the larger scale modern storefronts proposed. Commissioner Schulz said historic one-over-one sashes should be used on the second floor and storefront windows should have bulkheads to anchor building.

Commissioner Eichold left at this time.

Allen Miller said replication would be the right thing to do socially.

Chair Nelson thanked all participants and closed the discussion.

2) TUESDAY, SEPTEMBER 19: REACTIONS

Save Davis' Alan Miller, who was at the HMRC meeting, was again up through the night and put out the e-mail shown in Fig. 11.9 at 6:06 a.m. Tuesday morning.

There was no action at the demolition site on Tuesday. It seemed that "brick cleaning" was a piece-work job for which it was not easy to recruit day laborers, at least not in Sacramento in the Fall of 2000. Bowers paid ten cents a brick stacked on a pallet and a diligent worker could clean and stack about one pallet (500 bricks) a day.

Workers were recruited at visits to certain Sacramento street corners and parking lots where Latino day laborers-for-hire congregated. (Davis had no such places.) This day, Bowers was unsuccessful in recruiting anyone. Indeed, after several days of marginal or no success in recruiting, he settled into bringing a single old man who had worked for him on other demolition jobs to Davis in the morning and fetching him at the end of the day.

The front page of the Tuesday afternoon *Davis Enterprise* provided what might be considered the official declaration of the death of the Terminal Building (Fig. 11.20). Even so, most of the building was still standing and hope of some salvation still lingered with some people.

11.19. Save Davis email by Alan Miller, Tuesday morning, September 19.

```
X-POP3-Rcpt: jlofland@ike
Mime-Version: 1.0
X-Sender: sleeper@mail.omsoft.com (Unverified)
Date: Tue, 19 Sep 2000 06:06:10 -0700
To: (Save Davis)
From: ">>> Save Davis <<<" <mindx@omsoft.com>
Subject: Demolition Begins; Historic Commission Vague; Chen's Absent
X-Antirelay: Good relay from local net2 168.150.0.0/16
```

DEMOLITION BEGINS. Between 10 and 11am Monday the rear walls of the
Aggie Hotel were demolished. The front and mural remain standing as
of 5am on Tuesday. Most people passing by on 2nd or G Streets
probably never realized the destruction behind the facade.

BRICKS "SAVED." Mayor Ken Wagstaff showed up at the site with a
check and proclaimed that the bricks had been purchased and will be
stored.

HISTORICAL COMMISSION MEETING. The historical commission discussed
the design of the new building at length. Several members of the
public expressed various sentiments regarding their ideas about the
design. The idea of replicating the west wall window and brick
design was brought up by at least four public participants, yet
seemed to fall on vague ears. Federal guidelines, it was implied, do
not find it generally desirable to replicate a portion of a building
already destroyed. "Why bother?" was the mantra of the historical
commission. Two of the three members of the public who stayed at the
meeting late made the point that just because federal guidelines do
not find it desirable to replicate, in this case it may be quite
appropriate. Commission members seemed much more concerned with how
some as-yet-unspecified structure would fit in with some vague
architectural geometry of the downtown main street intersection. The
ridiculousness of these discussions is not the commissions fault: it
voted unanimously that this was a historical resource--a notion
ignored by our city council. The hotel should not be missing from
this central corner in the first place.

CHEN'S BETRAY DAVIS. In case you missed the Monday Enterprise, a
protest sign proclaiming the same as the introduction line to this
paragraph made the front page.

CHENS ABSENT. The burden of presenting the proposal was laid on city
planner Ken Hiatt with the complete absence of the Chens or their
architect. It was noted that the Chens chose not to come to the
meeting. Their absence was handled politically by the city
representatives present, but there was an underlying tone that their
absence was a profound act of cowardice and betrayal.

ALL TALK. The reality is this: despite supposed good-faith efforts
to save portions of the building, the Chen's decided to demolish it
as fast as possible before someone actually found a way to save a
wall or two. A last-ditch effort by the planning commission
(basically poo-pooed by some historical commission members as "well
they had to do something, all these members of the public wanted the
west wall saved") will likely yield us a pile of unusable bricks.

ANOTHER BRICK IN THE PILE. Historical commission members assured us
that these bricks cannot be used in recreating the west wall facade.
Since the bricks are not numbered and mapped, they will just be a
pile of bricks. Paid for with taxpayer money. (There was some talk
they could be incorporated in a 'sidewalk pattern' near the building.

>>> Save Davis <<<,9/19/00 6:06 AM -0700,Demolition Begins; Histori

Wow.)

WHAT'S LEFT?   Despite the historical commissions' general
disinterest, the planning commission did vote to look into
incorporating the brick and window design of the west wall into the
design of the new building's west wall.

CITY COUNCIL MEETING.   If you have any opinion about replicating the
west wall design or any other concerns regarding the Aggie Hotel, you
may wish to attend the city council meeting on Wednesday night.   It
will not be an agenda item, but we can be heard.   Whether any wall of
the building will still be standing by that time is unknown.

DISAPPOINTED IN OUR CITY.   A look at the vibrant historical
restoration of numerous brick-faced buildings in Woodland and
Winters, and one wonders what the hell is wrong with our city.   That
a unanimous recommendation by the historical commission was ignored,
that anyone could find that this building which welcomed travellers
from the railroad for decades to the main corner of town, that housed
the Antique Bizarre, Natural Foodworks, The Wardrobe, and La
Esperanza, that was the birthplace of several Davis bands, could be
found 'not of historical significance'--well, such a person must be

_____.

It's too damn bad that fate somehow landed the hotel in the hands of
people such as the Chen's, who found a friendly 3-2 council in the
year 2000 with their friend, the mayor, who refused to excuse himself
from voting despite an obvious conflict of interest, but led us all
to believe that an effort was being made to save some of the
building's elements.

THE RESULT OF OUR EFFORTS: rubble.

11.20. *Davis Enterprise* front page report on the demolition of the Terminal Building, September 19, 2000.

Historic hotel destroyed

75-year-old brick walls come down in 45 minutes

By Elisabeth Sherwin
Enterprise correspondent

On Monday morning a small group of people watched as the demolition of the city's historic downtown Terminal Hotel began.

It only took about 45 minutes for Stan Bowers of Valley Construction Co. to drive his excavator into the back of the 75-year-old brick hotel,

See HOTEL, Page A4

TUMBLING DOWN: The Terminal Hotel demolition began Monday. While the mural, above, cannot be saved, the bricks are being sold to the city. Mayor Ken Wagstaff hopes the bricks can be used in the site's new building.

Alison Portello/
Enterprise photos

HOTEL   From Page A1

bringing down the walls on two sides, exposing the building's innards.

The demolition was halted today while a work crew picks up the bricks. It's expected that demolition will continue later in the week and the building will be gone by Saturday.

Bowers maneuvered the jaws of his machine to remove a piece of timber from the rubble, which he gave to former Mayor Julie Partansky, an artist who said she would make something from the old wood.

In addition to Partansky, Heather Caswell, John Lofland, Bob Liebman, Betty Rivers and Rodney Robinson were among the onlookers. Building owners Grace and Lee Chen were not present. Mayor Ken Wagstaff arrived on the scene later Monday morning to arrange for the sale of the bricks to the city. On Monday night he released a statement saying that the mural on the north wall of the building, which is still standing today, could not be saved.

"While this news is disappointing," he said, "other factors are more encouraging."

Wagstaff said the brick from the west wall of the building will be salvaged with the city arranging for safe storage. The architect, Bill McCandliss, may be able to use this material in construction or design of the new building. And Wagstaff said he would seek support from his council colleagues to work with the mural artist, Terry Buckendorf, to re-create the mural either on the new building or at another suitable location.

Wagstaff said he would ensure that the design review process for the new building would provide the opportunity for the Historical Resources Management Commission and all interested parties to participate.

And on Monday evening the Historical Resources Management Commission and about a dozen members of the public met to discuss how the architect's plans for a new building at the Terminal Hotel location, 200 G St., fit into downtown. The consensus seemed to be: The new building doesn't work.

City staff member Esther Polito said the historical commission's role now is to act in an advisory capacity in determining whether the scale, design compatibility, material and general architecture of the proposed new building is in line with the four historic buildings nearby (the Brinley Building, the Anderson bank building, the Masonic Hall and the Southern Pacific Depot). Neither the Chens nor their architect were present at the meeting.

A member of the historical commission asked if the Chens had complied with the process that ended in the demolition of their building.

"More or less," said Ken Hiatt, associate planner for the city.

Hiatt said the Chens had been advised to attend city meetings but have chosen not to. Hiatt said he is convinced that the Chens want to see a beautiful building at the old location, but are keeping a low profile because the situation is getting emotional.

"The Chens have chosen not to show up due to fears of retaliation," he added.

Hiatt displayed the architect's drawings of the new building (which appeared in the Sunday Enterprise) and described the design for retail shops that would be on the first floor, offices on the second floor, residential units and townhouses on the third and fourth floors with a courtyard between, linking two separate buildings. The building fronting G Street could incorporate bricks from the old building. Nothing is final at this point.

Hiatt said the Chens had explored the possibility of underground parking for 12 spaces but found it would cost $38,000 to $50,00 per space. It would be cheaper for them to pay $8,000 per space in in-lieu parking fees to the city. The new building, said Hiatt, according to a complicated city parking formula, could require 58 parking spaces. The old building had required 41 parking spaces.

After Hiatt pointed out the features of the new building, members of the public and the commission had the opportunity to respond.

"I think a lot more thought has to go into the design," said Richard Hastings, a member of the state Historic Building Safety Board. "It really doesn't work."

"My feeling is the two buildings don't go together at all," added Betty Rivers.

"What really bothers me about this," added John Lofland, "is the compatibility of this design in relation to its surroundings, which is impossible to imagine." The architect, he said, should be required to show the new building in relation to the neighborhood, not standing alone.

"This is a poor effort to replicate a historic building," said Commissioner Jeanette Schulz. She said the proposed building is too high at four stories and that the overall Southern California design fails to fit with the downtown. She also didn't think the effort to save the old bricks was worth much either in terms of a functional building material or as a historical resource.

"And although it's not in our (commission's) purview to talk about parking, I will," she added. "We seem to be in a pattern of forgiving downtown parking requirements."

Wendy Nelson, commission chairwoman, reminded those gathered that downtown guidelines being developed recommend buildings be no more than three stories high, not four.

"We also talk about the need for senior and student housing," she said. She said renting to seniors who don't drive and students who bike would solve the parking problem.

"The Chens give lip service to doing what's best for the community," she said. "That's one way they can give back. And we don't have to bargain with them. We can just say: 'We want three stories, a courtyard, and a third-floor setback.' "

Terminal Hotel demons are the protesters

UPSIDE-DOWN THINK-ING ... in their zeal to demonize anyone we would dare to try to make a living in this town, a handful of folks occasionally cross the line between fair protest and ugly behavior ... that line was crossed again by a downtown protester who was pictured on the front page of Monday's newspaper ... the hand-painted sign he held — "CHENS BE-TRAY DAVIS" — was despicable ... for those who have been living in a cave the last six months, the Chens are a Davis family who owns the old Terminal Hotel building ... they have received approval to replace the building and build something new ... they have lived and worked in Davis for a long time and have been nothing but model citizens and a model family ... they went through all the appropriate channels — and in Davis there are many — to have their project approved ... they have not "betrayed" any-

one ... in fact, the sign-painter has it backward ... Davis has betrayed the Chens ...

EVEN MORE ON THE TER-MINAL HOTEL ... it's interesting that nobody called the Terminal Hotel the "Terminal Hotel" until recently ... and no one seemed to know whether we should preserve that gawdawful ride-'em-cowboy facade that wasn't part of the original building in the first place ... and truth be known, all those people protesting the destruction of a building that's not nearly as old as some of our esteemed citizens, would have been *opposed* to building the Terminal Hotel in the first place ... after all, it's an inescapable conclusion that the Terminal Hotel itself replaced either an existing structure or gobbled up open space ... either way, the current batch of protesters would have protested taking down the old building or constructing a building where formerly the deer and the

Bob Dunning
THE WARY I

antelope played ... the bottom line is this: if the residents of Davis believe this building should be preserved, then they should buy it and make the necessary upgrades to make it safe and habitable ... otherwise, leaves the Chens alone ...

AND ON THE FLIP SIDE ... while some folks wasted everyone's time by trying to turn the Chens into monsters, it was obvious from Sunday's headlines that others found meaningful ways to spend the weekend ... topping

the list were the 88 volunteers who turned out to haul out more than 5 tons of trash in and around Putah Creek ... they are true local heroes ... also to be praised are the handful of people who gathered recently for the first Davis Religious Forum on Racism ... these folks, too, are heroes, who have much to teach us ...

The Terminal Hotel is terminal

Saturday morning I hopped on the old Raleigh three-speed and pedaled at a leisurely pace to an open-air, on-site Planning Commission meeting at Second and G to see what was up with the old Terminal Hotel building. Specifically, I expected to learn what the building's owners, Grace and Lee Chen, and their architect, Bill McCandliss, were proposing for the site.

I was stunned (well, I'm never really stunned anymore) to learn that demolition of the Terminal Hotel would begin the next Monday morning.

That's yesterday, your time. After you read this you can drive by and determine whether the future of Saturday reflects the past of Tuesday.

And yet, even as I write, Mayor Ken Wagstaff has donned red cape and doffed eyeglasses, and is reportedly seeking a stay of demolition. So maybe you already will have learned that he did get the delay. It's hard to keep my tenses straight on this future historic stuff.

No one is expecting to save the whole building. But many people interested in historic preservation thought there was a gentleman's understanding with the owners, via the mayor, that they would incorporate some preservation into their new building.

In fact, right after a vote in City Council not to re-visit historic status for the Terminal Hotel, The Enterprise headline read, "City to Chens: Work with us on hotel."

But that was the past. As it stands (or perhaps falls) now, there is no plan to save bricks or pieces of the mural that might be bagged up like the Berlin Wall.

I should say, I don't half mind McCandliss' proposal for the site. By the way, he designed the materially hand-

Gerald Heffernon
LOOSE CANON

some mega-Nugget with the over-sized goddesses of fertility.

McCandliss, who speaks too softly for Saturday's G Street traffic and yet seems capable of spitting eight-penny nails, has offered a two-story fronting structure that "recalls" the soon-to-be-demolished hotel. Behind that are two set-back elements that soar (in Davis terms) to four stories and are capped with flat, Wright-ish roofs with deep overhangs.

Some people think the plan is out of scale. I'm not sure about the footprint and lack of parking, but I'm in favor of four-story buildings in Davis, or even 60-story buildings, as long as we require that the residents of tall buildings have cars that fold up like lawn chairs.

Besides, McCandliss' current design is a far sight better than the one the Chens had him draw up based on a Swiss-style lodge in Canada, the tortured aesthetics of which required an upper-story, visigothic on-gloming to McCandliss' core idea. Mercifully, that idea lasted less than a mayfly's life in City Hall.

I'm not a pure preservationist; sometimes I favor preserving a whole building and other times I'd prefer to start over from scratch with an unfettered contemporary building. The idea of partial preservation of the Terminal Hotel is only appealing because of its location and peculiar history

as a meeting place.

What is troubling is that those who hoped to see some part of the building kept intact —and most people thought that was the plan —were suddenly told that the building would be reduced to irretrievable dust.

The mural, for instance. Couldn't it be scored into one-foot sections, peeled off, and partly saved? Esther Polito, who wears both the historical and public art hats at the city, told me that the artist, Terry Buckendorf, might be interested in re-rendering the mural in its current double-historical framework; that is, a painting of the presumably lost Terminal Hotel with his mural on it.

It seems to me that incorporating some of the old pieces of the first mural would give this a nice, multi-layered quality. At the very least we could put small hunks of the painted stucco in baggies and sell them as memorabilia to raise money for an artists' retirement home.

That is what I wrote Sunday evening. At 10:00 Sunday night I get a hot tip that there is a large piece of wrecking equipment parked in back of the Terminal Hotel. Wagstaff's delay doesn't seem to have happened.

At 7:00 Monday morning I am sitting in a vehicle in back of the building, waiting. I feel like a private detective on a stakeout. We drink coffee and watch as the occasional person stops to take a picture of the mural and drives away. We take note of the volume of ridership on the San Francisco-bound train.

At 8:00, one of us calls the demolition man's office to see if the job is on. The office says he is on his way. About 8:20, Heather Caswell arrives and makes a protest sign. At 8:30, Jean Jackman arrives with a more ceremonial concept: black cloaks and a couple of 2-foot-long dried seed pods that

rattle, as in a death rattle. (I find out later this bit of theater doesn't happen).

She tells us that the demolition is scheduled to begin at 10:00. It's news to me. At 8:45 I go home and begin writing this. And now I'm waiting for a call to the actual demolition, or at least further news.

At 10:30, the demolition is already happening. I have to admire the relative surgical precision with which the demolition man uses a giant set of mechanical jaws to tear out sections of brick wall, bathtubs, and iron railings. I'm reminded of a Tyrannosauraus Rex. Only the top story of the back side of the building is removed, and then he stops.

Wagstaff quickly begins negotiating with him for the bricks on the front wall. It seems he, or the city, or the Chens will buy those bricks to be, theoretically, included in the new building in some form. The demo man estimates there will be about 7,500 usable bricks, at 40 cents a brick, cleaned, and he says he'll take a simple handshake on the deal. I'm guessing those bricks would be enough to face about half or two-thirds of a new wall in the same location.

To the suggestion of cutting the mural into sections, he says he's doubtful it will help. But he can pull down that wall to the inside so that the mural ends up on top, and he is willing to let the city salvage any recognizable pieces. He seems very accommodating.

And that's the death of the Terminal Hotel. The predicted gestation period for a new building is two years. Maybe it will have some of the DNA of the old building.

— Gerald Heffernon is a Davis resident. His column appears weekly.

11. 22. Gerald Heffernon, *Davis Enterprise*, September 19, 2000.

3) WEDNESDAY, SEPTEMBER 20: THE MAYOR ACCOUNTS

The failure of the Chens and their architect to appear and represent their project at the HRMC meeting on Monday created, I surmise, public appearance and legitimacy problems. Perhaps concerned about such problems and his own role and reputation in the Terminal Building matter, Mayor Ken Wagstaff asked the Chens and McCandless to appear before the City Council at its meeting two days later and to explain their actions and proposals.

Events were breaking too fast to schedule them on the formal agenda. Therefore, Wagstaff used what was called the "City Council, City Manager and City Attorney Communications" period as the time early in the meeting into which to insert his view of the matter, as well as to invite statements by Lee Chen and Bill McCandless.

Fig. 11.23 shows the Chens and McCandless waiting to make their statements to the Davis City Council. Fig. 11.24 is a video-captured picture from the cable broadcast of the meeting.

11. 23. Lee and Grace Chen (left and middle) and Bill McCandless (right), Davis City Chambers, September 20, 2000

11.24. Lee Chen as televised on Davis Cable Channel 7 addressing the Davis City Council, September 20, 2000. Betti Rakki, Davis City Clerk, is on the left.

11. 25. Excerpts from the statement of Lee Chen to the Davis City Council, September 20, 2000.

My name is Lee Chen. . . . I would just like to say something . . . because there is a misconception . . . .

Last June we talked to the Council, to say we will consult a structural engineer to see whether we would be able to preserve portion of the building and we did do that. We hired a very well known structural engineer, . . . Kit Miyamoto, from Sacramento . . . . After he look at the building, in his opinion it would be very costly to preserve the building, even portion of it . . . .

So after that we think maybe we'll be able to save couple of walls, the wall with the mural attached to it and also the west side, which. . . face G Street. So we look into that possibility. We had several contractor look into that possibility and we got couple of estimates. The cost to preserve . . . these two wall is about $200,000.

So we had several meetings with the Mayor and also with City Staff to discuss this issue. On August 18th . . . we finally conclude that it is really not . . . worthwhile to spend $200,000 of taxpayers money to save that two walls . . . . We make that conclusion . . . .

Now, at that time—that is, last month—we also informed the City since we cannot save that two wall, we hope —we inform the city, we say let us proceed demolition of building. And as you now see we did that last Monday. [Chen turns to the topic of saving bricks but Wagstaff interrupts him to determine the exact date the mural will be demolished. Chen continues:]

But anyway, . . . that's what happened . . . . Really it did not happen all of a sudden . . . . Most people say we betray them, we didn't tell them what happened. Actually, it take a couple of months to get to that stage.

In Fig. 11.25, I reproduce edited portions of my transcription of relevant portions of Mr. Chen's statement to the Davis City Council. Several aspects of this statement pose puzzles.

First, Mr. Chen says he got three construction estimates by August 18th. Why were none of them ever made part of the public record? Moreover, if these three estimates already existed, why did Bill McCandless also get yet another estimate from Harrison Construction well after that date——on September 8, according to the fax cover page shown in Fig. 10.32? Why was the Harrison Construction estimate made public (to Ken Hiatt at the very last minute), but not any of those supposedly gotten before August 18?

Second, if a definite decision to demolish all of the building was made on August 18, what are we to make of Stan Bowers' trip to Davis on July 27 in order to take out a Sidewalk Crossing

Permit for the purpose of demolishing the hotel (Fig. 10.22)? Bowers' July 27 trip would appear to mean that demolition had already been decided by July 27 and not on August 18.

I asked Mr. Bowers about the character of his demolition discussions with the Chens and he told me that there was never any talk of taking down only part of the building. From the start——and well before July 27—the deal was that he would take down and haul away *everything* on the site. If Mr. Bowers told me the truth, what are we to make of Mr. Chen's claim that a final decision to take down all the building was only made on August 18?

Third, Mr. Chen did not explain why people would have the misconception they appeared to have at the start of the on-site Planning Commission meeting of September 16. Did he not understand a decision must be communicated to others affected by it? Otherwise, when learning of a decision at the later date, when it is "too late," those affected are likely to feel they have been mislead or betrayed.

In this statement, Mr. Chen assumes that "everyone" knew the demolition decision was made on August 18th. In fact, I was not able to identity any one—City staff or otherwise, including the Mayor—who believed such a "conclusion" had been made at an August 18 meeting——or at any other meeting. Why would Mr. Chen assert the "conclusion" was known to "everyone" when it apparently was not?

Fig. 11.26 provides the terse, official version of the Wagstaff, Chen, and McCandless remarks at this meeting. A fuller description was provided in an *Enterprise* story the following day, which appears below as Fig. 11.30

A number of residents concerned about the course of these events also spoke in the open "Public Comments" time that followed the Wagstaff-Chen-McCandless speeches. The cryptic City version of what they said is reproduced as Fig. 11.27 and some of their remarks are reported in more detail in Fig. 11.30.

f.	Status of Terminal Hotel Demolition.	Mayor Wagstaff reported on the demolition of the Terminal Hotel and stated some of the bricks from the building have been preserved to possibly be incorporated in the new build.
		Lee Chen, owner of Terminal Hotel, stated that they did not rush into the demolition of the building but over many months worked with the city and architect to preserve portions of the building.
		Bill McCanless, architect, outlined the process that was established following city procedures. He pointed out that they have submitted the pre-application and conceptual drawings to the city.

11.26. City Council minutes of September 20, 2000 reporting the Wagstaff-Chen-McCandless account.

11.27. City Council minutes reporting speakers on the Terminal Building demolition, September 20, 2000.

Alan Miller Heather Caswell, Eric Nelson, Donna Lemonjello, Dick Hasting and John Lofland spoke about the Terminal Hotel demolition, preservation of the bricks from the building and possibility of a moratorium on issuing demolition permits within the proposed historic district until guidelines are in place.

Meanwhile, back at the demolition site on Wednesday, two workers were cleaning and stacking bricks. (Fig. 11.28)

11.28. Two workers "clean" bricks at the Terminal site, September 20, 2000.

Finally this Wednesday, Ken Hiatt formalized the City's arrangement regarding the G Street facade bricks and the mural. I have bothered to reproduce the letter here (Fig. 11.29) because it shows a quite serious City commitment in these matters that might or might not be honored as the months and years went on.

11.29. K. Hiatt to S. Bowers regarding Terminal Building bricks and the Arch Mural, September 20, 2000.

PLANNING AND BUILDING DEPARTMENT

23 Russell Boulevard – Davis, California 95616
530/757-5610– FAX: 530/757-5660 – TDD: 530/757-5666

September 20, 2000

Stan Bowers
Valley Construction Company
13721 Fair Oaks Blvd.
Citrus Heights, CA 95610

RE: **Terminal Hotel Face Bricks**

Dear Stan:

This letter is to confirm our conversation of September 18, 2000 in relation to the transportation and storage of the salvaged face brick on the west façade of the Terminal Hotel building at 200-206 G Street. As I understood from our discussion, the process for salvaging and transporting the bricks will be as follows:

1. Valley Construction will bring down west wall of the building sometime late this week, starting from second story portion, with an effort to preserve as many face bricks are reasonably possible;
2. The face bricks will be cleaned and palletized separately from the interior bricks and stored on-site until the bricks on the lower portions of the wall are removed, cleaned and palletized; and
3. You will contact me at least one day prior to when the bricks will be available for removal from the site and inform me as to how the city can best assist in the transport of the bricks to a city storage facility.

You are also aware of the city's and Chen's interest in potentially preserving any large portions of the mural on the north side of the building. As you have agreed, please contact Esther Polito (530-57-5626) and myself (530-757-5610) the day prior to when you anticipate this portion of the building to be demolished. We will arrange to have staff on-site during the demolition of this wall and assist in the effort to help preserve and transport any significant portions of the mural.

Thank you for your continued cooperation in these matters. Please do not hesitate to call me if you have any questions or with updates on the schedule of the demolition.

Sincerely,

KEN J. HIATT
Associate Planner/Downtown Coordinator

Cc: City Council Members
       Lee and Grace Chen

4) THURSDAY, SEPTEMBER 21 TO WEDNESDAY, SEPTEMBER 27: BRICK-CLEANING INTERLUDE

The level of activity subsided over the seven days following the Council meeting of Wednesday, September 20. These day were, though, only the "lull before the storm," which would come on Thursday, September 28.

In the meantime, there were the several small events depicted in Figures 11. 30 though 11.39 and which are explained in the caption boxes accompanying each.

Mayor leads discussion on Terminal Hotel fate

By Melanie Turner
Enterprise staff writer

An effort by Mayor Ken Wagstaff to help enlighten his colleagues about recent events relating to the Terminal Hotel led to about a one-hour discussion, including comments by members of the public who are concerned about the fate of the 75-year-old brick building.

Councilwoman Susie Boyd was absent Wednesday. She is on vacation in Spain.

Wagstaff on Wednesday said he simply wanted to make certain his colleagues were informed of the latest events relating to the former hotel as they have unfolded in the last week.

The Chens' contractor has begun demolition on the building and preliminary sketches for a new building were un-

veiled to the public and city Planning Commission on Saturday. Initial concerns were raised about a lack of parking, and the scale of the four-story proposal.

Wagstaff invited building owner Lee Chen and the Chens' architect, Bill McCandliss, to address the council.

Lee Chen said there has been a misconception that he and his wife, Grace, have sprung this demolition on the community "over night." The Chens have had a demolition permit for at least a year. Demolition to the building on the northeast corner of Second and G streets began Monday.

Stan Bowers, owner of Valley Construction Co., said earlier

See HOTEL, Page A7

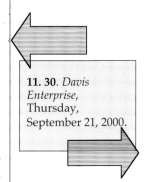

11. 30. *Davis Enterprise,* Thursday, September 21, 2000.

THE DAVIS ENTERPRISE **FROM PAGE ONE** THURSDAY, SEPTEMBER 21, 2000 A7

HOTEL
From Page A1

this week work to demolish the north wall, which has been covered since 1976 by a large mural depicting the historic Davis arches, would likely start some time early next week.

Chen said they have kept their promises by consulting with an engineer to learn if any portion of the building could possibly be saved. He said the cost of preserving the north and west walls—of interest to many in the community—is an estimated $200,000.

"It would be very costly to preserve the building, even a portion of it," he said. "...Our architect indicated to us that he could design a structure that would have a similar appearance on the west side."

The existing building is two stories and roughly 12,000 square feet. The proposed replacement building would be roughly double the size, and potentially four stories high.

Architect McCandliss emphasized to the council that city staff requested the Chens submit a pre-application before demolition took place and the latest drawing are "conceptual only."

While some have said at this point demolition is a known foregone conclusion, others said the two walls that several people had hoped to save—or at the very least the west wall along G Street—are still standing so there must be hope.

The mayor reminded the public that the council voted 3-2 to not uphold the Historic Resources Management Commission's unanimous recommendation to designate the building historic.

"It's tough. It's change," he said. "It's tough to let go of the past. But I would prefer to embrace the future."

Dick Hastings, a member of the state Historic Buildings Safety Board, said the public was under the assumption there would be time for discussions about what was to come prior to demolition.

"It was the first time we'd seen the drawings (on Saturday), and we were told Monday was demolition," he said.

"In my opinion both the city and the Chens are equally responsible for the neglect and poor planning that have taken place for the past year," said Heather Caswell, whose business, The Wardrobe, occupied a space in the old hotel for years. "Allowing demolition without a verifiable replacement project is not a good revitalization strategy. It hurts everyone, especially your downtown businesses."

She encouraged the council to create a policy to prevent such "poor planning." And, she urged the council to remember the city of Davis is now a Main Street city and must encourage ways to preserve some fabric of Davis' history. Finally, she urged the west wall be saved.

The proposal includes three sides of first-floor retail, second-floor service commercial and possibly residential, and third- and fourth-floor residential. McCandliss said the portion of the building on the corner of Second and G streets would be "reminiscent of the Terminal Hotel."

Alan Miller of Davis said he's pleased with the new design. He favors retail near the train station and more residential in the downtown. However, he has concerns about parking and he, too, believes efforts should be made to save the west wall.

While the mayor has ensured that many of the building's bricks will be saved for use in the new building, Miller said the bricks should be numbered and mapped in order to contribute some historic recreation of the west wall.

Eric Nelson advised the council to create a demolition ordinance to enable the city to take a proactive, rather than reaction approach—"rather than conduct last-minute salvage operations as the bulldozers are moving."

Efforts apparently are underway at the Planning Commission level to create such an ordinance.

Donna Lemongello, who said she's beside herself that the community is losing this 75 year-old building, told council members they must be numb by our fast-paced, modern society.

"What better place to spend money than on something of value," she said.

11. 31. The text below is excerpted from a letter to the *Davis Enterprise* that was not published because the Editor refused to accompany it with the "mountain resort" design the Chen's had submitted on August 30 (shown in Fig. 10.28).

The writer argued to the Editor that because the mountain resort design had never been published in the Enterprise, the letter made no sense without it. The Editor was not persuaded. The writer of the letter interpreted this refusal to print as an effort to protect the Chens.

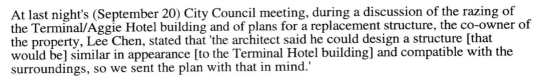

Editor
The Davis Enterprise

At last night's (September 20) City Council meeting, during a discussion of the razing of the Terminal/Aggie Hotel building and of plans for a replacement structure, the co-owner of the property, Lee Chen, stated that 'the architect said he could design a structure [that would be] similar in appearance [to the Terminal Hotel building] and compatible with the surroundings, so we sent the plan with that in mind.'

If what Mr. Chen said is true, how are we to explain the fact that the first conceptual design submitted by the Chens to the Planning Department on August 30 (and withdrawn a few days later in the face of near-universal sneers) proposes, as the accompanying sketch makes clear, a "mountain resort" type building that is neither "similar" nor "compatible"? (The currently-circulating design is arguably not much of an improvement, but at least it does offer a few more "reminders" of the sacrificed historic structure.)

There are important lessons to be drawn from the sad saga of the Terminal/Aggie Hotel building's demise, but we won't learn any of them if the central actors in the drama are allowed to re-write history in a way that obfuscates their motives and intents.

11.32. Thursday, September 21, the building stands as a ripped-open and metaphorically bleeding hulk subjected to a slow and agonizing death.

11.33. Someone used clothes pins to mount copies of this sign at several places on the fence around the building.

11. 34. Friday, September 24, Bowers fired up his excavator to move some debris in order to get at more bricks, displacing a pipe that punched through the Arch Mural. It was the first substantial damage to the mural.

11. 35. Sunday, September 24, preservationist Alan Miller made a last ditch public plea with signs on the Terminal site fence.

11.36. Monday, September 25, Miller began to elaborate a citizen critique of Chen and City actions and call for a freeze on demolition.

This was circulated by e-mail and as a flyer.

Wagstaff's phone answering machine quickly filled up and gave only the response that the machine was full and not taking messages.

Save the West Wall of the Aggie Hotel!

They are demolishing the Terminal Hotel, but the West Wall still stands. Mayor Wagstaff said the City would "work with" the Chens (Owners) to try "in earnest" to save the West and North Walls. The Chens stated the cost was $200,000, and the "City" and the Chens decided that was too much. Mr. Chen said these meetings (which did not include the general public or the planning or historical commissions) concluded on August 18. On September 16, it was announced building demolition would commence on Monday, September 18, which it did. During this month, the general public did not know of the buildings fate or that the plan to save the walls had been deemed "too costly."

WE are the city. The "City" which worked with the owners decided $200K was too much. The "City" never stated what an acceptable cost would be, or gave the citizenry a chance to find a way to make up the difference.

WE PROPOSE A 'SYMBOLIC BRICK' FUND-RAISER. Citizens would buy a symbolic brick and be commemorated on a plaque to be placed on the new building. Two-hundred $1000 bricks, or two-thousand $100 bricks (or a mix of the two) would cover the cost. The "City" had some sum in mind it was willing to pay (never stated), so some of this can be covered by the city and other sources. We propose a year be given to raise the funds.

The problem is the building started coming down before we had a chance to act! Therefore, we call on the mayor to stop the demolition of the West Wall and find the funds to shore up the West, and possibly North walls NOW!

Call Mayor Wagstaff at 758-3722 and tell him you would like the West Wall saved. WE ONLY HAVE A FEW DAYS! If you are willing to buy a brick or two, tell him that.

Wednesday, September 27, Mr. Bowers' people had assembled thirteen pallets of red bricks. This was sufficient to ask the company to whom he sold them to send its truck to pick them up. The removal is depicted in Figs. 11. 37-11.39.

11.37. A fork lift carried on the rear of a flat bed truck (shown in 11.39) picks up a pallet of bricks.

11.38. The fork lift places a pallet on the truck. (To the left, an unidentified man seen occasionally at the site over many ~~weeks, but who never spoke with anyone, observed the~~ work.)

11.39. Thirteen pallets of Terminal Building bricks load on a flatbed truck.

5) THURSDAY, SEPTEMBER 28: DEMOLITION AND CITY STAFF SCRAMBLE

At last, the big and final D for demolition day. Starting at about 10:00 a. m on Thursday, September 28, the building was reduced to a tall and flat stack of smashed wood, bricks, and debris by 4:30 in the afternoon. And even with this, Bowers, who operated the excavator, took an hour out for lunch and stopped another hour to fix a hole in a metal pipe caused by spilled battery acid that started a fire and brought out Davis fire trucks.

I will describe the demolition process itself and important episodes in it in the two chapters of Part III (chapters 12 and 13). Here, I report only the most basic facts of the day.

On the second floor, the hotel was constructed of two rows of rooms facing a center hall. Up to this day, Bowers had taken down the back wall, but not any rooms per se. Now he began by tearing down the row of rooms nearest to the excavator, those on the north and east. His progress toward the still-untouched Arch Mural is shown in Fig. 11.40. In Fig. 11.41 we see his machine finally reaching the Mural and pulling off a piece. But only about half of the Mural was now down. The rest of it was attached to the still-intact row of rooms on the west side of the building.

In prior conversations with City Staff and the Mayor, Bowers agreed to pause at this point so that staff could retrieve portions of about half the Mural then on the ground. In any event, it was close to noon and it was Bowers' habit to take an hour for lunch. (He regularly ate at what was then called the Paragon, at the southwest corner of Second and G.)

This gave the three city staff performing the physical task of loading mural remnants the space of an hour in which to work without fear of falling debris. Figs. 11.42 through 11.44 show aspects of this first phase of mural retrieval.

11.40. Bowers nears completion of pulling down the eastern row of Terminal Building hotel rooms. The mural is on the wall on the right.

11.41. The mural begins to fall. The man inside the fence facing away from us is running a high pressure water hose on the cracking parts in an effort to reduce the amount of dust.

'00 9 28

11. 42. Bowers paused for lunch. From the left, an intern, Wagstaff, Polito and Hiatt inspect portions of the Mural now on the ground. Notice that Polito is taking a picture of Wagstaff.

11.43. I had expected the City to deploy several trucks and burly workers to load the heavy pieces of the Mural, but it did not. Instead, there was one truck and three ordinary-size white-collar workers. The male among them, Ken Hiatt, is in action below.

11.44. The first of two flat-bed truck loads of mural pieces .

11.45. Bowers returned from lunch and, working from south to north, pulled down the western row of hotel rooms, and then the rest of the mural.

11. 46. The two rows of rooms down, Bowers continues on with pulling over the top half of the western wall.

11.47. The excavator was now safely away from the Mural. Hiatt left and Esther Polito and the intern remain to salvage pieces. In the end, Esther Polito drove away the second load of Mural pieces, accompanied by the intern.

News flashes from Terminal Hotel

By Alan C. Miller
Special to The Enterprise

The walls stand: The slow death of the Terminal Hotel continues. Demolition exposed living, working and playing rooms to the sky — places with so many memories now escaping to the ether. The mural wall and the west wall — the objects of most people's hopes for preservation — stand as of this writing. A plumbing pipe has punched grotesquely through the wall from the back. The stark reality of the demolition is now visible to all.

Buy-a-brick: In Fremont, a beloved high school facade was saved. Community members raised funding by purchasing symbolic "bricks." Also a six-figure project, they raised the money in one year. Our proposal is to hold a similar buy-a-brick fund-raiser here in Davis to save the walls.

There must have been some cost our city would have found acceptable to save the walls (or

Commentary

ing an appearance at the Council Chambers. An opponent who shows up is more honorable. (Any similarity to the first line of this paragraph to a line in a fairy-tale about three pigs, one of whom owns a brick structure, is purely coincidental).

Kill the umpire! However, at games the crowd doesn't boo an honorable opponent, they boo the umpire. The City Council is the umpire, and the mayor set himself up to be the hero-umpire by proclaiming he would "work with" the Chens to try and save a portion of the building. He apparently did that to the Chens' satisfaction. The Chens got to say it costs money, and the city got to say that's a good enough reason. The "earnest" search for a solution has produced demolition.

Wag flying at half staff: The Chens seem to have left the mayor flapping in the breeze. The public perception is that

Commission, which was supposed to be included in these talks, stated that she had no further input after June. Esther Polito of the city staff knows nothing of the Aug. 18 meeting. This "process" seemed to be up to the mayor and the Chens. It appears the mayor thinks he is "the city."

Tail wag staffing the dog. After Sue Greenwald stated she would have voted to designate the building historical, our distinguished mayor launched into an empty and clichéd speech in a noticeably patronizing and agitated tone: "You voted as Mike (Harrington) did to reopen the question. The other three council members voted no …. It's tough, it's change … it's tough to let go of the past, but I would prefer we embrace the future ….

"If anyone on this council tonight would like to ask that we take a 4-0 vote to see if the desire is here to get a court order and appropriate money

learning that an empty promise is as good as a lie if not better. With a good smoke screen you can make people think you are trying.

Done Dunning. Bob Dunning's assertion that those who wish to save the hotel would be the same people who would never allow it to be put up is laughable. Most of us fully favor the Chens' right to highly modify their structure for practical downtown purposes. All we ask is for a compromise that allows for historic preservation while allowing a profit for the owners. This is the responsibility (not requirement) which, we believe, goes along with owning a historic structure (as defined by the Historic Commission if not the City Council).

Dunning implied we should either buy the building or leave the "model citizen" Chens alone. He has a point. That citizens (the real "city") were not given a chance to explore funding ideas before demolition be-

was there?), and we can raise the difference. Contributor's names will be placed on a plaque on the building. Time is short. We need the mayor's leadership to work with us to designate funds to shore up the walls *now* while the fund-raising begins.

Why do we feel like mushrooms? The remainder of this piece will show that we, as citizens, were hidden from the so-called negotiations between the city and the owners.

Not by the hair on their Chenny Chen Chens: Wednesday night Mr. Chen gave a short speech to the council stating that they had done everything they were required to do. Their absence at the Historic Commission meeting was not appreciated, but they are commended for making any attempt at saving the walls was half-hearted, done behind closed doors, and futile. Some of us actually thought we were included in the words "the city" and would be informed of the progress of the "work with" talks.

What was the process that was supposed to go on between the city and the Chens to help save a portion of the wall? Mr. Chen mentioned a series of meetings concluding on Aug. 18, but was the citizenry informed of the results?

Wagstaff-gate? The Aug. 18 date indicates the mayor knew much earlier than he implied about the building's fate. Now we're into a Watergate-like "who knew and when did they know it?" cover-up scenario. The Historic Commission meeting was not appreciated, but Wendy Nelson of the Historical and prevent walls from coming down, I invite the motion. (Long pause). I do not hear the motion." He seemed annoyed and trying to evoke a dare—as if to show us it was hopeless; take your toys and go home.

Here I come to save the day. The mayor's symbolic Monday-morning hero gesture to save the bricks is just that. What we have is a pile of bricks with no agreement and no plan to put Humpty Dumpty back together again. The mayor says the Chens' architect "will be able to" use this material in the new building. These words have the same depth of promise as the promise to "work with" the city. There's no assurance, no plan, no feasibility or cost study. The Chens spent $3,000 on bricks they can sell later. We are gan by being informed of the outcome of the "Chen-City Work-With" negotiations is (to use Mr. Dunning's word) *disgusting*. These talks concluded a month before we knew the building was to be demolished. The mayor could help us right this wrong.

Is it sick to love a building? Some would say so, but whatever replaces our old friend, it is doubtful anyone will fight to save it in the year 2080. Some may profit from it, but no one will love it. Call Mayor Wagstaff today and support the buy-a-brick fund-raising proposal. The claw is moving toward the wall as you read this.

— Alan Miller is a 21-year Davis resident and a former resident the apartments in the Terminal Hotel.

11.48. Alan Miller Op-Ed column in the *Davis Enterprise*, September 28, 2000, the same day as the mural demolition. Events moved so fast and with so much uncertainty that Miller could still be talking here, in text written the previous evening and that went to press shortly thereafter, about saving part of a building that was demolished just hours before.

Mural falls

Demolition crews send the Terminal Hotel wall donning the popular mural of historic Davis crashing to the ground on Thursday.

Alison Portello/Enterprise photo

People stop to film, watch as walls come down

By Melanie Turner
Enterprise staff writer

A handful of people stopped to watch as the demolition finishing off the bulk of the controversial 75-year-old brick building on the northeast corner of Second and G streets began Thursday.

A couple of people videotaped the event, while others brought cameras to record the Valley Construction Company excavator ripping apart the old brick walls, exposing upstairs doorways and sinks, and chomping through the mural depicting Davis around the turn of the 20th century. Other passers-by seemed to hardly take notice.

The old brick building has been the subject of controversy in town as some have pushed to save at least some portion of the building, including the west wall and the north wall containing the mural of the old Davis arches.

Others, like Mayor Ken Wagstaff, have said, "I would prefer we embrace the future."

The building's owners, 34-year Davis residents Lee and Grace Chen, plan to construct a new three- to four-story building that will feature retail on three sides and residential units upstairs.

The building reportedly was bustling during World War II when it was a hotel serving people traveling by train. It's been known as the Terminal Hotel and Hotel Aggie.

Most recently, the building's upper story had been condemned for the last 15 years. The first floor housed La Esperanza, Hair Chalet, The Wardrobe and Natural Food Works.

"It served so many people for so long," said Mariesa Nyman, who stopped to watch the demolition. "I think the new building will serve a lot of people, too."

A 20-year Davis resident, Nyman said she felt it was necessary to tear the building down, given its poor condition.

"Change is sad, but sometimes you have to do it," she said.

John Lofland, who fought to have the building designated historic, said Thursday, in between taking snapshots of the action, "We've been struggling with this for so long we're all out of feeling."

Lofland had dubbed the Terminal Hotel, the across-the-street historic Anderson Bank building and the nearby brick Brinley Building a "matched set."

See TERMINAL, Page A3

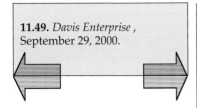

11.49. *Davis Enterprise ,* September 29, 2000.

TERMINAL From Page A1

The Historic Resources Management Commission recommended 18 months ago that the City Council designate the building as historic. The designation would have potentially slowed the demolition process and opened up opportunities to look at alternatives that may have been eligible for grant funding.

The council denied that request last September, on a 4-1 vote. Last June the council voted 3-2 to reaffirm that action, giving the Chens the go-ahead to demolish the building.

Associate planner Ken Hiatt has collected all the comments made at recent Planning Commission and Historic Commission meetings, at which a conceptual plan for a new building was presented. Hiatt will be compile those and forward them to the Chens and their architect, Bill McCandless.

A meeting is scheduled between the Chens, their architect, Hiatt, Historic Commission Chairwoman Wendy Nelson and city cultural services manager Esther Polito on Tuesday. The parties will review the comments, and the architect will use them to create a project that will be proposed for review and final approval.

The historic commission's role now is to act in an advisory capacity in determining whether the scale, design compatibility, material and general architecture of the proposed new building is in line with nearby historic buildings.

The final proposal eventually will be considered by the Planning Commission, potentially for final approval. The development proposal would go before the council only in the event that the proposal included, for example, a request that parking in lieu fees be waived.

11.50. The same day as the *Enterprise* final demolition report, Heather Caswell suggested some lessons to be learned from the Terminal Building episode.

|THE DAVIS ENTERPRISE |

FORUM

FRIDAY, SEPTEMBER 29, 2000

▶ LETTERS

Listen up, council

How many heritage buildings can the community sacrifice and still be Davis? In my opinion, both the city and the Chens are equally responsible for the neglect and poor planning that have taken place for the past year. Allowing demolition of the Terminal Hotel without a verifiable replacement project is not a good revitalization strategy. It hurts everyone ... especially our downtown businesses.

I encourage the City Council to create a demolition ordinance that will never allow poor planning such as this to take place again in our city. Now that new design guidelines have been organized, the City Council must better align our polices and ordinances and building codes to support our community's vision for a traditional-styled downtown.

In the past, the City Council has ignored recommendations made by the Historic Commission and the Planning Commission. I recommend that the City Council listen to our community before it's too late.

Heather Caswell
Davis

6) CLOSING REMARK

So ended the life of one of the dozen or so most historic buildings in Davis, California.

Even though the building qua building was dead, portions of its sundered and splintered carcass lay lifeless on the site for almost two months. They killed and smashed the building, but left its stinking and dust-spewing corpse for all to see and contemplate for several weeks.

This spectacle of sporadic smashing, pulling, grabbing and dropping parts of the carcass developed its own dynamic and became its own story. In the next two chapters, I tell that story.

III

DEMOLISHING
TWO MONTHS, FALL, 2000

The Terminal Building did not simply disappear. Nor, as SKY Engineering would have it, did it fall over in a wind or earthquake. Instead, Stan Bowers found the structure was quite sturdy and effort was needed to bring it down. But, down it came, methodically smashed into millions of little pieces that were gathered up in dozens of truck loads and carted to the Yolo and Sacramento County landfills.

• On his first day at the site, Monday September 18, I asked Bowers how long it would take him to demolish and haul away the entire building. Pausing only a second, he waved his hand as though this were merely a slight job and said "Oh, we'll be out of here by Friday next week." That would be twelve days. It was, in fact, 73 days before the site was down to bare earth.

I report his first estimate because it explains how I got into the peculiar activity of organizing my life for 73 days to document the removal of a building. The short answer is: I did not start out to spend 73 days at it. When Bowers said 12 days, I decided I could harness myself to a documenting task for a period that short. Had he said 73 days, I would not have been interested.

So, I started. But, at Day 12, while the building was down, removal had hardly started. However, I had now invested 12 days. This was a "sunk cost," an expenditure I could not get back and it had little value unless I made a further investment in covering the entire story.

When on Day 12—and on later days—I asked Bowers about his projection of completion, he was more indefinite but hopeful of completion "soon." However, by these later days, I was hooked. I had gone too far easily to throw away what I had done. And, I kept telling myself, the process could surely not take **that** much longer.

Also, I knew Bowers would not be paid the largest part of his contract until he finished. I was watching him accumulate thousands of dollars of out-of-pocket expenditures to keep the operation moving, however slowly. The Yolo County landfill did not extend credit; the dump truck was rented; the driver and others he hired were paid each week. Economic rationality demanded he not dawdle too much, I thought. Even so, I came to see he was less motivated by considerations of economy and cost than I had initially thought. So, the process dragged on.

• Several factors caused the process to take so long. **One**, Bowers seemed determined to squeeze as many pallets of cleaned bricks out of the building as he could. But, he also appeared to have only one reliable person to "clean" them (remove mortar clinging to them). This bottleneck slowed the task to a snail's pace. **Two**, there appeared to be only a handful of companies that bid on small demolitions. Such demolitions were a competitive and a "fire house" kind of activity. When a Sacramento Valley municipality wanted a structure demolished, companies bid, a contract was awarded, and work began immediately. Bowers worked in this market and was demolishing other buildings in other towns for some of the 73 days. **Three**, Bowers' "Valley Construction Company" seemed to be mostly him. As a "one man show," little happened when he was not there running things. **Four**, he liked to make clear to me and whoever else might be standing by that he did this kind of work because he enjoyed it rather than from economic necessity. In my assessment, he perceived differences between more and less "cost effective" ways to do things, but he was not particularly concerned to minimize his costs and to maximize his profits. His demolition activities were, I finally concluded, a kind of semi-retired hobby. Indeed, from Day 53 to Day 71 of the 73 days he was away on a vacation train trip from Sacramento, through Canada, to Niagara Falls, with an airplane return.

• The two chapters of this Part III consist largely of photographs. Unless otherwise credited, I took them. A hundred or so are presented. They have been selected from 67 rolls of color print film producing some 1,600 photographs I took over the eleven weeks.

• I treat the topic of demolishing from two vantage points.

In Chapter 12, I focus on the step-by-step increments of removing the building. This describes demolition as a **process**.

Demolition also involves distinctive moments that may or may not have a logical place in a process. Instead, events simply happened. We may think of these as **moments** and they are the subject of Chapter 13.

12

DEMOLITION PROCESSES

To examine something as a process is to inspect the steps though which it changes or develops. In the case of demolishing the Terminal Building, there were three such sets of steps (that is, processes). They differed in terms of their length and degree of drama. The first two did not last very long but were visually dramatic as well as very loud and dust-producing. The third lasted much longer and was, overall, much less dramatic in visual and auditory ways.

The first of the three took place the single day of Monday, September 18. In it, the rear walls of the building were torn off for the purpose of salvaging their brick.

The second more dramatic process played out over the two days of Thursday, September 28 and Friday, September 29. In the space of a few hours on each day, the Terminal Building went from a mostly intact structure to a shattered sea of rubble. This was achieved by a single, aging man showing the wear of his years. driving a likewise worn machine called an "excavator." It was amazing, indeed, to see how it was possible to smash something large and solid if one were diligent and had the right machine.

In contrast to the rapid-paced drama of these one and two-day processes, the third unfolded slowly over 73 days—the period over which the larger parts of the building were pulled and pounded into loadable rubble, put onto a truck, and hauled away. The going was slow importantly because it was sporadic. Periods of no action alternated with spates of smashing larger debris into smaller debris and loading it. Inexorably, though, the building disappeared.

In this chapter, I provide a photographic display of each of these three processes. They are presented in the order they are described above.

1) THE ONE-DAY PROCESS: SEPTEMBER 18

Aspects of the September 18 one-day process have already been depicted photographically as a phase of the "freeze failure" described in Chapter 11. Therefore, I will here only and briefly expand on that depiction.

I want to draw special attention to what we see in Fig. 12.1. It is the point at which Bowers made the first serious "hit" on the structure of the building. Even though anticipated, when that "first strike" actually happened, it was something of a shock.

12.1. First strike on the building itself, late Monday morning, September 18.

12.2. Smashing the interior so that the southern walls will fall forward rather than backward and onto Second Street.

12.3. Bowers has now worked around to the rear (east) wall.

12.4. With rear walls pulled off, the building is a set of exposed and gaping rooms, like this one.

12.5. The building at the end of the day on September 18, the end of the first process.

12.6. The pause from September 18th to the 28th was for the purpose of retrieving brick. These pallets were photographed September 24th.

12. 7. Wider view of pallets of bricks on September 25. In the background we are looking into rooms of the first floor apartments. On the right, there is an abandoned refrigerator.

2) THE TWO-DAY PROCESS: SEPTEMBER 28 AND 29

September 18th was only the warm up. The real action commenced September 28, the point at which Bowers figured he had gotten all the brick he could—13 pallets—from the current state of demolition.

Before the action began the morning of the 28th, Bowers' two helpers rummaged through the building and took out a motley collection of old toasters, radios, television sets and other items the owners had elected to leave behind. In Fig. 12.8 they are examining an item in a second floor hotel room.

Also in Fig. 12.8, we see that the medicine cabinet (shown in Fig. 12.4) has been removed from the wall. The two Bowers' workers seen there have removed all of them they could safely reach from several rooms. For better or worse, I stimulated this by asking one of the workers to salvage one for me as a gift to a person I knew who collected such objects and who had told me she would like to have one. Having gotten that one for me, they decided to take several of the others for themselves (and, by mobile phone, almost immediately sold them).

12. 8. Two Bower' workers made a last salvage tour before the major demolition began.

12.9 . As with the inner north wall, Bowers removed the inner (east) wall in increments. Here he is finishing an increment, ending at the first portion of the Arch Mural. The second floor room behind the excavator arm is the same room seen in Fig. 12.8, just above.

12. 10. Removing another increment of the structure.

12.11. Bowers once more reaches the Arch Mural and pulls off another portion of it.

12. 12. After "munching" at the Arch Mural back and forth along the inner east wall, Bowers finally cracks Davis.

12.13. Wide view of the demolition at the point where about half the building is down in rubble.

12. 14. At noon, the building is about half down and Bowers breaks for lunch. This break gives City staff time to salvage some of the mural, about half of which is now on the ground. (Figs 11.42 through 11.47 show additional pictures of this period.) From the left: E. Polito, K. Hiatt, S. Bowers, K. Wagstaff.

12.15. After lunch, the last of the Arch Mural is smashed down.

12. 16. Early in the afternoon, only the street walls of the building were standing. Here, Bowers starts to work on the second story of the west wall.

12.17. Working away.

12. 18. Working away.

12.19. The second story of the west wall is now down and Bowers has turned to the second story of the east-west wing.

12. 20. "The man" himself at work. He seemed thoroughly to enjoy what he was doing.

12.21. Another layer of the east-west wing needed to be removed before the south wall itself.

12. 22. An unsecured battery tipped over and the acid burned a hole in a brass hydraulic cable, igniting the fluid. Here Bowers is dismounting the flaming excavator as a worker turns the hose on the blaze. The fire department turns out, but is not needed. Bowers took the pipe to an Olive Drive muffler shop, had the hole welded, and was back at the demolition within about an hour.

12.23. Meanwhile, E. Polito and the intern continue to salvage Mural pieces.

12. 24. Unlike the north-south wing, Bowers took both stories of the south-facing wall down in one pass.

12.25. Smashing away.

12. 26. And more.

12.27. Bowers finally reached the southwest corner and with a big excavator stretch, pulled down the corner itself. With this, he called it a day at about 5: 00 p.m. Save for the first story western wall, the building was down.

12. 28. Friday, September 29 was the first day of hauling away the debris.

12.29. In this view we see the still-intact first-story western wall. For the first time since 1925, one could stand at the railroad tracks and see the Anderson Bank building (windows circled).

12. 30. The pattern of the bricks in the G Street facade was of special interest to some people, but little of it came down intact. Here is perhaps the largest chunk of the cornice visible before the lower level of the wall was pulled down.

12.31. Starting at the building's northwest corner, Bowers systematically pulled the wall and shade structure onto the rubble behind it.

12. 32. The corner lists before it falls.

12.33. The main entrance corner pulled down onto the ground.

12. 34. The building now down, attention turned to loading the truck. Four truck-loads were taken to the Yolo County Landfill on Friday and on this day, Saturday.

12.35. View from atop the rubble looking toward the Anderson Bank Building (left) and the Davis Barber Shop (right).

12. 36. Like some gigantic insect of prey, the excavator reposed triumphantly atop the rubble that was the Terminal Building.

12.37. View of the Terminal Building as a sea of rubble. (The Davis Barber Shop is on the left.)

3) THE 73 DAY PROCESS:
SEPTEMBER 18-NOVEMBER 29

Now we see the building disappear ever-so-slowly. For brevity's sake, I have edited the day-by-day chronicle down to only the more dramatic changes. These are depicted in Figs. 12.38 through 12.53.

12.38. DAY 1, morning, September 18.

12.39. DAY 1, afternoon, September 18.

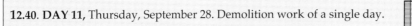

12.40. DAY 11, Thursday, September 28. Demolition work of a single day.

12.41, DAY 12, Friday, September 29, Bowers levels the first story of the west wall.

12.42. DAY 14. Sunday, October 1. Bowers' driver works Saturday and Sunday, hauling four loads a day.

12.43. DAY 16. Tuesday, October 3. Hauling slows to provide the brick cleaner time to salvage bricks.

12.44. **DAY 17,** Wednesday, October 4. The east wall and mural are leveled completely to the ground and debris pulled back from the sidewalk.

12.45. **DAY 18,** Thursday, October 5. Final few feet of the Mural removed and debris pulled off the parking lot roadway.

12.46. DAY 29, Monday, October 16. Removal is at a virtual standstill as brick is slowly and laboriously cleaned by the single cleaner, who Bowers personally transports back and forth to the site.

12.47. DAY 41, Saturday, October 28. The long brick-cleaning pause ends on Day 40, and hauling resumes.

12.48. DAY 46, Thursday, November 2. Hauling continues. Bowers is in the process of pulling the debris to the center of the lot. He works the excavator from the top of the pile.

12.49. **DAY 50,** Monday, November 6. The pile gradually declines. Over the past several days, Bowers has run the excavator down below street grade into the building basement for the purpose of pulling down its concrete walls.

12.50. **DAY 55,** Saturday, November 11. Bowers has finished breaking up the foundation and the concrete has been removed.

12.51. **DAY 59,** Wednesday, November 15. City staff has removed the five pallets of yellow/brown western facade bricks (bottom right).

12.52. DAY 72, Tuesday, November 28. Some remnants of the building remain, but the lot is essentially clear.

12.53.. DAY 73, Wednesday, November 29. The excavator gone, the demolition is complete.

4) FROM PROCESSES TO MOMENTS

In this chapter, I have depicted the demolition as a series of changes through time—as a process or processes. This is a useful perspective, but like all perspectives it leaves things out. One matter left out is the punctuating moment of special emotional or other note. I describe some of these in the next chapter.

13

DEMOLITION MOMENTS

Demolitions are marked by events or incidents that are not a necessary or logical part of them. Something important happens, but that "something" has a random relation to the logic of whatever is otherwise underway. There were several important "moments" of this kind during the demolition processes. I want here to relate the more salient of them.

In addition, some significant moments **were** integral parts of demolition processes that deserve more recognition than has so far been given. These are also reported in this chapter.

I present these moments in more-or-less the sequence they occurred. I say "more-or-less" because some are grouped, or the time-order otherwise changed, for the sake of brevity and/or clarity.

1) GAPING ROOMS
Over the eleven days the back wall was down but the main structure remained, I heard a number of people who paused at the site express sentiments such as these: "We are looking at history." "Think of all the people who stayed in those rooms." "Think of all the living done here." There was something eerie and haunting about looking into banks of open and gaping hotel rooms that were partly smashed but still much intact. The sight prompted a wistful, reflective mood, a sadness about all those wash basins used so many times over several decades that would never be used again (Fig. 13.1)

2) SHOP FAREWELLS
As reported, four businesses operated on the first floor of the G Street side of the building. From north to south, these were The Natural Foods Works, The Wardrobe, The Hair Chalet, and La Esperanza. The first two opposed demolition and wanted to remain in the building. Grace Chen ran the third. The proprietors of the last appeared to support the demolition and hoped to return to the new building.

These differences regarding demolition were expressed in the signs each posted indicating their closings and new locations. Fig. 13.2 shows the sheet of paper posted by Grace Chen. La Esperanza had a similar note. In contrast, the other two stores put up elaborate and colorful closing notices. Their respective windows have already been seen in Figs. 10.11 and 10.12. A more detailed aspect of the contrast is provided in Fig. 13.3.

In this same vein, in Chapter 10 (Fig. 10.14) we see the Wardrobe roof sign in the process of its careful removal as a treasured momento. This action was notable for its contrast with the treatment given the Hair Chalet's equivalent sign. Its owner simply left it behind on the roof of the shade structure. It got batted about in the debris of the hotel for some weeks until it was finally smashed. Fig. 13.4 is a picture of it I took on Day 37 (October 24).

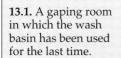

13.1. A gaping room in which the wash basin has been used for the last time.

GRACE HAS MOVED

TO

WEST LAKE PLAZA
SHOPPING CENTER

1260 LAKE BLVD.
SUITE #116

PH. (530) 753-2436

13.2. Farewell door sign of the Hair Chalet.

13.3. Portion of the Farewell door sign of The Wardrobe

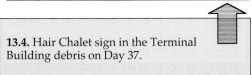

13.4. Hair Chalet sign in the Terminal Building debris on Day 37.

13.5. John Sheehy, excavator operator, truck driver, and rescuer of the Terminal Cafe cash register.

3) JOHN SHEEHY RESCUES THE TERMINAL CAFE CASH REGISTER

Fig. 13.5 reproduces a photo I took of John Sheehy, who was the person who actually loaded and hauled away the great bulk of the Terminal Building. Stan Bowers ran the show, did the showy smashings on various days, and performed many other tasks. But John did the steady, detail work of loading, hauling, and dumping.

Formally, John simply drove the truck Bowers was renting to haul away debris. According to John, he was supposed to be waiting around while the truck was loaded. But, years ago, Bowers had taught him to run the excavator and started to pay him extra also to load rather than just wait. So, John was working two jobs each day he was involved in a Bowers demolition.

When a demolition was underway, he was also willing to work every day a local landfill was open and accepted loaded trucks. So it was that he was working some Saturdays and Sundays and, in particular, Sunday, October 1 (Day 14).

On that day, he was operating the excavator near a gash in the ceiling of the still intact basement chambers of the building. Looking down into the basement he saw a variety of objects, including file cabinets and other office furniture. On one shelf, he spotted a large, very old cash register. Descending into the basement though the gash (Fig. 13.6), he worked his way through the debris (Fig. 13.7) to the cash register, picked it up, and threw it through a basement window onto the outside sidewalk. (It weighed at least a hundred pounds, so we know he was quite fit and strong.)

Knowing I was interested in Davis history, he explained that he had thrown it out for me and I could have it if I wanted it. I did. Fig. 13.8 shows it sitting in my minivan. (Subsequently, I donated it to the Hattie Weber Museum of Davis, where it became part of its permanent exhibition.)

13.6. John Sheehy climbs down into the Terminal Building basement, exploring for salvageable items.

13.7. View through a street-level window of the still not completely-collapsed basement .

4) WHERE DO YOU PUT AN ENTIRE BUILDING YOU DO NOT WANT?

With the building smashed down on September 29, Bowers' next problem was where to put all the pieces he had created. John Sheehy loaded his truck for the first time that day, but to where was he to go? Both men knew there was a "dump" in Yolo County, but neither knew where it was.

I was standing with them when they realized they had this problem, so they asked me where it was. Perhaps I should have been a die-hard preservationist and not told them, but I did. Worse still, I rummaged through the glove compartment of my minivan and located a AAA map of Yolo County that I gave them and on which I drew the route to the Yolo County Landfill.

Curious about exactly what happened at the landfill, I went with John one day and photographed an unloading. The key point in the process is shown in Fig. 13.9. In that picture we see that the truck bed tips up. With the rear gate open and the bed tilted up, the driver pulls forward and the contents slide out by gravity, leaving a thirty or so foot trail of debris

To the right in Fig. 13.9, one can see a caterpillar bulldozer. It was about to push this new debris into existing debris just left by garbage deliverers. The hotel, as such, would then be merged with garbage in general. In that way, the Terminal Building disappeared into the stream of Yolo County rubbish.

More broadly, the answer to the question, "Where do you put an entire building you do not want?" is: Smash it up and bury the pieces.

5) THE SECOND AND THIRD LOADS OF SALVAGED BRICK

The first load of bricks on pallets left the site on Day 10 (September 27). I previously treated their departure as an aspect of the failure to freeze demolition (Ch. 11, Figs. 11.37 through 11.39).

After that load, laboriously and over several weeks, Bowers' single but reliable brick cleaner eked out two more truck-loads of brick. The first of these left on Day 28 (October 2, Fig. 13.10). The second went out on Day 54 (November 10, Fig. 13.11).

This made a total of some twenty-five pallets of red brick salvaged from the building.

6) THE BRICK CLEANER

As reported, Bowers desired to have twenty people or more cleaning bricks at the site. But, efforts to recruit them were unsuccessful. He appeared to settle for what could be achieved by a single, older Mexican man who had worked for him on previous projects.

The work itself consisted of using an iron bar to knock mortar off a brick, a process called "cleaning." This was an extremely monotonous task, which explains why Bowers had trouble recruiting even laborers at the bottom of the hired-by-the-day work force. At the bottom, cleaning bricks was apparently the rock-bottom.

Bowers paid ten cents a brick and required they be stacked on a pallet—a pallet consisting of 500 bricks. An ordinary brick cleaner might do somewhat more than one pallet a day, thus making a little more than 50 dollars a day (which would be in the neighborhood of fifteen thousand dollars a year).

13.8. The rescued, perhaps Terminal Cafe, cash register sitting in the back of my minivan, Day 14 (November 1).

13.9. Dumping a load of smashed-up bits of the Terminal Building at the Yolo County Landfill.

Bowers called the brick cleaner "Jose," and spoke to him in single English words or very simple sentences. Jose did not appear to speak English or to understand it very well. Save for the occasional fellow brick cleaner present in the early days, he never interacted with anyone at the site except to respond as best he could when addressed by someone in English. (I never observed Bowers or any of his workers speak Spanish or seem to understand it.)

The sun was often out and day-long exposure to it was punishing. The old man used a stray sheet of plywood to devise a shade structure, as shown in Fig. 13.12.

Beyond cleaning, he had to tote the clean bricks to a pallet and stack them in an interlocking pattern. In Fig. 13.13, we see him starting a new pallet.

13.10. The second load of salvaged brick, Day 28 (October 2).

13.11.. The third load of salvaged brick, Day 54 (November 10).

13.12. The brick cleaner improvised a shade structure, under which he sat and "cleaned" bricks.

13. 13. The brick cleaner begins to lay the first layer of a new pallet of bricks.

7) SCRAP METAL

The building contained a number of metal "I beams," metal plates bridging the tops of windows, and diverse other metal objects. Bowers could have sent this scrap metal to the landfill along with everything else. He saved dumping costs, however, by giving it to a man who worked for him occasionally, who put it on his flat-bed truck and sold it to a scrap metal dealer.   Bowers told me the load shown in Fig 13.15 fetched the man about $60.00. He opined that this was not much, but "its sixty dollars he didn't have before."

The I beams were too long to fit onto the bed of a pickup truck, so they had to be bent. In Fig. 13.14, Bowers is in the process of bending an I-beam with the excavator.

13. 14. Bowers in the process of bending an I beam so that it will fit in the bed of a flat-bed truck.

13.15. Load of metal scavenged from the building.

8) THE BUILDING'S FAMOUS CORNER POST

Virtually every photograph of the Terminal Building contains a view of the post holding up the overhanging second-floor corner at Second and G streets. It was, in fact, a very heavy metal pipe. It became a piece of scrap metal kicking around in the debris of the site.

Although it had been there from Day 1, I finally noticed it on Day 18 (October 5). "Ah," I said, "an artifact to save!" I asked Bowers if I could buy it from him. He told me the price was "free," although he was willing to negotiate. So, I had only to take it away.

The problem was: to where? It was more than ten feet long and weighed perhaps two hundred pounds. What does one do with such an object? I consulted various history-minded people in Davis and got the same reaction from all of them: forget it. It is too big, heavy and presents too much of a storage problem.

So, I relented. It went off on a pickup truck with the other scrap metal (Fig. 13.16). At least occasionally, though, I think I made the wrong decision. This was particularly so when, many months later, I met a member of the Belenis family who had many fond memories of swinging on the post as a child and dearly wanted it saved.

13. 16. Portion of the iconic corner post of the building loaded as scrap metal. (The white arrow points to it.)

9) THE FENCE SIGN BROUHAHA

When The Natural Food Works and the Wardrobe closed, each had student customers who had left Davis for the summer. On returning, they would find that the stores had literally disappeared. Therefore, each store wanted to put a notice at the former location that directed returning customers to the new location.

Problem: The fence around the site was the obvious place for signs, but the Chens claimed the fence as their own and refused to give permission for its use. There was, indeed, acrimony on the matter, with charges that signs that were put up had been torn down and thrown away.

Two solutions were devised. One, The Natural Food Works placed a free-standing A-frame on the public sidewalk every day (and took it away every night). It is seen to the left in Fig. 13.17. Two, Heather Caswell enlisted the Executive Director of the Davis Downtown Business Association, Laura Cole-Rowe, to negotiate with the Chens for permission to have a fence sign. This agreement was achieved, but included the requirement that Ms. Cole-Rowe had personally to participate in placing the sign on the fence. In Fig. 13.17, we see her (on the left) fulfilling her agreement on the rainy Saturday afternoon of Day 41 (October 28).

13.17. Laura Cole-Rowe, Executive Director of the Davis Downtown Business Society (left) and Heather Caswell, owner of The Wardrobe (right), attach a sign announcing the store's new location to the demolition site fence.

10) THROWING BRICK

Bowers did not expect the brick cleaner to hunt through the debris for the bricks he cleaned. Instead, using the excavator, he (Bowers) would lift and smash pieces of the brick walls, creating piles of bricks that could then be cleaned.

Also, many smaller clusters of bricks and single bricks themselves were scattered through the rubble. In order to retrieve these bricks, one had carefully to climb onto the debris, bend over, pick up clumps or single bricks, and throw them into a clear location or into the "bucket" of the excavator.

From time to time, Bowers assembled his crew of four occasionally employed workers to engage in this process of "throwing brick." His initiating declaration would be: "Let's throw some brick." Fig. 13.18 shows this crew on Day 44 (October 31, Halloween). By this day, bricks had fallen into the partially excavated basement level, making "throwing brick" all the more challenging.

I mention "throwing brick" as one type of demolition moment because it was such exceptionally hard work. The workers clearly disliked it because, among other reasons, it required precarious bending over while standing on unstable and uneven materials. Unsurprisingly, most of the four were upright as much as they were bent over during these sessions (Fig. 13.18). (And, Bowers operated the excavator and exhorted the crew as much or more than he "threw brick" himself.)

11) OWNER VISITS

From time to time, Grace or Lee Chen visited the site. Grace Chen visited on Day 44 and told Bowers she was interested in buying enough Terminal Building brick to build a mailbox in front of her house. She also wanted to know the name of a mason who could construct such a structure. When she asked these questions, she was standing on the G Street sidewalk and Bowers was in the excavator atop a mound of rubble about 75 feet from her. In an impressive feat of memory, without pausing Bowers shouted the name and phone number of a mason to her. Not to be out performed by him in front of several onlookers (including me), Mrs. Chen loudly repeated the name and number and indicated she could remember both without writing them down.

13. 18. A session of "throwing brick," Day 44 (October 31). The "claw" of the excavator is configured as a bucket into which the five people working the site are to "throw brick." The black oval shows Bowers and his helpers rummaging for brick at the basement level.

During this same walk-about inspection of the site, Mrs. Chen chatted with the brick cleaner (Fig. 13.19). This was likewise an accomplishment since he did not speak Chinese or English and she did not speak Spanish.

In addition, she had a private conversation with Bowers. After she left the site, Bowers told me that she had said to him: "See that old man? [She pointed to me, some distance away.] He is against us and gave us trouble." Bowers took this to mean that she did not want him talking with me. But, he shrugged his shoulders and declared "I don't care about Davis stuff."

12) ONE PLAQUE RETURNS

Recall that on July 27, the two metal plaques attached to the Arch Mural were observed missing (Chapter 10, Figs. 10.19-21).

October 28, Bowers told me he thought he knew what happened to both of them. Then at the site on November 1 (Day 45), he handed me one of them, saying that he had not been able to locate the other and he had been told that it was broken and therefore of little use.

Because Bowers' demolition contract gave him ownership of everything on the site, in his view, the plaque belonged to him. (The City had long ago abandoned ownership of the mural.) He was clear that he was giving it to me personally and that I could do with it what I pleased.

13.19. Grace Chen, left, speaks with the brick cleaner, Day 44 (October 31).

13.20. Photograph of the Mural Arch plaque taken at the site the day of its return, Day 45 (November 1).

Using Bowers' logic, I was now the owner of this bit of Davis history. I gave thought to holding onto it until I was satisfied that appropriate units of the City of Davis could provide proper custody and care. That is, in my assessment one City administration after another had been too casual about retention and custody of historical documents and artifacts. But on the other side of that, I could not provide it any great degree of security. So, I decided to donate it to the Hattie Weber Museum of Davis, which was about as insecure as any place I would keep it. (Fig. 13.20 shows the returned plaque.)

13) CONCRETE REMOVAL

It was not overly difficult to pull down brick, tile, wood and plaster walls and smash them into truck-loadable pieces. However, all these materials were sitting on a concrete foundation and, worse still, a poured concrete basement.

The basement extended the entire width of the site from Second Street to the Davis/Ace parking lot and about one-quarter the depth of the site. Removal required that that this mass of concrete be broken into loadable chunks.

At first, Bowers used the excavator arm as a pounding sledge hammer and/or a pulling concrete cracker. We see him so engaged in these activities in Figs. 13.21 and 13.22.

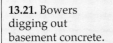

13.21. Bowers digging out basement concrete.

13.22. Pulling out the concrete foundation of the G Street wall.

But breaking up the deepest and largest portions of the basement required the additional and specialized large jack-hammer of a machine that is shown in Fig. 13.23. Like some giant, crazed woodpecker, it cracked the basement walls into chunks.

There was then the moving and loading of these heavy concrete chunks, as shown in Figs. 13.24 and 13.25.

13.23. Jackhammer machine breaking up a basement wall.

13.24. Pulling up a large chunk of foundation.

13.25. Loading a truck-sized piece of foundation/basement concrete.

14) FIRST "ARCHEOLOGICAL" ARTIFACTS

Working at removing some of the G Street wall foundation, on Day 40 (October 27) John Sheehy also struck a cache of long-buried trash. Shown in part in Fig. 13.26, it was mostly bottles, but also contained metal items, including a horse shoe. (The find was next to the site of the Place Livery, which was described in Chapter 2 and Fig. 2.5.)

13.26. Box of unearthed "artifacts" found near the G Street wall.

15) THE SEBASTOPOL DIGGERS

On Day 49 (Sunday, November 5), two men who told me they were from Sebastopol, California (a town some seventy-five miles from Davis) came onto the site. The older of the two (about age 50) had very long metal rods with handles that he pushed into the ground in various places in hopes of hitting solid objects. In one place, he hit something about six feet below the surface. The two of them began digging (Figs. 13.27 and 28).

The older man told me that he was an avocational California history buff who, when he had the time, visited demolition sites such as this in the hope of excavating historical objects, primarily bottles. His custom-fabricated and well-used probing rods, his purpose-configured shovels, the "digging suit" coveralls he wore, and other equipment he used, suggested, indeed, that this was an activity in which he engaged with some regularity.

Given that they were seeking to unearth Davis historical artifacts, I phoned Phyllis Haig, Curator of the Hattie Weber Museum of Davis, told her of the diggers, and suggested that she might want to come to the site and inspect what they were doing. She declined, explaining that she had obligations at the Yolo County Historical Museum in neighboring Woodland.

I showed the older digger the bottles John Sheehy had unearthed (seen in part in Fig. 13.26) and he commented in some detail on their styles, uses, and their places and periods of manufacture. For example, I was previously unfamiliar with such terminology as "pumpkin seed flask," "apocathary pot," and "Shasta soda bottle."

I observed as each of them switched off in digging—and I declined their invitation to help them dig. In Fig. 13.27, we see them at work. The hole they dug seemed to me quite deep. Each man was about six feet tall. At the point they stopped digging, the surface was above their heads when they stood upright in the hole (Fig. 13.28).

The long probe rods had given them faith they would come to something——and they did. A portion of what was thrown up out of the hole and laid out on the excavated dirt is shown in Fig. 13.29.

 I estimated that something like 200 objects—bottles in the vast majority—were dug up. Each of the men picked over their finds and placed what they wanted in their several plastic buckets. This done, there were about 75 objects they did not want and which they offered me.

13.27. Two men digging for artifacts on the site, Day 49, Sunday, November 5.

13.28. This man is about six feet tall and his head is below the surface as he stands in the hole he and this partner dug in a short period of time in this loamish Yolo County earth.

13.29. Bottles and a few other kinds of objects laid out on the side of a excavated mound of dirt.

I accepted them and placed them in several cardboard boxes I scavenged from the dumpster of a nearby restaurant. In Fig. 13.30, we see all the objects on a table in the patio of my home.

As wonderful as all these articles were, artifacts of this sort were (and are) not exactly my specialty, nor could I easily store and otherwise manage them. Seeking to find a proper home for them, I contacted the City of Davis Historical Resources Management Commission and the Hattie Weber Museum of Davis. In due course, I formally donated the collection to the City of Davis (save one small pharmacy bottle inscribed "J. W. Campbell, Davisville, Cal.")

13.30. Bottles and other objects dug up at the Terminal Building site (Photographed on Day 52, November 8).

16) SCATTERED PAPERS FROM THE BASEMENT

As the excavator lifted debris from the basement, it now and again grasped cardboard boxes filled with papers. Sometimes these boxes burst open and hundreds of sheets fluttered and scattered over the debris, as shown in Fig. 13.31.

Because the basement had also contained such strange objects as an early-model cash register, I hoped that by some miraculous act of neglect, I might stumble onto old Terminal Cafe and/or Hotel records. Stan and John were themselves curious about what might be found, so each time they struck boxes of paper, they paused and gave me time to scramble down into the excavation pit and scoop up the billowing documents.

Alas, I was not to be so fortunate as to find old Terminal records. The several thousand documents I examined all turned out to be merely the mundane business papers and commercial tribulations of an organization named Aggie Enterprises and other entities. (Oddly, some of the items were only about a year old, yet were being sent to the Yolo County Landfill.)

17) THE REDWOOD BEAMS FROM THE G STREET SHADE STRUCTURE

The posts holding up the ugly G Street shade structure and the frame of that structure were very large, redwood beams. In the early days of the demolition, a fair number of people coming by the site expressed interest in buying them. Each time, Bowers said the beams were already sold. I asked him who had bought them and he named a well-known Sacramento Valley developer.

13.31. A cloud of papers billow from a cardboard box burst open by the excavator.

As the days went on, the beams were literally kicked around the site. At one point toward the end and with the beams still there, I asked Bowers when and how they would leave. He responded that the deal with the developer had fallen through and they were going to the dump. In Fig. 13.32, we see some of them in a pile ready to load for the Yolo Landfill.

13.32. The last of the G Street shade structure redwood beams assembled to be loaded for the Yolo Landfill.

18) THE YELLOW G STREET FACADE BRICKS

Recall that the Chens had bought the yellow brick Bowers was going to salvage from the G Street façade for use in the new building (Ch. 11, Figs. 11.15 and 11.29). (Interestingly, preservationists did not propose or especially support this idea. Some even opposed it, regarding it as an empty gesture of "too little, too late." Others thought it was in bad taste akin to that of placing Lenin's embalmed body on public view.)

A little more than four pallets of yellow brick did, in fact, emerge from the building. These were removed from the site on Day 58 (November 14). Ace Hardware's forklift truck and driver were recruited for the task, as shown in Fig. 13.33.

Fig. 13.34 shows the four and a little more pallets stacked in the City's Corporation Yard. In front of them, we also see the saved remnants of the Arch Mural.

13.33. Davis Lumber forklift and driver load pallets of yellow bricks onto a City of Davis Parks truck, Day 58 (November 14).

13.34. Salvaged yellow brick and pieces of the Arch Mural in the City of Davis Corporation Yard (photographed December 8, 2000).

19) THE EXCAVATOR LEAVES, THE DEMOLITION ENDS

In other studies in which I have tried to fix the exact start and end of a social process, I have learned that this a very tricky and inexact task and is subject to several reasonable but differing reckonings. This is also true for the demolition of the Terminal Building.

That understood, I found it most useful to use the arrival and first use of the excavator and its cessation and departure as the way to mark the demolition's beginning and its end.

Using this marker, the demolition began when the excavator was delivered to the site late on Sunday, September 17. However, it was first put to use on Monday, September 18. The very drama of that first use recommended September 18 as Day 1.

The machine was last used on Monday, November 27, which was Day 71. But the process was not quite over. A last load of debris was to have been hauled later that week, but Bowers decided it was not worth keeping the excavator there for such a small amount of work. By telephone on Tuesday, he told me that the machine was needed to demolish a Victorian in downtown Sacramento and would be moved on Wednesday. (Ever the kidder, he invited me to come observe the process, and tried to get my goat with detailed descriptions of the intricate historic decoration of the building he would be smashing.)

It left the early morning of Wednesday, November 29, which was Day 73. In Fig. 13.35, we see the gentleman who specialized in moving these kinds of machines (and who had delivered it to the site), slowly coaxing it onto the detached platform trailer of his special trailer-truck.

13. 35. The excavator barely fit on the deck of the trailer on which it was hauled.

Given the degree of interest the *Davis Enterprise* had exhibited in the Terminal Building matter, I thought it might like to cover the departure, so I alerted the editor. She sent photographer Alison Portello and that afternoon the paper ran the picture and caption reproduced as Fig. 13.36. (Note the inaccurately benign term "grade" used in the caption to characterize the work of the excavator.)

Finally, leaving Davis along Second Street and the frontage road north of Interstate 80, in Fig. 13.37 we see the ungainly but effective truck with the excavator on it entering I-80 at the Yolo causeway on-ramp.

Thus ended the saga of the Terminal Building's demolition.

Hauling it away

Alison Portello/Enterprise photo

Frank Cook of The Gold River Co. straps down and cleans an excavator Wednesday that was used to grade the former site of the Terminal Hotel at Second and G streets. Property owners Lee and Grace Chen had the 75-year-old, 12,000-square-foot brick building torn down in September. They plan to construct a replacement building that's roughly twice that size. The drawings and a final application are being prepared to submit to the city.

13.36. *Davis Enterprise* coverage of the excavator's departure, Wednesday, November 29.

13.37. Its destruction work completed, the excavator left Davis on rainy and overcast Day 73—November 29, 2000.

IV

CONSEQUENCES AND CAUSES

There are two last, but very far from least, topics remaining to be treated.

- Left with a hole in the ground with a fence around it in November, 2000, what happened then? Various kinds of effects or consequences visible over the next two years are detailed in **Chapter 14.**

- After all is said and done, why did preservation fail? What might be the "causes" of preservation failing? This is the topic of **Chapter 15.**

14

CONSEQUENCES

Discussion of an event is not complete until we have considered its consequences or effects. Of course, the more time that has passed since the event, the more consequences or effects there are likely to be.

In the present case, this book was completed a little more than two years after the Terminal Building's demolition. For an event of this sort, two years is not a very long period over which to trace consequences. Presumably, many of the most important ones had not yet occurred. Indeed, the consequences I suggest here are rather modest. Nonetheless some interesting things had happened.

1) EMPTY, BLIGHTED HOLE

Although a new building within two years was promised and/or predicted at the time of demolition, the lot was still an empty and weed-filed hole on the second anniversary of demolition, September 18th, 2002.

14.1. Terminal Building site July 1, 2001, looking north along G Street with the G Street Plaza in the left distance, behind the sign with the word "security" on it. This view was virtually the same one year later.

Over the Winter and Spring of 2001 and of 2002, diverse and "volunteer" greenery (aka weeds) appeared (Fig. 14.1) and, for lack of water, turned to a brown fire hazard.

2) DAVIS ENTERPRISE "TOP 10" STORY

It was a custom of the *Davis Enterprise* to print an end-of-the-year assessment of the "top 10" Davis stories. According to the Enterprise's Bob Dunning, the list resulted from a "majority vote of select editors and reporters" of the paper (*Davis Enterprise*, December 31, 2000).

The Terminal Building demolition ranked fourth for the year 2000. The paper's summary of the entire list is reproduced in Fig. 14.2. All things considered, I think I would agree with this assessment of the story's importance in the political landscape of Davis.

I might note, though, that Bob Dunning groused that the list resulting from majority vote was not the same as his list. In particular, he distinguished between an event being "newsworthy" versus "important." When one did that:

> All that nonsense involving Madonna last month might have been deemed newsworthy, but it certainly wasn't important. The same with the false issue known as the Terminal Hotel Controversy.

The year's top 10 local stories

1 Alarmed by a sprawling community, Davis residents reacted at the ballot box in 2000, approving **Measure J and Measure O**. But growth and the high cost of housing are on the minds of UC Davis administrators, who begin wrestling with how to accommodate an influx of students, faculty and staff expected in the next decade. Former City Manager John Meyer is hired as a vice chancellor to oversee the preparations.

2 The unexpected **firing of Davis police Capt. Nick Concolino** generates a firestorm of controversy and an unprecedented vote of no-confidence in Chief Jerry Gonzales, who later resigns. Residents continue to lobby for Concolino's reinstatement.

3 The university reels as **three tragedies strike** in quick succession: a research trip to Mexico is marred by five fatalities in a boating accident; student David Thornton dies after a drinking binge on his 21st birthday; another student suffers serious stab wounds and her ex-boyfriend, Johnny Shao Tien, is arrested for assault and attempted murder.

4 The **Terminal Hotel** at Second and G streets is demolished over the protests of residents who wanted to preserve a mural on its north face. Owners Grace and Lee Chen hope to build a new retail/residential project there.

5 Yolo County's ag community, still reeling from the closure of the Hunt-Wesson cannery in late 1999, is dealt two more blows in 2000: **Spreckels Sugar Inc. and Del Monte Foods** announce the shutdowns of their Woodland plants, resulting in the loss of nearly 800 jobs.

6 A Woodland woman dies and her friend is seriously injured in a **hit-and-run traffic crash.** But the news turns more horrifying when police arrest a Woodland teen-ager for the crime and her mother, Lidia Ulloa, for attempting to conceal it. Both are imprisoned by year's end.

7 Residents and elected officials alike are outraged after **burrowing owl habitat in Mace Ranch is disced under,** probably killing the creatures, who are a species of special concern.

8 A fire in a breezeway at the **E Street Plaza** damages the electricity source and results in the closures of four businesses. Two stores reopen, but Davis Jewelers may never be back. Its owners have been charged with embezzlement for failing to return customers' property.

9 **Measure K,** a $26 million school facilities bond, [...] Davis school officials breathe a sigh of relief, then get to work on the massive task of building a new junior high school and two new elementary schools.

10 Longtime Davis store **Discoveries declares bankruptcy** and closes its doors, a sad day for many residents who recall the store as one of their favorite places to buy gifts.

14.2. *The Davis Enterprise*, December 31, 2000, "Top 10 local stories" for 2000.

In addition to the capsule summaries seen in Fig. 14.2, *Enterprise* writers provided somewhat expanded memorial capsules of each of the ten stories. The one for the Terminal Building is reproduced in Fig. 14.3. I provide it because it suggests the paper's attitude toward the matter in a way that did not come out so clearly in the many "straight" news stories it had done in 1999 and 2000.

I would characterize the attitude seen in Fig. 14.3 as snide put-down of what the writers perceived to be inappropriate caring for "antiquated landmarks." The summary also contains several factual errors, including the assertion that the campaigns involving the three places mentioned were "the same community members." In fact, there was little overlap among people actively involved in the Terminal Building and the other two matters.

4 **Farewell, hotel:** Davis residents once again proved their loyalty to antiquated landmarks by attempting to stop the demolition of the Terminal Hotel. The building had stood at Second and G streets downtown for more than 75 years.

The same community members who worked to save the Richards Boulevard underpass and the Boy Scout Cabin targeted their preservation efforts on the hotel, which featured a mural on the north face of the building. Owners Grace and Lee Chen expressed their desires before the City Council last summer to transform the hotel —

which was not up to safety codes and standards — into a new retail/residential complex roughly double the size of the 12,000-square-foot hotel. According to plans, the new complex could be as high as four stories in some places.

The Chens' plan drew protest from some residents, as well as the Historic Resources Management Commission, which recommended that the City Council grant the building a historic designation, which would allow it to be preserved. The council rejected the recommendation, opening the doors for the demolition.

In mid-July, three of four businesses that occupied the building relocated to other areas of the city. La Esperanza, a popular Mexican food restaurant, is still serving food at its second location, La Esperanza II, in the University Mall on Russell Boulevard.

On Sept. 18, the walls of the hotel came tumbling down, with a handful of protesters, City Council members and residents present. It is estimated that it will take up to two years before the new building is complete at the site.

14.3. December 31, 2000, *Davis Enterprise* year-end capsule write-up of the Terminal Building story.

3) PASSING FLURRY OF PLAZA SENTIMENT

As can been seen in the various photographs presented in chapter 12, removal of the building created a wide and open space at the northeast corner of Second and G streets. For the first time since 1926, people could look straight into the downtown from the train depot and visa versa.

This new and expansive experience gave rise to the rapidly communicated and widespread idea that a plaza at Second and G might be better than a new building. Business operators close to the area were especially vocal in feeling that a plaza would likely help them as much or more than the long shadow of a four story structure.

Despite this idea's popularity and the strength of sentiment supporting it, the proposal never went anywhere. The Chens were not interested, and, more important, no one was offering to buy the land from them for that purpose.

4) REDESIGNED AND APPROVED NEW BUILDING

Sentiment for a plaza also subsided because the Chens came forth with a revised plan for a building, one configured to meet objections to the previous design.

The design we saw in Chapter 10 (Fig. 10.29) featured an internal courtyard and four stores straight-up on the east side. These and other features caused it to be severely criticized by the Planning and the Historical Resources Management Commissions as being out-of-scale and character for the location (and perhaps not sufficiently "reminiscent" of the Terminal Building).

Architect McCandless responded to these and other criticisms with the configuration shown in Fig. 14.4. In this plan, the third and fourth stories were stepped back from all sides of the building and each featured glass as a way to de-emphasize their mass. The first two stories rose to about the height of the Terminal Building and had second-story design details intended to "recall" that building. With further tweaking, this new design was approved by the Planning Commission on September 18, 2001. Eerily, this date was one year to the day from the start of the Terminal Building demolition, September 18, 2000.

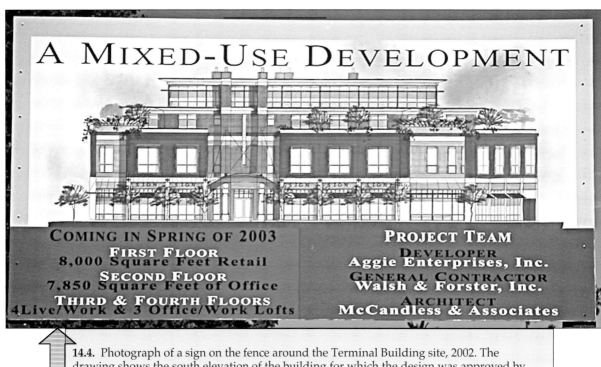

14.4. Photograph of a sign on the fence around the Terminal Building site, 2002. The drawing shows the south elevation of the building for which the design was approved by the Planning Commission on September 18, 2001.

5) PLAN TO USE THE BRICKS AND MURAL PIECES

The plan approved for the new building contained dozens of conditions, two of which pertained to using of the Arch Mural pieces and the salvaged bricks in the new building.

Numbered conditions 15 and 24, the exact text is reproduced in Fig. 14.5. At the time of the completion of this book, the owners had not yet come forth with plans for meeting either of these conditions.

On his own authority, Planner Ken Hiatt had authorized use of some of the bricks in connection with a map guide to the downtown that was erected at the southeast corner of Second and G in December, 2000 (Fig. 14.6).

Apparently to verify their authenticity, almost all the bricks were positioned so that one could read the identification of the brick-maker that was pressed into one edge of each during manufacture. (Normally, a brick is positioned so that one cannot read that name, for, the opposite edge was textured to be more attractive. For Davis history trivia buffs, the lettering is "Livermore F.B. WKS. S.F.")

15.   The owners shall work with the city to incorporate into the building or adjacent right-of-way, a didactic display of the Terminal Hotel Building as well as the "Davis Arches" mural. The display should be in a location accessible to the public such as the sidewalk area around the building or the main entry lobby to the upper floors. The owners shall contribute up to $3,000 towards the display.

24.   A proposal for reuse of the face bricks salvaged from the Terminal Hotel shall be submitted for review and approval of the Planning and Building Department prior to issuance of building permit. The bricks should be integrated into building accents and or the paving/landscape adjacent to the project site.

14.5. Conditions regarding use of the Arch Mural remnants and salvaged brick in a new building on the Terminal site.

14.6. Display map of the downtown at the southeast corner of Second and G. The bricks seen in the low wall/seat in the lower left are some of those saved from the Terminal Building demolition.

6) H STREET REALIGNMENT PLAN

The new building was designed to make the maximum allowable footprint on the lot. This created a new problem. Built to the maximum on the east side, the new wall would be only a few feet from H Street.

One of the arguments for tearing down the Terminal Building had been that it "faced away" from the train depot. Instead, any building should "face toward" the train depot with "open arms." McCandless designed "open arms" in the form of a restaurant space on the east side that looked toward the depot. But the windows and doors of that anticipated restaurant were next to the projected sidewalk. That sidewalk, in turn, abutted H Street. Almost everyone involved agreed that it would be much more "open arms" if there was room for a public plaza outside the restaurant between the sidewalk and the street.

Hence, there arose the idea of what came to be called the "H Street realignment." With the cooperation of the owner of Davis Lumber/Ace Hardware a plan to move H Street east and next to the tracks was developed. The concept began slowly to make its way the through the long and tortured budget, design and construction processes. In late 2002, it was still in only the early design stages. The actual realignment was years away, but would not delay the construction of the new building on the Terminal Building site.

7) DRAGGED-OUT DEMOLITION ORDINANCE

Even though, as we have seen in Chapter 5, demolitions were common in Davis over the 1950s-70s, there had been few in recent years. The sheer fact of one in 2000 was therefore attention-getting. Also, it occurred right downtown and next to the "multi-model center." A great many people therefore passed by it. Moreover, it now came to light that under the existing law demolitions were easy for an applicant to achieve.

These and other factors gave rise to citizen calls for a need to think about the legal conditions under which demolitions could be carried out. In October, 2000, the City Council directed staff to prepare a draft of options for a new ordinance.

Two years later, a draft with various options was still churning at the staff level and barely on agendas. This, though, was about par for the rate of progress of legislation in Davis.

8) AMBIGUOUS EFFECT ON PRESERVATION CONSCIOUSNESS AND ACTION

What effect did the Terminal Building demolition have on preservation consciousness and action in Davis? From the vantage point of two years, I would have to say the effect was unclear. Preservation matters did not seem to me to have gotten markedly better or worse.

Three buildings in the 1917 city were either demolished or on the block for demolition without public outcry or even modest comment. On the other hand, two other proposed demolitions had stirred citizen resistance and brought about favorable City action.

9) ADVANCED PRESERVATION SEMINAR

In the midst of the Terminal demolition, Laura Cole-Rowe, Executive Director of the Davis Downtown Business Association and active participant in the California and national Main Street programs, began to put forth the idea that the DDBA needed to make a special effort to educate Davis people on historic preservation.

As the press release in Fig. 14.8 relates, she and others were struck with how, in the Terminal episode, "even the more involved and informed on both sides often showed surprisingly limited and even erroneous understandings of the meaning and practical relevance of historical resources and preservation."

She recruited me to help in this activity, for which we applied and received a grant from the American Architecture Association Foundation. Two emergent matters shaped the program we organized.

First, in reflecting on what would be an effective form of such education, we came to think that the public in general was not the foremost or most strategic audience. Instead, the key audience should be the **owners** of buildings that might be historic and qualify for rehabilitation funds.

Second, at about the same time, it came to our attention that three people living close to Davis had in recent years teamed up to rehabilitate Sacramento Valley buildings to the Secretary's Standards and had qualified them for the Federal tax credit. These three were Roger Klemm, an architect practicing out of Placerville; Marcus Ullrich, a CPA with offices in Woodland and Davis; and David Wilkinson, an economic development specialist with Mercy Housing California in West Sacramento. This was a team of authentically preservationist developers. (They are described more fully in Fig. 14.8.)

This strategic audience idea and the discovery of this team organized our task. We conceived it as bringing Davis downtown commercial property owners into face-to-face contact with these preservationist developers. This took the form of about a dozen owners seated around a seminar table with Klemm, Ulrich and Wilkinson at the Hattie Weber Museum of Davis for almost three hours the afternoon of May 1, 2001.

But the point was not simply to bring these two groups together. Almost all of the grant was budgeted to pay for making a professionally done **videotape** of the seminar, so that yet other owners in Davis and elsewhere (and anyone else) could view the proceedings. We were very fortunate to have had skilled videographer Ray Johnston of Events Photography Video DJ in Davis available to do the production.

The resulting tape, which is available from the DDBA (Fig. 14.8) and in a number of libraries, is a very detailed and step-by-step description of Klemm's, Ulrich's and Wilkinson's preservation of buildings in Winters, Gridley, and Live Oak, California and their generalizations about the process of historical preservation. Indeed, they took special care to point up the general principles involved. In particular, Wilkinson underscored the general features of feasibility studies.

The educational problem at this level, though, is that these matters are technical. The seminar is not breezy, fast-paced and scintillating. It is unavoidably detailed and plodding, a fact that seemed not at all to bother the building owners attending the seminar, but does not make for popular television. I draw attention to this fact because much of the material one sees on historic preservation fails to communicate this technical nature—and this is a key problem that historic preservationists have not adequately faced.

We explored California-wide and nationwide distribution of the tape with the two leading historical preservation organizations by sending copies of it to appropriate people at each. Unfortunately, neither organization paid us the courtesy of even acknowledging receipt of the tape and our proposal, much less honoring us by turning us down. (I have since learned not to be surprised by such rude behavior. In sections 1 and 9 of Chapter 15 I speak further of the problem of disorganization among preservationists that prompts the public to perceive them as aloof and arrogant.)

10) LIVING-DEAD ICONS

The mural of the arch on the north wall of the Terminal Building and the building itself were (and remain) Davis icons. By "icon" I mean that both regularly showed up among the small number of physical things that people used symbolically to represent "Davis."

The vaguely "mission style" Southern Pacific train station was likely **the** most popular such item (as seen in Fig. 14.9), slightly outranking such objects as the UCD water tower, certain UCD buildings, and the Dresbach-Hunt-Boyer mansion.

But, right up there with all these was the Arch Mural and the Aggie/Terminal hotel.

Davis Downtown Business Association

P.O. Box 72497
Davis, CA 95617
(530) 756-8763
Fax (530) 756-6504

FOR IMMEDIATE RELEASE
FOR FURTHER INFORMATION, PLEASE CONTACT
LAURA COLE-ROWE, DAVIS DOWNTOWN BUSINESS ASSOCIATION
(530) 756-8763

Financial Incentives for Rehabilitating Older Commercial Buildings Video Available

Through a seminar made into videotape, the Davis Downtown Business Association seeks to bring the abstract and remote topics of "historical preservation" and "historic resources" down to the level of practical instructions and actions for residents of Davis.

This problem was put dramatically on display in Davis in 2000. In numerous debates over the preservation versus demolition of an historic downtown building called the Terminal Hotel, even the most involved and informed on both sides often showed surprisingly limited and often erroneous understandings of the meaning and practical relevance of historical resources and preservation.

Responding to this experience, DDBA's approach to achieving at least a partial remedy to this problem was to create a seminar in which the practical nuts and bolts of historical resources and preservation are shown in ways that bring them to life. Equally as important, the seminar was videotaped and is being made available throughout the community.

The seminar includes coverage of the following:

- The special provisions provided by the California State Historic Building Code to help owners of historic buildings

- Case studies of buildings successfully restored in nearby communities

- Tax incentives for preservation presented by a Certified Public Accountant.

- Survey of sources of funding outside the tax code and sources of technical assistance in old building rehabilitation.

The presenters for the seminar are:

Roger W. Klemm , founding Principal of Synthesis Design Group, Placerville, California, and his staff have worked on the restoration of over thirty-five historic structures in California and the West and in more than a dozen historic downtowns throughout California.

Marcus E. Ullrich, CPA, Managing Partner of Ullrich, Delvati CPAs, Woodland, California, has developed his own properties and advised clients with particular reference to the significant tax advantages that are available to developers of historic properties under the Federal Tax Code. Over the past twenty years, he has rehabilitated numerous historic properties.

David Wilkinson , an economic development specialist with California Mercy Housing, Sacramento, California, and a consultant, specializes in conducting feasibility studies of historic buildings, focusing on sources of funding.

The audience who participated in the seminar consisted of property owners of building in the historic conservation district (consisting of the original, 1917, city of Davis) that is now in the process of formation.

We hope that the long terms benefits of this project will include making the people of Davis more concretely knowledgeable about historic resources and historic preservation and therefore more comfortable with these ideas. Such changes would hopefully also lead them to become more active participants in these matters.

While some of the material will be specific to Davis, a good deal of the content is applicable anywhere in California.

This videotape will be shown on local public access television, and made available for viewing and copying at local libraries and in the offices of public and private organizations.

For further information, please call the Davis Downtown Business Association, 756-8763.

14.8. September 9, 2001 press release announcing the availability of the DDBA-produced videotaped seminar on "Financial Incentives for Rehabilitating Older Commercial Buildings."

Suddenly, in September, 2000, both, as physical objects, were gone.

However, even though physically destroyed, representations of both lived on in a twilight night of the living-dead. People and institutions change slowly. Even after two years, one could still buy Eastman Studios postcards of the Arch Mural in Davis stores. For quite a time, the City's web site and literature still listed the Arch Mural as one of Davis' items of "public art."

A large oil painting of Davis icons (shown in Fig. 14.9) that hung in the reception area of the City Parks and Recreation Department was relocated to the city council meeting room in 2001.

14.9. Photograph of an approximately four by six foot oil painting of Davis icons hung in the Davis Community Chambers, 2001. The black circle and white arrow point to the image of the Terminal/Aggie hotel that is the central feature of this painting.

This was ironic and even gruesome because, at its very center, is an image of the Terminal Building. One might even construe the relocation of this painting at the time it was done as an act akin to placing the head of a dead animal on trophy display. More gruesome still, the city's television channel began to use the painting as the background during periods of recess at televised meetings of the Planning Commission and City Council. As such, it was presented to the public in all its ironic living-deadness for long periods every month.

The painting was hanging in the chamber the evening of September 18, 2001, the meeting at which a new building on the Terminal site was approved by the Planning Commission. In the course of addressing the Commission on the proposed building, Alan Miller "pointed to the picture on the wall showing . . . sites to be seen in Davis and said, "hmm . . . well, I guess one of those is no longer with us" (Miller, 2001)

15

CAUSES
A SOCIOLOGY OF PRESERVATION FAILURES

So, why *did* preservation fail? The short and unsatisfying but true answer is: For a variety of reasons, no one of which was likely overwhelming or centrally determinative. Instead, an accumulating concatenation of either too weak or too strong variations in social conditions led to a series of preservation failures that ended in demolition.

This broad position may seem obvious and a weasel. It is, in fact, a contentious and not especially popular view of social causation. This is so because it rejects all forms of the major alternatives to it; namely, that there is one variable (or a small number of them) to which we should look in explaining many, most or even all social outcomes. The principle formulations of this master-variable view are quite familiar, social class, race and gender being among the more popular in recent decades. Considered over the longer term, other mono-causal formulations achieving some currency have included divine plans of assorted kinds, sex, shame, guilt, greed, envy, and the will to power.

There are of course also dangers when we move in the opposite, multi-variable direction. There can be so many variables that we wind up unable to say anything. One can well wonder, though, if many social outcomes are not in fact of this sort. It is only our strong need for easily graspable causal understanding that pushes us to impose simple explanations on complicated and indefinite causal complexes.

Be the dangers of single and multiple-cause thinking as they may, let me here strike a middle course. I work on the assumption of multiple causes but draw back from the abyss of an infinite number.

One way to begin to think about multiple causes is, first, to categorize or group conceivably relevant variables in terms of the social entities with which they are associated in a social setting. Second, these social entities can themselves be ordered in terms of their physical, social, and temporal distance from the outcome we want to explain. The most distant is considered first and closest is considered last.

Applied in this case, I think we can identify seven main classes of "social entities" operating in the Davis social setting that can, in turn, be ordered along the variable of distance from the outcome. Listing the most distant first, there are:

1) **External Organizations**
2) **Civic Culture**
3) **Community Groups**
4) **City Government**
5) **Citizen Action**

6) **Owners**
7) **The Building**

These "entities" are <u>not</u> variables. Instead, they are places in which to look for and to identify variables, which I will now do.

1) EXTERNAL ORGANIZATIONS VARIABLES

By "external organizations" I mean named, formally organized groups that had no offices or personnel in Davis, but who were recruited to the scene by people in Davis. In this case, these primarily consisted of engineering assessment firms and preservationist associations. In my appraisal, the actions of both these contributed to preservation failure.

<u>**UNFAVORABLE ENGINEER ASSESSMENTS.**</u> Recall that engineering firms twice assessed the building. The first one, hired by the owners, gave a markedly negative view (Fig. 7.5). The view was so alarming that a properly risk-averse City building department could not ignore its claims. It thereupon required the owners to pay for a second assessment by a different firm, one selected by the City. This assessment was much less alarmist. But it still pointed out what was true of virtually all California brick buildings of its period. It should undergo seismic retrofitting (Fig. 8.11).

Continuing down the risk-averse path, the City required a plan to achieve that upgrading and closed the building in the interim. All was not lost, but this series of events certainly, to me, figures importantly in any explanation of preservation failure.

<u>**WEAK OUTSIDE PRESERVATIONISTS**</u>. On the other side, a number of credible and professional outside preservationists were recruited, as described in Chapter 8 and Figs. 8.19, 8.27 and 8.37. Their appearances on the scene, however, were more in the nature of cameo roles in a motion picture rather than serious, full-scale performances. It was hit-and-run advocacy rather than involvement. Certainly, no one seemed changed by their visits or letters.

In saying this I of course understand that preservationists operate on severely constrained budgets and this fact goes a long way in explaining their behavior. (Let it be clear that my observations here are efforts accurately to describe causes rather than to lay blame.)

One of the ironies of the involvement of outside organizations is that, in the past, they sometimes fostered major preservation successes in Davis. I speak of the government grant programs that led to the important external funding of both the 1979 and 1996 surveys of cultural resources. Neither of these surveys were likely to happen without those grants (with consequent negative consequences on preservation). But, in the Terminal matter, the actions of external organizations had different effects.

2) CIVIC CULTURE VARIABLES

I use the term "civic culture" to draw attention to the tenor or atmosphere of public life in a community. In visiting large and small cities in several countries over many years, I have become a local newspaper and public affairs junkie, watching local government channels in places that have them (and, gasp, even watching their city council meetings).

I have been struck with variations among communities in such matters as how civilly people treat one another in policy debates; the left or right drift of the public discourse; the degree and sharpness of disagreement on key issues; and, the degree of optimism or pessimism that prevail in public discussion.

I have seen a few places in which a liberalism or a conservatism seemed to have triumphed, civility prevailed, public officials seemed to like one another even when they disagreed, and people optimistically believed that they could solve their problems. And, I have seen the reverse, places of very sharp disputes in which the public figures clearly disliked one another, and all the rest.

My explanation of why some civic cultures are sunny and others are stormy is not sanguine. In sunny civic cultures one political view has triumphed. The opposition has either left the field in despair or resigned itself to exist cheerfully in public life as always-on-the-short-end. Stormy civic cultures are the reverse. No faction can count on its dominance and the disputes over public actions are unending.

A DIVIDED AND GLOOMY CIVIC CULTURE. Davis in 1999-2000 and for much of its history struck me as exhibiting a "middling" civic culture along these lines. It was certainly not sunny, but then it was also not as stormy as some. Applying the weather metaphor a little further, perhaps gloomy is most apt. It was not fully stormy because the hard right had, in fact, been driven from political life in despair. So, the contests in Davis were between the middle and left, both broadly understood. The distances among positions on issues were not great and the acrimony was usually middling rather than intense.

I am aware that Davis was regularly stereotyped as a left-leaning Mecca of "all things right and relevant" and the "People's Republic of Davis." My view is that there was just enough reality to this stereotype to give opponents of it evidence that it existed. But, I think the "just enough" amounted to no more than about a third of the population. Although a minority, the "progressives" believed strongly, knew how to organize and campaign, and benefited from the plurality system used to elect members of the City Council. (Julie Partansky, for example was elected to her first term by 40% percent of those voting and was re-elected and became mayor by 39% of those voting.)

Against this third, there was another (more or less) third of Davis that strongly disapproved what they derisively labeled the "regressives." Terming themselves "moderates" and aligned with the Democratic Leadership Council element of the Democratic party, they were often difficult to distinguish from Republicans. And, a portion of them *were* Republicans.

Although there was, indeed, a great watershed shift in Davis politics in the early 1970s in which "progressives" were rather dominant for a time, the longer-term reality of the subsequent decades was a back-and-forth contest over who was temporarily "in charge." The upshot was a certain contained but continuing nastiness and hostility in the civic culture of Davis as the progressive and moderate thirds vied for support from the third-third who were indecisively in the middle. (My thanks to David Rosenberg, who explained all this to me some years ago—although not in these terms.)

When one side seemed to get too much of an advantage in policy matters, the storminess increased. This was particularly the case in 1998-2000 when Julie Partansky was mayor. Moderate City Council member Susie Boyd was legendary for her rudeness to Julie at Council meetings. I stress that this kind of behavior was not about personal relations or personalities. Instead, it was political struggle. Having a member of the Green Party as your mayor when you are a Republican-turned-conservative-Democrat could hardly make one cheerful. (Also indicative of the moderates as a political minority, Susie Boyd was elected to three Council terms by, in sequence, 44, 33, and 43% of those voting.)

Let me not be misunderstood. I do not think that sunny or stormy political cultures are necessarily better than the gloomy one seen in Davis. In each of these others, a topic like the

Terminal Building would either be approved without incident (sunny-left) or never even come up to for consideration (sunny-right). In a truly stormy political culture, the level of acrimony would be vastly higher. Scanning back over all the documents presented in previous chapters, I think the relative mildness with which the dispute was carried on is quite evident.

DUNNING DISSING. Then we add to this mix one Bob Dunning, the house columnist of the *Davis Enterprise*. Dunning grew up in Davis, graduated from Davis High School in 1964, attended UCD as an undergraduate, and earned a law degree on the same campus (graduating in the same class as David Rosenberg). However, he never practiced law. Instead, he was also an avid fan of organized sports and went to work as a sports reporter for the *Enterprise*. Gradually he began writing "color" columns on sports and then on other topics.

Eventually, the paper made him a straight columnist, a job he had held perhaps two decades at the time of the Terminal Building affair. Many years ago, Dunning had aligned himself with the moderates of Davis and he voiced the Enterprise's rapid-growth and development line. In 2001, the paper announced that when his column did not appear on Sunday, it would replace him with "On the Light Side," a feature devoted to "those fun, quirky or humorous stories that don't always make it into the paper" (*Davis Enterprise*, September 23, 2001). This replacement practice might be read as telling us not to take Dunning seriously.

Be his relation to his employer as it may, he routinely attacked "regressives"(using that word) and he was especially without mercy regarding Julie Partansky, with whom he seemed almost obsessed at times. Claiming that his insulting put-downs of her were simply good fun and only jokes, he was fond of characterizing her as one or another kind of creature from outer space (e.g. "our Councilwoman from Mars").

His wisdom on other matters was likewise curious. He wrote, for example, that the 9-11 bombers of the World Trade Center "are a bunch of punks who enjoy blowing things up . . . they have no ideology . . . they have no religion . . . " (*Davis Enterprise*, September 18, 2001) [The three dot format is the original, not my deletions.]

He was of course hated by the progressive third of Davis and loved by the "moderate" third. One progressive, for example, characterized him as a "cramped personality, a self-preoccupied whiner with narrow interests and limited vision." For moderates, though, he was a paragon of good judgement, grace, and humor.

It therefore came as no surprise when Dunning began to use his column to make snide remarks about the Terminal Building campaign and campaigners, as we have seen in Figs. 8.38, 8.43, 10.18, and11.21. Although his influence may not have been great, his typical nastiness likely did not help the preservationist side. (Over time, though, I fear he contributed to degrading the quality of public discourse in Davis by encouraging people to think of policy matters as mere jokes.)

PRESERVATION AS A PROGRESSIVE CAUSE. In this gloomy and divided Davis civic culture, historic preservation had become rather more associated with the progressives than with the moderates. I was so naively provincial when I became involved in these kinds of matters that I thought preservation more left than right in its location on the political spectrum. But, as I began to look at the national scene, I found I was wrong. Preservation is a political wild card that has quite varied supporters *and* opponents.

But, in Davis, the die was cast and cast unfortunately. As a consequence, the Terminal Building cause came to be seen, in many eyes, as a progressive ("regressive") cause. This did not help. Indeed, we know that Susie Boyd worked very actively for demolition (e. g. Fig. 8.21). She may well have been all the more galvanized by her well-known antipathy toward the then-leading progressive, Julie Partansky (who was the only Council member to vote for designation in 1999).

The identification of the Terminal matter with the progressives was especially unfortunate because some prominent Davis moderates and even conservatives **did** support saving the building. I have in mind, in particular, Phyllis Haig, the fact of whose support (and people like her) was not publicized nearly enough.

<u>WEAK PRESERVATION CULTURE</u>. In the absence of detailed and sophisticated survey interviews, it is difficult to assess the breadth and depth of public commitment to historical preservation in Davis. Not having such data, I can only offer the impression, based on the history presented in Chapters 5 and 6, that public support was relatively limited and weak. The Terminal Building affair animated a number of Davisites, but there was no collective action **on either side** of the magnitude seen in Davis history with regard to many other matters. Such significantly more-mobilizing concerns over the decades included the Vietnam war, women's reproductive rights, gay rights, rape prevention, the siting of group homes for certain disabled in residential neighborhoods, the construction of a sports complex, and a number of environmental matters.

I have looked at other cities in terms of the number and scale of local-history and preservation organizations and activities as they compare to Davis. My impression is that a fair number had, in 1999-2000, much more robust complexes of preservation institutions and activities. They featured such entities as a real museum, a city historical society, one or more full-time historical officers employed by the city, a historical commission with teeth and grit, regular historical celebrations, and the like. Davis, in contrast, had none of these.

Even what snobbish middle-class Davis regarded as crude working-class Woodland (its nearest neighbor) was many cuts above Davis in preservation institutions and associated consciousness: a national register historic district, an annual "Stroll Through History" which celebrated and educated the public about architecture and history with guided walking tours and open houses (rightly claimed to be the largest such event in California), on-going historic preservation campaigns, and on and on.

(Amazing Woodland projects have included rehabilitation of the Hotel Woodland, for which the City of Woodland "commissioned a thorough feasibility study that demonstrated that it could be saved"[Wilkinson, 2001]. Ironies of ironies Bill McCandless was the lead architect on that project and had earned a reputation as a preservationist because of it, even speaking at preservation conferences. Davis was obviously a different kettle of fish for him, a situation in which he reversed course and advocated demolition, and in which he was no help on the matter of a feasibility study [e. g. Figs. 8.21 and 10.32].)

This relatively low level of preservation consciousness and institutional development in Davis had, of course, its own causes. **First**, Davis was a very small place historically—much, much smaller than Woodland or even Dixon—so there was never much to feel preservationist about. (And, even with a small downtown stock, in the 1950s-70s era of "cowboy" development, almost two-thirds of all of it was torn down or moved out-of-town [Lofland, 2000]).

Second, in the first decades after World War II, the old downtown elites turned on their own town. It was as much the G Street merchants as anyone else who led the broad and long term project to demolish "old" Davis and to build a new one.

In addition, and **third**, these local elites were joined in this project by the new university elites. Many of them regarded the existing small town as a Sinclair Lewis *Main Street:* A provincial backwater that needed to be transcended and made cosmopolitan.

Fourth, the unfortunate association of preservation with the progressives and their skepticism about Davis population growth encouraged a pseudo-preservationism in moderates that was difficult to counter. Moderates claimed to be preservationist, but *this* building (or underpass, or whatever) lacked merit.

Importantly, pseudo-preservationism is seen far beyond Davis, which helps us understand its less than obvious agenda. Bemoaning the flattening of historic downtowns around the world, travel maven Arthur Frommer provides this telling typification of the declarations of those doing the flattening:

> The landmark is an "eyesore," a "hunk of junk." We wouldn't dream of destroying a truly distinguished building, they say, but this one just doesn't make it—its pedestrian, not really first rate (Frommer, 2000).

Last, in my assessment, Davis preservationists (as well as local history people) were not especially assertive or sophisticated in promoting and building local history/preservationist culture and institutions. The professionalization of preservation in the late 1970s and early 1980s (Ch. 6, section 1) may well have exacerbated this problem because of its mandate to present preservation as a technical subject.

The upshot was a preservationist/local history presence in Davis that could too easily be perceived by ordinary people as insular and aloof. (Episodes fostering this perception included such a basic discourtesy as, in mid-2001, the HRMC never responding to a letter from the DDBA Design Committee offering to help in surveying historical resources. The powers-that-were felt no response was needed.) (In the United States more generally there is some evidence that preservation and local history as social movements are in danger of losing their respective visions and falling into bureaucratic trances, a view effectively articulated by Jack Elliot with regard to preservation [see, e.g. Elliot, 2000, 2002]. Among occupations, professional preservationists, in particular, may soon find themselves ranking in public esteem in the vicinity of IRS agents, who perform work that is similar to theirs in a number of ways.)

3) COMMUNITY GROUPS VARIABLES

Most fundamentally, a community is composed of named, formally organized groups of the private sector. Commonly, these are classified by institutional realm or area of life, as, for example, business, industry, professions, religion, education, culture, recreation, and so on.

A SMALL NUMBER OF A NARROW RANGE OF GROUPS REACTED. Without quite knowing the implications, I am struck in retrospect with how few groups of any kind were moved to have an opinion one way or the other on the Terminal Building (or on historical preservation per se). Mainly, only two organizations of businesses took stands (The Davis Chamber of Commerce and the DDBA) and the Yolo County Historical Society. That was about it.

BUSINESS GROUP OPPOSITION OR TIMIDITY. And, the positions they took were either in support of demolition (Fig. 8.7) or tepid caution (Fig. 10.5).

Fairly early-on, Heather Caswell drew up a petition to be signed by downtown merchants that advocated DDBA involvement and Terminal Building preservation. This was circulated to the extent that twenty-three signatures were obtained. But (as sometimes happens in citizen campaigns), this effort stoped at twenty-three merchant signatures and even this considerable achievement was never presented to the City Council, made known in the *Davis Enterprise*, or otherwise publicized.

HISTORICAL GROUP LIMPNESS. Very puzzling, the organization presumably most dedicated to preservation, the Yolo County Historical Society, did no more than write a single, short letter (Fig. 8.20). Had not Heather Caswell gone to one of their Board meetings and asked them to help, it seemed likely they would not even have done that.

DESCENDENT ALOOFNESS. The descendents of the two families who initially owned and operated the Terminal Building were in a broad way a community group. Members of these families maintained a polite but firm distance from the events of 1999 and 2000. Efforts to see if any of them had pictures of and artifacts from the cafe and the hotel were met with courteous explanations that none of them had any, or that the locations of possible items were uncertain. Whatever the meaning of these behaviors, it was hard to see this descendant aloofness as helpful in preserving the building.

NEWS COVERAGE. With a mindset attuned to identifying causes of preservation failure, one can too easily overlook or underplay variables that work to forestall or present failure; that is, that work in the direction of preservation success.

One of these is the variable of the amount and nature of coverage given by the local press. In this case, I would have to say that one of the strongest variables working in the direction of preservation success was the regular, abundant and fair coverage given by the *Davis Enterprise*. Of course, there was the harmful "Dunning dissing" (section 2, above), but I think that the Dunning effect was small compared to the enormous help the *Enterprise* provided in printing everything the campaign asked it to print and in electing to do many news stories and background features.

4) CITY GOVERNMENT VARIABLES

Variables involving city government can be divided into elected officials, city staff and citizen commissions, and the political situation of 1999-2000.

COUNCIL MAJORITIES COULD FLAUNT HISTORICAL FACTS WITH IMPUNITY. For reasons difficult to understand, on both occasions the building came before the City Council the majority chose to **ignore** the claim of the HRMC that the building occupied a significant social place in Davis history.

I use the word "ignore" in order to distinguish this reaction of the Council majorities in 1984 and 1999 from other reactions they **could** have had; namely, they could have **rejected, questioned, doubted, or rebutted** the claims of such significance.

Instead, they stated that they did not want to trouble the owners with waiting a year to demolish the building and/or they thought the building was ugly and therefore without merit.

Given that all of them had taken an oath to uphold the law, this ignoring the claimed facts is all the more interesting. But, to the causal point to be made here: They could ignore and flaunt the historical facts because they did not expect to be punished beyond the ordinary hazards an elected official faces in casting any vote. And there was no punishment.

Council-member decisions to ignore the historical facts did not pass unnoticed, as we have seen in several items published in the *Enterprise*. One of the real crowd-rouser talks at the June 11, 2000 celebration was that of Historic Resources Management Commission Chair Wendy Nelson, who engaged in a call-and-response with the audience on this very matter (Chapter 9, Fig. 9.24). Because of the salience of this point, I reproduce the Nelson crowd call-and-response engagement in Fig. 15.1.

Wendy Nelson's "Call and Response" With the G Street Plaza Celebration Crowd
On Designating the Terminal Building a Historical Resource

I am very proud to be a member of the Historic Resources Management Commission that unanimously voted to designate the Terminal/Aggie hotel a historical resource.

 One of the reasons I am very proud is that I do not see us as an ordinary commission because we are not an ordinary city. We are a Certified Local Government. Because that is so, our Commission is made up of professionals. Among our commissioners there are historians, preservations, architects, cultural resources managers, historic and prehistoric archeologists.

The Historic Resources Management Commission serves in an advisory capacity to the Council and to other City entities and we serve as the stewards of our city's historical resources.

We maintain an inventory . . . of historic resources . . . . It is from those historic resources in our inventory that . . . we take special care in designating special resources to the category of City of Davis Historic Resource.

The Terminal Hotel has been brought forward to the Council for designation twice, once in 1984 and most recently in 1999. The most recent time, as I said, it was a unanimous vote from the Commission. Unfortunately, both times the Council voted against designation.

So we might ask, "What's the criteria for designating a historical resource?" What is so difficult? What is it about our Terminal Hotel that our Council has a hard time seeing it as historic?

So I 'm going to take a minute here and I 'm going to tell you what the criteria are for designation. And as I go through

them— I 'm only going to list four of them —at the end of each one I want you to tell me whether you think—you as amateurs out there, not professionals like the Commission—what you think . . . . Let's see if you think it should be designated.

Criteria A: " **It exemplifies or reflects valued elements of the city's cultural, social, economic, political, aesthetic, engineering, archeological, or architectural history."**

Remember only one of these [is needed for designation].

WHAT DO YOU THINK? [Crowd roars "YEAH"]

 Criteria B: "**It is identified with persons or events important in local, state or national history."**

WHAT DO YOU THINK? [Crowd roars "YEAH"]

Criteria C: "**It reflects significant geographical patterns, including those associated with different eras of settlement and growth, particular transportation modes, or distinctive examples of park or community planning."**

WHAT DO YOU THINK? [Crowd shouts "YEAH"]

Criteria D: "**It embodies distinguishing characteristics or an architectural style, type, or period, or method of construction, or is a valuable example of use of indigenous materials or craftsmanship."**

WHAT DO YOU THINK? [Crowd shouts "YEAH."]

Oh, thank you!

15. 1. Excerpt from "The Building, The Commission, the Council," the three-minute story told by Wendy Nelson, Chair, City of Davis Historical Resources Management Commission, at the Celebration of Terminal Hotel History on the Davis G Street Plaza, June 11, 2000. Details on this event were given in Chapter 9 (and Nelson pictured in Fig. 9.24). (The bold face type used for the four criteria is my editorial addition.) Nelson is quoting from the *Davis Municipal Code,* Chapter 40, "Zoning," Section 40.23.060,"Historical resource/district designation criteria."

VERY LIMITED STAFF AND VOLUNTEER RESOURCES. I draw particular attention to ignoring rather than questioning or rejecting HRMC claims because the case for significance, **as presented** in both 1984 and 1999, was not, in my view, all that strong. The Council majorities could have reasonably questioned the quality and quantity of the documents asserting the case for designation, but they did not.

If the case was not developed with very much documentation, why was this? The answer is that the burden of such research fell on a single staff person assigned only about a third time to HRMC matters. All eight of the members of the HRMC worked full-time, had families, and served as unpaid volunteers. Hence, the development of this case—as well as other cases---was rather on the fly.

The causal relevance of these limitations is that even though the Council majorities did not make a public matter of it, it was also hard for anyone supporting designation to stress the point that the evidence was overwhelming (although a few people did make that claim anyway). (I am **not** saying the building did not merit designation, only that the research to make a lead pipe case had not been done.)

This limitation of resources also operated at the level of the HRMC's dealing with and advising the owners during the period when it **may** have been possible to send them on the rehabilitation route. The owners were made aware of the various federal and state programs that they could conceivably have used, but the advising appears never to have become specific to their building.

THE POLITICAL SITUATION OF 1999-2000. The political situations of governments differ in the degree to which there is easily "space" on the public agenda at a given moment for preservation issues or not. At one extreme, a government can be so preoccupied with pubic safety challenges, budget shortfalls, or the like, that preservation issues seem unimportant, relatively speaking, and are pushed aside. At the other extreme, a government with few or no serious challenges may be open to thinking about preservation issues for want of much else to think about.

Davis in 1999 and 2000 tended to the former extreme rather than to the latter. The *Enterprise* summary of the year 2000's top ten stories, reproduced in Fig. 14.2 of Chapter 14, summarized the challenges. The top stories of 2000 (as well as of 1999) were sprawl and the UC Davis announcement that it was about to begin a new era of major growth. These feared or impending changes spawned growth-control Measures J and O, which pre-occupied city officials and the public.

Exacerbating these problems, UC Davis hired away fabled Davis city manager John Meyer to organize its new growth! A city department head nearing retirement was appointed acting city manager and it was more than a year before a new manager was recruited and started work. Due to the importance of the city manager in the Davis version of the city manager system, this was a long period of a government essentially on-hold and lacking leadership.

Co-incident with these problems, a popular police captain was fired for a reason or reasons officials refused to disclose and this created, as reported in the *Enterprise*, "a firestorm of controversy and an unprecedented vote of no confidence in Chief Jerry Gonzales, who later resigns" (*Davis Enterprise*, December 31, 2000). There were also protracted City Council struggles over the General Plan, as well as other controversies of import (Fig. 14.2).

The upshot of the combination of these and additional issues was a political situation in which preserving the Terminal Building not was not among the more troubling matters of the day. Any human, even including Davis City Council members, can seriously focus on only a limited number of troubling topics. Beyond whatever that capacity for focus is for a given person, attention wanes or ceases. I fear that in Davis in 1999-2000, the Terminal matter was either low on (or not on) officials' lists of critically troubling topics.

Reflecting on it, I suppose one might even agree with Bob Dunning and fault the *Enterprise* editors for voting the Terminal matter as high as fourth on its list of the top ten stories of the year 2000 (Chapter 14, section 2).

5) CITIZEN CAMPAIGN VARIABLES

There were at last two variables of note relating to the preservationist campaign.

LACK OF KNOWLEDGE AND EXPERTISE. Months after the Terminal matter was over, I and others learned some basic facts about historic preservation that no one on any side appeared to understand (or at least said in public) during the 1999-2000 campaign.

These facts included the requirement that in order to be eligible for the twenty percent level of federal tax incentive, a building had itself to be on the National Register of Historic Places or listed as a contributor as part of a district that was on the National Register. Achieving either of these listings required a rather involved process of application to the California Office of Historic Preservation and a public hearing. Salient here, not understanding these necessities, no one in Davis was even talking about undertaking either process, much less actually engaged in them. (However, by age alone the building was eligible for the ten percent level of credit.)

In addition, when I and others began to talk to people who had actually rehabilitated buildings under the Federal program, we learned that such projects "pencil" better when done with relatively larger buildings involving budgets on the of order of at last a million dollars. In this perspective, the Terminal Building was a relatively small project (Klemm, Ullrich and Wilkinson, 2001).

We also did no understand the conventional wisdom among informed developers that rehabilitation with tax incentives can be profitable, but not **as** profitable as constructing a entirely new and **larger** building on a site. Therefore, an owner who sought **absolutely to maximize** profits (not simply to make a decent profit), had little or no reason to be interested in preserving or rehabilitating her or his building.

Moreover, in this period there was little or no discussion of the "adverse impact" provisions of the California Environmental Quality Act (CEQA), which may have allowed a court challenge of the City's demolition permit. Certainly, no one undertook such a court petition (or, to my knowledge, engaged in serious discussion of the possibility). (Interestingly, in connection with a late 2002 proposal to lower the windows in the Anderson Bank Building—just across the street from the Terminal Building site—City staff made serious and frequent reference to CEQA and that Act figured centrally in denying the proposal.)

These and other limits of knowledge among the preservationist campaigners (as well as among everyone else), meant that, in some significant sense, none us knew what we were talking about. Worse, we did not know that we did not know what we were talking about.

LACK OF NUMBERS. As I have alluded to regarding the strength of preservation culture, the campaigners were organized but not large in numbers. They could get up to a couple of dozen people in the Council Chambers at critical times. This was a respectable number and signaled a serious political matter, but it was not large. Historically, a number of other issues mobilized people in the hundreds and presented the standing room only spectacle of packed-in humanity.

(Curiously, one of the campaign's strongest suits was the *Enterprise* Letter to the Editor feature. As can be read in the Chapters of Part II, there was quite a stream of pro-preservation letters. Some were encouraged by the organizers, but many came from people not personally known to any of them.)

6) OWNER VARIABLES

Owners of preservation-relevant buildings obviously vary in ways that can promote or retard the failure or success of preservation. Most evidently, an owner can simply be against preservation and that clear position can easily figure as a strong causal factor that explains preservation failure. (Or, in some cases, other factors can overcome such owner resistance.) In this case, there are reasons to believe that the owners were not unambiguously against preserving their building in some fashion or form. Although we clearly can never know what they **"really"** believed on this matter, a number of their private and public professions over time suggested at least an openness to the idea of preservation.

OWNER MYSTIFICATION. Looking back over the variables reviewed above, there is a theme of hardly anyone really having or presenting a detailed, technical and realistic picture of what rehabilitation or preservation was about. A number of people spoke with the owners and/or wrote them on these topics, but without much specificity. My impression, indeed, is that even the idea of a "feasibility study" was not well understood by a number of people who proposed one. (In this respect, it is of note that the architect who finally came to be the main advisor of the owners led them away from rather than toward preservation/rehabilitation and did not do a feasibility study.)

The upshot, I hazard to guess, is that the owners were mystified or even baffled by all the preservation/rehabilitation talk that swirled around them over the months. Given that the topics were, in fact, arcane and technical, such bafflement should not surprise us. From the perspective of what I have learned about this area since the Terminal matter ended, I look back with the recognition that I did not myself, at that time, have an adequate understanding of what was involved at the "on the ground" level of rehabilitating a specific building. (And, those who claimed expertise in these matters in this scene were unhelpful or even prone to promote mystification themselves.)

OWNER STEALTH? In perusing preservation publications I have been struck by the frequency with which one encounters reports of **owner stealth** as a variable. A preservation disagreement between an owner and other groups begins to take shape. The owner responds by quickly and stealthily demolishing the building.

Some of these present high drama, as in a bulldozer driver who was instructed to "get in there and get it down before they get another injunction." So he struck "just after nightfall on a early winter Saturday afternoon" (*Preservation News*, February, 1981, p. 3). A historic house owned by a county was taken down by means of a quick vote taken "at a sparsely attended Friday night meeting that was supposed to be devoted to small administrative matters . . . The next morning the house . . . [was] toppled" (*Preservation News*, December, 1980, p. 10). Owners of historic houses in remote locations have simply torn them down without telling anyone, as in a case in which "they removed every trace. It was like it was never there" (*Preservation News*, December, 1980, p. 2).

So, this can certainly be a potent variable in preservation failure!

The reader can review the materials presented in Chapter 10 and 11 and draw her or his own conclusions about the degree to which owner stealth was a factor in the Terminal Building case.

7) BUILDING VARIABLES

At least two variables involving the physical features of the building itself seemed to operate in the direction of preservation failure.

THE SHADE STRUCTURE AND VISUAL INTELLIGENCE. Sometime about 1960, someone had "town and countryized" the west side of the building by adding a shake roof shade structure to it (seen in Fig. 5.28, as well as in many other pictures). I say "town and country" because this was the shade structure style of the earliest (1950s) California suburban malls, several of which were named "town and country." In those malls, however, the buildings matched the rustic character of the shade overhangs.

But here, there was a severe mismatch between the 1950s pseudo-Old-West structure and the 1920s commercial brick building. Curiously, although the City's file on the Terminal Building contained records of a variety of other permits for work on it, there were no records on the shade structure. In line with the "lets throw out the old" spirit of the 1950s-70s (Chapter 5), perhaps there never was a permit.

The upshot was that the building seemed ugly to many people who looked at it naively. A person needed a reasonably high level of visual intelligence and sophistication to "see" the building without the shade structure. Sadly, too few people appeared to have that much visual intelligence.

GENERAL DETERIORATION. All buildings require maintenance—roofs must be replaced, wood painted, plumbing repaired, and so on. It is beyond dispute that the building had been neglected for a very long time. Already at the time the final owners purchased it in 1977, it was in bad shape. Indeed, the amount of work required to achieve City permission to operate it as a hotel seemed to have figured in the decision to, in effect, close that part of the building.

By 1999-2000, the deterioration had advanced much farther and was obvious even to the casual observer. This fact prompted some to think that the decay had gone so far that the time had come to get rid of it. (Achieving this perception is, of course, what is meant by the well-known and widely-observed strategy of "demolition by neglect.")

8) EVIDENTIAL UNCERTAINTY

Having offered the above multi-factor account, I feel it is important to place it in the context of forms of evidence for such accounts and how this one relates to them.

For our purposes, we may think of causal accounts as being grounded in three kinds of data collection and analysis. First, there are causal accounts derived from the random assignment of "subjects" to **experimental** treatments. Second, there are causal accounts derived from the **statistical** controls possible when working with a large number of cases on which measurements have been made. And third, there are causal accounts derived from the close inspection of a single **case**.

For reasons we need not review here, the confidence we can have in a causal account declines as we move from the experimental to the statistical to the case. For better or worse, the method used in this book is that of the case rather than of the experiment or of statistical manipulation. It is the shakiest basis on which to mount a causal account. But, since it is the only one we have, we must choose between no account and a shaky one. I have chosen the latter.

For this reason of evidential uncertainty, what I have said above should be read with tentativeness and caution.

Here, near the end, I want also to reiterate what I said at the beginning about framing questions. One can legitimately disagree with my organizing this inquiry in terms of answering the question, "Why did preservation fail?" An alternative view might be that there was nothing to preserve, so there was no preservation to fail.   In that other view, the question might be, "Why did demolition succeed?"

I doubt the empirical details of one's answer would be that much different, but the approach certainly would. So, empirical work can take us a good distance, but in the end values couch how we organize inquires.

9) CONCLUDING REFLECTIONS

Accepting the fragility of case causal-accounts, what might we nonetheless venture in a summary way about why preservation failed?

I think two variables were seen in strong form with striking frequency among the various groupings. The first was **lack of knowledge** at the level of what was, as a practical matter, involved in getting a preservation process underway. Second and concomitant, there was **lack of experience** with preservation at the level of having previously coordinated the preservation of at least one building.

It later came to light that even the various architects were merely architects and had never themselves organized a preservation project. Architectural knowledge was an indispensable skill in preservation, but far, far short of the construction cost and financial expertise necessary to make a preservation project happen (Klemm, Ullrich and Wilkinson, 2001; section 10 of Chapter 14).

Likewise, non-architects who claimed preservation knowledge and experience had been or were primarily government employees, or government contract firms, rather than private sector preservationist developers. These people could cite laws and give you booklets, but they had never themselves actually done what such documents described as possible. As a consequence, interactions with them had an abstract and remote character (mere "book learning") regarding actual preservation.

Of course, most people in the Terminal drama were not as close to preservation matters as people such as architects and government specialists. For them, preservation was truly a foreign country, a nice place to visit, perhaps, but not one to which one had gone and returned to tell the tale.

Without claiming it would have changed the outcome, let me venture this "hypothetical." The **absence** from this situation of even one preservationist developer with a proven record of conducting valid feasibility studies and of completing rehabilitation of historic buildings significantly contributed to preservation failure. Indeed, this may have been among the strongest of variables that contributed to preservation failure.

Stated in the reverse: No one involved in the Terminal matter (in **any** group) could with credibility and competence explain in detail how preservation of the Terminal Building might (or might not) happen.

Of course, some will say that the owners were never actually open to preservation—despite what they said—and the entire exercise was meaningless because of this. This may be true, but there is no way we can ever know for certain.

But, we do know, I think, that the owners and others never had access to a credible preservationist alternative. There **was** a push for a feasibility study that failed. What was missing, though, was an appreciation that the very idea of a "feasibility study" itself needed to be explained and placed in the context of a larger preservation process.

A preservationist developer with a solid history of well-founded feasibility studies and success with historic buildings could have made that case.   But no such person was present and the case was never made.

Instead, we saw a quagmire of groping, milling, hesitation, and flailing about on all sides. Events drifted and in the absence of credible alternatives, demolition happened.

SOURCES, METHODS, ACKNOWLEDGEMENTS

For me, this is an unusual book because of the large differences in units of time making up the story. In Part I, the time-units are, primarily, decades and even longer. Then, in Part II, the units reduce to, mostly, years and months. Finally, in Part III, the prime units are days, hours, and minutes.

These differences in the scale of time signal differences in sources and types of data, methods of analysis, and kind of debts I have to the many people who helped me.

1) HEYDAY HISTORY: CHAPTERS 2, 3 and 4

The first three chapters of Part I are traditionally "historical," here meaning that hardly anyone who lived during the period covered is now alive. One is therefore almost entirely dependent on the written record. In the case of this book, that written record was primarily microfilm copies of the *Davis Enterprise*.

Fortunately, before deciding to write this book I had previously completed a project that required that I read a great deal of that newspaper covering the early decades of the twentieth century. My quest was for information on an area now called "Old North Davis" (Lofland, 1999). Almost nothing of that neighborhood's origin and development was known and one key source of information was the microfilmed *Enterprise*.

Even though I was specifically searching for Old North items, I could not resist photocopying a variety of other stories I found delightful. In three-ring binders, these photocopies came to consume some two feet of shelf space. (Fortunately, the dime per copy slot device attached to the Davis Branch Library photocopy machine virtually never worked and I was spared the chore of feeding it a huge number of dimes. I thank the Branch librarians—especially Jay Johnstone—for trusting me to pay lump sum amounts of my own assessment.)

When the June 11, 2000, G Street Plaza event was scheduled (Chapter 9), I went back and reviewed these photocopies for information on the building. I was excited to discover that, without realizing it, I had a compiled a nice record of social doings in and around the Terminal Building. Initially, I assembled these reports for an exhibit at the June 11 celebration (seen, for example, in Fig. 9. 6). Having done that work, it was easy then to re-process the stories as they appear in Chapters 2, 3, and 4.

My reading of *Enterprise* microfilm was not without error and early-on I missed some important aspects. Happily, Davis resident Betty Rivers also read the *Enterprise* on microfilm from time and time. It was from her I learned the building was constructed in two phases in 1924 and in 1926-27, a fact my previous readings had missed.

2) NEGLECT HISTORY: CHAPTERS 4 and 5

As reported in section 8 of Chapter 1, the 1950s through the 1990s were decades of Davis' explosive growth and transformation. Forming a nuanced view of these changes and their relation to Davis local history and preservation—and therefore to the Terminal Building—was no easy task and one on which I spent several months.

I was able to spend any time at all—much less months—because of five people who made invaluable records of those decades available to me and/or who spent considerable time relating events to me.

The first of these five was Debbie Davis, the Editor of the *Davis Enterprise*. Desiring to clear clutter out of the paper's printing plant and knowing of my interest in Davis history, in January, 2001 she gave me 83 bound volumes of the *Davis Enterprise* covering late 1966 through 1983. Stacked waist-high on a pallet, the Enterprise's forklift truck was needed to place this heavy object onto the bed of a medium-sized pickup-truck—squeezing the bed down to just slightly touching the tires (this is partially pictured in Sherwin, 2001a).   Day-after-day for some weeks, I immersed myself in these volumes. At the end of each session in which I wrestled with these awkward objects, my hands were almost entirely black with newspaper ink.

Second, in July of this same year, the heir of deceased Professor and Mrs. Hubert Heitman was selling their former home. He asked the realtor, Cynthia Gerber, to help him dispose of several boxes and paper bags of issues of the *Davis Enterprises* found in storage rooms on the property. Mrs. Gerber thought the Hattie Weber Museum of Davis, rather than the county landfill, was the appropriate place to take these bags and boxes, which she did. Now called the Heitman Enterprise Collection at the Museum, it contains a large portion of the issues of that paper from the late 1950s through the mid-1960s, including the entire year of 1964 (of which, previously, there were no known copies *at all*) (Sherwin, 2001b). I spend much time reading all these papers.

The methodological importance of these "hard copy" *Enterprises* is that they freed me from the constraints of both a library microfilm machine and the only other existing hard copy, those in bound volumes kept by the UC Davis Department of Special Collections.

The *Enterprise* photos from the 1950s-90s seen in Chapters 4 and 5 were scanned from these hard copies. This results in the best available quality because: 1) the microfilm version contains limited gray-scale; 2) the huge bound volumes in UC Davis Special Collections are, as a physical matter, virtually unscannable; and, 3) the Davis Enterprise says it has no files of its old photographs. Therefore, the original newspapers provide the best surviving versions we have of a vast number of photographs taken by and used in the *Davis Enterprise*.

Moreover, these papers were available to me in my own study and at my own computer equipment. This was a locale much more conducive to slow and deliberate inspection than the reading rooms of either the Davis Branch Library (with microfilm) or the UC Davis Special Collections Department (with bound volumes) (as marvelous as both those institutions otherwise are).

Together, these collections provided me a unique and unfettered access to a detailed chronicle of Davis history. So, my debts to Debbie Davis and Cynthia Gerber are great, indeed. (I, however, only scratched the surface of this record for the limited purposes of this book. These rich Enterprise materials are available to all other serious researchers and I hope that they will use them for a variety of other types of projects.)

Third, Phyllis Haig was a participant in virtually all 1960s-1990s local history and preservationist activities, an assertion that cannot be made about anyone else. As important,

Mrs. Haig saved pretty-much every document that came her way in these involvements. Moreover, she **took notes** on a very large portion of the meetings she attended over the decades. These items resided in eight storage boxes in her garage and she was extraordinarily generous in allowing me to review all their contents and to photocopy whatever I desired. The account of Davis local history and preservation spanning Chapters 5 and 6 would be enormously poorer (and perhaps non-existent) without this assistance.

Fourth, Robin Datel saved her files from the period she was active as a historical commissioner and very kindly loaned them to me for this research.

Fifth, several detailed conversations with Esther Polito about events of the late 1980s and 1990s were indispensable in helping get the historical record right. She also did me the very great favor of looking up a number of dates and Council and Commission votes.

In addition to theses five, I want also to acknowledge the very helpful observations on and insights about this period related to me by Bob Black and Lynn Campbell.

3) PRESERVATION FAILURES: CHAPTERS 7, 8, 10, 11
The focus and methodological work changes sharply when we come, in Part II, to what we might call the four "struggle" chapters, those numbered 7, 8, 10, and 11.

In these, my decision was to let the story tell itself as much as possible by means of the public record. The public record here consists of two main parts: 1) newspaper accounts, and 2) documents **produced by** and **given to** the City of Davis. The text I provide is the minimum needed to tie the public record together.

As anyone would expect, there was, of course, also a "back-story," a private spate of jockeyings among the most involved parties that was done behind closed doors and out of public view. Only occasionally did I get a glimpse of what went on in it and who its more hidden participants seemed to be. (For example, I am told that early-on Heather Caswell had serious discussions with the owners about her—together with others—buying the building.)

I made little effort to dig out this back-story. I made this decision for two reasons. One, it seemed to me that what we saw on the surface and in public were sufficient to provide us a basic understanding of what happened and the causes of it. While an elaborate and **accurate** back-story would be interesting (and, especially, amusing), I doubt if it would substantially change our understanding. Two, reports of who said what and what "really" happened in the back-story are especially contentious and the subject of competing and contradictory claims. I might have been able to assemble a set of these contradictory claims. But, I would still be left with having to report that I could not know which were more true and which were less true.

As I said in Chapter 1, I decided to write this book on September 18, 2000, the day demolition began. This means that I had not previously been collecting either form of the public record—the newspaper reports or the City documents.

Subsequently, I went back to old *Enterprises* to assemble the rather detailed record we see in Chapters 7, 8, 10 and 11. I thought I had it all, but then I learned that Phyllis Haig was independently clipping and pasting in a scrapbook every *Enterprise* item on this matter! I asked her to let me check her record against the one I had put together. I found that her chronicle was more complete than mine. She graciously allowed me to photocopy items I had missed, thus saving me hours in front of a microfilm reading machine. In Chapters 7, 8, 10 and 11, her clippings are distinctive in having detailed identifying information from the paper pasted above them.

As can also be seen in these four chapters, the City document record is even more complicated that the one in the *Enterprise*. City documents are public records and, by law, I could examine and photocopy all the pertinent Terminal Building files. Even so, their meaning, sequence, and context was not always clear. When puzzled, I would ask city planner Ken Hiatt for elaboration and clarification. He was always an exceedingly cooperative and helpful guide though this maze.

On a variety of these "struggle" matters, I have learned a great deal in conversations with Laura Cole-Rowe and Gerald Heffernon. I thank them for sharing their insights with me and offering much good advice.

4) CELEBRATION: CHAPTER 9

The celebration of Terminal and Davis history held on the G Street Plaza on June 11, 2000 posed a special problem of data. Heather Caswell and I were the lead organizers. At the time of its preparation and performance, I was not thinking of writing a book on the Terminal matter. This meant that I did not even bring a camera and take any pictures on that day, much less make any sound or motion picture images. I was, instead, attending to backstage matters of making sure the event went as planned (which it did).

So, when I decided to write a book, there was the question locating visual data on the event. As it happened, Davis residents Laima Druskis and Sunny Shine had, on their own, shot a large number of still photographs of pretty much everything. Indeed, they presented a box of them to Heather and I in the way that people at any special event show one another pictures taken of it.

Liama and Sunny are credited in Chapter 9 and I am happy again to thank them.

Integral to the four "struggle" chapters and the celebration chapter is, of course, the work of Heather Caswell. At one level, I am indebted to her in the odd sense that there likely would have been little story to tell without her. Had she not been very important in catalyzing citizen action to save the building, the structure might well have gone down without much of a murmur.

At another level, she recruited me to be part of the loose band of activists energized to try to save the building. Importantly through her, I knew about the struggle as it went along.

Her role in all this was so important that I have thought it appropriate to dedicate the book to her, shared with the more than one-hundred year history of Davis published in the *Davis Enterprise*. Together, they provided a very large portion of the data for this book.

5) DEMOLITION: CHAPTERS 12 and 13

The two pages introducing Part III provide an account of the data and methods regarding demolition "processes" (Chapter 12) and "moments" in those processes (Chapter 13). I will therefore not repeat that material here.

With regard to the demolition, I am very pleased to thank Stan Bowers for treating me in a consistently genial and helpful manner over its 73 days—and beyond. He went out of his way to let me know what was happening in many matters and to point up aspects of the situation at the demolition site that I would otherwise have missed.

In November, 2002, I gave him a draft of this book to review. He responded by telling me he had located the second missing plaque from the Terminal Arch Mural (Chapter 13, section 12).

Further, if I would come and pick it up at his suburban Sacramento home, I could have it. I went and got it. Thanks, Stan.

Likewise, his chief associate, John Sheehy, was always very helpful, most spectacularly in rescuing the Terminal Cafe cash register from the building's basement (Chapter 13, section 3), but in many other concrete ways as well.

6) REVIEWERS AND ADVISORS

On completing the first draft in late October, 2002, I was concerned that I did not want to print anything about anyone who appeared in the book in any important way without first giving them an opportunity to read and respond.

To this end, I went through the draft and counted the names of everyone who seemed to me to be a "principal participant." In my estimation, there were 29 such persons. (Given all the letters, events, consultant reports, and such, the list of names of everyone mentioned is obviously much, much longer.)

Because the manuscript was some 350 pages long in hard copy, I tried to keep my costs under at least some control by producing it in Adobe Acrobat (pdf) on a compact disk. Accompanied by hard copy of the front matter and Chapter 1, I delivered or sent this package to the 29 principal participants. In addition, I offered hard copy for those who could not read the document on a CD. Six of the 29 asked me for hard copy, which I supplied.

In the space of three months, I had heard back from only a few. I saw several of these people regularly or from time-to-time. When seeing them, I would sometimes raise the question of why I had not heard from them on the draft and would be told it was, indeed, in the stack of things they planned to read. Jokingly I said to some of them that "silence is consent" and that I would not be sympathetic with complaints they might have **after** printing.

In addition, I asked a number of other people knowledgeable about preservation and/or Davis affairs but not involved in the Terminal matter to review the draft.

Despite being a "picture book" of a sort, I am aware that the manuscript is long and tells a complicated story. I am therefore all the more appreciative that quite a few people actually did wrestle with it in detailed and extremely helpful fashions.

Because of them, this book is quite significantly improved over the draft that each read. My very heartfelt thanks to each of these readers:

Lynn Campbell	Merrily DuPree	Joann Leach Larkey	Wendy Nelson
Heather Caswell	Jim Frame	Lyn Lofland	Ken Wagstaff
Robin Datel	Phyllis Haig	Stephen Mikesell	Mike White
Mark DuPree	Mike Harrington	Scott Neeley	David Wilkinson

Among these hardy helpers, I owe a special debt to three who, without me asking them, read the manuscript in proof-reader detail and caught an enormous number of typing and kindred errors: Merrily DuPree, Jim Frame, Lyn Lofland.

As with previous books I have written, I owe Lyn Lofland a profound debt. She believed in the value of this work and helped at every step to bring it to a respectable public product. Although I did the work, I do not think I could have carried it through without her love and support.

I have tried to make this book as complete and accurate as possible. But, like every other inquiry ever conducted, it surely still contains errors of substance and style and of commission and omission. The reader should therefore bring a critical mindset to it. And in turn, I hope the reader will bring a critical mindset to the criticisms generated by that critical mindset.

John Lofland
Davis, California
March, 2003

REFERENCES

Allport, Gordon W. and Leo Postman. 1947. *The Psychology of Rumor.* New York, NY: Holt.

Amato, Joseph A. 2002. *Rethinking Home: A Case for Writing Local History.* Berkeley, CA: University of California Press.

Amery, Colin. 2001. *Vanishing Histories: 100 Endangered Sites From the World Monuments Watch.* New York, NY: Harry N. Abrams, Inc.

Architectural Resources Group. 1996. *City of Davis Cultural Resources Inventory and Context Statement.* San Francisco, CA: The Firm.

Barthel, Diane L. 1996. *Historic Preservation: Collective Memory and Historical Identity.* New Brunswick, NJ: Rutgers University Press.

Becker, Howard S. 1974. "Photography and Sociology." *Studies in the Anthropology of Visual Communication.* 1:3-26.

————. 1995. "Visual Sociology, Documentary Photography, and Photojournalism." *Visual Sociology* 10:5-14

————. 2002. "Visual Evidence." *Visual Studies* 17:3-11 (No. 1).

Berger, Peter. 1963. *Invitation to Sociology: A Humanistic Perspective.* Garden City, NY: Anchor Books.

California, State of. 1975. *State Historical Building Code.* Title 24. Building Standards, Part 8.

Chadwyck-Healey, Inc. 1999. *Davis, California Sanborn Maps* [a compact disk]. Ann Arbor, MI: Chadwyck-Healey.

Choay, Francoise. 2001. *The Invention of the Historic Moment.* New York, NY: Cambridge University Press.

City of Davis. 1996. *Core Area Specific Plan.* Davis, CA: The City of Davis.

————. 2001. *Davis Downtown and Traditional Residential Neighborhood Design Guidelines.* Davis, CA: The City of Davis.

Connor, Hap. 2002. "History Is in Our Hands: The National PSA Campaign for Preservation." *Forum News.* IX (No. 2), 1-2, 6 (November-December).

Davies, Richard O. 1998. *Main Street Blues: The Decline of Small Town America.* Columbus, OH: Ohio State University Press.

Davis Enterprise, The. ed. 1996. *Those Who Make Memories.* Davis, CA: The Davis Enterprise.

Datel, Robin, 1982-86. *Datel Collection.* (Private collection of documents from her service on the Davis Historical Commission.)

————. 1985. "Preservation and a Sense of Orientation for American Cites." *The Geographical Review.* 75:125-141.

Datel, Robin and Dennis Dingemans. 1988. "Why Places Are Preserved: Historic Districts in American and European Cities." *Urban Geogaphy* 7:37-52 (no. 1).

Elliott, Jack D., Jr. 2002a. "Radical Preservation: Toward a New and More Ancient Paradigm." *Forum Journal* 16: 50-56 (No. 3, Spring).

————. 2000b. Radical Preservation, the Web Site. http://www.radicalpreservation.com.

Fransway, Rebecca (Producer). 2000. *Terminal Building Celebration.* Davis, CA: Davis Community Television. (Videotape made on June 11, 2000 and shown on Davis Community

Television several times that June. Copy archived at the Hattie Weber Museum of Davis.)

Fidelity National Title Insurance Company. 2001, *Chain of Title Guarantee, Order No. 125806, Lot 15, Block 19, City of Davis.* Apr: 70-252-04. Irvine, CA.

Fitch, James. 1982. *Historic Preservation: Curatorial Management of the Built World.* NY: New York: McGraw-Hill.

Fitch, Mike. 1998. *Growing Pains: Thirty Years in the History of Davis.* Davis, CA: The City of Davis Website (www.city.davis.ca.us/city/parks/histres/30years/toc.html).

Fogelson, Robert M. 2001. *Downtown: Its Rise and Fall, 1880-1950.* New Haven, CT: Yale University Press.

Friedman, Donald. 1995. *Historical Building Construction: Design, Materials, Technology.* New York, NY: W. W. Norton.

Frommer, Arthur, 2000. "Historic Preservation, Travel and You: There's a Direct Link Between Respect for the Past and Tourism." *Author Frommer's Budget Travel Magazine.* July-August, pp. 24-27 (and Frommer's Web Site, Aurthur Frommer's Budget Travel Online, frommer.com).

Gaddis, John Lewis. 2002, *The Landscape of History: How Historians Map the Past.* New York, NY: Oxford University Press.

Haig, Phyllis. 1963-80. *Haig Collection.* (Eight storage boxes of the records of preservation activities in Davis, the private collection of the owner.)

Hata, Nadine Ishitani. 1992. *The Historic Preservation Movement in California, 1940-1976.* Sacramento, CA: Office of Historic Preservation, California Department of Parks and Recreation.

Hamer, David. 1998. *History in Urban Places: The Historic Districts of the United States.* Columbus, OH: Ohio State University Press.

Heirich, Max. 1971. *The Spiral of Conflict: Demonstrations at Berkeley 1964-1965.* New York, NY: Columbia University Press.

Historic Environments Consultants. 1980. *Cultural Resources Inventory Final Report.* Sacramento, CA: The Firm.

Kammen, Carol. ed. 1996. *The Pursuit of Local History: Readings in Theory and Practice.* Walnut Creek, CA: AltaMirra Press.

————, 2003. *On Doing Local History, Second Edition.* Walnut Creek, CA: AltaMirra Press.

Klemm, Roger, David Wilkinson, and Marcus Ullrich. 2001. *Financial Incentives for Rehabilitating Older Commercial Buildings.* (Videotaped seminar with downtown Davis commercial building owners, May 1.) Davis, CA: Davis Downtown Business Association.

Koenig, Fredrick. 1985. *Rumor in the Marketplace: The Social Psychology of Commercial Hearsay.* Dover, MA: Auburn House.

Konicki, Leah. n.d. *Rescuing Historic Resources: How to Respond to a Preservation Emergency.* Washington, DC: National Trust for Historic Preservation.

Kriesberg, Louis. 1982. *Social Conflicts.* Englewood, NJ: Prentice-Hall.

Kunstler, James Howard. 1993. *The Geography of Nowhere: The Rise and Decline of America's Man-made Landscape.* New York, NY: Simon & Schuster.

————. 1996. *Home From Nowhere: Remaking Our Everyday World in the 21st Century.* NY: Simon & Shuster.

Landmark Preservation Council of Illinois. 1994. *How to Save a Landmark.* Chicago, IL: Landmark Preservation Council of Illinois.

Larkey, Joann Leach. 1969. *Davisville '68: The History and Heritage of the City of Davis, Yolo County, California.* Davis, CA: The Davis Historical Landmark Commission.

Larkey, Joann Leach and Shipley Walters. 1987. *Yolo County: Land of Changing Patterns, An Illustrated History.* Northridge, CA: Windsor Publications, Inc.

Lee, Antoinette. 2002. "From Tennis Shoes to Sensible Pumps: How Historic

Preservation Went From a Passion to a Profession." *AASLH History News.* 57, #3, 18-21 (Summer).

Lepore, Jill. 2001. *Encounters in the New World: A History in Documents.* New York, NY: Oxford University Press.

Liss, Helene. 2000. *Demolition: The Art of Demolishing, Dismantling, Imploding, Toppling & Razing.* New York, NY: Black Dog & Leventha.

Livingston and Blayney City and Regional Planners. 1961. *Davis Core Area Plan.* San Francisco, CA: Livingston and Blayney [Additionally published with a front page titled "Core Area Report Supplemental Data, January 1, 1965].

Lofland, John. 1999. *Old North Davis: Guide to Walking a Traditional Neighborhood.* Woodland, CA: Yolo County Historical Society.

—————. 2000. *Davis Heritage Buildings, How Many to Start With, How Many Left?* Yolo County Historical Booklet Series, Number 7. Woodland, CA: Yolo County Historical Society.

—————. 2001. *Davis City Council Elections, 1917-2000.* Yolo County Historical Booklet Series, Number 8. Woodland, CA: Yolo County Historical Society.

Lofland, John and Phyllis Haig. 2000. *Davis, California, 1910-1940s.* Charleston, SC: Arcadia.

Lofland, John and Lyn H. Lofland. 1995. *Analyzing Social Settings: A Guide to Qualitative Observation and Analysis.* Belmont, CA: Wadsworth Publishing.

Longstreth, Richard W. 1998. *History on the Line: Testimony in the Cause of Preservation.* Ithaca, NY: Historic Urban Places, Inc.

Lowenthal, David. 1998. *The Heritage Crusade and the Spoils of History.* New York, NY: Cambridge University Press.

National Park Service and The National Conference of State Historic Preservation Officers. 1995. *Preserving Your Community's Heritage Through the Certified Local Government Program.* Washington, DC: National Park Service.

National Trust for Historic Preservation. 1976. *Directory of Landmark and Historic District Commissions.* Washington, DC: National Trust for Historic Preservation.

Miller, Alan. 2001. E-mail to the author, September 20.

Miller, Charles Richard ["Dick"]. no date. *A History of John D. "Jack" Miller, Jr. While He Was Chief of the Davis Volunteer Fire Department Covering the Years June 1934 Thru November 1940* (Printed by the author, copy in the Archives of the Hattie Weber Museum of Davis, Davis, CA).

Moe, Richard and Carter Wilkie. 1997. *Changing Places: Rebuilding Community in the Age of Sprawl.* New York, NY: Henry Holt.

Murtagh, William J. 1997. *Keeping Time: The History and Theory of Preservation in America, Revised Edition.* New York, NY: John Wiley.

Parker, Donald Dean. 1943. *Local History: How to Gather It, Write It, and Publish It.* New York, NY: The Social Science Research Council.

Partansky, Julie. 1992. Personal binder of documents on the Old North alleys anti-paving campaign.

Rabun, J. Stanley. 2000. *Structural Analysis of Historic Buildings: Restoration, Preservation, and Adaptive Reuse Applications for Architects and Engineers.* New York, NY: Wiley.

Robin, Peggy. 1995. *Saving the Neighborhood: You Can Fight Developers and Win.* New York, NY, Wiley.

Rome, Adam. 2001. *The Bulldozer in the Countryside: Suburban Sprawl and the Rise of American Environmentalism.* Cambridge, UK: Cambridge University Press.

Rosnow, Ralph L. and Gary Alan Fine. 1976. *Rumor and Gossip: The Social Psychology of Hearsay.* New York, NY: Elsevier.

Russo, David J. 1988. *Keepers of Our Past: Local History Writing in the United States, 1820s-1930s.* New York, NY: Greenwood Press.

Schwartz, Richard. 2000. *Berkeley 1900: Daily Life at the Turn of the Century.* Berkeley, CA: RSB Books.

Seidman, Rachel Filene. 2001. *The Civil War: A History in Documents*. New York, NY: Oxford University Press.

Sherwin, Elisabeth. 2001a. "A Peek At the Past: John Skarstad, left, University Archivist at UC, Davis, and John Lofland, Professor Emeritus, leaf through a bound volume of the Davis Enterprise." *Davis Enterprise*, January 15.

————. 2001b. "'64 Davis Enterprise Issues Found." *Davis Enterprise*, July 11.

Shibutani, Tamotsu. 1966. *Improvised News: A Sociological Study of Rumor*. Indianapolis, IN: Bobbs-Merrill.

————. 1968. "Rumor." Pp. 576-580 in Davis Sills, Ed. *International Encyclopedia of the Social Sciences*. Vol. 13. New York, NY: Macmillan.

Steven, Michael E.. & Steven Burg. 1997. *Editing Historical Documents: A Handbook of Practice*. Walnut Creek, CA: AltaMira Press.

Stevens, Robert E. and Philip Sherwood. 1982. *How to Prepare a Feasibility Study: A Step-by-Step Guide Including 3 Model Studies*. Englewood Cliffs, NJ: Prentice-Hall.

Suttles, Gerald D. 1972. *The Social Construction of Communities*. Chicago, IL: The University of Chicago Press.

Swanke Hayden Connell Architects. 2001. *Historic Preservation: Project Planning and Estimating*. Kingston, MA: R. S. Means Co., Inc.

Terrell, Greta. 1996. *Getting To Know Your 20th-Century Neighborhood*. Washington, DC: National Trust for Historic Preservation.

Tyler, Norman. 2000. *Historic Preservation: An Introduction to Its History, Principles, and Practices*. New York, NY: W. W. Norton.

Taylor, William H. Jr., 1980. "Introduction." Pp. 5-7 in Historic Environment Consultants, *Cultural Resources Inventory: City of Davis*. Sacramento, CA: The Firm.

Weinberg, Nathan. 1979. *Preservation in American Towns and Cities*. Boulder, CO: Westview.

Wilkinson, David. 2001. E-mail correspondence with the author.

————. 2002. E-mail correspondence with the author.

Wood, Byrd and Liz Weaver. 2000. *Basic Preservation Procedures*. Washington, DC: National Trust for Historic Preservation.

Woodward, C. E. 1961. "Core Area Planner's Semi-final Report Calls for 'Do or Die'." *Davis Enterprise*, August 3.

BY AND ABOUT THE AUTHOR

BY THE AUTHOR

Davis History and Preservation Books, Booklets, and Web Site

*Old North Davis: Guide to Walking a Traditional
    Neighborhood* (1999)
Davis, California 1910s–1940s (co-author, 2000)
*Davis Heritage Buildings: How Many to Start
    With? How Many Left?* (2000)
Davis City Council Elections, 1917-2000 (2001)

Picture Map Supplement to the Book Old North Davis
    (2001)
www.davishistoricalsociety.org (co-editor,
    2002 - —)
Demolishing a Historic Hotel (2003)

Other Books

Doomsday Cult (1966, enlarged edition 1977)
Deviance and Identity (1969, republished 2002)
Analyzing Social Settings (co-author, 1971, 1984,
    1995, 2003)
Doing Social Life (1976)
Interaction in Everyday Life (editor, 1978)
Crowd Lobbying (1982)
Symbolic Sit-ins (co-author, 1982)

Protest (1985)
Peace Action in the Eighties (co-editor, 1990)
Peace Movement Organizations and Activists (co-editor,
    1991)
Polite Protesters (1993)
Social Movement Organizations (1996)
Handbook of Ethnography (co-editor, 2001)

ABOUT THE AUTHOR

A Professor of Sociology Emeritus at the University of California Davis, since the mid-1990s John Lofland has been involved in Davis, California historical research and historic preservation.

For this work, he has received the Sacramento County Historical Society's Award of Merit for Publication, the City of Davis' Preservation Appreciation Award, and the Davis Downtown Business Association's Volunteer of the Year Award. In 2002, he was elected the first President of the newly-formed Davis Historical Society.

In his academic career, he was the founding editor of the *Journal of Contemporary Ethnography,* served as President of the Society

for the Study of Symbolic Interaction and of the Pacific Sociological Association, and as Chair of the American Sociological Association's sections on Collective Behavior and Social Movements and the Sociology of War and Peace. He is a recipient of the Society for the Study of Symbolic Interaction's G. H. Mead Award for outstanding lifetime contributions to the study of human behavior and social life.

His previous book-length inquires include studies of the Unification Church—the "Moonies"—in America in the 1960s, protest demonstrations at the California State Capital in the 1970s, and the American peace movement of the 1980s.

He is a graduate of Swarthmore College (B. A., 1958), Columbia University (M. A., 1960), and the University of California, Berkeley (Ph. D., 1964).

Cover design by
Dino Gay
Woodland, California

Internal design and composition by
Davis Research
Davis, California

Printing by
Walsworth Publishing Company
Marceline, Missouri